Elements of
discourse understanding

Elements of discourse understanding

Edited by
ARAVIND K. JOSHI
BONNIE L. WEBBER
IVAN A. SAG

CAMBRIDGE UNIVERSITY PRESS

Cambridge
London   New York   New Rochelle
Melbourne   Sydney

Published by the Press Syndicate of the University of Cambridge
The Pitt Building, Trumpington Street, Cambridge CB2 IRP
32 East 57th Street, New York, NY 10022, USA
296 Beaconsfield Parade, Middle Park, Melbourne 3206, Australia

First published 1981

Printed in the United States of America

Library of Congress Cataloging in Publication Data

Main entry under title:

Elements of discourse understanding.

Papers from a workshop held in May 1978 at the
University of Pennsylvania.

Includes index.

1. Discourse analysis – Data processing – Congresses.
2. Psycholinguistics – Congresses. I. Joshi, Aravind,
1929–   . II. Webber, Bonnie Lynn. III. Sag,
Ivan A., 1949–   .
P302.E4   001.51   80-29393
ISBN 0 521 23327 5

Contents

v

Contributors

Herbert H. Clark
Department of Psychology
Stanford University
Stanford, CA 94305

Catherine R. Marshall
Bell Laboratories
Whippany, NJ 07981

Gerald Gazdar
School of Social Sciences
University of Sussex
Brighton, England BN1 9QG

Barbara J. Grosz
SRI International
Menlo Park, CA 94025

P. N. Johnson-Laird
Laboratory of Experimental
  Psychology
University of Sussex
Brighton, England BN1 9QG

Aravind K. Joshi
Department of Computer and
  Information Science
University of Pennsylvania
Philadelphia, PA 19104

S. Jerrold Kaplan
Department of Computer Science
Stanford University
Stanford, CA 94305

Donna M. Kwilosz
Department of Psychology
The Johns Hopkins University
Baltimore, MD 21218

Wendy G. Lehnert
Department of Computer Science
Yale University
New Haven, CT 06520

Mitchell Marcus
Bell Laboratories
Murray Hill, NJ 07974

George A. Miller
Department of Psychology
Princeton University
Princeton, NJ 08544

C. Raymond Perrault
Department of Computer
  Science
University of Toronto
Toronto, Ontario, Canada

Philip R. Cohen
Bolt Beranek and Newman, Inc.
Cambridge, MA 02138

Ellen F. Prince
Department of Linguistics
University of Pennsylvania
Philadelphia, PA 19104

Stanley J. Rosenschein
SRI International
Menlo Park, CA 94025

Ivan A. Sag
Department of Linguistics
Stanford University
Stanford, CA 94305

David L. Waltz
Coordinated Science Laboratory
  and Department of Electrical
  Engineering
University of Illinois at
  Urbana/Champaign
Urbana, IL 61801

Bonnie Lynn Webber
Department of Computer
  and Information Science
University of Pennsylvania
Philadelphia, PA 19104

William A. Woods
Bolt Beranek and Newman, Inc.
Cambridge, MA 02138

Editorial preface

In May 1978, a workshop was held at the University of Pennsylvania on topics in "Computational Aspects of Linguistic Structure and Discourse Setting." Its aim was to bring together a small group of researchers actively engaged in using discourse characteristics and human cognitive and inferential processing capabilities as a rich source of explanation for linguistic phenomena. This volume consists of edited versions of the papers submitted by the invited participants (linguists, psychologists, and researchers in artificial intelligence), as well as an introduction noting some links among the papers.

This workshop would not have been possible without the support of the Alfred P. Sloan Foundation, which has furnished funds for the Program in Cognitive Science at the University of Pennsylvania. Assistance also came from both the Departments of Computer and Information Science, Linguistics, and Psychology, which helped in all the mechanics of workshop production. We thank them all. Thanks are also due to Dr. Lila Gleitman and Dr. Rochel Gelman, who helped with the initial planning of the workshop, and to our students, who took care of the nitty-gritty with patience and good humor – Kathy Ball, Bill Dolsen, Bruce Kaufman, Eric Mays, Kathy McKeown, Steve Platt, and Tom Williams.

Finally, our special thanks go to our authors for their promptness and cooperation and also to the editors of Cambridge University Press, who worked closely with us on this volume.

Introduction

BONNIE L. WEBBER, ARAVIND K. JOSHI, and
IVAN A. SAG

The original versions of the chapters appearing in this volume were presented and discussed at a workshop in May of 1978 sponsored by the Sloan Foundation at the University of Pennsylvania, entitled "Computational Aspects of Linguistic Structure and Discourse Setting."[1] They were written by the participants in response to a list of suggested topics that emphasized discourse structure and function.[2] Authors were asked to use this list as a guideline, but were free to interpret the theme of the workshop broadly and to discuss various aspects of language structure and discourse setting that were of particular interest to them. Preliminary drafts of these papers were distributed at the workshop (except for those by Gazdar and Prince), and final drafts were received over the next several months.

The approach to discourse taken in all but one of the chapters illustrates important roles played by each of the following processes or structures, and hence, the need to understand them clearly in order to compile a useful account of discourse:

a. Utterance meaning
b. The discourse participants' evolving model of what underlies the discourse
c. Their similarly evolving models of each other
d. Situational characteristics (e.g., task-based, perceptual, etc.)

These factors affect what things are said and how, as well as what is left implicit in a discourse – left, that is, to reasoning.[3]

Although these themes do not exhaust the significant features of discourse, they do provide an interesting, and we hope useful, organizing strategy for introducing the majority of the works included in this volume.

The one exception to this thematic presentation is the chapter by Marcus on deterministic parsing. Its place here reflects its important contribution relating deterministic computation to independently

1

motivated linguistic concepts. Because of its special nature, this chapter will have an introduction of its own, which includes a discussion of the possible relations of the work Marcus describes to discourse processing.

Utterance meaning

Five of the chapters – those by Johnson-Laird, Woods, Waltz, Miller and Kwilosz, and Gazdar – discuss issues involved in what, and how, utterances mean. "How" implies an activity, and appropriately so, for each of these authors shows that deriving the meaning of an utterance involves an active process of comprehension.

Johnson-Laird is concerned with a psychologically valid theory of utterance meaning and advances here the notion of "mental model" as the basis for such a theory. In this approach, utterances provide clues to the building of mental models, which are then accessible to procedures people have for manipulating and interrogating them. He presents two types of examples to illustrate and justify his approach – discourses involving spatial descriptions and ones involving quantified sentences. As to the former, he shows how, within a mental-model account, the meaning of a relational term like "behind" or "to the right of" can be expressed as a procedure, in a way that can be used by other procedures, for constructing or verifying the corresponding spatial relation in a model. The procedure representing a relation, in fact, takes a verification (or construction procedure) as an argument and delivers up a new procedure. The resulting procedure applies as if the items involved in the relation were on a graph laid out in front of a viewer. The meaning of a quantified sentence, on the other hand, involves another type of construction within the model – setting up appropriate tokens that do or do not, according to the type of quantifier, exhibit the properties delineated in the utterance.

Woods' chapter also stresses procedures involved in utterance meaning, but in a different way. Woods develops here a two-stage approach to a natural language semantics. In the first stage, an utterance is assigned one or more interpretations in a nonambiguous, finely discriminating internal language. In the second stage, the semantics of that language are characterized. It is in this second stage that procedures are involved – not procedures that an understanding system executes in response to an utterance or in deciding whether to believe an assertion to be true, but rather abstract procedures that may be partially or fully evaluated as the need arises, in real or in hypothetical circumstances. The internal language, whose semantics is specified by these procedures, is discussed here at length, including its role in developing a taxonomy of experience, thereby relating language to perception.

Waltz is also concerned with the relation between language and perception, and in his chapter explores design issues for a system that has both vision and language. This exploration is grounded in his complementary beliefs that perception can conveniently be viewed as a process of "description building" and that the understanding of natural language utterances about scenes is based on our abilities to *use* these descriptions to drive processes of "picture building" and "event simulation." Like Johnson-Laird, Waltz sees the meaning of an utterance as ultimately procedural, with the pictures we build as mimicking – via event simulations – the dynamics of the world.

The fourth chapter discussing utterance meaning is that by Miller and Kwilosz, who are concerned with the meanings attributable to one specific class of utterances: those containing modal verbs and, possibly, a negative element as well. Drawing on experiments on how people group positive and negative modal sentences for similarity, Miller and Kwilosz show the inadequacy of traditional modal logics as a semantics for natural language modals. In particular, they show that to be adequate, any theory must take into account people's general situational knowledge. As in Johnson-Laird's discussion of spatial relational terms and in Prince's account of specific indefinite determiners, what Miller and Kwilosz find constant in the use of a given modal is that the speaker has made (and that the listener, consequently, is invited to make) a particular inference: that on the basis of general knowledge, given the prevailing situation, the proposition that the utterance expresses follows inferentially.

In Gazdar's chapter, another aspect of utterance meaning and its role in discourse is highlighted, that of speech act recognition and interpretation. Speech acts are associated with the intent of utterances in discourse. Gazdar here presents a general characterization of the notion of speech act (and its related notion, illocutionary force), followed by a clear exposition of the issues involved in relating utterances to the speech acts they achieve. An issue related to this is that of how an interrogative sentence can, on some occasions of use, manifest a request. Lehnert's chapter provides some interesting discussion of this topic.

Discourse models

One way of explaining the relationship between a discourse and the external or hypothetical situation it concerns is to postulate mental models of that situation that the participants are building or have already built. Several of the authors discuss such mental models, or discourse models, and the role that they play in discourse.

As mentioned in the previous section, the theory of meaning that Johnson-Laird advances is based on the notion of mental models. They provide, as he shows, a systematic way of explaining people's understanding and, at times, misunderstanding of utterances, as displayed in the inferences they draw from them.

Johnson-Laird also points out another role that mental models may play besides that which they do in the immediate discourse: that of allowing people to acquire higher-order knowledge of the relations like "on the right of" portrayed therein. Such knowledge would include properties like transitivity and almost-transitivity, the latter of which holds of "on the right of," which is transitive except when objects are arranged circularly.

Webber's interest in mental models lies in how more formal (or structural) aspects of the discourse shape the model of the underlying situation that a listener might develop. Taking the viewpoint that one function of discourse is to get a listener to synthesize a model of the underlying situation (i.e., the entities it involves, along with their properties and interrelations) that is an *adequate counterpart* of the speaker's own, Webber considers the problem of accounting for definite anaphora (definite pronouns and noun phrases) occurring in the discourse. These anaphora are taken as intending to specify entities within the speaker's discourse model and, the speaker hopes, their counterparts in that of the listener. In her chapter Webber considers one aspect of the model synthesis process – how entities are created and described in response to indefinite noun phrases – and attempts to account for this in a way that will mesh with how they are later accessed anaphorically.

A listener's belief in the adequacy of the *counterpart* discourse model s/he has built in response to the speaker's utterances may be a leap of faith or more actively reassured. Regarding the latter, there is an interesting discussion in Waltz's chapter concerning how a listener can dynamically "run" event simulations in order to check the consistency and plausibility of the "picture" s/he has constructed in response to the speaker's utterances. One specific example discussed here is a listener's plausible response, in terms of event simulations, to the somewhat bizarre "My dachshund bit the mailman's ear."

One significant property that may or may not be attributed to a discourse entity is that of having an *externally existing* counterpart. In her presentation, Prince considers the entities evoked by indefinite noun phrases and whether or not counterpart existence would be ascribed to them. She contrasts specific and nonspecific indefinites on this point and shows that only the specific indefinite causes a listener to associate with the newly evoked entity an external counterpart whose existence at least the speaker is assumed to believe in. Prince also notes that if the listener ascribes some credibility to the speaker, the listener will attribute external existence to the counterpart as well.

Rosenschein also supports the importance of discourse models by providing here a formal framework for characterizing how the discourse participants' mental states change over time in response to perceived events, including of course the discourse itself. Whereas Webber, Johnson-Laird, and Prince discuss the evolving content of the participants' mental models, Rosenschein seeks to describe formally the relationship maintained over time between their beliefs, actions, and goals. He suggests an initial set of axioms that characterize and interrelate these constructs. An interesting point of contact with Gazdar lies in Rosenschein's use of these axioms, along with a formally stated "cooperativity principle," to provide a formally reasoned account of the following short, after-dinner exchange, the speech act accomplished by its second utterance:

> J: I'm finished now.
> S: I don't have any money.

Models of participants' beliefs

The convoluted intricacies of "I believe that you believe that I believe . . ." have been noted in many places – from *Peanuts* comic strips to R. D. Laing's paradoxical *Knots*. The many roles that belief modeling and its attendant notion of "mutual belief" or "shared knowledge" play in discourse understanding are illustrated in several of the chapters in this volume.

Clark and Marshall focus on definite reference, showing how a seemingly impossible-to-acquire state of shared knowledge among the discourse participants forms the primary foundation for successful referring expressions. They show, in fact, several ways in which this "mutual knowledge paradox" may be resolved, presenting in the process a taxonomy of the ways knowledge comes to be regarded as shared by the discourse participants. This notion of mutual knowledge has a usefulness for language understanding far beyond the needs of definite reference alone. Their chapter also presents a historical overview of the notion of "mutual" or "shared" knowledge as it has been discussed in the philosophical, linguistic, and computational literatures.

Perrault and Cohen also discuss successful referring expressions – in this case, apparently anomalous (albeit successful) ones in which the speaker does not believe that the description s/he is using can, in fact, be truthfully ascribed to the intended referent. They point out that such expressions can successfully refer if certain criteria that they spell out about the speaker's and hearer's beliefs about each other and the external context are indeed satisfied.

Grosz notes another type of belief about the other and its effect on the discourse. That is, she shows that the differential status conferred upon the discourse participants by the task they are cooperating on will lead to different expectations on the part of each as to how the other will use language. She notes, for example, that an apprentice to a task will often use physical as opposed to functional descriptions in constructing referring expressions, whose use an expert engaged in helping him or her will understand and accept.

Prince's chapter demonstrates how the use of specific indefinite noun phrases reflects upon both a speaker's beliefs about a listener and his or her beliefs about the underlying situation. We remarked upon this latter point in the preceding section, discussing Prince's thesis on the existential presuppositions of specific indefinites. As to the former point, Prince notes that in hearing a specific indefinite, a listener will infer that the speaker is not assuming that the listener is "familiar" with the intended individual via some sort of mutual knowledge. This discussion complements well a similar point in Clark and Marshall's discussion of specific definites.

Kaplan, on the other hand, discusses certain consequences of people's misjudgments in their beliefs about each other vis-à-vis alterations in the flow of discourse. In particular, he considers questions, with respect to the problem of identifying and correcting a questioner's mistaken assumptions about the extension of a given referring expression. He notes the importance of pointing out such mistaken assumptions, lest the answer to a question perpetuate the misconception.

Complementing Kaplan's concerns, Lehnert shows the important role that one's assessment of another person's knowledge plays in formulating an answer to his or her question. She points out its influence on the answerer's judgment of what information would be new to the questioner (i.e., not already given or inferred), as well as on the level of technicality at which a response is made.

Another interesting tie with Kaplan's chapter is Lehnert's discussion of how knowledge-state assessment may influence the potential respondent's reception of a question. If it is one whose answer the respondent feels the speaker already knows, Lehnert notes that the respondent may wonder what's wrong. Kaplan points out another possibility: that the question reflects an incorrect presumption on the speaker's part, one to whose correction the respondent should cooperatively attend.

Situational characteristics

Not only the situation being discussed but also the situation in which the discussion is taking place has important effects on the discourse. The most obvious is, of course, people's use and interpretation of deictic expressions, but there are many more subtle ones, several of which are pointed out in the chapters by Grosz, Perrault and Cohen, and Lehnert.

In Grosz's chapter, it is the task on which the discourse participants are cooperating that is analyzed for its influence on the discourse. Grosz shows how the task structure in addition to defining the roles of the participants, defines in part a focusing structure (what the participants are concentrating on), which in turn strongly influences how things are referenced and described.[4] For example, she points out that if a subtask involves a particular screw being adjusted, the fact that the larger task of which it is a part involves many screws does not detract from the speaker's ability to use the singular definite noun phrase "the screw" to refer to that screw, and that screw alone.

The situational effect on discourse pointed out in the paper by Perrault and Cohen has to do with the observation that a speaker's ability to use an inaccurate description to refer successfully depends crucially on how that reference will be determined by the listener. For example, an inaccurate description like "the woman with the martini" will not be successful if the listener attempts to verify it by dropping hydrometers in people's drinks.

Lehnert discusses another situational effect, on the interpretation of negative utterances. In particular, she considers appropriate replies to questions that require enumerating or characterizing a set of items that do *not* exhibit a given property (e.g., "Who isn't here today?"). Such answers must be constrained to avoid the ridiculous, and one constraint comes from situational expectations (in this case, "Who, of those who should be here, isn't?").

Deterministic parsing

As we mentioned, one chapter in this volume is concerned with sentence level processing and not discourse processing. In it, Marcus explores the hypothesis of determinism, which claims that natural language can be parsed by a computationally simple mechanism that does not use backtracking, contains no hidden parallelism, and does not destroy any partial structures built during the computation.

Marcus's main purpose is to show how certain specific properties (constraints) of natural language, in particular, the subjacency principle and the specified subject constraint, are natural consequences that follow from the structure of a grammar interpreter based on the determinism hypothesis.

Linguistic theories postulate constraints – universal, one hopes – on the structure of language. One basis for such constraints may be the processing mechanisms involved in language production and comprehension. Processing mechanisms have been, up until now, primarily a concern of computational linguists. However, we believe that deliberately looking for such correspondences should be a major thrust of both the linguistic and computational linguistic methodologies.

Even if one does not accept the determinism hypothesis, or it turns out to be only partially valid, explaining its consequences has given deep insights into the structure and processing of natural language. Marcus's chapter is a significant contribution in this direction.

Turning our attention again to discourse, a determinism hypothesis may also be interesting to consider for discourse processing, to see what insights it might provide into the structure of discourse. For example, what sort of structural units might be needed in order for a fixed look-ahead scheme to be formulated analogous to Marcus's parser? Whereas this is all very speculative, the point we want to make is that investigating the consequences of strong hypotheses for discourse processing may be a fruitful strategy, even if these strong constraints are not completely valid.

By focusing on four themes that struck us particularly, we have clearly not done justice to the range of material the chapters cover. We hope now that readers will proceed to derive enjoyment and knowledge from this material just as we have done in presenting it.

NOTES

1 Gazdar and Prince were unable to be present at the workshop; their chapters were received subsequently.
2 Suggested topics: (1) nature and function of descriptions – referential and attributive descriptions, manipulation of multiple descriptions; (2) the structure of dialogue and discourse setting; (3) question-answering –

intensional vs. extensional responses, direct and indirect answers; (4) anaphora in discourse; (5) meaning representations – logical representations and their role in natural language processing; (6) procedural semantics; (7) inferences in context.

3 All the chapters touch upon reasoning and inferential processes in one way or another, either primarily from the point of view of the speaker deciding what to say (cf. Clark and Marshall, Kaplan, Lehnert, Perrault and Cohen) or from the point of view of the listener, deciding on how to interpret it (cf. Gazdar, Grosz, Johnson-Laird, Miller and Kwilosz, Prince, Rosenschein, Waltz, Webber, Woods). Each is interested in appropriate representations and procedures that will enable the computation of necessary inferences and prevent the derivation of irrelevant ones (i.e., that will enable the characterization of the class of appropriate inferences). Related to this matter is the issue of accounting for the fact that often there is a pronounced bias in favor of some types of inferences at the expense of other equally valid ones, an issue that is related to the complexity of an inference. This last issue has not received much attention in this volume, although Johnson-Laird refers to some of his work in this direction.

4 This focusing structure is, of course, part of *both* the speaker's and the listener's mental models of the discourse. Grosz shows how, for these models to be adequate counterparts, their focusing structures must correspond, each to the other.

1

Definite reference and mutual knowledge

HERBERT H. CLARK and CATHERINE R.
MARSHALL

Jack thinks
    he does not know
  what he thinks
    Jill thinks
    he does not know
But Jill thinks Jack does know it.
So Jill does not know
    she does not know
  that Jack does not know
  that Jill thinks
  that Jack does know
and Jack does not know he does not know
  that Jill does not know she does not know
  that Jack does not know
    that Jill thinks Jack knows
what Jack thinks he does not know

Jack doesn't know he knows
and he doesn't know
  Jill does not know.

Jill doesn't know she doesn't know,
  and doesn't know
    that Jack doesn't know Jill does not know.
They have no problems.

Knots, by R. D. Laing

In speaking and listening people make essential use of a great deal of
world knowledge that they "share" with each other. The question is,
what kind of "shared" knowledge do they use, and how? Recently, in
looking at how people plan definite reference, we came on one answer
to this question that made us distinctly uneasy. It seemed to suggest
that expressions like *the cold asparagus, the mess I made,* and *that animal*
require speakers to check a list of facts or beliefs that is infinitely long.
Under the most plausible assumptions about how they would actually
check that list, they should take an infinitely long time to decide on
each noun phrase. However, if there was anything we were certain

10

about, it was that noun phrases like these are ordinarily selected in a *finite* amount of time – in a few seconds or less. We were at an impasse. The argument for an infinite amount of processing time seemed impeccable, but so did the evidence against it. What we had was a processing paradox, which for reasons that will become clear later we called the *mutual knowledge paradox.*

Like all paradoxes, of course, this one rests on several critical assumptions, and when these assumptions are weakened in one way or another, the paradox can be resolved in several ways. These different resolutions, however, each have their own consequences, and depending on which one we accept, we are led to rather different models for the production and understanding of speech. It is important to decide, then, which way the mutual knowledge paradox is most plausibly resolved.

But we are interested in this paradox only as a way of getting at the two central questions of this chapter: (a) What type of shared knowledge is needed for language use? and (b) how is that shared knowledge in practice assessed and secured? The area of language in which we will take up these questions is definite reference, but even our interest in definite reference is secondary to our concern with the two questions of mutual knowledge. The way we will proceed, then, is to set out the mutual knowledge paradox, describe two ways of resolving it, and argue that one of them is the more usual resolution. We will then suggest that the answers to these two questions bear directly on current theories of language structure and language use, in particular on the characterization and processing of definite reference.

The mutual knowledge paradox

Imagine that there is a Marx brothers film festival on at the Roxy, with one film showing each night for a week. Against this background consider the following scenario:

> *Version 1.* On Wednesday morning Ann reads the early edition of the newspaper which says that *Monkey Business* is playing that night. Later she sees Bob and asks, "Have you ever seen the movie showing at the Roxy tonight?"

Our interest is in Ann's use of the definite referring expression *the movie showing at the Roxy tonight,* term *t*, by which Ann intends to refer to *Monkey Business*, referent *R*. What does Ann have to assure herself of in order to make this reference felicitously? That is, under what conditions does Ann have good reason to believe that Bob won't get the wrong referent or have to ask for clarification, as with "Which movie do you mean?" The answer we will develop is that she must be certain that once she has made her reference he and she can establish certain shared knowledge about the identity of that referent. Although not all aspects of this scenario are applicable to all other instances of definite reference, we will take up the more general case later.

An obvious first condition is that Ann herself know that the expression *the movie showing at the Roxy tonight* uniquely describes the movie *Monkey Business* – for example, there aren't two movies showing tonight instead. We will describe this knowledge as "*t* is *R*," that is, "the movie at the Roxy tonight is *Monkey Business*." So, Ann must be certain that after her reference the following condition will be true:[1]

(1)   Ann knows that *t* is *R*.

But is this enough? Obviously not, for what is missing is even the simplest notion of shared knowledge. Specifically, (1) gives no assurance that on the basis of her reference Bob himself will realize that *the movie at the Roxy tonight* uniquely describes *Monkey Business,* a realization that is surely a sine qua non of a felicitous reference. The way Ann's reference may fail can be illustrated by a variation on our original scenario:

> *Version 2.* On Wednesday morning Ann and Bob read the early edition of the newspaper and discuss the fact that it says that *A Day at the Races* is showing that night at the Roxy. Later, after Bob has left, Ann gets the late edition, which prints a correction, which is that it is *Monkey Business* that is actually showing that night. Later, Ann sees Bob and asks, "Have you ever seen the movie showing at the Roxy tonight?"

Although this version satisfies condition (1), Ann has clearly made her definite reference without the proper assurances. She has no reason to think that Bob will realize that the film she is referring to is *Monkey Business.* He is most likely to think it is *A Day at the Races.* The reason why her reference isn't felicitous is clear. She has not assured herself that after she had made her reference Bob will know that *the movie showing at the Roxy tonight* uniquely describes *Monkey Business.* So Ann must satisfy this condition:

(2)   Ann knows that Bob knows that *t* is *R*.

At first, conditions (1) and (2) may appear to be enough, but it is easy to show that they aren't. Consider this variation:

> *Version 3.* On Wednesday morning Ann and Bob read the early edition of the newspaper, and they discuss the fact that it says that *A*

Day at the Races is showing that night at the Roxy. When the late edition arrives, Bob reads the movie section, notes that the film has been corrected to *Monkey Business,* and circles it with his red pen. Later, Ann picks up the late edition, notes the correction and recognizes Bob's circle around it. She also realizes that Bob has no way of knowing that she has seen the late edition. Later that day Ann sees Bob and asks, "Have you ever seen the movie showing at the Roxy tonight?"

The scenario satisfies conditions (1) and (2). Ann knows that the movie is *Monkey Business* and that Bob knows that it is too. But she believes that he believes that she still thinks it is *A Day at the Races.* He is very likely to take her reference as one to *A Day at the Races* instead of *Monkey Business.* Her reference is infelicitous because she hasn't satisfied this condition:

(3) Ann knows that Bob knows that Ann knows that *t* is *R*.

The third condition, however, is still not enough, as we can illustrate with yet another version of the original scenario:

Version 4. On Wednesday morning Ann and Bob read the early edition of the newspaper and discuss the fact that it says that *A Day at the Races* is playing that night at the Roxy. Later, Ann sees the late edition, notes that the movie has been corrected to *Monkey Business,* and marks it with her blue pencil. Still later, as Ann watches without Bob knowing it, he picks up the late edition and sees Ann's pencil mark. That afternoon, Ann sees Bob and asks, "Have you ever seen the movie showing at the Roxy tonight?"

This version satisfies conditions (1), (2), and (3). Ann knows that the movie is *Monkey Business;* she knows that Bob knows it too – she saw him look at the late edition; and she knows that he knows that she knows it too – she saw him notice her pencil mark on the correct movie in the late edition. Yet Ann is still not completely justified in thinking Bob will know she is referring to *Monkey Business.* If she looks at the world from his point of view, she should reason like this: "She knows that the movie is *Monkey Business.* But she thinks that I, Bob, think it is *A Day at the Races,* and so by her reference, she must think I will pick out *A Day at the Races.*" But if her reference may get Bob to pick out *A Day at the Races,* it is infelicitous. So we must add another condition for Ann to be sure of:

(4) Ann knows that Bob knows that Ann knows that Bob knows that *t* is *R*.

Can we now stop with the confidence that condition (4) is enough? Not if we can dream up a scenario that satisfies (1) through (4) but still doesn't justify a felicitous reference. With a little difficulty, we can:

Version 5. On Wednesday morning Ann and Bob read the early edition of the newspaper and discuss the fact that it says that *A Day at the Races* is playing that night at the Roxy. Later, Bob sees the late edition, notices the correction of the movie to *Monkey Business,* and circles it with his red pen. Later, Ann picks up the newspaper, sees the correction, and recognizes Bob's red pen mark. Bob happens to see her notice the correction and his red pen mark. In the mirror Ann sees Bob watch all this, but realizes that Bob hasn't seen that she has noticed him. Later that day, Ann sees Bob and asks, "Have you ever seen the movie showing at the Roxy tonight?"

Complicated as this scenario is, it is possible to see that Ann should not in good conscience have made this definite reference. Putting herself in Bob's shoes again, she should reason like this: "Ann knows that the movie is *Monkey Business,* and she knows that I know that too. Yet she believes that I think she thinks the movie is *A Day at the Races,* and so by her reference, she should think I will decide she is referring to *A Day at the Races.*" But if her reference gets Bob to pick out *A Day at the Races,* it is infelicitous. So we must add condition (5):

(5)   Ann knows that Bob knows that Ann knows that Bob knows that Ann knows that t is R.

Can we be confident that condition (5) is enough? Indeed, we can be sure that it isn't, no matter how fast we seem to be narrowing in on what Ann must be sure of. What these versions show is that there is a way *in principle* of demonstrating that the last piece of embedded knowledge is insufficient. The method is this: Corresponding to Ann's condition (1) is an analogous condition that Bob must assure himself of if he is to be certain she is referring to *Monkey Business.* The condition is this:

(1′)   Bob knows that t is R.

For Ann to be sure that her reference succeeds in bringing about this knowledge, she must put herself in Bob's shoes, reason as he would, and make sure she could identify the intended referent uniquely. What we did in constructing Version 2 was to create a scenario in which (1) held after Ann's definite reference, but Ann couldn't know whether (1′) held or not. This led us to add condition (2), *Ann knows that Bob knows that t is R,* the equivalent of *Ann knows that* (1′). But just as Ann needs to make sure her reference will bring about (2), Bob has to come to know (2′):

(2′)   Bob knows that Ann knows that t is R.

But then (2′) is something else Ann must make sure her reference will bring about, as we showed in creating Version 3, and this led to condition (3). Corresponding to (3), however, is Bob's (3′), which we used in creating Version 4. In principle, we could use this procedure to construct countermanding versions ad infinitum.

The paradox

This view of what Ann has to be sure will result from her use of *the movie showing at the Roxy tonight* suggests a processing paradox. On the one hand, Ann has an infinity of conditions, like (1) through (5), to assure herself of, and that should take her an infinite amount of time. On the other hand, she is surely able to use *the movie showing at the Roxy tonight* as a definite reference, when the circumstances are right, in a finite amount of time. Hence the paradox.

You might rightly complain, however, that the paradox contains a number of hidden assumptions, one or more of which are probably suspect. We see the underlying assumptions to be roughly these:

> *Assumption I.* Ann ordinarily tries to make definite references that are felicitous – ones for which Bob won't get the wrong referent or have to ask "Which one?"
> *Assumption II.* To make such a felicitous definite reference Ann must assure herself of each of the infinity of conditions (1), (2), (3), (4), and so on.
> *Assumption III.* Each of the conditions (1), (2), (3), (4), and so on takes a finite (though small) amount of time or capacity to check.
> *Assumption IV.* Ann ordinarily makes each definite reference in a finite amount of time, on the order of a few seconds.

Assumption I is simply that Ann always tries to make herself understood. She doesn't just blurt out a definite reference and hope against hope that it will work. She chooses her references deliberately and with care. Assumption II merely restates what we have just argued in Ann's reference to *Monkey Business* – that it appears to require her to check an infinity of conditions. Assumption III states a processing assumption that is common to almost every psychological model for such a process – that an infinite number of mental operations cannot be carried out in a finite amount of time (Sternberg, 1966; Townsend, 1972). And Assumption IV states the obvious empirical observation that when people refer to things, they don't take much time in doing it.

The mutual knowledge paradox can be resolved, therefore, by throwing out one or another of these assumptions. Assumptions III and IV seem impossible to get rid of. At least, doing so would take a great deal of argument. The burden of the paradox, then, falls on Assumptions I and II. Which one, if not both, should we drop? We will return to this question once we have looked more closely at the Frankenstein monster we have created for "shared" knowledge.

"Shared" knowledge

In common parlance, "shared" knowledge has several definitions. Ask your aunt what it means for the two of you to share knowledge that the mayor is an embezzler, and she would probably say, "It means that you know he is an embezzler, and so do I." If p is the proposition that the mayor is an embezzler, then the first definition of shared knowledge comes out like this:

> A and B share$_1$ knowledge that p =$_{def.}$
> (1)   A knows that p.
> (1')   B knows that p.

Or your aunt might give a more complicated answer: "It means that both of us know that he is an embezzler, and furthermore, I know that you know he is, and you know that I know he is." This leads to a second definition of shared knowledge:

> A and B share$_2$ knowledge that p =$_{def.}$
> (1)   A knows that p.
> (1')   B knows that p.
> (2)   A knows that B knows that p.
> (2')   B knows that A knows that p.

We can define a series of types of "shared" knowledge merely by extending the list of statements. These can be denoted by the appropriate subscript on *share*. Shared$_4$ knowledge contains statements down to (4) and (4'), shared$_n$ knowledge, statements down to (n) and (n'). None of these finite definitions, of course, describes the "shared" knowledge required of Ann and Bob after her reference to *Monkey Business*. For that we need something more.

Mutual knowledge

What is required, apparently, is the technical notion of *mutual knowledge*. It has been defined and exploited by Lewis (1969) and Schiffer (1972) for dealing with close cousins of the problem we have raised here. Mutual knowledge is Schiffer's term, whereas Lewis's term for the same thing is common knowledge. We have chosen Schiffer's term, which seems more transparent and less open to misinterpretation. Schiffer defines mutual knowledge as follows:

A and B mutually know that $p =_{def.}$
(1)　　A knows that p.
(1′)　　B knows that p.
(2)　　A knows that B knows that p.
(2′)　　B knows that A knows that p.
(3)　　A knows that B knows that A knows that p.
(3′)　　B knows that A knows that B knows that p.
et cetera ad infinitum.

Mutual knowledge is the same as shared$_\infty$ knowledge. With the appropriate changes in the definitions, we can also talk about mutual beliefs, mutual expectations, and other mutually held propositional attitudes.

Harman (1977) notes that the infinity of statements in this definition of mutual knowledge can be represented more succinctly in a single self-referential statement of the following kind:[2]

A and B mutually know that $p = _{def.}$
(q)　　A and B know that p and that q.

Cohen (1978) uses a similar representation. In some ways, this definition captures our intuitions about mutual knowledge even better than Schiffer's definition. A visual metaphor will help. Imagine that the proposition p is that the mayor is an embezzler, which Ann and Bob come to know by viewing a picture of the mayor altering the books in the city treasurer's office – he was caught red-handed by a local newspaper photographer. Now by Harman's definition, it is as if Ann and Bob are viewing not only the picture of the mayor's embezzlement, but also a picture of them looking at this picture. That second picture, of course, shows them looking at both pictures, the second of which shows them looking at both pictures, and so on ad infinitum. This definition seems to capture the kind of omniscience Ann and Bob possess about their knowledge of the mayor's embezzlement.

Yet this definition per se doesn't change what Ann and Bob have to assess. Ann must check whether for the Marx brothers example she and Bob know that t is *Monkey Business*. But she must also check to see whether she and Bob know that q, and q is that she and Bob know that t is *Monkey Business* and know that q'. That is, she must check to see whether she and Bob know that she and Bob know that t is *Monkey Business*, and, for q', whether she and Bob know that she and Bob know that she and Bob know that t is *Monkey Business* and that q'', and so on. So just the fact that mutual knowledge can be captured in a single statement doesn't absolve Ann and Bob from checking each of an infinity of statements. Although the representation *looks* simpler, its assessment isn't necessarily simpler.

The form in which mutual knowledge will be most useful, however, is slightly different from either of these two definitions. Note that both definitions represent mutual knowledge as an omniscient observer would see it, an observer who can say both what A knows and what B knows. But in our Marx brothers examples, Ann was not omniscient. She needed only half the conditions in Schiffer's definition – those numbered *without* primes. It is easy to see that what she needed is equivalent to this:

A knows that A and B mutually know that p.

The effect of this single recursion is to erase all the primes in Schiffer's definition. This assertion says, for example, that A knows that $(1')$. With $(1')$ spelled out, it says that A knows that B knows that p. But this is equivalent to (2). All the other primes get obliterated in the same way. So from Ann's vantage point, she must determine that she knows that she and Bob mutually know that p, and from his vantage point, he must determine that *he* knows that he and she mutually know that p.[3] Most of the time, however, we will speak informally of A determining merely that A and B mutually know that p, and of B determining merely that A and B mutually know that p. These might be called *one-sided definitions of mutual knowledge*.

Uses of mutual knowledge

The notion of mutual knowledge was originally devised by Lewis to handle some ordinary problems of coordination raised by Schelling in his book *The Strategy of Conflict* (1960). Take the grandfather of all coordination problems:

You are to meet somebody in New York City. You have not been instructed where to meet; you have no prior understanding with the person on where to meet; and you cannot communicate with each other. You are simply told that you will have to guess where to meet and that he is being told the same thing and that you will just have to try to make your guesses coincide. (Schelling, 1960, p. 56)

According to Lewis, you will want to go where the other person will go, namely, where you expect him to go. But you expect him to go where he will expect you to go. Where is that? Where he will expect you to expect him to go, of course. And so on. In short, the two of you will go where you mutually expect the other to go. Whether your mutual expectations are accurate or not is another matter.

If you repeatedly meet your friend at the same place, Lewis argues, you will eventually firm up your expectations and set up a regularity that can be called a convention. It may become a convention, for example, that the two of you meet, whenever you are supposed to meet in New York City, at the lost-and-found booth of Grand Central Station. But to do so, the two of you must mutually know, among other things, that both of you will go to that booth and that both of you expect each other to go to that booth. In Lewis's formulation, mutual knowledge is indispensable to the definition of convention. It is also, therefore, indispensable to the definition of language because, as Lewis shows, a language like English is in part a system of such conventions.

An application of mutual knowledge closer to our own examples is found in Schiffer's reformulation of Grice's definition of speaker meaning in natural language. Very briefly, his application goes like this. As Grice (1957, p. 385) defined this meaning, "'S [the speaker] meant something by x' is (roughly) equivalent to 'S intended the utterance of x to produce some effect in an audience by means of the recognition of his intention.'" But this definition will not work, Schiffer shows, unless the speaker and audience mutually know, among other things, the effects particular utterances are intended to produce. Schiffer was forced to this conclusion by a series of counterexamples to Grice's definition devised by Strawson (1964), by Searle (1965), and by Schiffer himself. Strawson's and Searle's counterexamples had led to minor repairs in Grice's definition, but Schiffer's, like ours, showed that it was always possible in principle to devise problematic scenarios for "shared" knowledge with fewer than an infinite number of steps. Schiffer's solution was to incorporate the notion of mutual knowledge directly into the definition of speaker meaning, just as Lewis had incorporated it directly into the definition of convention.

Mutual knowledge, then, is ubiquitous. It is an essential ingredient in convention, in meaning, and in language in general. It isn't surprising that it should be an essential ingredient in definite reference too.

Uses of "shared" knowledge

How have other investigators defined "shared" knowledge? Most haven't. The great majority have avoided the problem by not mentioning any interaction between the speaker and listener (for example, J. Anderson, 1976, 1977, 1978; R. Anderson et al., 1976; Ortony and Anderson, 1977; Schank and Abelson, 1977). Others have avoided the problem by limiting the universe of discourse to precisely what the speaker and listener both know. In Winograd's (1972) understanding program, for instance, the commander of the computer "robot" knows what the robot knows and cannot entertain the possibility that there are things the robot knows that he doesn't know. This has been characteristic of most models within psychology and artificial intelligence.

Within linguistics and philosophy only a handful of investigators have addressed the problem of "shared" knowledge. Several have discussed shared knowledge in a general way, but without saying which kind of shared knowledge they mean. Karttunen (1977, p. 155), for example, talked about a "conversational context," the set of propositions the speaker and addressee can take for granted at that point in the discourse. Later, Karttunen and Peters (1975) introduced the notion of "common ground" or the "common set of presumptions." This consists of the set of propositions "any rational participant [in an exchange of talk] is rationally justified in taking for granted, for example, by virtue of what has been said in the conversation up to that point, what all the participants are in a position to perceive as true, whatever else they mutually know, assume, etc." (p. 286). Karttunen and Peters did not say whether they meant "mutually know, assume, etc." in the technical sense or not. (See also Hawkins, 1978, and McCawley, 1979.)

On several occasions, investigators have committed themselves to specific kinds of shared knowledge. Clark and Haviland (1977), for example, discussed a processing strategy, the given-new strategy, that appeared to require nothing more than shared$_2$ knowledge. Prince (1978) in proposing the notion of tacit assumptions, took up examples that required various amounts of shared knowledge, but didn't bring in anything more than shared$_3$ knowledge. Kempson (1975) explicitly committed herself to shared$_4$ knowledge in discussing the set of propositions that constitute the speaker and hearer's "shared knowledge – knowledge they believe they share" (p. 167). She specifically listed knowledge statements (1), (2), (3), and (4), and no others. In an early paper, Stalnaker (1977) characterized pragmatic presupposition as equivalent to shared$_4$ knowledge: "A proposition P is a pragmatic presupposition of a speaker in a given context just in case the speaker assumes or believes that P, assumes or believes that his addressee believes that P, and assumes or believes that his addressee recognizes that he is making these assumptions, or has these beliefs" (p. 137).

Finally, a few investigators have been explicit in their use of mutual knowledge. In a later paper, Stalnaker (1978) replaced his earlier shared$_4$ knowledge with the notion of "common ground": "Presuppositions are what is taken by the speaker to be the *common ground* of the participants in the conversation, what is treated as their *common knowledge* or *mutual knowledge* [Stalnaker's emphasis]" (p. 321). Similarly, Nunberg (1977), in accounting for definite reference and other pragmatic problems, introduced the notion of "normal beliefs," which are based on mutual knowledge. And Cohen (1978), in his computational model of speech acts and reference, made essential use of mutual beliefs too.

As this brief survey shows, at least some investigators have felt the need for a notion of shared knowledge. When they have been specific, they have used notions ranging from shared$_2$ to mutual knowledge. There have been almost as many names for shared knowledge as investigators: conversational context, common ground, common set of presumptions, shared sets, contextual domain, tacit assumptions, pragmatic presuppositions, normal beliefs, and mutual beliefs. Yet these investigators have not taken up the question that would resolve the mutual knowledge paradox: How is shared knowledge assessed in the process of speaking or understanding? Before turning to this question, however, we must take up definite reference itself.

Definite reference

Although definite reference has begotten a vast literature in linguistics, philosophy, artificial intelligence, and psychology, there is still little consensus about its essentials. In this brief section, we cannot hope to do justice to that literature or provide that consensus. Yet to be able to examine the role mutual knowledge plays in definite reference, we need a model for definite reference, no matter how tentative. For this purpose, we will adopt Hawkins' (1978) model of definite reference and modify it a bit to handle some observations of Nunberg (1977) and to make it more closely resemble a related model of Clark and Clark (1979). The only claim we make for this model is that it is a reasonable first approximation – good enough at least to allow us to examine the role of mutual knowledge.

The location theory of the definite article

In Chapter 3 of his book *Definiteness and Indefiniteness* Hawkins reviews the major nongeneric uses of the definite article *the* and then proposes what he calls the location theory of the definite article. He takes up only some uses of the demonstratives *this* and *that;* he doesn't discuss pronouns or proper names. Although his theory is more restrictive than we desire, it is a place to start.

According to the location theory, the speaker performs three acts in using the definite article:

   a. He introduces a referent (or referents) to the hearer.
   b. He instructs the hearer to locate the referent in some shared set of objects.

    c. He refers to the totality of the objects or mass within this set that satisfy the referring expression.

To take an example, imagine that Ann told Bob *Bring me the apples*. By this she introduces to him some referents, namely apples. She instructs him to locate apples in some set of objects that she and he share knowledge about. She then refers to the totality of apples in that set – namely, all of the apples. If Ann had said *Bring me the apple*, the shared set of objects would contain exactly one apple, and by referring to the totality of objects within this set, she would have referred to that apple uniquely.

As (b) makes clear, the referent is to be located in a shared set of objects. Where do these shared sets come from? Hawkins argues that they are based on shared knowledge – he doesn't specify which kind – and are inferred "either from previous discourse or from the situation of utterance" (1978, p. 168). As evidence, Hawkins discusses the eight major uses of the definite article put forth by Christopherson (1939) and Jespersen (1949):

1. *The anaphoric use.* In *I bought a lathe, but the machine didn't work right,* the utterance of *a lathe* sets up a "shared previous discourse set," which can subsequently be identified as the referent of *the machine*.

2. *The visible situation use.* In a situation where a bucket is visible to both the speaker and listener, the speaker can say *Pass me the bucket*. The visible bucket constitutes a shared set of objects, which can then be identified as the referent of *the bucket*.[4]

3. *The immediate situation use.* A speaker can use *Do not feed the pony* even though the pony is not visible so long as its existence can be inferred from the situation. Then it is the inferred pony that constitutes the shared set of objects to which *the pony* refers.

4. *The larger situation use based on specific knowledge.* Bob may know the particular store Ann shops at every day, and so it is a shared set of objects. Ann can then refer to it without further explanation, as in *I'm going to the store.*

5. *The larger situation use based on general knowledge.* Ann and Bob know as a general fact that American towns of a certain size each have one city hall. The city hall of Spearfish, the town they happen to be going through at the time, therefore constitutes a shared set of objects that Ann can refer to, as in *I wonder where the city hall is.*

6. *The associative anaphoric use.* In *A car just went by and the exhaust fumes made me sick,* the car is a "trigger" to the "associate" exhaust fumes, and so with the mention of a car, people have a set of associates, which constitutes a shared set of objects. According to Hawkins,

"speaker and listener share knowledge of the generic relationship between trigger and associate" (1978, p. 125).

7. *The unavailable use.* Take *Bill is amazed by the fact that there is so much life on earth*, in which *the fact that there is so much life on earth* introduces new information unknown to the listener. To account for this apparent counterexample to (b), Hawkins takes a transformational approach, arguing that the sentence is derived from *That there is so much life on earth is a fact which Bill is amazed by*. In this source, *a fact* is now indefinite, and so the location theory can be preserved. The unknown information introduced in *The woman whom Max went out with last night was nasty to him*, which contains a "referent-establishing relative clause," is handled in a similar way, and so is the unknown information in *I don't like the color red*, which contains a nominal modifier.

8. *The unexplanatory modifier use.* In *The first person to sail to America was an Icelander*, the definite noun phrase picks out a unique person, whoever he may be, from the set of people who have sailed to America. This is what Donnellan (1966) has called an *attributive* rather than a *referential* use of the definite noun phrase. It picks out "whatever or whoever fits that description," whereas a referential use is "merely one tool for calling attention to a person or thing," and "any other device for doing the same job, another description or name, would do as well" (p. 285). Attributive uses are not intended to secure the mutual knowledge of the identity of the thing being picked out (although they may), and so they should not be assimilated, as they appear to be by Hawkins, with the referential uses, which *are* intended to secure mutual knowledge of the identity of the referent. Our concern is with referential uses, and so we will not consider the unexplanatory modifier use or any other attributive uses any further.

Modifications of the location theory

Like all other current theories of definite reference, the location theory has its problems. At least two of these problems are critical to our enterprise.

The first problem has to do with a condition Hawkins places on the composition of the shared set of objects in (b): "The hearer must either know or be able to infer that the intended object has the property that is used to refer to it in the descriptive predicate" (1978, p. 168). This condition says that for *the ham sandwich*, the hearer must know or be able to infer that the referent is a ham sandwich. This, however, cannot be correct – at least not without qualification.[5] Nunberg (1977) has pointed out systematic examples in which the referent does not have to have the property of the descriptive predicate. Imagine a waiter in a restaurant pointing to a ham sandwich and saying to another waiter *The ham sandwich is sitting at table six.* In this utterance, *the ham sandwich* is used to refer to the customer who ordered the sandwich, and that customer is obviously not a ham sandwich. Or imagine Ann pointing at her watch and saying *This watch now costs a hundred dollars,* by which she means "an instance of the type of watch this watch is would now cost a hundred dollars" (her own battered watch no longer having much value). Indeed, as Nunberg shows, deferred reference like this is common. To handle such cases, Nunberg introduces the notion of reference function. This is a function the hearer computes on each occasion to get him from the "designatum" (the ham sandwich or watch) to the intended referent (the customer or kind of watch).

The way we will handle this is to distinguish direct from indirect reference precisely on the analogy of direct and indirect illocutionary force. To begin with illocutionary force, *Do you know the time?* can be said to have a *direct* illocutionary force, "Do you have the knowledge of the time?", by virtue of which a speaker can convey a second *indirect* illocutionary force, "Please tell me the time" (Searle, 1975). In his utterance, the speaker intends to convey both illocutionary forces, although the direct meaning may not be intended to be taken seriously (Clark, 1979), and it may convey the indirect meaning by one or another conventional means (Morgan, 1978). Analogously, *the ham sandwich* can be said to have a *direct* referent, the ham sandwich on the plate in front of the waiter, by virtue of which the waiter can indicate a second *indirect* referent, the man who ordered the sandwich. In uttering *The ham sandwich is sitting at table six,* the waiter intends to refer to both objects – the sandwich and the person – although the thing that he is saying is sitting at table six is always the indirect referent. The relation between the direct and indirect referents is determined by Nunberg's reference function.

The condition Hawkins places on the composition of the shared set of objects, then, doesn't need to be changed, as long as we say he is dealing with *direct* definite reference. That is what we will do. We assume that theories of indirect definite reference will proceed along the lines set out by Nunberg as to what constitutes the intended reference function on any particular occasion. As he demonstrates, discovering those functions will not be an easy matter.

The second problem lies in the chronological order of (a) the time of acquisition by the speaker and listener of their shared knowledge of the required set of objects and (b) the moment of the reference act itself – the moment when the speaker utters the referring expression. Call these two moments Moment$_{SK}$ and Moment$_{RA}$, respectively (SK for shared knowledge and RA for reference act). Although Hawkins doesn't say so explicitly, he seems to assume that Moment$_{SK}$ must precede Moment$_{RA}$. That is, the speaker can only refer to sets of objects he and his listener *already* share knowledge about. This assumption pervades Hawkins' discussion of the first six uses of the definite article, and it seems to motivate his transformational treatment of the seventh.

Is this assumption correct? Clearly not. It appears possible to find counterexamples to the assumption for all eight uses of the definite article. Take the anaphoric use. Contrary to the assumption, it is easy to get an anaphor before its "antecedent," as in *Before he could steal anything, a burglar who had broken into our house was frightened away.* Or take the visible situation use. Contrary to the assumption, Ann can felicitously ask Bob *Please pass the salt* without his realizing there is any salt around. Indeed, it is her reference that induces him to assume there must be salt in view and to look for it. Or take the larger situation use based on general knowledge. Also contrary to the assumption, Ann can felicitously tell Bob *The fourth root of 81 is the number of sisters I have* without assuming that Bob *already* knows what the fourth root of 81 is. She need only assume that he can readily figure it out. In each of these examples, Moment$_{SK}$ comes *after* Moment$_{RA}$, and the shared knowledge is brought about in part by the reference act itself.

But if Moment$_{RA}$ can precede Moment$_{SK}$, there is less reason to posit transformational sources for the seventh use of the definite article. For an alternative analysis, consider Ann's assertion to Bob *The woman Max went out with last night was nasty to him*, where Ann is introducing the woman referred to for the first time. Referent-establishing relative clauses like this, as Hawkins notes, must be anchored to object sets that are already shared, in this instance Max. Ann could not have said, for example, *The woman some man went out with last night was nasty to him*, because *some man* doesn't provide such an anchor. If this is so, Bob can form an object set for this utterance by very much the same procedure as he would for *I wonder where the city hall is*, the fifth use of the definite article. For Ann and Bob it is general knowledge that men like Max often go out with women, ordinarily one woman on any one night, and so Bob can form the set of objects Ann is referring to, namely, the woman Max went out with last night. The requirement, then, seems to be not that Bob already have a shared set of objects, but that he be able to form one based on general or particular mutual knowledge and on the fact that the reference act occurred.

With these two modifications, we can reformulate the location theory in slightly different terms. Tentatively, we suggest the following convention:

The direct definite reference convention. In making a direct definite reference with term *t* sincerely, the speaker intends to refer to

1. the totality of objects or mass within a set of objects in one possible world, which set of objects is such that
2. the speaker has good reason to believe
3. that on this occasion the listener can readily infer
4. uniquely
5. mutual knowledge of the identity of that set
6. such that the intended objects or mass in the set fit the descriptive predicates in *t*, or, if *t* is a rigid designator, are designated by *t*.

We will not try to justify this formulation in detail, but a few observations are in order. The main point of the convention is this: For a speaker to refer to a thing, he must be confident that because of his speech act the identity of that thing will become mutually known to him and his listener. It doesn't have to be mutually known beforehand, but of course if it were, the listener's inferences would be all that much easier. Ordinarily, to *become* mutually known, the referent must at least be anchored to something that is already mutually known via an anchor cable that is already mutually known. To understand Ann's *I wonder where the city hall is*, Bob doesn't need to believe that the city hall of that town is mutually known, but merely that he and she mutually know about that town (the anchor) and that they mutually know that towns of that size ordinarily have a single city hall (the anchor cable). In condition (6), we have added the notion of a rigid designator, as defined by Kripke (1972, 1977), to take care of proper nouns. In Kripke's theory, *George Washington*, say, is a rigid designator, because it designates the same thing in all possible worlds. In our convention, to use *George Washington* Ann must have good reason to believe that Bob can figure out who it is that the term rigidly designates.

Heuristics for assessing mutual knowledge

For felicitous reference, the speaker and listener must establish certain kinds of mutual knowledge. Simpler notions of "shared" knowledge will not do – as witness Ann's reference to *Monkey Business*. In the light of Lewis's and Schiffer's arguments, this conclusion isn't terribly surprising. Definite reference is an example par excellence of something speakers and listeners achieve through coordination, and coordination is ordinarily achieved on the basis of mutual expectations. Moreover, definite reference is governed by conventions, and mutual knowledge is an indispensable part of conventions.

But what about the mutual knowledge paradox? It is unthinkable that speakers and listeners assess mutual knowledge by working serially, statement by statement, through an infinity of statements. As we noted earlier, this paradox rests on two debatable assumptions:

> *Assumption I:* Ann ordinarily tries to make definite references that are felicitous.
>
> *Assumption II:* To make a felicitous definite reference, Ann must assure herself of each of the infinity of statements (1), (2), (3), (4), and so on.

The inevitable conclusion is that one or both of these assumptions must be weakened and the infinite process replaced by finite heuristics.

The obvious thing to weaken first is Assumption I. In ordinary speech Ann may sometimes guess at what Bob knows – perhaps guessing wildly– and turn out expressions of definite reference that are far from felicitous. Much of the time this may not matter because her references may be close enough to succeed anyway. And when they don't go through, Bob will look puzzled, ask for clarification, or show other evidence of misunderstanding, and Ann can reassess what she thinks Bob knows and repair her reference. Indeed, repairs of this kind appear to occur often in spontaneous speech, suggesting that speakers don't always satisfy Assumption I with the precision that our Marx brothers examples might have suggested. Perhaps, then, the felicitous reference is an ideal that in practice is rarely reached.

Yet surely it is an ideal people strive for because they will want to avoid misunderstanding whenever possible. What heuristics will enable them to approach this ideal if not reach it? We will suggest two families of heuristics. The first, which we will call truncation heuristics, results in a permanent weakening of Assumption I. The second family, which we will call copresence heuristics, retains the possibility of felicitous definite reference, as in Assumption I, but solves the problems posed by Assumption II.

Truncation heuristics

The stickler in assessing mutual knowledge statement by statement is that there is an infinity of such statements, and that is too many to check. What if people checked only a few of them – like the first four? The task could then be carried out in a finite, even short, period of time, and that would resolve the mutual knowledge paradox. But if they did this, they could not be guaranteed a felicitous definite reference on each occasion, and Assumption I would no longer hold. Heuristics of this kind will be called *truncation heuristics*.

What makes these heuristics plausible is that they ought ordinarily to lead to few references that are infelicitous. Imagine that Ann always verifies the statement *Ann knows that Bob knows that Ann knows that Bob knows that t is R,* which is condition (4) for mutual knowledge. On actuarial grounds, if condition (4) holds, it should be highly likely that conditions (5) through infinity hold too. So although errors can occur, they should occur rarely and only in complicated situations.

What makes this a *family* of heuristics is that there are several checking procedures a speaker might use. First, imagine that Ann, in referring to *Monkey Business* with the noun phrase *the movie showing at the Roxy tonight,* checks conditions (1) through (4). This might be called the *progressive checking strategy* because Ann starts at the beginning of the list and works so far down. Where she stops depends on her desire for precision. The more precise she wants to be, the farther down the list she will want to check. Second, imagine that Ann checks condition (4) and no others. This might be called the *selective checking procedure.* Once again, the condition Ann picks out to check depends on her precision. The more precise she wants to be, the farther down the list she will want to enter.[6]

Neither of these procedures guarantees a felicitous definite reference because both lead to something less than full mutual knowledge of the referent. Yet in special circumstances there are heuristics that *can* lead to a felicitous reference – so long as the listener draws the right inferences. These heuristics will be called the *augmented truncation heuristics.*

Consider this variation on Version 4:

> *Version 4a.* On Wednesday morning Ann and Bob read the early edition of the newspaper and discuss the fact that it says that there is a double feature playing that night at the Roxy – *Monkey Business* followed by *A Day at the Races.* Later, Ann sees the late edition, notes that *A Day at the Races* has been canceled, and marks the notice with her blue pencil. Still later, as Ann watches without Bob's awareness, Bob picks up the late edition and sees Ann's pencil mark. That afternoon, Ann sees Bob and asks, "Have you ever seen the movie showing at the Roxy tonight?"

Like Version 4, this scenario satisfies conditions (1), (2), and (3), but it also satisfies (4*):

(4*)   There is no R^* such that Ann believes that Bob believes that Ann believes that Bob believes that t is R^*.

Here R^* is a unique referent that fits the description *the movie showing at the Roxy tonight*. Because the reference is singular and there are actually two movies for which condition (4) holds, there is no R^* that fits this description.

These conditions can be enough for a felicitous reference if Ann can count on Bob drawing the right inferences. She could reason this way: "Bob knows that I know that the movie tonight is *Monkey Business*. But because we discussed the early edition, he believes that I believe he thinks there are two movies showing. I can disabuse him of this belief by using a *singular* definite reference. Because he knows I know that *Monkey Business* is the only movie playing, he will infer that I know that he knows that too – even though he doesn't know I know that. He should be able to infer:

(3′)   Bob knows that Ann knows that Bob knows that t is R.

But because this is my, Ann's, conclusion, I know or believe the equivalent of (4):

(4)   Ann knows that Bob knows that Ann knows that Bob knows that t is R.

Reasoning further, I know that this is something Bob could infer, which gives way to (4′), hence my (5), and his (5′), hence my (6), and so on ad infinitum. Voila! He and I mutually know that t is R." In Version 4, it should be noted, Ann could not have reasoned this way precisely because that version doesn't fulfill condition (4*).

When will augmented truncation strategies work? That depends on the precision Ann wants. Imagine a Version 2a (analogous to Version 4a), in which Ann had seen the late edition of the newspaper canceling *A Day at the Races*, but had no idea whether Bob had seen that notice. So she would fulfill:

(1)   Ann knows that t is R.
(2)   There is no R^* such that Ann knows that Bob knows that t is R^*.

In this version, although she might be sure that Bob realized she was referring to a single movie – he *could* have thought she made a speech error and intended to say *movies* – she has no reason to think he would be able to figure out which one. In an analogous Version 3a, in which she saw Bob look at the late edition but realized he didn't know she had seen it, she could have some confidence he would figure out which. But what Bob really needs to know is that she knows the movie is *Monkey Business*, as in Version 4a. Higher-order versions should make her even more confident he will draw the right inferences.

What we have described, then, is a constellation of conditions that Ann, with certain auxiliary assumptions, can take as good evidence Bob will pick out the right referent. There are probably other such constellations, but all of those we have considered require at least three or four conditions for a reference to be felicitous.

Difficulties with truncation heuristics

In principle, truncation heuristics seem capable of doing the job. They may even allow for felicitous definite reference. We suspect that they may be used on at least some occasions. Version 4a is not such an implausible scenario for people to handle roughly as we suggested. In fact, for scenarios like Version 4a, we have asked subjects to tell us what is being referred to by expressions analogous to *the movie showing at the Roxy tonight*. These subjects appeared to use procedures very much like the truncation heuristics, especially the augmented truncation heuristics. As the scenarios became more complex, they tended to have more difficulty as this analysis would predict. So these heuristics are possible.

But are they plausible as the way people *normally* assess mutual knowledge in making definite reference? We believe not. Our doubts lie in two areas. First, it isn't easy to deal with reciprocal statements as complicated as condition (4). It is implausible that people ordinarily check these conditions per se. Second, the evidence people need in order to verify these conditions anyway suggests a radically different family of heuristics, namely, the copresence heuristics.

Reciprocal knowledge statements, like condition (4), seem unlikely mental objects for people to assess. Recall that in Version 4 of our Marx brothers scenario, we created a situation in which Ann didn't believe that Bob knew that she knew that he knew that the movie that night was *Monkey Business,* a violation of condition (4). The scenario wasn't easy to understand. The main sticking point was in grasping condition (4) and deciding that it wasn't true. Why is condition (4) so difficult to grasp, and to disconfirm?

There are probably two main reasons. One is that recursive statements about propositional attitudes are themselves difficult to grasp. For example, *John Dean knew that Nixon knew that Haldeman knew that Magruder knew that McCord had burgled O'Brien's office in the Watergate Apartments* describes a pipeline of gossip that is difficult to keep straight. When these statements are also reciprocal, with the pipeline turning back on itself, the difficulty seems to increase with the square of the number of recursions. Parallel to the last example is the following *reciprocal* statement: *John Dean knew that Nixon knew that John Dean knew that Nixon knew that McCord had burgled O'Brien's office in the Watergate Apartments.* It isn't just that *utterances* of these sentences are difficult to grasp. Rather, their content appears to be inherently hard to keep track of. Any statement more complex than condition (4) can be obliterated by one glass of decent sherry.

Studies of children suggest that the ability to deal explicitly with reciprocal knowledge develops quite late in childhood. In one study (Miller et al., 1970), children were asked to describe cartoons of people thinking of people thinking of people. These children found reciprocal relations much more difficult to describe than nonreciprocal ones. In addition, no more than half the twelve-year-olds were able to deal with reciprocal relations like condition (2), and fewer than a third were able to deal with reciprocal relations like condition (3). In another study (Barenboim, 1978), it was found that children spontaneously talk very little about other people's thoughts (like condition 2) until age twelve, or about other people's thoughts about other people's thoughts (like condition 3) until age sixteen (see also Flavell et al., 1968). All these studies required rather a lot from children – explicit talk about recursiveness and reciprocity – yet they suggest that recursive reasoning even two levels deep is not easy for children under age twelve. The trouble is that children much younger – six to eight years of age (Maratsos, 1976; Warden, 1976) – appear to use definite reference felicitously, at least much of the time. And even younger children sometimes spontaneously repair definite references to take account of what their listeners know (E. Clark and Andersen, 1979). So although studies of children give us anything but a knockdown argument, they do suggest that the truncation heuristics are not very plausible.

The more basic argument against the truncation heuristics is to be found in what counts as evidence for the truth of conditions (1), (2), (3), and so on. Take condition (3), *Ann knows that Bob knows that Ann knows that t is R.* Obviously, Ann won't have this statement represented per se in memory for any arbitrary *t* and *R*. Ann doesn't go through life creating such statements for every object she or anyone else might potentially refer to. Rather, what she needs is a piece of information from which she can deductively or inductively *infer* condition (3). Imagine, for example, a version of our original scenario in which Ann and Bob look at the late edition's correction to *Monkey Business* together. It would be hard to think of better evidence Ann could appeal to for the truth of condition (3).

Ann's knowledge that she and Bob looked at the correction together, however, is infinitely more useful than that. It is also about the best evidence Ann could appeal to for the truth of all the rest of the infinity of conditions. That is, with this evidence, Ann can jump immediately to full mutual knowledge. If that is so, why would she ever check conditions one by one – even a truncated list of them? She would be better off making sure of the back-up evidence itself. This is precisely the principle that underlies the next family of heuristics, the copresence heuristics.

Copresence heuristics

What kind of evidence can Ann appeal to in order to verify simultaneously the infinity of conditions? If Ann knew, she could in principle satisfy Assumption I and make definite references that were felicitous. She would resolve the mutual knowledge paradox instead by circumventing Assumption II, which otherwise forces her to verify an infinity of conditions one by one. We will argue that what she generally needs is evidence of *triple copresence* – of certain events in which Ann, Bob, and the target object are copresent, as when Ann, Bob, and the notice about *Monkey Business* were openly present together Wednesday morning. The trick is to say what counts as triple copresence – as being "openly present together" – and to say how this can lead to inferences of mutual knowledge.

When Lewis and Schiffer hit on the notion of mutual knowledge, they each recognized the need for a finite means of handling the infinity of conditions. Their solutions were essentially the same. If A and B make certain assumptions about each other's rationality, they can use certain states of affairs as a basis for *inferring* the infinity of conditions all at once. This solution is elegant, for it satisfies everyone. It fits people's intuitions that they mutually know certain facts, and that they yet arrive at this knowledge simply and easily, as if in one short step.

This solution is best illustrated with an example adapted from Schiffer: Ann and Bob are sitting across a table from each other, and there is a single candle between them. Both are looking at the candle, and both see the other looking at it too. The proposition p is that there is a candle on the table. Consider the scene from Ann's point of view. Clearly, she has direct evidence for the truth of (1):

(1)   Ann knows that p.

But she knows other pertinent information too. First, she has evidence that she and Bob are looking at each other and the candle simultaneously. We will call this the *simultaneity assumption*. Second, she assumes that he is not only looking at her and the candle, but also *attending* to them. We will call this the *attention assumption*. Finally, Ann assumes that Bob is normal and if he were in her shoes he would be drawing the same conclusions she is. We will call this the *rationality assumption*.

Now if Bob is attending to the candle and is rational, he has evidence for (1'):

(1') Bob knows that *p*.

This, however, is Ann's conclusion, and so she has evidence for (2):

(2) Ann knows that Bob knows that *p*.

But if Bob is rational, he will be drawing the inference that corresponds to hers – his equivalent of (2) – namely (2'):

(2') Bob knows that Ann knows that *p*.

Once again, this is Ann's conclusion, and so she has evidence for (3):

(3) Ann knows that Bob knows that Ann knows that *p*.

In like fashion, Ann would be justified in iterating this process through the remaining knowledge statements (4) through infinity, and Bob would be justified in doing the same for his.

This method for inferring mutual knowledge can be formalized as follows (adapted from Lewis):

> *Mutual knowledge induction schema*. A and B mutually know that *p* if and only if some state of affairs *G* holds such that:
> 1. A and B have reason to believe that *G* holds.
> 2. *G* indicates to A and B that each has reason to believe that *G* holds.
> 3. *G* indicates to A and B that *p*.

G is called the *basis* for the mutual knowledge that *p*. In the candle example, *G* (for "grounds") is Ann and Bob's evidence of triple copresence and their auxiliary assumptions. Ann and Bob each have reason to believe that *G* holds. These grounds *G* indicate to each of them that the other has reason to believe that they hold. And the grounds *G* indicate to both of them that there is a candle on the table. By the induction schema, Ann and Bob mutually know that there is a candle on the table.

The point of this schema is that Ann and Bob don't have to confirm any of the infinity of conditions in mutual knowledge at all. They need only be confident that they have a proper basis *G*, grounds that satisfy all three requirements of the induction schema. With these grounds, Ann and Bob tacitly realize, so to speak, that they could confirm the infinity of conditions as far down the list as they wanted to go. Because they could do so in principle, they need not do so in fact. This is what gives the copresence heuristics their power. Once one has found proper grounds for mutual knowledge, that is enough.

Mutual knowledge can then be treated as a single mental entity instead of an infinitely long list of ever more complex mental entities. That is, what Ann would represent to herself is not (1), (2), (3), and so on ad infinitum, but merely this: *Ann and Bob mutually know that p*. This obviously leads to an important savings in memory. Just as it is implausible that Ann ordinarily checks a large number of conditions like (1), (2), and (3), so is it implausible that she ordinarily stores these conditions separately in memory. Whenever she needs one of these conditions, she can generate it by a rule such as this (an adaptation of Harman's definition of mutual knowledge): If A and B mutually know that p, then q, where q is that A and B know that p and that q. On demand Ann can deduce, for example, that if she and Bob mutually know there is a candle on the table, then she knows that Bob knows that she knows there is a candle on the table. So with the mutual knowledge induction schema there is simplification in memory too, and the simpler memory structure makes good intuitive sense.[7]

What do the grounds G for the mutual induction schema look like? In the candle example, Ann's grounds consisted of two parts. The first was her direct visual evidence of triple copresence – that there was a candle on the table and that Ann and Bob were simultaneously looking at each other and at the candle. As an event she experienced, this information is relatively fleeting. The second part was her assumptions about the situation – that Bob was consciously attending, that he was doing so simultaneously with her, and that he was rational. These assumptions are more lasting. Ann can assume that Bob is chronically rational, and that if he appears to be looking alertly at a scene, he is attending to it at that moment. These are assumptions she would make for any event of this kind.

There are other grounds too. Some of them are like the candle example but consist of weaker evidence of triple copresence and stronger auxiliary assumptions. For there is a trade-off between the evidence and assumptions loosely as follows:

Evidence + Assumptions + Induction Schema = Mutual Knowledge

Because the induction schema is fixed, the weaker the evidence Ann has at her disposal, the stronger the assumptions she must make in order to satisfy the induction schema and infer mutual knowledge. Still other grounds don't use triple copresence at all. It is instructive to classify the grounds that are most commonly used.

Varieties of mutual knowledge

Mutual knowledge can be classified in various ways. For our purposes it ought to be classified to show its grounds – its sources in a person's experience – because we are interested in how it is secured in the making of definite reference. One main division is between lasting and temporary kinds of mutual knowledge, and another is between several kinds of temporary mutual knowledge. A third division is between *generic* and *particular* knowledge.

Generic knowledge is knowledge about *kinds* of things (about kinds of objects, states, events, and processes), whereas particular knowledge is knowledge about *individual* or *particular* things (about particular objects, states, events, and processes). What we know about dogs in general (that they are animals, that they are domesticated, that they come in many species, and so on) is generic knowledge. What we know about Rin Tin Tin (that he once lived in Hollywood, that he was in several movies, that he was fed caviar, and so on) is particular knowledge. These two types of knowledge are ordinarily expressed in two different ways. Generic knowledge comes in generic sentences like: *Lions roar; A canary is a bird; Rooms each have a floor, a ceiling, at least three walls, at least one door, and they may have windows, carpets, lights, and so on.* Particular knowledge normally comes in nongeneric sentences that refer to particular things, like: *That lion roared just now; Our canary is yellow;* and *The room I am in now has a floor, a ceiling, four walls, two doors, a skylight, a desk, a bookshelf, and so on.* With definite reference, speakers refer to individuals – things in particular knowledge. Yet in doing so, they often need to draw on generic knowledge too.

Community membership

Even when Ann is not acquainted with Bob, she can assume there are generic and particular things the two of them mutually know. The basic idea is that there are things *everyone* in a community knows and assumes that everyone else in that community knows too.[8] In the broad community of educated Americans, for example, people assume that everyone knows such *generic* things as these: Cars drive on the right; senators have terms of six years and representatives terms of two years; and steak costs more than hamburger. They also assume everyone knows such *particular* things as these: George Washington was the first president of the United States; Colorado is west of Pennsylvania; there was a great depression between World Wars I and II. Once two people establish that they belong to the community of educated Americans, they can assume that they mutually know all of these things. We will call this mutual knowledge based on community membership.

But Ann belongs simultaneously to many communities and subcommunities, each of which has its own distinct areas of knowledge. At one and the same time Ann could be a high school graduate, a nineteenth-century-history buff, a San Francisco Forty-Niner football fan, a psychiatrist, a Palo Alto home owner, an American, a Californian, a skier, a speaker of Spanish, and a person of Scottish extraction. For each of these communities, she will have acquired facts she assumes are nearly universal within that community, and she must keep straight which facts are universal for which communities. She would not want to meet another person of Scottish ancestry and assume mutual knolwedge of Freud's theory of neurosis or the Spanish word for beautiful.

The trick is to judge community membership, and there are many ways of doing that. Ann may judge Bob to be an American by his accent, a Palo Alto home owner by his attendance at a meeting of such home owners, a nineteenth-century-history buff by his description of the German revolution of 1848, a psychiatrist by his announcement of that fact, and a person of Scottish ancestry by his surname MacPherson. Not only will Ann use these signs in her judgements, but Bob will provide them intending her to use them for that purpose. In ordinary conversation people go to some trouble to establish the communities of which they are members just so that their definite references will succeed. An illustration of this point can be found in Schegloff's (1972) account of how people formulate references to places, as when giving directions.

Before Ann and Bob can assume mutual knowledge of what is universally known within a community, they must mutually know that they both belong to that community. Ann might know, for example, that Bob and she belong to the Stanford University community. But unless he comes to know that, to know that she knows that, to know that she knows that he knows that, and so on, he can misinterpret such references as *the church, the library,* and *the president.* It is easy to imagine a series of Marx-brothers-like examples that demonstrate this. Ann could establish mutual knowledge of their Stanford community membership by her reference itself, as in *Memorial Church, Meyer Library,* and *Stanford's president,* but this won't always be possible. Requiring mutual knowledge of community membership introduces a new problem: How do Ann and Bob initially come to mutually know they belong to the same particular community? We suggest that they use one of the copresence heuristics discussed in the next section.

Mutual knowledge of community membership makes an excellent basis G for the mutual knowledge induction schema. Let us suppose that G is "Ann and Bob mutually know that they are both educated Americans." The induction schema requires three things. By requirement (1), Ann and Bob must have good reason to believe G. Indeed, they do. They mutually know they are both educated Americans, which entails that they mutually know G itself. By requirement (2), G must indicate to Ann and Bob that each has reason to believe that G holds. This requirement is fulfilled in the same way. And by requirement (3), G must indicate to Ann and Bob that, for example, American Independence was declared on July 4, 1776. This holds because they assume that every educated American knows the date of American Independence. By the induction schema, it follows that they *mutually* know that American Independence was declared on July 4, 1776.

It is instructive to spell out the two main assumptions required here for mutual knowledge of proposition p. First, Ann must believe that she and Bob mutually know they belong to a particular community. Let us call this assumption *community comembership*. And second, Ann must believe that everyone in that community knows that particular proposition p. Let us call this assumption *universality of knowledge*. Mutual knowledge of this type, then, has a basis G with two assumptions:

1. Community membership: community comembership, universality of knowledge.

Right away we should note two obvious problems. First, communities are not well defined. At what point should a person be considered an educated American, or a member of the Stanford University community, or a nineteenth-century-history buff? Deciding community membership is not a simple task. And second, the two assumptions may vary in strength or certainty. Ann may be certain Bob is an educated American, but less certain that he is a psychiatrist. This is akin to the first point. And she may be more certain an educated American will know that George Washington was the first president of the United States than that Colorado is southwest of South Dakota. The strength of these two assumptions, of course, will affect how certain Ann is that the definite references she is making are felicitous.

Mutual knowledge based on community membership is generally preserved over long periods of time. Once Ann and Bob mutually know they are educated Americans, they are likely to retain that knowledge for use in reference to all sorts of things. And with a constant source of fresh evidence, that mutual knowledge is continually being renewed. Mutual knowledge of the next three types, in contrast, is ordinarily relevant only for short periods of time. It may be used only once and then dropped. Its most distinguishing characteristic is that it is based on evidence that is in a sense more direct.

Physical copresence

The strongest evidence for mutual knowledge that people are generally prepared to accept is what we will call *physical copresence*. An example par excellence is the scene with Ann, Bob, and the candle. Not only are the three of them physically and openly present together, but Ann, say, can readily assume that Bob is attending to this fact, is doing so at the same time she is, and is rational. The physical, or perceptual, evidence Ann possesses is so strong that her three auxiliary assumptions can be relatively trivial. It is rare that she would have reason to think, contrary to the attention assumption, that Bob was catatonic, hypnotized the right way, or very nearsighted, or, contrary to the rationality assumption, that he was too brain-damaged or too young to possess the mutual knowledge induction schema. So with this evidence, once Ann has assured herself of these minimal assumptions, it is trivial for her to refer to *this candle*. Mutual knowledge of the candle has already been secured, and all she has left to do is make sure its identification is unique.

When the time period of physical copresence is placed with respect to the moment of the reference act itself, we can distinguish three varieties of physical copresence. Imagine that Bob isn't paying attention to the target candle, but it is easily within view. Ann can then say *this candle*, which gets Bob to look at it and complete the physical copresence of him, her, and the candle. This could be called *potential physical copresence*. When Ann and Bob are actually focusing on the candle as she says *this candle*, we have a case of *immediate physical copresence*. And when Ann and Bob have looked together at the candle but have stopped before she says *that candle*, we have an instance of *prior physical copresence*.

On the face of it, these three types of physical copresence differ in how strong they are as evidence. The immediate type is the strongest. The potential type is slightly weaker, for Ann must assume that Bob can discover the target candle and bring it into view simultaneously with her. Let us call this the *locatability assumption*. The prior case is also weaker, for Ann must assume Bob can recall the earlier copresence of him, her, and the candle. Let us call this the *recallability assumption*. If Ann is to use evidence of physical copresence to secure the mutual knowledge necessary for her definite reference, she will need the following auxiliary assumptions:

2. Physical copresence
   a. Immediate: simultaneity, attention, rationality
   b. Potential: simultaneity, attention, rationality, locatability
   c. Prior: simultaneity, attention, rationality, recallability

(Simultaneity, attention, and rationality refer to the assumptions we described earlier.) So far so good. The stronger the evidence, the fewer auxiliary assumptions are needed here.

Linguistic copresence

Many things that are referred to have only been mentioned in conversation. Imagine Ann saying to Bob *I bought a candle yesterday*. By uttering *a candle*, she posits for Bob the existence of a particular candle. If Bob hears and understands her correctly, he will come to know about the candle's existence at the same time as she posits it. It is as if Ann places the candle on the stage in front of the two of them so that it is physically copresent. The two of them can be said to be in the *linguistic copresence* of the candle. Ann can then make a definite reference to the candle, as in *The candle cost me plenty*.[9]

The world in which a thing is claimed to exist can be real or imaginary, past, present, or future. *A deer and a unicorn were grazing beside a stream when the unicorn complimented the deer on his beautiful extra horn.* These two beasts live in an imaginary world, on an imaginary stage, which is quite enough for their linguistic copresence with the speaker and listener. (The question of worlds is too complicated to consider further here, but see McCawley, 1979, and Prince, 1978.)

Unlike physical copresence, linguistic copresence can never be "immediate," that is, simultaneous with the definite reference for which it is used. *A candle* cannot be spoken at the same time as *the candle*. It must come either before, as in *I bought a candle, but the candle was broken*, or afterward if *the candle* is pronominalized, as in *Because it was broken, I returned a candle I had just bought to the store*. In parallel with physical copresence, these two cases can be called prior and potential linguistic copresence, respectively.

To refer to an object that is linguistically copresent, Ann need not use the same term as was used with the potential or prior mention of it. Because a lathe is a machine, and also an inanimate thing, she could say *I bought a lathe, but the machine/it didn't work right.* Note that because not all machines are lathes, it would ordinarily be odd to say, with the same intended interpretation, *I bought a machine, but the lathe didn't work right.*

What auxiliary assumptions are needed for linguistic copresence? To begin with, there are the assumptions of simultaneity, attention, and rationality. Ann and Bob must be attending to Ann's utterance of *a candle* simultaneously, and both must be rational. There is also a complex assumption we will call *understandability.* Ann must assume that Bob will penetrate her indefinite reference, *a candle,* and understand that she is sincerely positing the candle's existence in some world. And as before, prior linguistic copresence requires the assumption of recallability, and potential linguistic copresence the assumption of locatability. Recalling and locating linguistic objects, however, may not be the same as recalling and locating physical objects; so these two assumptions may be either stronger or weaker than those for physical copresence. Putting them all together, we have:

3. Linguistic copresence
    a. Potential: simultaneity, attention, rationality, locatability, understandability
    b. Prior: simultaneity, attention, rationality, recallability, understandability

Fairly clearly, linguistic copresence is ordinarily weaker evidence for mutual knowledge than physical copresence. Whereas seeing is believing, hearing about something requires more – the extra understandability assumption. Both types of copresence are difficult to compare with mutual knowledge based on community membership, whose auxiliary assumptions are so different.

Mixtures

Very often mutual knowledge is established by a combination of physical or linguistic copresence and mutual knowledge based on community membership. Imagine Ann saying to Bob *I bought a candle yesterday, but the wick had broken off.* In uttering *a candle,* Ann establishes the linguistic copresence of him, her, and the candle, but not of him, her, and the wick. To refer to the wick she has to assume that when Bob accepts the existence of the candle, he also accepts the existence of the wick. He and she mutually know that they belong to the community of educated people for whom it is universally known that candles have wicks. By referring to *the wick,* she can therefore secure mutual knowledge of the identity of the wick that belongs to this particular candle. Ann's use of *a candle,* then, establishes what we will call the *indirect linguistic copresence* of her, Bob, and the wick.

Indirect copresence of this kind may be based on a less certain association than that between candles and wicks (see H. Clark, 1977, 1978; Clark and Haviland, 1977; Haviland and Clark, 1974; and others). For example, a candle has only a *likelihood* of having a wrapper associated with it and only a *low possibility* of being made of bayberries. Yet that is enough to allow Ann to establish their mutual knowledge with her references in *I bought a candle yesterday, but the wrapper was torn* and in *I bought a candle yesterday, and the bayberry smelled great.* Indirect copresence can be very indirect indeed.

There can also be indirect *physical* copresence. A physically present candle, for example, may have a price, which is then indirectly present too. When Ann and Bob are looking at a candle, Ann says *The price was $3,* referring to the candle's price that is indirectly copresent and thereby establishing mutual knowledge of its identity.

Both types of indirect copresence require mutual knowledge based on community membership. That knowledge may be generic, as with candles having wicks, wrappers, bayberries, and prices, but it may also be particular. Imagine that Ann and Bob belong to a small community in which it is universally known that Charlie has a broken left leg. That broken leg is then indirectly copresent with the mention of Charlie. Ann could say to Bob *I saw Charlie yesterday, and the leg is getting better.*

What assumptions are required for inducing mutual knowledge from indirect copresence? If we think of the copresence of the wick as parasitic on the copresence of the candle, then there are first the assumptions of physical or linguistic copresence, whichever is the parasite's host. There is next an assumption we will call *associativity.* It must be mutually known in the community that the parasite is certainly, probably, or possibly a particular part of, or in a particular role with, the host. The two major types of indirect copresence, then, require these assumptions (where parentheses enclose assumptions that are optionally needed depending on the subtype of the host):

4. Indirect copresence
   a. Physical: simultaneity, attention, rationality, (locatability or recallability), associativity
   b. Linguistic: simultaneity, attention, rationality, (locatability or recallability), understandability, associativity

As this listing shows, indirect copresence is always weaker than direct copresence with the parasite's host. The four major types of mutual knowledge are summarized in Table 1.

Types of reference

Traditional linguistic theories tell us that definite reference comes in different kinds. But if definite reference secures mutual knowledge of the identity of R, and if this mutual knowledge is ordinarily inferred from states of affairs G, then definite reference should be classifiable by these grounds G. We will argue that the traditional classifications are indeed based on these grounds G. This argument is important for two reasons. It is indirect evidence that copresence heuristics are used in making definite reference. And it suggests that definite reference cannot be fully explained without bringing them in.

Deixis, anaphora, and proper names

The three basic types of definite reference are deixis, anaphora, and proper names (Lyons, 1977). Deictic expressions are used to point to things in the nonlinguistic situation. In Ann's *I want that, I* refers to the speaker Ann, and *that* refers to the object she is pointing at. Anaphoric expressions are used to refer to things introduced into the conversation itself. In Ann's *I bought a candle, but the thing was broken, the thing* refers to the candle introduced by Ann's utterance of *a candle*. Deixis is often construed to cover anaphora too, but we will stick with its narrower sense. Contrasting with both deixis and anaphora are proper nouns, as in *George Washington had a knotty mouth*. In Kripke's (1972, 1977) proposal, each proper noun rigidly designates the same individual regardless of context.

With this classification, the fit between definite reference and mutual knowledge seems clear. Deixis corresponds to physical copresence; anaphora corresponds to linguistic copresence; and proper names correspond to community membership. The fit could hardly be more obvious. Yet deixis, anaphora, and proper names are categories that are primarily based on functional characteristics. It is worthwhile to look more closely at a few of their structural properties.

The prototypical deictic expressions are demonstratives, as when the speaker gestures at something and says *that*, or *that woman*. These gestures are used to establish immediate physical copresence. They make certain that the speaker and listener come to look at the same object simultaneously. As Hawkins (1978, p. 111) points out, *that* can

Table 1. *Four types of mutual knowledge and their auxiliary assumptions*

Basis for mutual knowledge	Auxiliary assumptions
1. Community membership	Community comembership, universality of knowledge
2. Physical copresence	
a. Immediate	Simultaneity, attention, rationality
b. Potential	Simultaneity, attention, rationality, locatability
c. Prior	Simultaneity, attention, rationality, recallability
3. Linguistic copresence	
a. Potential	Simultaneity, attention, rationality, locatability, understandability
b. Prior	Simultaneity, attention, rationality, recallability, understandability
4. Indirect copresence	
a. Physical	Simultaneity, attention, rationality, (locatability or recallability), associativity
b. Linguistic	Simultaneity, attention, rationality, (locatability or recallability), understandability, associativity

replace a "visible situation use" of the definite article, as in *Look out for the table,* where the table is visible, but not an "immediate situation use," as in *Beware of the dog,* where the dog is somewhere around but not visible. This contrast coincides with our distinction between direct and indirect physical copresence. When there is a candle between Ann and Bob, the candle is physically present, but its price is only indirectly present (unless there is a price tag). Ann can say *That candle is beautiful,* but not *That price is high.* The choice of *that* is governed in part by whether the basis for mutual knowledge is direct or indirect physical copresence.

In anaphora, the prototypical expressions are definite pronouns and definite descriptions, although demonstratives can be used too. In *I met a woman yesterday; the woman/she was a doctor,* the noun phrases *the woman* and *she* are used to refer to a woman already established by linguistic copresence. The type of linguistic copresence is critical. When it has been established in a previous sentence, the speaker can choose either definite descriptions or pronouns, depending on other factors. When it is established in the same sentence as the definite reference, the choice is highly constrained, as summarized, for example, by Lasnik (1976). In *The woman decided she would operate,* the second reference to the woman must be the pronoun *she.* When there is potential linguistic copresence, it must "command" the definite reference in a technical sense of command. In *She decided that the woman would operate,* it is impossible for *she* to refer to the same person as *the woman.*

Indeed, there appear to be stringent requirements on the basis for mutual knowledge that will allow pronouns. Chafe (1974) has argued that the referents of pronouns must be in the listener's consciousness, "on stage," at that point in the conversation. If so, the conditions on pronouns tie in directly with the assumptions of recallability and locatability. When the referents are recallable, or locatable, within immediate as opposed to long-term memory, the speaker can use a pronoun; otherwise, he cannot.

Demonstratives can be used for anaphora only under special conditions. In *I met a woman yesterday: that woman was a doctor, that* attracts contrastive stress and implies there is a contrasting set of women. It is not used for simple cases of linguistic copresence. And in discourse *this* and *that* are distinguished precisely by the kind of linguistic copresence they require. To refer to something established by prior copresence, one can use either *this* or *that,* but to refer to something yet to be established – potential linguistic copresence – one must use *this.*

Anaphora can be summarized this way. It is prototypically expressed with pronouns or definite descriptions. The expression that is appropriate depends on the type of linguistic copresence: whether it is potential or prior, whether it "commands" the definite reference or not, and whether it is available in immediate or long-term memory, among other things. Anaphora can also be expressed with demonstratives, yet the demonstrative that is appropriate again depends on whether the linguistic copresence is potential or prior. The choice of definite reference, then, is heavily determined by the basis for the mutual knowledge it establishes.

Proper names are the prototypical way of referring to things that are mutually known by community membership. When a particular is widely known in a community, it tends to get a proper name – a rigid designator that doesn't change from one conversation to the next. That is, it is the universally known things within a community that get so named. Note what get proper names: people (*George Washington*), places (*Valley Forge*), and prominent events (*the Revolutionary War*). The few trees, rocks, or animals that get proper names have to be prominent, like *The Great Redwood, Standing Rock,* and *Rin Tin Tin.* There is probably no grain of sand, glass of water, or ream of typing paper that has ever received a proper name.

Many universally known particulars, however, are referred to with definite descriptions instead of proper names; for example, *the sun, the moon,* and *the snowfall last winter.* Historically, many of these have come to be treated as proper names, as in the change from *the great swamp* to *the Great Swamp,* from *the civil war* to *the Civil War,* and from *the supreme court* to *the Supreme Court.* Sometimes the definite descriptions even become proper nouns, as in *the earth* to *Earth* and *the first world war* to *World War I.* Pronouns and demonstratives apparently cannot be used for reference to things that are mutually known on the basis of community membership, except in rare cases. They require a more direct basis for mutual knowledge.[10]

Eight uses of the definite article

Another classification of definite reference already noted is Christopherson's, Jespersen's, and Hawkins' eight uses for the definite article. Two of these uses are obvious cases of deixis and anaphora. The rest reflect mixtures and fall under our heading of indirect copresence.

The "visible situation use," as in *Pass me the bucket* for a visible bucket, is a clear example of physical copresence, but there are three other uses that are indirect physical copresence. The "immediate situation use," as in *Do not feed the pony* for a nonvisible pony, relies on the physical copresence of a fenced-in yard, supplemented by generic knowledge that such a yard could contain a pony. The "larger situation use based on specific knowledge" relies on the physical copresence of, say, Ann and Bob in a particular situation, with mutual knowledge based on community membership completing the identification of the referent. Ann and Bob mutually know, for example, which store Ann ordinarily goes to in a community; so as long as she and Bob are physically copresent in the neighborhood, she can refer to that store as *I'm going to the store.* The "larger situation use based on general knowledge," as in *I wonder where the city hall is* for a new town, has a similar basis.

The "anaphoric use" is a plain example of linguistic copresence, and the "associative anaphoric use," as in *A car just went by and the exhaust fumes made me sick,* a case of indirect linguistic copresence. Within a community, cars are known to produce exhaust fumes, knowledge that along with the linguistic copresence of the car is enough to secure mutual knowledge of the fumes being referred to.

There are several subtypes of "unavailable use" of the definite article. The first is the "referent establishing relative clauses," as in *The woman Max went out with last night was nasty to him.* These always "relate the new, unknown object [here, the woman] either to other objects in the previous discourse set, or to participants in the speech act, or else they identify entities in the immediate situation of the utterance" (Hawkins, 1978, p. 137). So they are cases of indirect linguistic or physical copresence via mutual knowledge based on community membership. A second subtype is the "associative clause," as in *the beginning of World War II,* another case of indirect copresence because it is mutually known among educated people that wars have beginnings, and so one can indirectly identify the beginning of a mutually known war. A third subtype is the "noun complement," as in *the idea that he is in Caracas* and *the fact that the world is round.* One way to view these is to say there is a set of possible ideas, and a set of possible facts, and these sets are mutually known based on membership in the community of thinking, perceiving humans. Any individual fact or idea can then be identified merely by being specified. The fourth type, "nominal modifiers," as in *the color red,* would work the same way.

Deixis as fundamental

According to many linguists (for example, Lyons, 1975), deixis is the source for all definite reference. In Indo-European languages, the pronouns (like English *he, she, it,* and *they*) and the definite articles (like English *the*) are historically derived from demonstratives (like English *this* and *that*). Thorne (1972, 1974) has argued that the definite article is fundamentally locative – that is, deictic. *The woman* designates not merely a particular woman, but a particular woman in a particular place. All the world's languages appear to have demonstratives and personal pronouns, but many do not have definite articles. In these languages, when a definite reference has to be made absolutely clear, a demonstrative is used, as in *that woman* (Moravcsik, 1969). That is, demonstratives are stretched to cover other nondeictic kinds of definite reference. And in language acquisition, E. Clark (1978; Clark and Sengul, 1978) has argued that deixis is also fundamental. Children refer to things by pointing long before they begin to speak, and their first referring expressions, usually *that, there,* or *look* in English, are almost invariably accompanied by pointing. The weaker forms of definite reference – the pronouns and definite article – are acquired only later. Proper nouns, our incommensurate case, however, come in very early (E. Clark, 1973).

If, as we have argued, physical copresence is the fundamental type of copresence, then it follows that deixis should have primacy in definite reference. The idea is this: Physical copresence is the prototype of what it means for a thing to be mutually known. It is such good evidence that it needs only weak auxiliary assumptions to serve as a basis G in the mutual knowledge induction schema. The other types of copresence each require stronger assumptions, as if they were defective types of copresence in which one or another of the essential conditions of physical copresence hadn't been fulfilled. If physical copresence is primary, then deixis too should be primary. It is significant that there is such a convergence of evidence from historical linguistics, language universals, and language acquisition.

To summarize, when definite reference is divided into types, these correspond to different bases G by which mutual knowledge of the identity of the referent is established. And among these types, deixis appears to be primary. All this evidence is in line with the copresence heuristics – in particular with the use of physical, linguistic, and indirect copresence and of community membership.

Reference repairs

In conversation people often say one thing, repair what they have just said, and then go on (see Clark and Clark, 1977, pp. 260–71). Ann might say *I ran into Ralph – you know, the guy who works in our clinic – the other night at the symphony*. Or she might say *I ran into Ralph the other night at the symphony*, to which Bob would ask *Who is Ralph*, to which Ann would reply *You know, the guy who works in our clinic*. Both types of repairs – self-repairs and other-repairs – are common in everyday speech, although self-repairs predominate (Schegloff et al., 1977).

Repairs of definite reference, what DuBois (1975) has called *reference editing*, give further evidence for the copresence heuristics. The argument is this. One reason speakers repair definite references is to make them more likely to succeed. In our examples, Ann wants to make it more likely Bob will identify the person she was referring to. In making these repairs speakers have two broad options. They can provide more information in the reference itself. This way the basis G on which they and their listeners come to mutually know the identity of the referent will become clearer. This might be called a *horizontal repair*. Or they can strengthen the type of copresence on which their reference is based. This might be called a *vertical repair*. Of these repairs, some should increase the success of a reference, and others should not. If our proposal is correct, those that increase success

ought to be just those that provide stronger types of copresence –
direct instead of indirect, physical instead of linguistic, immediate
instead of potential. The evidence is that they are.

Horizontal repairs

Most reference repairs are horizontal. They ensure greater success by
providing more precise information about the referent without changing the type of basis G on which its identity becomes mutually known.
Consider these four cases.

1. *Physical copresence.* Imagine telling a librarian with a gesture, *I
want that.* He prompts, *Which one?* You reply, *The book right there on the
second shelf.* He prompts again, *I still don't see which one.* You reply, *The
green book on the second shelf from the bottom of that bookcase.* These references all rely on potential physical copresence. What changes with
each repair is the precision with which the referent is specified. This
you accomplish by adding descriptors that refer to other potential
physically copresent items – *right there, the second shelf, the bottom, that
bookcase.* Each addition, you believe, makes it more likely that the right
book will be identified uniquely. Each new piece of information
strengthens the basis G on which the identity of the referent can be
mutually known. Horizontal repairs of *prior* physical copresence work
the same way.

2. *Linguistic copresence.* Imagine this interchange. Ann: *A doctor I met
last night introduced me to a lawyer, and she gave me some advice.* Bob: *Who
did?* Ann? *The lawyer.* In this repair Ann has disambiguated her reference by providing one more descriptor – that the referent is a lawyer.
This descriptor, like the reference itself, is based on prior linguistic
copresence. She could not have added *the woman in black* or *the person
near the piano* or *the rich one,* which do not make contact with information Ann has provided linguistically, but she could have said *the person
the doctor introduced me to* or *not the doctor* or *the one I talked to second.* To
be effective, horizontal repairs must add or alter descriptors, not de-
lete them. It wouldn't make sense for Ann to say *A woman I met last
night introduced me to her daughter, and the older one, I mean she, gave me
good advice.* Cooperative repairs – and that is what we are talking
about – must lead to a more precise identification of the referent.

3. *Indirect copresence.* Imagine Ann's report: *I tried to get downtown
yesterday but the bus – the one I was riding in – broke down.* The bus is
identifiable only on the basis of indirect copresence, and the repair
adds other evidence of indirect copresence, namely that Ann *rode* on
the bus. Like the previous two types of repairs, the more information

the listener is provided with, the more successful the reference is judged to be.

4. *Community membership.* When references rely on community membership, there are several ways of making horizontal repairs. One is to add more information, as in *I met Nina – Nina Baker,* or as in *I hated the war – the Vietnam War.* Another is to change the community basis for the reference, as in *I like my new colleague – you know, Elizabeth Adams.* Here both the original reference and the repair rely on community membership. What the repair does is change the community from one in which it is universally known who the speaker's colleague is to one in which it is universally known who Elizabeth Adams is. This change in community must strengthen either the certainty it is mutually known that the speaker and listener belong to that community or the certainty that the referent is universally known in that community.

Vertical repairs

The principle of repairs is that they *strengthen* the basis G on which mutual knowledge of the identity of the referent can be inferred. With this principle we can examine vertical repairs, ones that replace one kind of copresence by another, to see if we can order the types of copresence for their strength. If our proposal is correct, the types of copresence should order themselves from strongest to weakest according to the number and kind of auxiliary assumptions they require. Indeed, that is what we will demonstrate.

1. *Physical copresence.* Among types of physical copresence, immediate physical copresence should be the strongest because it requires the fewest auxiliary assumptions – and it is. Ann: *The book over there is mine.* Bob: *Which one?* Ann, picking up a book and showing it to Bob: *This one.* In her repair Ann has moved from potential to immediate physical copresence. If she had moved in the reverse direction, from inmediate to potential physical copresence, her repair would have been nonsense. Or imagine Ann: *The book I just showed you is mine.* Bob: *Which book was that?* Ann, picking up a book and showing it to Bob: *This one.* Ann's repair here goes from prior to immediate physical copresence, and it too would be nonsensical in the reverse direction. Recall that the basis G for potential and prior physical copresence requires the auxiliary assumptions of locatability and recallability, respectively. What these and similar repairs show is that some such assumptions are necessary and that G can be strengthened by turning to direct evidence that doesn't need them – namely, immediate physi-

cal copresence. As Searle (1969, p. 88) has argued, the limiting case of referring to something is physically showing it (along with a suitable expression).

Physical copresence is stronger when it is direct than when it is indirect. Ann, still staring at Bob and the candle: *The price was too high.* Bob: *What price?* Ann: *The price of this candle.* And physical copresence is stronger, all other things being equal, than linguistic copresence. Ann: *I was just reading a book on your bookshelf, and it was terrific.* Bob: *What book?* Ann, picking out a book and showing it to Bob: *This one.* Repairs like these, then, are evidence for the auxiliary assumptions of associativity and understandability that we said were required for indirect physical copresence and for linguistic copresence.

2. *Linguistic copresence.* When things are not physically showable, repairs have to be made that move up to the strongest kind of linguistic copresence. Ann: *I bought a candle today; the seal was broken.* Bob: *What seal?* Ann: *The seal on the wrapper around the candle.* This repair moves the evidence up from indirect to direct linguistic copresence. It suggests that the assumption of associativity is not a trivial one. And within linguistic copresence, a repair can be made that strengthens the recallability or locatability of the linguistic copresence. Ann: *I think your idea is excellent.* Bob: *What idea?* Ann: *A moment ago you mentioned going to a movie tonight.* This repair brings back into linguistic copresence an idea Bob had failed to recall.

3. *Community membership.* Community membership cannot be ordered for strength in relation to physical, linguistic, or indirect copresence because its auxiliary assumptions are not comparable with those of the other three types. It can apparently be either stronger or weaker than physical or linguistic copresence, depending on the purpose for the repair. Take this exchange: Ann: *I was just talking to the woman standing right over there* (pointing). Bob: *Who is she?* Ann: *Nina Baker, the artist.* Contrast it with this interchange: Ann: *I was just talking to Nina Baker, the artist.* Bob: *Who is she?* Ann: *The woman standing right over there* (pointing). In the first exchange, the woman's physical appearance was not as significant an identification for Bob as her role in Ann and Bob's community. In the second, it is the other way around, as if Bob knows little about Nina Baker in the community and now at least can identify her physically. These repairs bear out the claim that the community membership has auxiliary assumptions that are not comparable with the others.[11]

The several bases G we proposed earlier – physical, linguistic, and indirect copresence and community membership – are only one way of cutting up the territory. They provide a tidy geography in which each basis has associated with it a few assumptions, such as simultaneity, recallability, understandability, and community comembership. A more thorough survey of repairs might suggest a different geography with slightly different auxiliary assumptions. Still, such a survey would rely on the logic we have just been using. Every repair that is judged to strengthen a reference should be associated with the elimination or simplification of one or more auxiliary assumptions. Such a survey should lead to a more complete map of the copresence heuristics themselves.

To summarize, repairs of definite reference bear witness to people's use of copresence heuristics. When a speaker makes such a repair, he tacitly reassesses his evidence for mutual knowledge of the identity of the referent, and his repair is an attempt to strengthen that evidence. The way he strengthens it is to try to find fresh evidence that needs weaker or fewer auxiliary assumptions.

Organization of memory

The copresence heuristics, with their voracious appetite, can be satiated only by the right kinds and amounts of factual fodder. How is this fodder organized? What does the storehouse of data the heuristics feed on look like? The arguments we have offered so far suggest a rather different view of memory from those of most current models of understanding and production.

One traditional view of definite reference is that its primary function is to pick out particular individuals – individual objects, states, events, or processes (see Strawson, 1974). What this view has suggested to most investigators is that in processing definite reference people search memory for the particulars actually referred to. They can't, of course, find the particulars themselves, but they can find *referential indices* corresponding to them. Each index is a stand-in, so to speak, for the referent itself. Imagine that Bob's memory contains a set of referential indices for entities represented as $E_1, E_2, E_3, \ldots E_n$, and that E_3 is the referential index for *Monkey Business*. When Ann uses the definite description *the movie showing at the Roxy tonight*, he is supposed to search this list and settle on the intended referent E_3. Although current models of comprehension differ in their specifics, virtually all of them assume this kind of search for the intended referent, including those of Anderson (1976), Clark and Haviland (1977), Kintsch (1974), Kintsch and van Dijk (1978), Rumelhart et al. (1972), Schank and Abelson (1977), and Winograd (1972), to name just a few.

All of these models, however, are incomplete. Bob cannot search memory for E_3 alone, for that would hardly guarantee that E_3 was mutually known to him and Ann. In most cases, he must search for an *event* that involves not only E_3 but also E_1, Ann, and E_2, him. This event, call it E_4, has to be evidence of their physical, linguistic, or indirect copresence. Or when community membership is concerned, he must search for an individual E_3 that everyone in a community he (E_1) and Ann (E_2) both belong to knows. In none of the models just mentioned does the listener search for such an event or for such a community-wide individual.

Components of memory

Our point can be made with a metaphorical view of memory as a personal archive, or library, in which there are several different kinds of reference books. Most theories of understanding require memory to contain a grammar of English and a dictionary. With these two books, the listener can parse sentences and figure out what they mean. But to handle definite reference, the listener needs more.

What most current models of comprehension add is an elaborate kind of telephone book. In a definite reference like *the man in the red shirt*, Bob is told the name and address of the individual whose referential index he is seeking. All he needs to do is search the telephone book for this name and address, and the book will tell him the right referential index – the telephone number that connects his name and address (the reference) with his physical person (the referent). The telephone book must be a sophisticated one, like the Yellow Pages, in which the names and addresses are organized and cross-classified according to some scheme. But in effect it is a mere listing of descriptions of individuals paired with their referential indices.

Such a telephone book won't do, however, because it doesn't contain the right kind of information. Take Ann's telephone book. For her to be able to make a successful definite reference, the book would have to distinguish those names and addresses she knew Bob knew from the rest, and it would have to make the same distinction for everyone else she might potentially talk to. Although that satisfies condition (2) for mutual knowledge, it doesn't do anything more. Her book would also have to distinguish those names and addresses she knew Bob knew she knew from the rest, satisfying condition (3), and those she knew Bob knew she knew Bob knew from the rest, satisfying condition (4), and so on. Very quickly, her book would grow unmanageably large. The telephone book, in effect, is an embodiment of Assumption II, which is just the assumption we want to circumvent in order to avoid the mutual knowledge paradox.

What the copresence heuristics require instead is a pair of books, a diary and an encyclopedia. Bob's diary is a personal log that keeps an account of everything significant Bob does and experiences. When Ann uses the reference *the man in the red shirt,* Bob must find in memory an individual who fits that description – a man in a red shirt. But he knows that he must search his diary for an entry that gives evidence of the physical, linguistic, or indirect copresence of him, Ann, and that man. That is, he must seek out an *event* that he can use along with certain auxiliary assumptions as the basis G for inductively inferring mutual knowledge of the identity of that man. This is far more complicated than searching a telephone book for a number. Every event he searches for involves the referent plus two other individuals, and that takes more specification than the referent alone.

Not all parts of the diary will be equally accessible. The more recent events ought to be more accessible, and there is evidence to suggest that they are. In several studies, people were found to take less time to understand definite references that relied on linguistic copresence the more recently the antecedent event occurred (Carpenter and Just, 1977; Clark and Sengul, 1979; Lesgold et al., 1979). And events that are more significant ought to be more accessible too. However, too little is known to be able to say much more about the organization of the diary. Our point is that such a diary is needed to account for genuine cases of felicitous definite reference.

Bob's second book is an encyclopedia, which he needs for mutual knowledge based on community membership. It will have recorded in it all the generic and particular knowledge Bob believes is universal to each community he belongs to. Instead of being organized in the conventional way – alphabetical by subject matter – it might take this form: Chapter 1 would contain the knowledge every human being is assumed to know, Chapter 2 the additional knowledge every American is assumed to know, Chapter 3 the additional information (over Chapters 1 and 2) that every Californian is assumed to know, and so on. Within each chapter there would be sections on biographical, geographical, historical, and other types of information. And there would be special chapters for the additional specialized knowledge possessed by psychiatrists, by Palo Alto homeowners, and by whatever other communities and subcommunities Bob may happen to belong to. Happily, subject matter and communities tend to go hand in hand – psychiatry is known by psychiatrists, and the rules and regulations for owning homes in Palo Alto by Palo Alto homeowners – and so the encyclopedia doesn't have as complicated an organization as it might first appear.

It is the encyclopedia that Bob consults for references that require mutual knowledge based on community membership. Imagine that Bob and Ann mutually establish through months of companionship that they both belong to certain communities – those corresponding, say, to Chapters 1 through 8, 11, 15, and 33 in Bob's encyclopedia. When Ann uses the reference *George Washington,* Bob must search just those chapters for an individual with that name. He must also consult those chapters for her references that rely on indirect copresence. When she says *I went to buy a candle but the price was too high,* he will find what is known about candles, determine that each has a price, use this information to create an individual (or rather, its referential index) that corresponds to the price of the candle she mentioned, and identify it as the referent of *the price.* Creating such referential indices via indirect copresence is known to take people longer than merely identifying referential indices that are already present. People understand *The beer was warm* more quickly after *Mary got some beer out of the car,* where the beer is directly copresent, than after *Mary got some picnic supplies out of the car,* where the beer is only indirectly copresent (Haviland and Clark, 1974).

A great deal has been said about the organization of such an encyclopedia. Minsky (1975) has proposed that people have "frames" for what such things as rooms consist of in general and what specific rooms consist of. Schank and Abelson (1977) have made a similar proposal for "scripts" of what people should and actually do do in such activities as going to a restaurant. Rumelhart and Ortony (1977) have proposed "schemata." Yet in none of these proposals is there any consideration for how this knowledge might be compartmentalized according to what information is mutually known by a community or by two individuals, as required for definite reference.

The diary and encyclopedia are not independent of each other. They must be cross-indexed by the individuals they contain – as when someone speaks of George Washington, the Revolutionary War, and 1776 and then refers to them all in *He led the army then.* And certain diary entries will be duplicated in the encyclopedia, as when Bob sees a news item on CBS television and supposes that it is universally known by the community of people who habitually watch CBS television.

Speaker models and listener models

The memory described so far seems entirely too large and unwieldy for everyday use. It seems to go against people's intuition that talk is easy, that getting the right information at the right time is effortless and straightforward. Their intuition is based, we suggest, on the fact that the diary and the encyclopedia are compartmentalized into useful units. In conversation the units that are pertinent at any time can be prepared for selective access.

Imagine, at a party, turning from talk with an English speaker to talk with a French one. You are likely to feel you are changing gears – as if you are putting away your English dictionary and grammar and pulling out your French ones. Our suggestion is that you make similar shifts whenever you change interlocutors. You prepare yourself selectively to talk to, or listen to, that particular person or group of people. You do this by selecting pertinent parts of the diary and encyclopedia for ready access.

The way a speaker prepares is by accessing his model of the listener, and the listener accesses his model of the speaker. When Ann talks to Bob, she creates in memory a model of what is in Bob's mind – his knowledge, his perceptions, his current thoughts – and she constantly updates it. Bob carries along a similar model of what is in Ann's mind. These models must include the right diary entries and encyclopedia chapters. Ann's model of Bob would contain all those chapters of her encyclopedia that correspond to communities she knows he belongs to. However, she knows she can refer only to individuals in those communities she knows they mutually know they *both* belong to. She may know Bob is a chess addict, but realize he doesn't know she knows. So her model may include Chapters 1 through 11, 16 through 24, 38, and 55, but of those only Chapters 1 through 8, 16 through 18, and 55 are mutually known. Her model of him also contains all those diary entries that involve Bob in some way. It is these she consults when deciding whether she can establish mutual knowledge of the identity of most individuals she wants to refer to. Ann's model of Bob, in short, contains just those parts of her diary and encyclopedia that will be useful for getting him to understand her, whatever she may want to talk about. It will also contain just those parts that will allow her to understand him and all his actions.

The suggestion is that we carry around rather detailed models of people we know, especially of people we know well. If Bob is a close friend of Ann, she may even have a special chapter in her encyclopedia for him, as if he and she form a community of two people. It is hard to underestimate the importance of these models. At a cocktail party, as Ann turns from Bob, her close friend, to Charles, her cousin from out of town, her model of the listener will change radically, and so will the way she refers. Diary entries are particularly important here. If she has just told Bob about her theory of the Marx brothers' success in Hollywood, she cannot immediately expect Charles, who has not heard what she told Bob, to understand references to things she told Bob. She must keep track – careful track – of what she told each of them. Though her Marx-brothers theory may be uppermost in her mind as she turns to Charles, she has to explain it over again to him if he is to understand her. People who tell someone the same gossip, or joke, or piece of news twice without realizing it are considered impolite or absentminded. They have failed in the social imperative of keeping their models of each particular listener straight.

How do we build these models in the first place? In certain circumstances we can watch our model of a person being erected block by block. One of these is in formal introductions, which are designed to lay the foundations of our model of the other person in the first few seconds and to add onto it prefabricated sections quickly and easily.

Imagine Ann at a party of academics bumping into Ed. "Isn't the weather just great!" she tells Ed. The weather one can always refer to, because it is mutually identifiable by people in the same locale. The convention of always talking about the weather at the beginnings of conversations and in new conversations has an obvious basis in mutual knowledge.

"Yes, it is," replies Ed. "My name is Ed Taylor. I'm a psychiatrist working here at the Palo Alto VA hospital." With this, Ann can add to her model of Ed not only, say, encyclopedia Chapters 1 and 2 – for being human and being American, which she could gather from his reply alone – but also Chapters 3 through 11, 15 and 25, for being a Californian, a Palo Altoan, a psychiatrist, and so on. This is typical of self- and third-party introductions. They allow one to build up great chunks of the model of the other person. They are intended to accomplish just that so that the two now have something to talk about, things they can felicitously refer to.

"How do you do. And I'm Ann Horton, and I work in the psychiatry department at Stanford." With this, Ann has established mutual knowledge of the universal information in these chapters. She was able to refer to Stanford University and its psychiatry department just because she knew Ed was a member of the Palo Alto community and the community of psychiatrists, and so her reference would secure mutual knowledge of the identity of these two places. "What kind of psychiatry do you specialize in?" she might go on, continuing to establish mutual knowledge of larger and larger spheres of experience.

In summary, people's memory must be organized to enable them to get access to evidence they will need to make felicitous references. What that implies is that their memory must contain a diary of significant personal experiences cross-indexed with an encyclopedia organized both by subject matter and by the communities who possess the knowledge. It also suggests that people have selective access to information that is pertinent to each person they talk to. They have a model of what is in the other person's mind, a model they have built up from previous contact and which they continue to update as they go on talking. It is that model that enables people to make and understand references so quickly and accurately.

Conclusions

Definite reference is one of those phenomena in language that seem so obvious that it is hard to see what there is to explain. We have tried to shatter this illusion by posing the mutual knowledge paradox, which is this: To make or interpret definite references people have to assess certain "shared" knowledge. This knowledge, it turns out, is defined by an infinite number of conditions. How then can people assess this knowledge in a finite amount of time? From the beginning, we knew the paradox was illusory – one or more of its assumptions had to be incorrect. Yet we found it a useful magnifying glass for looking into the processes by which people use and understand definite reference.

The resolution of the paradox we favor for most circumstances is that people assess mutual knowledge by use of the copresence heuristics. They search memory for evidence that they, their listeners, and the object they are referring to have been "openly present together" physically, linguistically, or indirectly. Or they search memory for evidence that the object is universally known within a community they and their listeners mutually know they belong to. With such evidence they can infer mutual knowledge directly by means of an induction schema. There is no need to assess an infinite number of conditions, and the paradox collapses.

The copresence heuristics have important consequences for definite reference. They help determine people's choice of noun phrase for each definite reference. For physical copresence, as in deixis, people prototypically use demonstratives. For linguistic copresence, as in anaphora, they prototypically use pronouns or definite descriptions. And for community membership, they prototypically use proper names, especially proper nouns. The heuristics also determine in part how people repair inadequate or unsuccessful definite references. The idea is that each repair should strengthen the basis on which mutual knowledge of the referent is established. The copresence heuristics, by spelling out the trade-off between direct evidence and certain auxiliary assumptions, tell how that basis can be strengthened.

And these heuristics require a memory that is organized around diary entries and around communities in which knowledge is universally shared. Currently, the memory assumed in most models of comprehension and production is not organized this way.

What all this suggests is that our views of comprehension and production are in need of reform. We have tried to shatter the illusion that definite reference is simple and self-evident by demonstrating how it requires mutual knowledge, which complicates matters enormously. But virtually every other aspect of meaning and reference also requires mutual knowledge, which also is at the very heart of the notion of linguistic convention and speaker meaning. Mutual knowledge is an issue we cannot avoid. It is likely to complicate matters for some time to come.

NOTES

Although this chapter bears a strong superficial resemblance to the paper with the same title presented at the Sloan Workshop on Computational Aspects of Linguistic Structure and Discourse Setting, it differs from the earlier one in several fundamental ways, thanks to comments by the workshop participants and other colleagues. We are indebted to Eve V. Clark, Mark D. Jackson, Philip N. Johnson-Laird, Lawrence M. Paul, Christine A. Riley, Neil V. Smith, and especially Robert Stalnaker for a number of detailed suggestions. Our paper "Reference Diaries," which was based on that earlier paper, should also be replaced by this presentation. We were supported in this research by National Institute of Mental Health grant MH-20021, the Center for Advanced Study in the Behavioral Sciences, a National Endowment for the Humanities Fellowship to HHC, and a Danforth Fellowship to CRM.

1   One important caveat here. Often all Ann will be able to check is her belief or assumption or supposition instead of her *knowledge* that t is R. Which propositional attitude is appropriate – knowledge, belief, assumption, supposition, or even some other .term – depends on the evidence Ann possesses and other factors. For simplicity we will use *know* as the general term, but we could replace it with *believe* or certain other terms without affecting our argument.

2   Another way to represent this is as two interreferring statements of this kind:

> A and B mutually know that p =_{def.}
>   (r)   A knows that p and that r'.
>   (r')   B knows that p and that r.

In some ways this representation is preferable, for unlike the single self-referential statement, it does not assume that if A knows that A knows that p, then A knows that p. Although this assumption may be justifiable for the verb *know*, it is not so obviously justifiable with *believe* or *assume* or *suppose* in place of *know*.

3 This one-sided mutual knowledge can be represented in a self-referential definition (see note 2) as follows:

A knows that A and B mutually know that $p =_{\text{def.}}$
(r)   A knows that p and that: B knows that p and that r.

4 "Visibility" is obviously too restricted a term here and should be replaced by "perceptability" to encompass taste, smell, and hearing, as in *where is the awful smell/taste/noise coming from?* This is part of our reason for later using the term "physical" as opposed to "visual" for such cases.

5 It cannot be correct for other reasons either. In Donnellan's (1966) example "Who is the man drinking a martini?", the definite reference *the man drinking a martini* refers to a particular man even if the speaker is mistaken and the man happens to be drinking water; moreover, such a reference will generally succeed (see also Donnellan, 1968). The complication of this sort of misdescription and its relation to mutual belief are thoroughly discussed by Perrault and Cohen (this volume). There is a related problem in deception (see Bruce and Newman, 1978).

6 There may seem to be no real difference between the selective and the progressive checking strategies because for shared knowledge the truth of condition (4), for example, entails the truth of conditions (1), (2), and (3). For shared beliefs or suppositions or other propositional attitudes, however, this entailment no longer holds. If Ann believes that Bob believes that the movie showing at the Roxy tonight is *A Day at the Races*, that doesn't imply that *she* believes it is *A Day at the Races*. In the more general case, these two strategies are distinct.

7 When mutual knowledge is treated as a primitive, it follows that most cases of non–mutual knowledge will require a more complex memory representation than mutual knowledge. As a consequence, they ought to be more difficult to understand. Our Marx brothers scenarios bear out this prediction. Versions 2, 3, 4, and 5 were successively more difficult to understand. The knowledge we had to keep in mind required more and more conditions, and these conditions themselves became more and more complex. The version for mutual knowledge, where Ann and Bob openly discussed the showing of *Monkey Business* at the Roxy, was the easiest to understand. Apparently, the mutual knowledge we had to represent for it was simple.

8 Of course, we must qualify the notion that *everybody* in a community needs to know a thing before it is taken to be mutual knowledge within that community. We can do that informally by replacing *everybody* with *almost everybody,* and *universal* by *almost universal,* or we can do it more formally by introducing parameters that specify the probabilities (see Lewis, 1969, pp. 76–80). This qualification is needed if we want to account for why certain references that are otherwise justifiable on the basis of community membership and community knowledge occasionally fail.

9 Written language, as in books and on signs, we assume, is derivative from spoken language and requires an extended notion of copresence. In *Pride and Prejudice,* for example, Jane Austen assumed her readers would be rational comprehending people who would take in her words serially, as if spoken, etc., etc. She could pretend, in other words, that she was speaking her novel to each reader and that linguistic copresence would be established that way. Signs often rely on an extended notion of physical

copresence as well. For example, *Break this glass to sound alarm* makes sense on a fire alarm, but not pinned to the back of a professor's coat. Nevertheless, we are mindful of the differences between written and spoken language and expect them to complicate the copresence heuristics in various ways.

10 One exception, pointed out to us by a native, is the Highland Scottish use of *himself* as a proper name for the local laird or head of a clan, as in *Himself was angry with Ian today.* Its highly marked form helps to make its proper-name status clear.

11 What an adequate answer to a *who*-question consists of has been taken up by Boer and Lycan (1975) in their paper on "knowing who." They argue that the answer to "Who is X?" is always relative to some purpose and that its ultimate answer is always an attributive use of the definite description. So the *ultimate* answers – and the ultimate repairs – go beyond our paper, which is about referential uses.

REFERENCES

Anderson, J. R. 1976. *Language, Memory, and Thought.* Hillsdale, N.J.: Erlbaum.

Anderson, J. R. 1977. "Memory for Information about Individuals." *Memory and Cognition* 5:430–42.

Anderson, J. R. 1978. "The Processing of Referring Expressions within a Semantic Network." In D. L. Waltz, ed. *Theoretical Issues in Natural Language Processing—2.* New York: Association for Computing Machinery, pp. 51–6.

Anderson, R. C., Pichert, J. W., Goetz, E. T., Schallert, D. L., Stevens, K. V., and Trollip, S. R. 1976. "Instantiation of General Terms." *Journal of Verbal Learning and Verbal Behavior* 15:667–79.

Barenboim, C. 1978. "Development of Recursive and Nonrecursive Thinking about Persons." *Developmental Psychology* 14:419–20.

Boer, S. E., and Lycan, W. G. 1975. "Knowing Who." *Philosophical Studies* 28:299–344.

Bruce, B., and Newman, D. 1978. "Interacting Plans." *Cognitive Science* 2:195–234.

Carpenter, P. A., and Just, M. A. 1977. "Integrative Processes in Comprehension." In D. LaBerge and S. J. Samuels, eds. *Basic Processes in Reading: Perception and Comprehension.* Hillsdale, N.J.: Erlbaum.

Chafe, W. L. 1974. "Language and Consciousness." *Language* 50:111–33.

Christopherson, P. 1939. *The Articles: A Study of Their Theory and Use in English.* Copenhagen: Munksgaard.

Clark, E. V. 1973. "What's in a Word? On the Child's Acquisition of Semantics in His First Language." In T. E. Moore, ed. *Cognitive Development and the Acquisition of Language.* New York: Academic Press, pp. 65–110.

Clark, E. V. 1978. "From Gesture to Word: On the Natural History of Deixis in Language Acquisition." In J. S. Bruner and A. Garton, eds. *Human Growth and Development: Wolfson College lectures 1976.* Oxford: Oxford University Press, pp. 85–120.

Clark, E. V., and Andersen, E. S. 1979. "Spontaneous Repairs: Awareness in the Process of Acquiring Language." Paper presented at the biennial meeting of the Society for Research in Child Development, San Francisco. March.

Clark, E. V., and Clark, H. H. 1979. "When Nouns Surface as Verbs." *Language*, 55:767–811.

Clark, E. V., and Sengul, C. J. 1978. "Strategies in the Acquisition of Deixis." *Journal of Child Language* 5:457–75.

Clark, H. H. 1977. "Inferences in Comprehension." In D. LaBerge and S. J. Samuels, eds. *Basic Processes in Reading: Perception and Comprehension.* Hillsdale, N.J.: Erlbaum.

Clark, H. H. 1978. "Inferring What Is Meant." In W. J. M. Levelt and G. B. Flores d'Arcais, eds. *Studies in the Perception of Language.* London: Wiley.

Clark, H. H. 1979. "Responding to Indirect Speech Acts." *Cognitive Psychology,* 11:430–477.

Clark, H. H., and Clark, E. V. 1977. *Psychology and Language: An Introduction to Psycholinguistics.* New York: Harcourt Brace Jovanovich.

Clark, H. H., and Haviland, S. E. 1977. "Comprehension and the Given–New Contract." In R. O. Freedle, ed. *Discourse Production and Comprehension.* Norwood, N.J.: Ablex Publishing, pp. 1–40.

Clark, H. H., and Marshall, C. R. 1978. "Reference Diaries." In D. L. Waltz, ed. *Theoretical Issues in Natural Language Processing—2.* New York: Association for Computing Machinery, pp. 57–63.

Clark, H. H., and Sengul, C. J. 1979. "In Search of Referents for Nouns and Pronouns." *Memory and Cognition* 7:35–41.

Cohen, P. R. 1978. "On Knowing What to Say: Planning Speech Acts." Unpublished doctoral dissertation, University of Toronto.

Donnellan, K. S. 1966. "Reference and Definite Descriptions." *Philosophical Review* 75:281–304.

Donnellan, K. R. 1968. "Putting Humpty Dumpty Together Again." *Philosophical Review* 77:203–15.

DuBois, J. W. 1975. "Syntax in Mid-Sentence." In *Berkeley Studies in Syntax and Semantics,* Vol. 1. Berkeley, Calif.: Institute of Human Learning and Department of Linguistics, University of California, pp. III-1–III-25.

Flavell, J. H., Botkin, P. T., Fry, C. L., Wright, J. W., and Jarvis, P. E. 1968. *The Development of Role Taking and Communication Skills in Children.* New York: Wiley.

Grice, H. P. 1957. "Meaning." *Philosophical Review* 66:377–88.

Harman, G. 1977. "Review of *Linguistic Behavior* by Jonathan Bennett." *Language* 53:417–24.

Haviland, S. E., and Clark, H. H. 1974. "What's New? Acquiring New Information as a Process in Comprehension." *Journal of Verbal Learning and Verbal Behavior* 13:512–21.

Hawkins, J. A. 1978. *Definiteness and Indefiniteness: A Study in Reference and Grammaticality Prediction.* London: Croom Helm.

Jespersen, O. 1949. *A Modern English Grammar on Historical Principles, Vol. 7.* Copenhagen: Munksgaard.

Karttunen, L. 1977. "Presupposition and Linguistic Context." In A. Rogers, B. Wall, and J. P. Murphy, eds. *Proceedings of the Texas Conference on Performatives, Presuppositions, and Implicatures.* Arlington, Va.: Center for Applied Linguistics, pp. 149–60.

Karttunen, L., and Peters, S. 1975. "Conventional Implicature in Montague

Grammar." In *Proceedings of the First Annual Meeting of the Berkeley Linguistic Society,* Berkeley, Calif.: Berkeley Linguistics Society, University of California, pp. 266–278.

Kempson, R. M. 1975. *Presupposition and the Delimitation of Semantics.* Cambridge: Cambridge University Press.

Kintsch, W. 1974. *The Representation of Meaning in Memory.* Hillsdale, N.J.: Erlbaum.

Kintsch, W., and van Dijk, T. A. 1978. "Toward a Model of Text Comprehension and Production." *Psychological Review* 85:363–94.

Kripke, S. 1972. "Naming and Necessity." In D. Davidson and G. Harman, eds. *Semantics of Natural Language.* Dordrecht: D. Reidel.

Kripke, S. 1977. "Speaker's Reference and Semantic Reference." *Midwest Studies in Philosophy* II:255–76.

Lasnik, H. 1976. "Remarks on Coreference." *Linguistic Analysis* 2:1–22.

Lesgold, A. M., Roth, S. F., and Curtis, M. E. 1979. "Foregrounding Effects in Discourse Comprehension." *Journal of Verbal Learning and Verbal Behavior* 18:291–308.

Lewis, D. K. 1969. *Convention: A Philosophical Study.* Cambridge, Mass.: Harvard University Press.

Lyons, J. 1975. "Deixis as the Source of Reference." In E. L. Keenan, ed. *Formal Semantics of Natural Language.* Cambridge: Cambridge University Press.

Lyons, J. 1977. *Semantics,* Vols. 1 and 2. Cambridge: Cambridge University Press.

McCawley, J. D. 1979. "Presupposition and Discourse Structure." In C. K. Oh, ed. *Syntax and Semantics,* Vol. 13, *Presupposition.* New York: Academic Press.

Maratsos, M. P. 1976. *The Use of Definite and Indefinite Reference in Young Children: An Experimental Study of Semantic Acquisition.* Cambridge: Cambridge University Press.

Miller, P. H., Kessel, F. S., and Flavell, J. H. 1970. "Thinking about People Thinking about People Thinking about . . . : A study of Social–Cognitive Development." *Child Development* 41:613–23.

Minsky, M. 1975. "A Framework for Representing Knowledge." In P. Winston, ed. *The Psychology of Computer Vision.* New York: McGraw-Hill, pp. 211–77.

Moravcsik, E. A. 1969. "Determination." *Working Papers in Language Universals.* Stanford, Calif.: Stanford University, 1:64–98.

Morgan, J. L. 1978. "Two Types of Convention in Indirect Speech Acts." In P. Cole, ed. *Syntax and Semantics,* Vol. 9, *Pragmatics.* New York: Academic Press, pp. 261–80.

Nunberg, G. D. 1977. "The Pragmatics of Reference." Unpublished doctoral dissertation, City University of New York.

Ortony, A., and Anderson, R. C. 1977. "Definite Descriptions and Semantic Memory." *Cognitive Science* 1:74–83.

Prince, E. F. 1978. "On the Function of Existential Presupposition in Discourse." In *Papers from the Fourteenth Regional Meeting, Chicago Linguistics Society.* Chicago: Chicago Linguistics Society, University of Chicago, pp. 362–76.

Rumelhart, D. E., and Ortony, A. 1977. "The Representation of Knowledge in Memory." In R. C. Anderson, R. J. Spiro, and W. E. Montague, eds. *Schooling and the Acquisition of Knowledge.* Hillsdale, N.J.: Erlbaum.

Rumelhart, D. E., Lindsay, P. H., and Norman, D. A. 1972. "A Process Model for Long-Term Memory." In E. Tulving and W. Donaldson, eds. *Organization of Memory.* New York: Academic Press, pp. 197–246.

Schank, R., and Abelson, R. 1977. *Scripts, Plans, Goals, and Understanding: An Inquiry into Human Knowledge Structures.* Hillsdale, N.J.: Erlbaum.

Schegloff, E. A. 1972. "Notes on a Conversational Practice: Formulating Place." In D. N. Sudnow, ed. *Studies in Social Interaction.* New York: The Free Press, pp. 75–119.

Schegloff, E. A., Jefferson, G., and Sacks, H. 1977. "The Preference for Self-correction in the Organization of Repair in Conversation." *Language* 53:361–82.

Schelling, T. C. 1960. *The Strategy of Conflict.* Oxford: Oxford University Press.

Schiffer, S. R. 1972. *Meaning.* Oxford: Oxford University Press.

Searle, J. R. 1965. "What is a Speech Act?" In M. Black, ed. *Philosophy in America.* London: Allen and Unwin, pp. 221–39.

Searle, J. R. 1969. *Speech Acts: An Essay in the Philosophy of Language.* Cambridge: Cambridge University Press.

Searle, J. R. 1975. "Indirect Speech Acts." In P. Cole and J. L. Morgan, eds. *Syntax and Semantics,* Vol. 3, *Speech Acts.* New York: Seminar Press, pp. 59–82.

Stalnaker, R. C. "Pragmatic Presuppositions." In A. Rogers, B. Wall, and J. P. Murphy, eds. *Proceedings of the Texas Conference on Performatives, Presuppositions, and Implicatures.* Arlington, Va.: Center for Applied Linguistics, pp. 135–48.

Stalnaker, R. C. 1978. "Assertion." In P. Cole, ed. *Syntax and Semantics,* Vol. 9, *Pragmatics.* New York: Academic Press, pp. 315–32.

Sternberg, S. 1966. "High-speed Scanning in Human Memory." *Science* 153:652–4.

Strawson, P. F. 1964. "Intention and Convention in Speech Acts." *Philosophical Review* 73:439–60.

Strawson, P. F. 1974. *Subject and Predicate in Logic and Grammar.* London: Methuen.

Thorne, J. P. 1972. "On the notion 'definite.'" *Foundations of Language* 8:562–8.

Thorne, J. P. 1974. "Notes on 'Notes on "On the notion 'definite.' " ' " *Foundations of Language* 11:111–14.

Townsend, J. T. 1972. "Some Results Concerning the Identifiability of Parallel and Serial Processes." *British Journal of Mathematical and Statistical Psychology* 25:168–99.

Warden, D. A. 1976. "The Influence of Context on Children's Use of Identifying Expressions and References." *British Journal of Psychology* 67:101–12.

Winograd, T. 1972. *Understanding Natural Language.* New York: Academic Press.

2

Speech act assignment

GERALD GAZDAR

Consider the following sentence:

(1) *You will go home tomorrow*

The conditions under which (1) would be true are given, straightforwardly enough, in (2):

(2) *You will go home tomorrow* is true w.r.t. an addressee α and day of utterance n if and only if α goes home on day $n + 1$.

There's a sense in which (2) tells us all there is to tell about the meaning of (1), and yet if (1) is uttered in a conversation, the addressee will certainly derive more from the fact of its utterance than follows merely from (2). He may find it to be an assertion, a question, a prediction, an order, a reply, and so on. He may find it to be more than one of these things at the same time, he may find it to be possibly one, possibly another, but not both together. However, he is unlikely to find it to be a confession, a suggestion, an adjudication, an expression of gratitude, or a dedication. What he does take it to be will play a large part in determining how he responds to it when it becomes his turn to speak. Thus he may reply with (3) if he takes it to be an assertion,

(3) *How do you know*

with (4) if he takes it to be a question,

(4) *Yes*

with (5) if he takes it to be a prediction,

(5) *That's what you think*

and with (6) if he takes it to be an order,

(6) *Okay*

In discussing the issues raised by such observations, I shall assume that the reader is familiar with the notions of illocutionary force and

64

speech act as introduced and discussed by Austin (1962) and Searle
(1969). In the first place, and least controversially, a theory of speech
acts is needed as part of a(ny) theory of utterance meaning.[1] Second,
conversationalists, whether computational or human, must be able to
recognize and interpret utterances as, for example, assertions, questions, orders, predictions, and so on, if they are to be able to respond
appropriately to them. Simply knowing the conditions under which
(1) would be true is not sufficient to allow a response to be made. Note
that I'm not claiming that a theory of speech acts constitutes a theory
of utterance sequencing,[2] but only that an account of the recognition
and interpretation of speech acts is a necessary component of such a
theory. And finally, a theory of speech acts is the crucial ingredient of
any theory of the truth conditions of utterance reports. Consider (7)–
(10) as reports of the utterances of (1) by John:

(7) *John asserted that I would go home tomorrow*
(8) *John asked me if I was going home tomorrow*
(9) *John predicted I would go home tomorrow*
(10) *John told me to go home tomorrow*

These sentences could be used to truly report some utterance by John
of (1), but they do not have the same truth conditions despite the fact
that what is being reported could be the utterance of the same sentence in each case. So there are at least three reasons why we need a
theory of speech act recognition and interpretation: (a) as part of a
theory of utterance meaning, (b) as part of a theory of utterance
sequencing, and (c) as part of a theory of the truth conditions of
utterance reports.

Consequently, this chapter addresses itself to two issues:

(i) What kind of thing is a speech act or an illocutionary force?
(ii) What is the relation between utterances and the speech acts they
achieve?

Question (i), which will be discussed in the first half of this paper, is
intended generically – there is a whole series of particular questions of
the form "What kind of thing is a promise/permission/warning/etc.?"
but I shall be concerned with those questions only incidentally, and
only insofar as they have a bearing on the more general questions.
The generic question is, of course, only legitimate if the particulars
subsumed under it form some kind of natural class (i.e., if promises,
permissions, warnings, etc. are entities of the same type). This is a
widely, if implicitly, made assumption in the literature, and I shall
make it also without further discussion. Question (ii) has two aspects.
On the one hand there are general issues concerned with whether, for

example, each utterance can be associated with exactly one speech act, or, to take another example, whether there exists some subset of sentences having the property of invariantly inducing a unique speech act assignment, independent of context. These issues, which I shall consider in the latter part of the chapter, have been largely neglected in the linguistics literature. And, on the other hand, there are issues concerned with how, for example, one can account for the fact that some interrogative sentences on some occasions of use manifest requests. In the early 1970s there was some influential and enlightening discussion of this kind of issue, but it will not be considered directly here.[3]

In order to address the questions of what kind of things speech acts and illocutionary forces are, I'm going to spell out some assumptions, define some familiar terminology, and introduce some notation.[4]

Let D be the set of sentences of a natural language. I shall assume that the members of D are equipped, as it were, with their full structural descriptions and are thus syntactically and lexically disambiguated. I shall further adopt a very liberal view of what is to count as a sentence; thus the NP utterances of Yanofski (1978) will be considered sentences for the purposes of the present discussion, as will "elliptical" answers to questions, and so on. Sentences have properties by virtue of their syntax; for example, they may be declarative, interrogative, subjunctive, imperative, exclamative, or optative.[5] I shall assume that these -ive properties are syntactic properties (characterized in terms of, e.g., word order, absence of subject, presence of wh-words, etc.) and leave entirely open, for subsequent consideration, the relations these properties may or may not bear to illocutionary force. The failure to distinguish, for example, the (syntactic) property of being interrogative from the (pragmatic) property of being a question, has given rise to considerable confusion and equivocation in the recent literature (e.g., virtually everything written by proponents of the "Performative Hypothesis"; see Gazdar, 1979, pp. 15–35, for critical discussion).

I shall let M be the set of contexts in which sentences may be uttered. For most of the discussion which follows it won't matter too much what contexts are taken to be, but I will return to the issue when we get around to addressing question (i). Now that we have a set D of sentences and a set M of contexts, we may define the set of utterances E to be the crossproduct of D and M ($E = D \times M$). An utterance then is an ordered pair consisting of a sentence and a context (i.e., the context in which the sentence is uttered). When $e = \langle d, m \rangle$, I shall sometimes use e_0 and e_1 to refer to d and m, respectively. It may well be that there are constraints on the set of sentence–context pairings, in which case the set of (normal) utterances will be a proper subset of the crossproduct, but that issue need not concern us for the moment.

So much for utterances. What about speech acts and illocutionary forces? Because we have two terms available to us, and because I need to make a certain distinction, I propose to use them differently. Under the usage adopted here, "a request to pass the salt," "a request to quit standing on the speaker's foot," and "a request to close the window" will count as different speech acts but as speech acts that manifest the same illocutionary force (i.e., the force of requesting). But requesting, promising, warning, questioning, and so on, are distinct illocutionary forces. Let F be the set of illocutionary forces (we shall worry what an illocutionary force is later). As we have set things up, one component of a speech act will be a member of F, but it is less clear what the other component should be. Searle (1969) and Katz (1977) maintain that this other component is a "propositional content." Thus Katz (1977, pp. 10–11) tells us that (11) and (12) have the same propositional content, but have different illocutionary forces:[6]

(11) *Someone will eat the cookies*[7]
(12) *Who will eat the cookies*

This seems straightforward until one considers (13):

(13) *Will someone eat the cookies*

Example (13) appears to have the same propositional content as (11) [and hence also (12)] and the same illocutionary force as (12), namely, that of questioning. But that means that (12) and (13) have the same propositional content and the same illocutionary force and are therefore instances of the same speech act – which they plainly aren't. One might attempt to escape this dilemma (which neither Katz nor Searle show any signs of being aware of) by distinguishing two illocutionary force subtypes corresponding to polar and *wh*-interrogatives. This doesn't help, as can be seen from (14)–(17):

(14) *Someone ate something*
(15) *Who ate something*
(16) *What did someone eat*
(17) *Who ate what*

To judge from (11) and (12), these will be assigned the same propositional content, (14) will be distinguished as being of assertoric illocutionary force, and (15)–(17) will be regarded as having *wh*-question illocutionary force. But (15), (16), and (17) represent intuitively distinct speech acts despite having the same propositional content and the same illocutionary force according to this sort of theory. Further sub-categorization of questions won't help because English allows indefinitely many *wh*-words in interrogative sentences.

There's a straightforward way out of this problem. Instead of treating speech act assignments as pairs consisting of an illocutionary force and a propositional content, we treat them as pairs consisting of an illocutionary force and a content, where the set of contents is identified with the set of sentence meanings.[8] On this account, (15)–(17) can be said to have the same illocutionary force but different contents. Take (15) and (16): The speech act canonically done by utterance of (14) will consist of the illocutionary force of questioning together with the meaning of the sentence *Who ate something*. The speech act canonically done by utterance of (16) will consist of the illocutionary force of questioning together with the meaning of *What did someone eat*. On anybody's theory of the semantics of interrogative sentences the meanings of *Who ate something* and *What did someone eat* are going to be distinct. For example, on Hamblin's (1973) theory, the meaning of the former will be the set of all propositions each of which is expressed by a sentence of the form π *ate something* where π ranges over persons, whereas the meaning of the latter will be the set of all propositions each of which is expressed by a sentence of the form *Someone ate* τ where τ ranges over things.[9]

Let J be the set of sentence meanings. Then the set of speech act assignments A is a subset of the crossproduct of F and J ($A \subseteq F \times J$). Where $a = \langle f, j \rangle$, I shall sometimes use a_0 and a_1 to refer to f and j, respectively. I shall assume that the semantic theory for the language provides us with a function $[] \in J^D$ that maps sentences of the language (members of D) into their meanings (members of J). Thus $[d] \in J$ when $d \in D$, and $[Who\ ate\ what] \in J$ if *Who ate what* $\in D$. For the purposes of what follows I shall assume that declarative sentences express propositions and that interrogative sentences express sets of propositions, but these assumptions are not crucial to the claims made. I shall not make any assumptions respecting the meanings of imperative, exclamative, and optative sentences.[10]

Let us now return to the first question we set ourselves:

(i)   What kind of thing is a speech act or an illocutionary force?

The answer I propose giving to the "What is a speech act?" question is one that emerges, implicitly or explicitly, from much of the more formal work that has been done on speech acts in the last ten years.[11] A speech act is a function from contexts into contexts. Thus an assertion that ϕ is a function that changes a context in which the speaker is not committed to justifiable true belief in ϕ into a context in which he is so committed.[12] A promise that ϕ is a function that changes a context in which the speaker is not committed to bringing ϕ about into one in which he is so committed. A permission to ϕ is a function that changes a context in which ϕ is prohibited into one in which ϕ is permissible. And so on. For the purpose of actually defining such functions we could follow Hamblin (1971) and take contexts to be sets of "commitment-slates," one for each participant to the discourse, where a commitment-slate is a set of propositions representing the commitments of that participant. Hamblin is only concerned with defining what he refers to as "information-oriented" systems, systems that include such speech acts as assertions, questions, answers, inquiries, retraction-demands, and retractions. Consequently the contents of his commitment-slates are entirely alethic (or epistemic). However, there would seem to be no problem of principle in incorporating deontic propositions into commitment-slates (and hence into contexts) in order to allow the definition of such speech acts as promises, permissions, prohibitions, requests, and so on. Independent motivation for requiring contexts to contain both alethic/epistemic and deontic information is provided by the highly context-dependent semantics required for modal verbs like *can* and *must* (see Kratzer, 1977, for relevant discussion). Note that the familiar "common ground" view of context can be defined on the basis of the set-of-commitment-slates view: The common ground is simply the intersection of the set of commitment-slates.

Speech acts will, in general, be partial functions – that is, they won't be defined for every context. You can't permit something that is already permitted, or prohibit something that is already prohibited, confirm something that has not already been mooted, request something that has already been granted, and so forth. Let X^Y stand for the set of all partial functions from Y into X.[13] We can stipulate that the set of speech acts A^* (the reason for this choice of notation will become apparent shortly) is a subset of the set of partial functions from M into M ($A^* \subseteq M^M$). If speech acts are functions from contexts into contexts, then what are illocutionary forces? Well, as we have used the terminology, speech acts are formed by combining an illocutionary force with a sentence meaning. And we don't have much choice about what sentence meanings are (the semantic determines that). So an illocutionary force, say that of promising, has to be something that takes a sentence meaning, say the proposition [*speaker will arrive on time*], to give a speech act, in this example the speech act of promising to arrive on time, which is itself a function from contexts into contexts. Given our assumptions and stipulations, an illocutionary force can only be one thing, namely, a function (possibly partial) from sentence meanings into speech acts. Thus $F \subseteq (M^M)^J$. At least some members of F will be partial functions because at least some illocutionary forces won't be defined for some types of sentence meaning. For example, one cannot assert things that are not propositions; thus $f([who\ ate\ what])$ will be undefined when f is the illocutionary force of asserting. Likewise one cannot promise to do things in the past. It will be remembered that earlier we introduced the notion of a speech act assignment and stipulated that the set A of speech act assignments was a subset of $F \times J$. You may be wondering at this point what the relation is between A and A^*, and why we need both types of entity cluttering up our ontology. The answer is that speech act assignments don't really have any independent ontological status at all; they're just hypothetical entities introduced to simplify the discussion in the latter half of this paper.[14] The set of speech acts A^* is straightforwardly definable in terms of A: $A^* = \{a_0(a_1): a \in A\}$. The members of A^* don't allow us to discriminate the illocutionary force from the content of the speech act, whereas the members of A do. Hence the need for the latter. But the members of A are not the kind of thing that speech acts are, whereas the members of A^* are. Hence the need for the latter.

Many speech acts seem to be incremental in their effects on the contexts they apply to. That is, the context that results from their taking place consists of the original context plus something. For example, an assertion that ϕ has the effect of adding the speaker's commitment to the justifiable true belief that ϕ to the context. If we assume, for the sake of simplicity, that contexts are just sets of propositions, then we can say that a speech act $\alpha \subseteq A^*$ is incremental if and only if, for all contexts m, $m \subseteq \alpha(m)$.[15] It is legitimate to ask at this point whether all speech acts are incremental in this sense. The answer, interestingly, is no. There exists a class of speech acts described by such verbs as *abolish, countermand, downgrade, exempt, permit, renounce, rescind, retract,* and *revoke,* whose effect on the context is not incremental.[16] What such acts have in common is that they require there to be something in the context when the act takes place, something that is not there afterward. Take the case of permission to ϕ: If I permit ϕ, then it must be the case that ϕ is prohibited in the context that obtains prior to the act of permitting ϕ. As a result of that act, ϕ is no longer prohibited. The act of permitting ϕ has the effect of removing or deleting the prohibition on ϕ from the context. If we attempt to formulate permission to ϕ so that it is incremental, then we will end up defining a function that has inconsistent contexts as its range, contexts in which ϕ is both prohibited and permitted.[17]

Our second question:

> (ii) What is the relation between utterances and the speech acts they achieve?

can be reformulated as

> What are the properties of the function that maps utterances into speech acts?

I shall assume that there is some (possibly partial) function $ that has utterances (E) as its domain and sets of speech act assignments $(\mathscr{P}A)$ as its range ($\$ \in (\mathscr{P}A)^{(E)}$). We take the range to be sets of speech act assignments in order not to exclude the possibility that some utterances may be associated with more than one speech act (as I shall take up shortly). And we map into speech act assignments (A) rather than speech acts (A^*) for reasons of formal convenience; because each member of A uniquely determines a member of A^*, there is no issue of principle here.[18] I shall sometimes refer to speech act assignments elliptically as speech acts in what follows. In this section I shall consider some rather general properties that the function $ might be thought to possess.

The first question to ask about $ is whether it is a partial or total function. Because we have defined E as simply the crossproduct of D and M, we have allowed all kinds of bizarre sentence–context pairs to be utterances. Consider, for example, (18) uttered by a blue-collar worker to the managing director of the company he works for, in a context in which it is clearly not intended as a joke:

(18) *I hereby fire you*

What kind of speech act could that possibly be? It clearly isn't an act of firing, and it doesn't seem interpretable as an assertion (because the sentence uttered is blatantly false). We could multiply examples ad nauseam, but there's no point – the conclusion is inescapable. Because some utterances are just too bizarre to be treated as speech acts at all in the sense in which we are using the term in this paper, $ must be a partial function. Let $E' \subset E$ be that subset of utterances for which $ is defined. We can regard E' as being the set of "normal utterances" (see Heringer, 1972, p. 6), that is, those utterances that achieve some speech act. I shall sometimes refer to normal utterances elliptically as utterances in what follows. In saying that (18) wouldn't be any kind of recognizable speech act in the context given, I'm not claiming that such an utterance wouldn't have any effect on the context. But we don't want to call every act of speaking which changes the context a "speech act."

The next question is whether $ assigns a unique speech act to each utterance. Is it the case that for all e in E', $\$(e)$ is a singleton? If so, then we can say that $ is uniquely assigning. Turner (1976, p. 244) remarks that "there is no reason *a priori* to suppose that a *single* utterance is limited to the doing of a single action." Nevertheless, some theorists have maintained that $ is uniquely assigning; thus Heringer (1972, p. 6) asserts that "a given utterance under normal circumstances must be the performance of one and only one illocutionary act." Now dialogues along the lines of (19) are by no means uncommon:

(19)   A: *You will go tomorrow*
        B: *Is that a question or an order*

In such cases the context is insufficient to allow the addressee to arrive at the speaker's intended speech act. However, it is at least arguable that A's utterance is in some sense deviant and that, given the nature of the context, he should have uttered a sentence that would have made his intention transparent. And if (19) is a deviant case, then we cannot use it to establish that $ is not uniquely assigning. Turner (1976) and Weiser (1974) have discussed cases where speakers deliberately exploit the speech act opacity that natural languages allow. Imagine, for example, an utterance that, in context, could either be a request to ϕ or a question about ϕ, but not both simultaneously. The addressee, if he wants to avoid refusing the request can ignore that part of the assignment and respond to it as if it were simply a question. Conversely, the speaker, if he is accused of having made a (possibly unreasonable) request, can deny it and claim merely to have intended a question. The conclusion Weiser (1974, p. 729) has drawn from such observations is worth quoting: "the complex intention of a speaker to produce a sentence with two possible meanings on a single occasion is beyond the descriptive capacity of any current approach to pragmatics that involves speech acts." Again, it could be argued that such cases involve exploitations of the speech act assignment apparatus and should not be regarded as counterexamples to the claim that $ is uniquely assigning.

Unlike Heringer, Searle has never maintained that utterances uniquely determine a speech act:

It is important to realize that one and the same utterance may constitute the performance of several different illocutionary acts. There may be several different non-synonymous illocutionary verbs that correctly characterize the utterance. For example suppose at a party a wife says "It's really quite late." That utterance may be at one level a statement of fact; to her interlocutor, who has just remarked on how early it was, it may be (and be intended as) an objection; to her husband it may be (and be intended as) a suggestion or even a request ("Let's go home") as well as a warning ("You'll feel rotten in the morning if we don't"). (Searle, 1969, pp. 70–1)

Searle is making two separate claims here: first, that speech act assignment is relative to recipient, and second, that a single utterance may have two distinct assignments with respect to the *same* recipient. The recent literature offers us a number of examples that support this second claim. Levinson (in press, p. 9) gives the following fragment:

(20) A: *Would you like another drink*
     B: *Yes I would, thank you*

and points out that B's utterance shows A's utterance to have been both a question and an offer: "the *yes* answers the question and the *thank you* acknowledges the offer." And Allwood (1978) discusses (21):

(21) A: *Stop flirting with my wife*
     B: *I've got something in my eye*
     A: *I know you are lying*

as follows:

We see that there are many ways of construing A's first remark. For example, it could be a request and an accusation. B's first remark qualifies as a statement, an extenuation and an explanation. A's second remark could be a statement, an objection and a renewed accusation. (Allwood, 1978, p. 11)

Consider also in this connection the following dialogue:

(22) A: *What do you need*
     B: *Four at thirty three*
     A: *Okay, will do*

B's remark here is an instance of what Turner (1976) calls "double duty utterances"; in this case it is both an answer to A's question and the request to which A agrees. More exotic, but otherwise analogous, is the utterance of the word *over* in the course of a game of cricket. This, as Levinson (1979, p. 368) points out, functions simultaneously "as both a statement that six turns at bowling have now transpired since the last cry and as an instruction to reverse the bowling." It seems then that we may conclude, in the light of these examples, that $ is not uniquely assigning.

Sadock (1974, p. 11) has claimed that "generally speaking, it is the case that there is associated with a single sentence one and only one illocutionary force." Interpreted uncharitably this makes an even stronger claim than Heringer's (which was about utterances, not sentences) and is falsified, a fortiori, by the examples noted above. But we could construe Sadock as claiming that although utterances may be associated, one of the speech acts the utterance is associated with has an illocutionary force that is uniquely determined by the nature of the sentence uttered. Formally this is equivalent to the claim that there exists a function $\mathcal{F} \in F^D$ such that for all $e \in E'$, $\mathcal{F}(e_0) \in \{a_0 : a \in \$(e)\}$. I shall refer to this claim as the "literal meaning hypothesis." Under the literal meaning hypothesis, $\mathcal{F}$ might be roughly defined as follows:

(23)   *If e_0 contains a performative prefix, then $\mathcal{F}(e_0) = f$ where f is the illocutionary force named by the performative verb in the prefix. Otherwise:*
       $\mathcal{F}(e_0) = question$, *when e_0 is interrogative*
       $\mathcal{F}(e_0) = request$, *when e_0 is imperative*
       $\mathcal{F}(e_0) = assertion$, *when e_0 is declarative*

Searle appears to subscribe to a version of the literal meaning hypothesis that incorporates something closely resembling (23). In commenting on examples such as (24) and (25):

(24)   *Can you pass the salt*
(25)   *Would you mind not making so much noise*

he writes as follows:[19]

In cases where these sentences are uttered as requests, they still have their literal meaning and are uttered with and as having that literal meaning. I have seen it claimed that they have different meanings "in context" when they are uttered as requests, but I believe that is obviously false. (Searle, 1975, pp. 69–70)

For Searle the literal meaning of interrogative syntax is question illocutionary force; likewise imperative syntax means requesting, and declarative syntax means asserting. Searle admits that the "literal meaning" may, on occasion, be defective. That is, in his terms, one or more of the felicity conditions for the "literal" illocutionary act may fail to obtain in a given context of use. In many contexts (24) will be defective with respect to every felicity condition pertaining to questioning according to the list given by Searle (1969, p. 66). And yet Searle would still maintain that (24) retains its "literal" illocutionary force in such contexts. Levinson (in press, p. 18) argues against Searle on the basis of the following example:

(26)   *May I remind you that your account is overdue*

On Searle's position (26) has the literal meaning of a request for permission to remind, but, as Levinson points out, "it cannot possibly actually function as a request for permission to remind, since reminding is done in uttering the sentence without such permission being granted."

There is some experimental work that has a bearing on the literal meaning hypothesis. Benjamin compared memory for illocutionary force for two short polemical pieces that differed only in that one used interrogatives in certain places where the other had declaratives. His results show that addressees are quite insensitive to the syntax (and hence "literal meaning") of rhetorical questions: "listeners who hear a speaker ask a rhetorical question in an argumentation context generally perceive the speaker to have asserted the statement which the question implies" (Benjamin, 1972, p. 4). Reeder (1975) showed that young children match utterances only according to their contextually determined illocutionary force and completely without reference to the illocutionary force that Searle would say was part of the meaning of the sentence uttered. And Clark and Lucy (1975, p. 67) conclude, of their experiment on interrogative and declarative sentences used as requests, that "quantitatively, all the sentences behaved according to their conveyed, not their literal, meaning." The literal meaning hypothesis commits one to a perverse view of certain request–reply sequences. Consider example (27), which comes from the script of a TV series and was brought to my attention by Ken Reeder (personal communication, 1975):

> (27) Cannon: *Do you mind if I use your two-way radio*
> Police Officer (handing microphone to Cannon): *Sure*

On Searle's view, Cannon's utterance is literally a question as well as being a request. The police officer's reply, then, is presumably both an admission that he does mind (in answer to the question) and an affirmative response to the request. There's a more plausible story about this example, but it isn't really one that can be told by anyone who subscribes to the literal meaning hypothesis. If that hypothesis is an empirical one, and not one that is simply true by stipulation, then it seems to me that the considerations adduced strongly suggest that the hypothesis is false. At best, there is no evidence whatsoever that suggests that it might be true.

The failure of the literal meaning hypothesis has two important consequences. The first has to do with the relation between semantics and pragmatics. As Levinson (1979, p. 30) puts it, it gives us "reason to think that illocutionary force has nothing to do with semantics, and should rather be handled entirely in pragmatics. Not all linguists seem to see this." One of those who does is Hausser:

Syntactic mood does not determine the speech act. Rather, syntactic mood *participates* with all the other linguistic properties of a given surface expression ϕ in delimiting the set of use-conditions of ϕ. Since there is no one to one relation between syntactic moods and speech acts, it would be a mistake to implement speech act properties in the semantic characterization of syntactic mood. (1978, p. 176)

The other consequence is that the relation between syntactic mood and illocutionary force in the so-called direct cases (e.g., imperative used for requesting, interrogative used for questioning) becomes no less problematic than the so-called indirect cases. Schegloff makes the point as follows:

Even where an utterance is in the linguistic form of a question [i.e., has interrogative syntax, G.G.], and seems to be doing questioning, the latter will not be adequately accounted for by the former. For if the question form can be used for actions other than questioning, and questioning can be accomplished by linguistic forms other than questions, then a relevant problem can be posed not only about how a question does something other than questioning; but how it does questioning; not only about how questioning is done by non-question forms, but how it gets accomplished by a question form. (1976, p. E3)

It appears then that the sentence uttered may not of itself determine the illocutionary force component of any of the speech acts assigned to the utterance. But does the sentence uttered constrain the content component of (any of) the speech act assignments in any way? The answer to this question is probably yet, but the relation is not nearly as straightforward as consideration of examples like (28) and (29) might lead one to believe:

(28)   *I had eggs for breakfast*
(29)   *Are you hungry*

Suppose that (28) is uttered in context m_1 and is heard to be (at least) an assertion that the speaker had eggs for breakfast. And suppose that (29) is uttered in a context m_2 and is heard to be (at least) a question as to whether the addressee is hungry. Then we have that:

$$\langle assertion, I\ had\ eggs\ for\ breakfast \rangle \in \$(\langle I\ had\ eggs\ for\ breakfast,\ m_1 \rangle)$$
$$\langle question, Are\ you\ hungry \rangle \in \$(\langle Are\ you\ hungry,\ m_2 \rangle)$$

On the basis of such examples one might wonder whether all speech act assignments had as their content the meaning of the sentence uttered (i.e., whether for all $e \in E'$ and $a \in \$(e), a_1 = e_0$). The case of interrogatives used as requests shows that this cannot be so. Consider the utterance of (30) in a context m_3 where it is heard to be (at least) a request that the addressee pass the salt:

(30)   *Can you pass the salt*

We shall have something like:

⟨*request, You will pass the salt*⟩ ∈ $(⟨*Can you pass the salt, m_3*⟩)

but certainly not:

⟨*request, Can you pass the salt*⟩ ∈ $(⟨*Can you pass the salt, m_3*⟩)

so the content of the speech act is not identical to the meaning of the sentence uttered. And if, as suggested by our discussion of the literal meaning hypothesis above, some utterances of (30) will have no question assignment, then there will be some context m_4 such that:

⟨*question, Can you pass the salt*⟩ ∈ $(⟨*Can you pass the salt, m_4*⟩)

in which case it is unlikely that we can even maintain that all utterances have some speech act assignment with a content identical to the meaning of the sentence uttered (i.e., it is probably not the case that for all $e \in E'$ there is some $a \in (e) such that $a_1 = e_0$). Note that if one wishes to hold, as some have done, that the utterance of sentences with performative prefixes can determine a singleton speech act assignment set containing only an assignment with the illocutionary force named by the performative, and excluding, for example, an assignment that involves the assertion that the act named is taking place, then one is forced to the conclusion just noted. For example, context m_5 may be such that:

{⟨*demand, I will be set free*⟩} = $(⟨*I demand to be set free, m_5*⟩)

Let us consider S in the light of Searle's expressibility principle which he states as follows:

For any meaning X and any speaker S, whenever S means X then it is possible that there is some expression E such that E is an exact expression of or formulation of X. (1969, p. 20)

The word "possible" here serves simply to exclude obvious counterexamples arising from languages that lack various lexical items. In the remarks below I shall assume that D is fully equipped in that respect. Searle draws the following conclusions from his expressibility principle:

It enables us to equate rules for performing speech acts with rules for uttering certain linguistic elements, since for any possible speech act there is a possible linguistic element the meaning of which (given the context of utterance) is sufficient to determine that its literal utterance is a performance of precisely that speech act. To study the speech acts of promising or apologizing we need only study sentences whose literal and correct utterance would constitute making a promise or issuing an apology. (1969, p. 21)

Searle seems to be claiming here that for any speech act α there is some sentence d such that, for all contexts m, the utterance of d in m will constitute the performance of exactly the act α. This claim can be expressed as follows:[20]

(31) $(a \in A)\ (\exists d \in D)(m \in M)[\$(\langle d,\ m \rangle) = \{a\}]$

Assuming (31), Searle goes on to claim that the study of speech acts can be reduced to the study of a certain set of sentences, definable as D' in the present framework:

(32) $D' = \bigcup_{a \in A}\ \{d \in D:\ (m \in M)[\$(\langle d,\ m \rangle) = \{a\}]$

D' can only stand as a surrogate for A or A^* if (31) holds because only in that case will it be true that D' contains at least one sentence for each speech act. In the case of speech acts having the illocutionary force of requesting, we can probably arrive at something like the set of sentences Searle needs by selecting just those with preverbal *please*. But the relation preverbal *please* bears to requesting is exceptional because most illocutionary forces lack such a "disambiguator." The only plausible general candidate for guaranteeing (31) is the explicit performative construction, and, indeed, this seems to be what Searle has in mind. But explicit performatives do not suffice to guarantee (31). Thus Sacks (cited in Schegloff, 1976, p. D11) has observed in transcripts of conversations that many occurrences of *I bet* . . . and *I promise* . . . are neither acts of betting nor promising, but function instead as attempts to close down sections of the conversation. Furthermore, explicit performatives, or any other means, will often be quite incapable of achieving some speech act simply because that speech act would be unintelligible or impossible in the context concerned (cf. (18), above). For example, (33) can be a warning, but if I want to be absolutely sure that my utterance is taken to be a warning, then I can utter (34) instead:

(33) *There's a rabid dog in the kitchen*
(34) *I warn you that there's a rabid dog in the kitchen*

However, in most contexts, (35) cannot be a warning, and, in those contexts, adding a performative prefix, as in (36), doesn't help. The speaker will be heard as making a joke, or being ironic, or performing some such activity.

(35) *There's a marshmallow in the kitchen*
(36) *I warn you that there's a marshmallow in the kitchen*

Finally, it may be observed that in many contexts in which asserting, requesting, questioning, and so forth, are possible acts, utterance of the corresponding performative sentences are not possible ways of achieving those acts. A simple experiment will establish this: Try sustaining an otherwise everyday conversation with someone who is neither linguist nor philosopher in which each sentence you utter spells out in a performative prefix the illocutionary force of the speech act you intend.

For these reasons it seems rather unlikely that (31) can be maintained. But if it can't be, then Searle's corollary to (31), which is that we only need study the sentences that fall under its rubric (i.e., the members of D', on the assumption that (31) holds) in order to learn about illocutionary force, must be abandoned. Methodologically this is an important consequence because much linguistic work on speech acts (i.e., that done within the framework of the "Performative Hypothesis") has implicitly assumed Searle's corollary and restricted itself to the consideration of sentences rather than utterances. The strongest expressibility condition that is even potentially defensible in this domain probably looks something like (37):

$$(37) \quad (a \in A)(m \in M)[(\exists d \in D)[a \in \$(\langle d, \ m \rangle)] \to$$
$$(\exists d \in D)[\{a\} = \$(\langle d, \ m \rangle)]]$$

and (37) doesn't even guarantee that D' is nonempty.

NOTES

This work was supported in part by a British Academy Overseas Fellowship and by NSF Grant BNS-76-20307 (Peters and Karttunen, UT).
I am indebted to Brian Butterworth, Richard Coates, Dave Good, Lauri Hollings, Phil Johnson-Laird, Hans Kamp, Lauri Karttunen, Ruth Kempson, Ewan Klein, Bill Ladusaw, Steve Levinson, Christopher Longuet-Higgins, John Lyons, Stan Peters, Ellen Prince, Andy Rogers, Aaron Sloman, and Mark Steedman for their critical comments on earlier drafts.

1 The rest of such a theory will include at least a theory of conversational implicature and a theory of presupposition. See Gazdar (1979) for specific proposals.
2 Levinson (in press) offers convincing arguments against identifying the theory of utterance sequencing with a theory of speech acts plus a syntax (stated in terms of speech act categories) for conversational structure.
3 See Gordon and Lakoff (1971), Heringer (1972), Forman (1974), and, more recently, Brown and Levinson (1978), Heringer (1977), Levinson (1979, in press), Morgan (1978), and Steedman and Johnson-Laird (1980).
4 The formalism in this paper serves a largely clarificatory purpose, appearances notwithstanding. The various definitions and stipulations are being used, not so much for theory construction, but rather for the precise

evaluation of certain widely held, but imprecisely expressed, theoretical positions respecting speech acts and illocutionary force.

5 See Lyons (1977, pp. 747–8) and Sadock and Zwicky (in press), for discussion of such syntactic properties.

6 Katz uses the term "propositional type" to refer to what I and most other people call "illocutionary force."

7 Examples sometimes stand for sentences and sometimes utterances, and sometimes they do duty for both. The surrounding text should enable the reader to work out their status in any particular case.

8 I shall ignore throughout aspects of sentence or utterance meaning having to do with presuppositions or the types of conversational implicature discussed at length in Gazdar (1979). I shall also ignore the existence of indexical expressions like *I, you, now, here*, and so on.

9 Lauri Karttunen (personal communication, 1978) tells me that the idea that interrogative sentences express sets of propositions originates with Stahl (1956). See also Karttunen (1977) for an interesting variant of the theory. Strictly speaking, on my formulation of Hamblin's theory, π and τ range over names of persons and things, respectively, so we need to assume, irrelevantly, that all persons and things in the domain have names.

10 See Hausser (1978) and Schmerling (1978).

11 I have in mind Davies and Isard (1972), Hamblin (1971), Isard (1975), Kamp (1973, 1976, 1978), Lewis (1979), Stalnaker (1978), and Steedman and Johnson-Laird (1980).

12 As a theory of assertion, this is a gross oversimplification; see Stalnaker (1978) and Rogers (1978) for remedial discussion.

13 This notational convention is borrowed from Scott (1969, p. 153). Note that $X^Y \subseteq X^{(Y)}$.

14 I'm glossing over a problem here. If Kamp (1973, 1976, 1978) is correct, then one probably can't make any force–content distinction of the kind built into the members of A. But I don't think this problem materially affects the, largely negative, conclusions reached in the latter half of this paper.

15 This definition is formally, though not conceptually, highly dependent upon one's assumption respecting the nature of contexts: If we had taken the members of M to be sets of worlds rather than sets of propositions, as we might well have done, then the definition would have had to stipulate that $\alpha(m) \subseteq m$.

16 These verbs are taken from Fraser (1974, p. 147). They all fall into his category of "verbs of legitimizing." Not all members of that category have the requisite property, but no members of any of his other categories appear to have it.

17 This view of permission, and of its significance, is due to Kamp (1973); a similar analysis of retraction is to be found in Hamblin (1971).

18 But see note 14, above.

19 Perrault et al. (1978, p. 129) endorse this view of Searle's by prefacing the quotation I give with the phrase "Searle (1975) correctly suggests that." But later in the same paper they appear to reject the literal meaning hypothesis: "A crucial part of understanding indirect speech acts is being able to recognize that they are not to be interpreted literally" (ibid., p. 130).

20 Of course, it is not clear from Searle's prose exactly what scope relations the context quantification bears. But because only (31) allows the definition of an interesting D', as in (32), it seems reasonable to suppose that (31) conveys Searle's intentions.

REFERENCES

Allwood, J. 1978. "On the Analysis of Communicative Action." *Gothenburg Papers in Theoretical Linguistics,* 38.

Austin, J. L. 1962. *How to Do Things with Words.* Oxford: Oxford University Press.

Benjamin, R. 1972. "The Rhetorical Question: Its Perception by Listeners." Mimeo, San Diego University.

Brown, P., and Levinson, S. C. 1978. "Universals in Language Usage: Politeness Phenomena." In E. N. Goody, ed. *Questions and Politeness: Strategies in Social Interaction.* Cambridge: Cambridge University Press.

Clark, H. H., and Lucy, P. 1975. "Understanding What Is Meant from What Is Said: A Study in Conversationally Conveyed Requests." *Journal of Verbal Learning and Verbal Behavior* 14:56–72.

Davies, D. J. M., and Isard, S. 1972. "Utterances as Programs." In D. Michie and B. Meltzer, eds. *Machine Intelligence 7.* Edinburgh: Edinburgh University Press, pp. 325–39.

Forman, D. 1974. "The Speaker Knows Best Principle." *Papers from the Tenth Regional Meeting, Chicago Linguistics Society,* pp. 162–77.

Fraser, B. 1974. "An Analysis of Vernacular Performative Verbs." In R. W. Shuy and C.-J. N. Bailey, eds. *Towards Tomorrow's Linguistics.* Washington, D.C.: Georgetown University Press.

Gazdar, G. 1979. *Pragmatics: Implicature, Presupposition, and Logical Form.* New York: Academic Press.

Gordon, D., and Lakoff, G. 1971. "Conversational Postulates." *Papers from the Seventh Regional Meeting, Chicago Linguistics Society,* pp. 63–84.

Hamblin, C. L. 1971. "Mathematical Models of Dialogue." *Theoria* 37:130–55.

Hamblin, C. L. 1973. "Questions in Montague English." *Foundations of Language* 10:41–53.

Hausser, R. 1978. "Surface Compositionality and the Semantics of Mood." *Amsterdam Papers in Formal Grammar* 2:174–93.

Heringer, J. T. 1972. "Some Grammatical Correlates of Felicity Conditions and Presuppositions." *Ohio State University Working Papers in Linguistics* 11:1–110. Also distributed by IULC.

Heringer, J. T. 1977. Pre-sequences and Indirect Speech Acts. *Southern California Occasional Papers in Linguistics* 5:169–79.

Isard, S. 1975. "Changing the Context." In E. L. Keenan, ed. *Formal Semantics of Natural Language.* Cambridge: Cambridge University Press, pp. 287–96.

Kamp, J. A. W. 1973. "Free Choice Permission." *Aristotelian Society Proceedings, New Series* 74:57–74.

Kamp, J. A. W. 1976. "The Formal Semantics and Pragmatics of Nonindicative Speech Acts." Paper presented to the 3rd Groningen Round Table, Mathematical Linguistics: Semantics for Natural Languages, Groningen.

Kamp, J. A. W. 1978. "Semantics versus Pragmatics." In F. Guenthner and H. Schmidt, eds. *Formal Semantics and Pragmatics for Natural Language*. Dordrecht: Reidel, pp. 257–87.

Karttunen, L. 1977. "Syntax and Semantics of Questions." *Linguistics and Philosophy* 1:3–44.

Karz, J. J. 1977. *Propositional Structure and Illocutionary Force*. New York: Thomas Crowell.

Kratzer, A. 1977. "What 'Must' and 'Can' Must and Can Mean." *Linguistics and Philosophy* 1:337–55.

Levinson, S. C. 1979. "Activity Types and Language." *Linguistics* 17:365–99.

Levinson, S. C. In press. "The Essential Inadequacies of Speech Act Models of Dialogue." In H. Parret, M. Sbisa, and J. Verschueren, eds. *Possibilities and Limitations of Pragmatics*. Amsterdam: John Benjamins, B.V.

Lewis, D. 1979. "Scorekeeping in a Language Game." *Journal of Philosophical Logic* 8:339–59.

Lyons, J. 1977. *Semantics 2*. Cambridge: Cambridge University Press.

Morgan, J. L. 1978. "Two Types of Convention in Indirect Speech Acts." In P. Cole, ed. *Syntax and Semantics 9: Pragmatics*. New York: Academic Press, pp. 261–80.

Perrault, C. R., Allen, J. F., and Cohen, P. R. 1978. "Speech Acts as a Basis for Understanding Dialogue Coherence." *Theoretical Issues in Natural Language Processing* 2:125–32.

Reeder, K. 1975. "On Young Children's Discrimination of Illocutionary Force." *Pragmatics Microfiche* 1.5:D8–G4.

Rogers, A. 1978. "Remarks on the Analysis of Assertion and the Conversational Role of Speech Acts." *Proceedings of the Fourth Annual Meeting, Berkeley Linguistics Society*, pp. 190–201.

Sadock, J. M. 1974. *Toward a Linguistic Theory of Speech Acts*. New York: Academic Press.

Sadock, J. M., and Zwicky, A. M., In press. "Sentence Types." In S. Anderson et al., eds. *Language Typology and Syntactic Fieldwork*. New York: Academic Press.

Schegloff, E. A. 1976. "On Some Questions and Ambiguities in Conversation." *Pragmatics Microfiche* 2.2:D8–G12.

Schmerling, S. F. 1978. "Toward a Theory of English Imperatives." Mimeo, University of Texas at Austin.

Scott, D. 1969. "Advice on Modal Logic." In K. Lambert, ed. *Philosophical Problems in Logic*. Dordrecht: Reidel.

Searle, J. R. 1969. *Speech Acts*. Cambridge: Cambridge University Press.

Searle, J. R. 1975. "Indirect Speech Acts." In P. Cole and J. Morgan, eds. *Syntax and Semantics 3: Speech Acts*. New York: Academic Press, pp. 59–82.

Stahl, G. 1956. "La Logica de las Preguntas." *Anales de la Universidad de Chile* 102:71–75.

Stalnaker, R. C. 1978. "Assertion." In P. Cole, ed. *Syntax and Semantics 9: Pragmatics*. New York: Academic Press.

Steedman, M. J., and Johnson-Laird, P. N. 1980. "The Production of Sentences, Utterances and Speech Acts: Have Computers Anything to Say?" In B. Butterworth, ed. *Language Production*. London: Academic Press.

Turner, R. 1976. "Utterance Positioning as an Interactional Resource." *Semiotica* 17:233–54.

Weiser, A. 1974. "Deliberate Ambiguity." *Papers from the Tenth Regional Meeting, Chicago Linguistics Society,* pp. 723–31.

Yanofski, N. 1978. "NP Utterances." *Papers from the Fourteenth Regional Meeting, Chicago Linguistics Society,* pp. 491–502.

3

Focusing and description in natural language dialogues

BARBARA J. GROSZ

When two people talk, they focus their attention on only a small portion of what each of them knows or believes. Some entities (objects or relationships) are central to the dialogue at a certain point and hence are focused on more sharply than others. More important, much of what each participant knows is not clearly in view at all; it is neither considered by the speaker in choosing what to say and how to say it, nor by the hearer in interpreting an utterance. Not only do speaker and hearer concentrate on particular entities, but they do so using particular perspectives on those entities. In choosing a particular set of words with which to describe an entity, a speaker indicates a perspective on that entity. The hearer is led, then, to see the entity more as one kind of thing than as another. For example, a single building may be viewed as an architectural wonder, a house, or a home, and a single event may be viewed at one time as a selling, another time as a buying, and still another as a trading.

Focusing is an active process.[1] As a dialogue progresses, the participants shift their focus to new entities or to new perspectives on entities previously highlighted by the dialogue. Furthermore, an actor is involved in focusing (as the term is used in this paper). If an entity is in focus, it is the object of someone's focusing; it cannot be impersonally in focus. When I use the constructions "highlighted," "focused on," or "in focus," there is always an implicit actor doing the highlighting or focusing. Finally, the entities that the speaker and hearer focus on are entities in their shared reality.[2] Focusing, then, is the active process, engaged in by the participants in a dialogue, of concentrating attention on, or highlighting, a subset of their shared reality.

The relationship between language and focusing is two-way: What is said influences focusing; what is focused on influences what is said. The speaker provides clues for the hearer both to what s/he is currently focused on and to what s/he wants to focus on next. These clues may be linguistic or may derive from shared linguistic or nonlinguistic

84

knowledge. The hearer depends on shared beliefs about what entities are highlighted to interpret such things as the appropriate sense of a particular word, and the object or event corresponding to a definite description. The link between the entities discussed in an utterance and the entities focused on when the utterance is spoken is thus an important aspect both of producing and of understanding that utterance.

The use and interpretation of definite descriptions in dialogue demonstrate the importance of focusing to dialogue participants.[3] This chapter examines the relationship between focusing and definite description and the implications of this relationship for computer systems for natural language processing. The following section presents an example that illustrates this relationship. The section entitled "Descriptions" discusses definite descriptions from both the speaker's and the hearer's perspectives and presents problems that arise for both participants whose solutions are influenced by how the participants are focused. The section "A focus representation" describes some initial mechanisms that were used to incorporate focusing in a computer system constructed to participate in task-oriented dialogues. The section on "Focus in discourse" addresses some problems that arise in computationally capturing the notion of focusing, and discusses other aspects of dialogue with which focusing mechanisms must be coordinated in a natural language processing system, in order to deal with the problems introduced in the preceding sections.

An example

To begin, I want to examine a sample dialogue between two people, an expert and an apprentice, cooperating to complete a task. It illustrates several important aspects of the role of focusing in communication. The sample comes from a corpus of task-oriented dialogues collected in situations simulating direct interaction between a person and a computer (Grosz, 1977; Deutsch, 1974; Walker, 1978).[4] The particular task being performed is disassembly of an air compressor.

(1) E: First you have to remove the flywheel.
(2) A: How do I remove the flywheel?
(3) E: First, loosen the two allen-head setscrews holding it to the shaft, then pull it off.
(4) A: OK.
(5)   I can only find one screw. Where's the other one?
(6) E: On the hub of the flywheel.
(7) A: That's the one I found. Where's the other one?
(8) E: About ninety degrees around the hub from the first one.

(9)   A: I don't understand. I can only find one. Oh wait, yes I think I was on the wrong wheel.
(10)   E: Show me what you are doing.
(11)   A: I was on the wrong wheel and I can find them both now.
(12)   The tool I have is awkward. Is there another tool that I could use instead?
(13)   E: Show me the tool you are using.
(14)   A: OK.
(15)   E: Are you sure you are using the right size key?
(16)   A: I'll try some others.
(17)   I found an angle I can get at it.
(18)   The two screws are loose, but I'm having trouble getting the wheel off.
(19)   E: Use the wheelpuller. Do you know how to use it?
(20)   A: No.
(21)   E: Do you know what it looks like?
(22)   A: Yes.
(23)   E: Show it to me please.
(24)   A. OK.
(25)   E: Good. Loosen the screw in the center and place the jaws around the hub of the wheel, then tighten the screw onto the center of the shaft. The wheel should slide off.

First, consider the use of the phrase "the two screws" in (18) to refer to the two setscrews holding the pulley on its shaft and the use of the phrases "the screw in the center" and "the screw" in (25) to refer to a part of the wheelpuller.[5] Because most objects do not have proper names, definite descriptions are a primary means of identifying objects. However, as in this dialogue, the same description may be used to identify different objects at different times. When (25) was uttered, the two screws mentioned in (3) through (18) were the most recently mentioned objects that could be referred to by a phrase such as "the screw," but they were no longer focused on by the dialogue participants – they were no longer relevant to either the dialogue or the task – and hence were not considered as possible referents for either "the screw in the center" or "the screw" in (25).

One can see in this example that the most recently mentioned object that satisfies a description may not be the object identified by that description. What entities a speaker and hearer are focused on influences both the kinds of descriptions they use and how their descriptions are interpreted. In utterance (3), the expert indicates that he is focused on, and concurrently gets the apprentice to focus on, the two subtasks involved in removing the pulley. In particular, the two allen-head setscrews involved in the first task are brought into focus; they continue to be in focus through the first part of (18). The initial clause of (18) indicates the completion of the task involving the screws and hence suggests that the apprentice will shift her attention to some new task (she might not – she could still say something more about the screws). She does make such a shift in the second clause of (18) ("but I'm having trouble getting the wheel off"). In (19), the expert indicates that he has followed this shift (note that he might have asked a question about the screws – e.g., "How loose are they?" – and thereby continued to focus on them and the associated task) and narrows focusing from the task of removing the flywheel to a particular tool involved in that task. In this context, it is clear that the phrase "the screw" cannot refer to either of the setscrews, but must refer to something else.[6]

This dialogue also indicates some of the ways in which focusing is manipulated in a dialogue. In particular, it illustrates how the structure of the entities being discussed (the "domain") influences focusing and hence the structure of the discourse. The dialogue concerns the performance of a task; its topic is that task. As a result, the way in which the apprentice and expert focus, and hence the structure of the dialogue,[7] are closely linked to the structure of the task. Information about the structure of entities in the domain provides one kind of clue to how focusing can change. What about general linguistic clues to focusing? What information in words themselves or in sentence structure can influence focusing? The use of "but" in (18) illustrates one kind of linguistic clue to focus. The indication of contrast suggests a shifting of focus to the entities described in the clause following the "but." In fact, this shift does occur and the remainder of the fragment concerns things involved with "getting the wheel off."[8]

The final point I want to make with respect to this fragment concerns the relationship between how the speaker and hearer are focused and how differences in focusing affect understanding. It is clearly crucial for speaker and hearer to be able to distinguish their own beliefs from each other's beliefs. What about focus? We are concerned here not with the consistent difference in focusing that results from the speaker being one step ahead of the hearer (closing this gap is one goal of an utterance), but rather with whether speaker and hearer purposely maintain differences in focusing over several interactions (as they do with beliefs). An analysis of the dialogues we collected indicates that, in most cases, whether or not a speaker and hearer are focused similarly, they speak as though they were. Speaker and hearer assume a common focus; they usually do not have distinct models of each other's focus. That is, the speaker assumes that the hearer, in understanding an utterance, has followed any shift in focus indicated by that utterance and is, to the extent it matters, focused on the entities the speaker intended (from the perspective the speaker intended). It is only when a difference in focusing results in some fairly major incompatibility that a problem is detected. The interchange in (5) through (11) illustrates what happens when the two participants in a dialogue believe erroneously that they are focused on the same entity. Initially, the apprentice is focused on the motor pulley, which she thinks is the flywheel. Because the expert is not aware of this (he probably doesn't even consider the possibility), his responses are not very helpful.

Descriptions

One of the key ways in which the influence of focusing on dialogue is manifest is in the definite descriptions used. There is a two-way interaction between definite descriptions and focusing: (1) What entities a speaker and hearer concentrate on (and from what perspectives) influences the manner in which they describe entities, and (2) how entities are described influences how the speaker and hearer continue to focus their attention. Two specific problems relating to descriptions are strongly influenced by focusing. From the speaker's perspective, there is the problem of what to include in a description. From the hearer's perspective, there is the problem of what to do when a description doesn't correspond to any known entity – when it doesn't "match" anything.

Generating descriptions

Three factors that influence the production of a description are: (1) the information speaker and hearer share about the entity being described, (2) the perspectives they have on it, and (3) the use of redundancy. The following fragment of dialogue illustrates the first two of these factors.[9]

> E: OK. Now we need to attach the conduit to the motor. The conduit is *the covering around the wires that you . . . were working with earlier*. There is a small part . . . oh brother.
> A: Now wait a s . . . the conduit is the cover to the wires?
> E: Yes and . . .
> A: Oh I see, there's a part that . . . a part that's supposed to go over it.
> E: Yes.
> A: I see . . . it *looks just the right shape* too. Ah hah! Yes.
> E: Wonderful, since *I did not know how to describe the part*.

The problem that arises here is that there is no simple shape-based description for the object the expert needs to identify, so he must find some other shared information on which to base his description (see Downing, 1977; Chafe, 1979). The problem is complicated because the expert and apprentice do not share a visual field. If they did, the expert could point (if they and the object being pointed at were all in the same location) or use relative location (e.g., "it's next to the red-handled screwdriver").[10] The expert's solution in this case is to anchor the description on the basis of a past action the apprentice performed and then to describe the object functionally (i.e., to describe its function rather than its shape). Functional descriptions often enable bypassing other more complex descriptions. The statement "it is used for doing x" or "it has the right shape for doing x" may be used to communicate complex shapes and structures. As always, the success of such descriptions depends on the hearer's ability to determine what such an object is like, or to pick out the object from a set.

The fragment also illustrates the problems that arise when two participants in a dialogue have different perspectives on what is being described. The expert's orientation is basically functional; he has a model of what is going on, of how the compressor works, and of how it goes together. His descriptions are based on this model. The apprentice's orientation is basically visual or shape-based. He can see the parts and can tell by trying whether they fit. This discrepancy is even clearer in the following fragment, where from the functional perspective of the expert we get the descriptions "pump" and "cooling fins," whereas from the shape-based perspective of the apprentice, the same objects are described as "thing with flanges" and "little ribby things":

E: Remove the *pump* and the belt.
A: Is this *thing with flanges on it* the pump?
E: Point at "the thing with flanges on it" please.
A: I'm pointing at the thing with flanges on it. These *little ribby things* are flanges.
E: Yes, the thing you are pointing at is the pump. The little ribby things are *cooling fins*.

In this fragment, one can see the expert and apprentice working toward a shared view, trying to establish, or check that they have established, a common referent and hence a common focus.[11] An implicit goal in a dialogue is to establish this commonality – the effort this requires is very clear here. One way in which misunderstandings arise is that the participants in a dialogue fail to establish this common ground but *think* they have done so. (This happened with the flywheel and motor pulley in the initial dialogue fragment.) Not only do such mismatches occur, they are difficult to detect and often go unnoticed until a fairly major problem arises.

A further problem that arises in producing a description is deciding how much information to include in it. The linguistic description of an object must distinguish it from all others currently focused on by the speaker and hearer.[12] But the situation is more complicated than this. It is clear from an analysis of the task-oriented dialogues and from other data (Freedle, 1972) that the description of an object seldom contains only the minimal amount of information necessary to distinguish it. Descriptions, like the rest of language, are often redundant.[13] What appears to be the case for physical objects is that the speaker describes an object not in the minimum number of "bits" of information, but rather in a manner that will enable the hearer to locate the object as quickly as possible. Clear distinguishing features (e.g., color, size, and shape) are part of a description precisely because they eliminate large numbers of wrong objects and hence help the hearer to isolate the correct object more quickly.

The use of redundant information (and not just distinguishing information) to speed up the search for a referent can be seen easily from an example. If someone asks "What tool should I use?" the response "The red-handled one." may not be satisfactory even if there is only one red-handled tool, because processing such a description requires considering too many alternatives. The phrase "the red-handled screwdriver" is more helpful, because it limits the search to screwdrivers. In giving a description that minimizes the time it takes the hearer to identify the referent of a referring expression, a balance must be reached. Too much information is as harmful as too little because all parts of the description must be processed to make sure the object is the correct one. Furthermore, the hearer may wonder whether he is mistaken if he thinks he has determined the referent but there is more description to process (see Grice, 1975). Using the phrase "the red-handled screwdriver with the small chip on the bottom and a loose handle" to identify the only red-handled screwdriver will probably both increase the hearer's search time and confuse the hearer. Rather than minimizing either the communication time (including processing of the description) or the search time alone, the combination of communication time and search time must be minimized. A speaker should be redundant only to the degree that redundancy reduces the total time involved in identifying the referent.

Matching a description

As the preceding discussion illustrates, a major role of descriptions is to point; the speaker is directing the hearer's attention to some entity.

For the hearer, focusing is crucial in providing a small set of items from which to choose that entity. Being able to so restrict attention is necessary both for identifying the correct referent (as the interpretation of the phrase "the screw" in the initial dialogue fragment illustrates) and for constraining search time (see Grosz, 1977).

One problem that arises for a hearer, especially a computer system in the role of hearer, is what to do when a reference does not correspond to (or match) any known entity.[14] If the description suffices to distinguish the entity being pointed at from others that are currently focused on, then the mismatch does not matter. But, what does "suffice to distinguish" mean? The question of what kind of mismatch is significant depends on more than the entities in focus. For example, the difference between yellow and green may not matter when a yellow-green shirt is being distinguished from a red one; it does matter when picking lemons.

In addition, the hearer must decide whether or not an inexact match should even be considered. In the usual use of definite descriptions, to identify some entity in the domain of discourse, inexact matches are always acceptable. Donellan (1966) distinguishes this referential use from an attributive use for which an inexact match is not possible: "In the attributive use, the attribute of being the so-and-so is all important, while it is not in the referential use" (p. 102). But the distinction in the terms that Donnellan makes it poses a problem for a hearer because it is the speaker's intent, and not the speaker's beliefs,[15] that distinguishes attributive from referential uses of a description. This means that the hearer (whether a person or a computer system) must be able to detect this intent. In certain cases (e.g., descriptions of entities that do not yet exist), the attributive use is usually clear. In using the phrase "the winner of the 1984 Nobel Peace Prize," a speaker is describing a person whose identity is not yet known; there is no other way to describe that person (yet).[16] There are other instances in which the distinction relies on knowledge outside the dialogue in which the reference occurs (in particular, what the hearer believes the speaker wants). It seems that for this problem the dialogue participants must rely on the potential for clarification available in further dialogue. If a hearer misinterprets an attributive use of a description, the speaker can explicitly indicate the need for an exact match.[17]

To summarize, the importance of focusing to both the interpretation and the generation of definite descriptions comes from the highlighting function it serves. By separating those items currently highlighted from those that are not, focusing provides a boundary around the entities from which the entity being either described or identified must be distinguished. For generation purposes, this boundary circumscribes those items from which the entity being described must be distinguished, and thus provides some means of determining when a description is sufficiently complete. This boundary is useful for interpretation in providing a small set of items from which to choose. If an exact match cannot be found in focus, it is reasonable to ask if any of the items in focus comes close to matching the definite description, and, if so, which is the closest.

A focus representation

We turn now to the question of how to integrate mechanisms for focusing into a computer system, in particular into a language processing system. Suppose the system has a knowledge base that encodes the portion of the world the system knows about, and that this knowledge base contains formal elements that stand for entities in that world. Then the system needs a means of highlighting those elements in its knowledge base that correspond to the entities currently focused on and must be able both to use this highlighting (e.g., to interpret and generate descriptions) and to change it appropriately as the dialogue progresses.[18] In this section I will describe focusing mechanisms that were incorporated in a computer system constructed to participate in task-oriented dialogues. The representations described in this section are used by the procedures that determine the referents of definite noun phrases.[19] Some of the limitations of these mechanisms will be discussed in the following section.

A key characteristic of the focusing mechanisms I will describe is that they segment the knowledge base of the system into subunits. Each subunit, called a focus space, contains those items that are focused on by the participants in the dialogue during a particular part of the dialogue. This segmentation is structured by ordering the spaces in a hierarchy that corresponds to the structure of the dialogue. To illustrate the focusing mechanisms, I will consider how they are used for interpreting the phrases "the screws," "the screw in the center," and "the screw" in the initial dialogue fragment.

Figure 1 illustrates a piece of the encoding of the knowledge about the task and objects being discussed in this dialogue fragment.[20] There is a particular air compressor, AIRCOMPRESSOR1, which has as one of its parts a pump, PUMP1, which in turn has as one of its parts a flywheel, FLYWHEEL1. (The arcs labeled h.a.p. are a shorthand for the representation of these has-as-part relationships.) The arc labeled e from PUMP1 to PUMPS indicates that PUMP1 is an element of

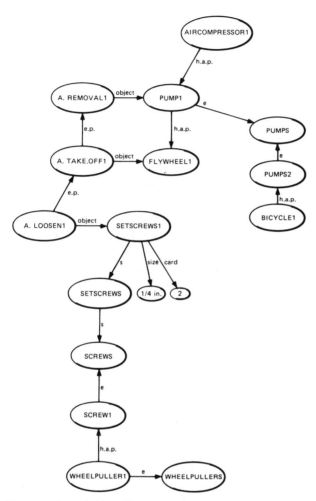

Figure 1. A partial encoding of the domain.

PUMPS (as is PUMP2, a part of some bicycle, BICYCLE1). In addition, there is a removal operation, A.REMOVAL1, which involves
PUMP1 and has an event-part (indicated by the arc labeled e.p.), a
taking-off operation A. TAKEOFF1. This taking-off operation has an
event-part A.LOOSEN1 that involves two quarter-inch setscrews,
SETSCREWS1, a subset of the set of all SCREWS.

Consider the situation just before (18) is uttered. The loosening of
the setscrews is the primary focus of the dialogue at this point. It is

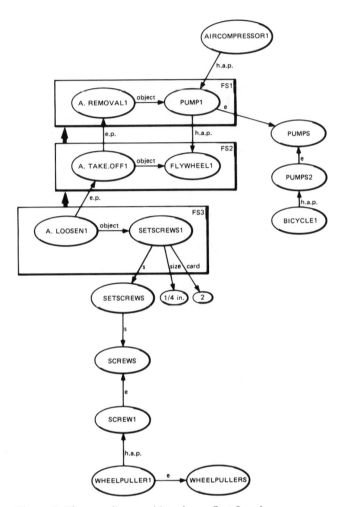

Figure 2. The encoding partitioned to reflect focusing.

viewed here as part of taking off the flywheel, which in turn is focused on as part of the pump removal. Figure 2 shows the network of Figure 1 partitioned to reflect this focusing. The nodes and arcs of the network have been separated into spaces. Space FS1 highlights removing the pump, space FS2 taking off the flywheel, and space FS3 loosening the screws. The heavy arrows between spaces indicate the hierarchy of focus. Space FS3 is the primary focus at this point in the dialogue. As long as this is the focusing situation, the phrase "the screws" will be taken to refer to SETSCREWS1, the two setscrews involved in the loosening operation. When the apprentice indicates that this operation is complete [in (18)], the potential for closing space FS3 arises. If this were to happen, as it indeed does in this dialogue fragment, focus would shift back to space FS2. Notice that once space FS3 is closed, SETSCREWS1 are no longer in focus. In particular, they are no longer considered candidates as referents for definite noun phrases. This situation could change of course – a reference to the loosening operation (e.g., "when I was loosening the setscrews") would reopen space FS3; discussion of another operation involving the setscrews would bring them back into focus in another focus space.

The interpretation of utterances (19)–(25) requires expanding the fragment of encoded knowledge to include some task (or process) information. Figure 3 shows in shorthand some of the information needed to understand the subtasks that participate in the task of removing the flywheel. The double arrows indicate the succession of task steps.[21] The dashed line between A.TAKE.OFF1 and the space labeled PLOT1 indicates an indirect pointer from the taking-off task to its subtasks and the objects involved in those subtasks. In particular, we can see that the task breaks down into two subtasks, a loosening (A.LOOSEN) and a removal operation involving a tool (A.RE-MOVE.WITH.TOOL), and that the removal operation uses a wheel-puller as its tool. This information is recorded on a separate space to indicate that it is only a template.[22] The node A.LOOSEN1 is an instantiation of the template subtask A.LOOSEN. The instantiation is made when the real task of loosening the setscrews [mentioned in utterances (3)–(18)] is performed.

This encoding of task information also plays a role in shifting focus. In addition to highlighting those items *explicitly focused* on by the dialogue participants by placing them on focus spaces, the focusing mechanisms differentially access certain information associated with these items. In particular, the subactions and objects involved in a task are *implicitly focused* on whenever that task is focused on. In this case, the dashed line to the space PLOT1 indicates certain entities implicitly focused on by the taking-off operation.

Concepts that are implicitly focused on are separated from those that are explicitly focused on (i.e., they are not added to focus spaces) for two reasons. First, there are numerous implicitly focused entities, many of which are never referred to in a dialogue. Including such entities in focus spaces would clutter them, weakening their highlighting function. Second, references to implicitly focused items may indicate a shift of focus to those items, making it useful to distinguish those references from others.

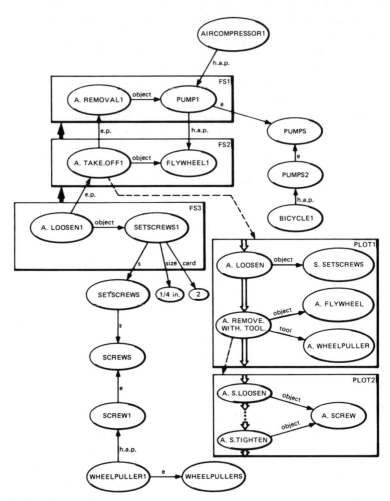

Figure 3. Implicit focus.

Utterance (18) results in focusing on the task following A.LOOSEN1, in this case the removal operation involving a wheelpuller. The dashed line from A.REMOVE.WITH.TOOL to PLOT2 indicates which entities are implicitly focused by the mention of the use of the wheelpuller. It is in this context that the definite noun phrases in (25) are resolved. The indirect pointer from A.REMOVE.WITH.-TOOL is followed, and the screw A.SCREW is found as a possible referent for "the screw in the center." Two things remain to be done.

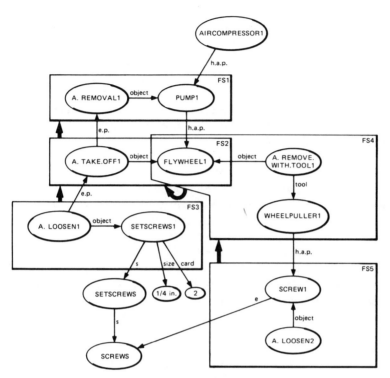

Figure 4. Updated focus partitioning.

First, a check must be made to see that A.SCREW satisfies this description. Second, a real screw corresponding to A.SCREW must be identified. Once this is done, we have the situation of Figure 4, where instantiations of the information in the plot spaces of Figure 3 have been made, and the "real" wheelpuller screw SCREW1 is in explicit focus.

Focus in discourse: prospects and problems

The preceding section described focusing mechanisms incorporated in a computer system for task-oriented dialogues. These include structures for highlighting elements of a knowledge base, operations on those structures, procedures that use them for interpreting definite noun phrases, and procedures for updating them. The implementation provides for two kinds of highlighting, explicit and implicit, and uses task information to determine shifts in focus. An *explicit focus* data structure contains those elements that are relevant to the interpretation of an utterance because they have been discussed in the preceding discourse. In addition, the focusing mechanisms provide for differential access to certain information associated with these elements. In particular, the subactions and objects involved in a task are implicitly highlighted whenever that task is highlighted. That is, *implicit focus* consists of those elements that are relevant to the interpretation of an utterance because they are closely connected to task-related elements in explicit focus.

There are several directions in which these mechanisms must be extended for a system to be able to deal with the general problems posed by focusing and definite descriptions in dialogue. First, the only clues to changes in focusing that are used by the system are clues based on shared knowledge about the structure of entities in the domain (in particular, the structure of the task). Linguistic clues and the interaction between different kinds of clues remain to be examined. Second, the highlighting of explicit focus and implicit focus is used in interpreting definite descriptions, but an exact match is required; the question of what constitutes an inexact match has not yet been faced. Third, although the highlighting structures provide for focusing on different aspects of an entity, the deduction routines do not use this information in accessing information about an entity in focus. Finally, the question of how the focusing mechanisms interact with representations of belief has not been addressed. The following sections examine the problems posed by each of these extensions in more detail.

Ranges of focusing and clues to shifts in focus

The term *focus* (as well as *theme*) is sometimes used (e.g., Halliday, 1967) to refer to prominence in a sentence, a more local phenomenon than focus as discussed here. It is clear that a speaker and hearer are focused not only globally on some set of entities but also more locally, and that this more local focusing affects the way in which a particular idea is expressed in an utterance. This raises the question of how sentential focusing interacts with the more global focusing discussed in this chapter. When does the way in which an utterance is phrased not only highlight certain entities, but also change the global focusing of the dialogue participants? An answer to this question requires looking more closely at what kinds of clues a speaker can use to shift focus.[23]

A speaker's clues on how to focus may be linguistic or may come from knowledge about the relationships among entities being discussed. Linguistic clues may be either explicit, given directly by certain words, or implicit, deriving from sentential structure or from rhetorical relationships between sentences. In the model described in Grosz (1977), both implicit focus and the procedures for shifting focus are based on clues that derive from knowledge a speaker and hearer share about the structure of the entities being discussed; they use a representation of the task to decide when and how to shift focus.[24] For the focusing mechanisms to be useful for discourse in general, they must be extended to take care of the linguistic clues that a speaker may use. In particular, two kinds of implicit linguistic clues must be understood and their use for shifting formalized.

First, there are the global linguistic clues that come from patterns of relationships between sentences, such as paraphrase and elaboration (Grimes, 1975; Halliday and Hasan, 1976). For example, by elaborating on some element of a sentence, a speaker shifts focus to that element (really the entity expressed by that element). A major question here is how to recognize when such patterns occur (see Hobbs, 1976). Perhaps more important, there is the question of whether recognizing the patterns requires knowing how the focus of attention in the two sentences is related. It may be that such global patterns are more useful in setting expectations about where focus may be in the succeeding utterances than in determining the focus in any particular utterance.

The second kind of implicit clue comes from the syntactic form of an utterance. Sidner (1979) presents rules for determining focus, based on thematic relations and syntactic structure. A particularly important aspect of her work involves the recognition that focusing is only *predicted* by a single utterance and that the "potential focus" must be confirmed by succeeding utterances. That is, the question of whether an utterance changes global focus cannot be answered on the basis of the individual utterance. Rather, an utterance can only suggest a global shift in focus. This expectation may then be confirmed in a following utterance if the speaker continues. If the hearer speaks next, s/he may choose to accept or reject this shift.

Inexact matches: the problems that remain

Before the focusing mechanisms can be extended to handle inexact matches, two major problems must be addressed: determining how to decide whether an inexact match is close enough and determining how to decide between accepting an inexact match and considering a shift in focus. For the first problem, focusing makes it possible to determine the closest match, but not to decide whether that match is close enough. For example, if a red ball and a green ball are in focus, then the red ball comes closest to matching the description "the red block" but not close enough to be considered the referent of that phrase. For the second problem, if no exact match can be found in explicit focus, the matching procedures must decide whether to accept a referent that inexactly matches a description or to consider the possibility that the speaker wants to focus on some new entity. For example, should a hearer confronted with the phrase "the red spot" in the situation just described look for a red spot on one of the balls? Answers to these questions require research on some fundamental issues in semantics and on speech errors.

Focusing and perspective

Focusing involves not only highlighting certain entities, but also highlighting certain ways of viewing those entities. For example, a doctor may be viewed as a member of the medical profession or as having a role in a family. In the process of focusing on some entity, the speaker also chooses a certain perspective on that entity and, as a result, focuses on that entity from that perspective (Fillmore, 1978; Halliday, forthcoming). Fillmore says:

> The point is that, whenever we pick a word or phrase, we automatically drag along with it the larger context or framework in terms of which the word or phrase we have chosen has an interpretation. It is as if descriptions of the meanings of elements must identify simultaneously "figure" and "ground."
> To say it again, whenever we understand a linguistic expression of whatever sort, we have simultaneously a background scene and a perspective on that scene. (1978, p. 74)

The perspective from which an entity is viewed influences how further information about that entity is accessed. The representation of focus presented in Grosz (1977) allows for differential access to properties of an entity, but this addresses only one part of the problem.[25] Using the initial perspective from which an entity is viewed for differential access does not rule out considering a concept differently from the way it has already been portrayed. Instead, it orders the way in which aspects of the concept are to be examined. One of the problems this raises is how to decide: when to consider a switch in perspective, when to abandon deriving properties or searching items implicitly focused by an initial perspective, and when to examine other aspects of the entity.

Another problem that relates to perspective is how perspective influences the particular description a speaker chooses. Does global focus give an indication to a speaker of which properties to choose? The fragments of dialogue in the example section contained several illustrations of the effect of differences in how a speaker and hearer were focused on communication. This suggests that focusing, though often quite useful, can cause problems for people; similar problems may be unavoidable in a natural language processing system.

Focusing and beliefs

An additional aspect of focus that has not yet been addressed is its interaction with a representation of beliefs. The dialogue fragments in the section on description pointed out some of the problems that arise when the two participants know different things about the entity being described. It is important, then, for a speaker to be able to separate his or her own beliefs from what s/he believes the hearer knows or believes. It seems equally clear from the dialogues, however, that focusing is not one of the things that is separate for the two participants. There is a pervasive assumption by speaker and hearer that they share a common focus (this is, in fact, an important part of how and why focusing works). Of course, the speaker is always a step ahead of the hearer in shifting focus, but communication only ensues if the shift is clearly indicated to the hearer. The main extension that seems to be needed here is to coordinate the focusing mechanisms with an encoding of knowledge that distinguishes beliefs (rather than, as is now the case, with some uniform encoding of knowledge that does not distinguish between speaker and hearer), and a reasoning system that can reason about knowledge and beliefs (e.g., Moore, 1979; Cohen, 1978).

Summary

Focusing is the active process, engaged in by the participants in a dialogue, of concentrating attention on, or highlighting, a subset of their shared reality. Not only does it make communication more efficient, it makes communication possible. Speaker and hearer can concentrate on a small portion of what they know and ignore the rest. The importance of focusing in communication is clearly demonstrated by the definite descriptions that are used in dialogue. For a natural language processing system to carry on a dialogue with a person it must include mechanisms that computationally capture this focusing process. This chapter has examined the requirements that definite descriptions impose on such mechanisms, discussed focusing mechanisms included in a computer system for understanding task-oriented dialogue, and indicated future research problems entailed in modeling the focusing process more generally.

NOTES

The work reported herein was supported by the National Science Foundation under Grant No. MCS 76-22004 and by the Advanced Research Projects Agency of the Department of Defense under Contract No. N00039-78-C-0060. I would like to thank Gary Hendrix, Jerry Hobbs, David Levy, Ann Robinson, Jane Robinson, Candy Sidner, and Brian Smith for discussing the ideas in this paper and commenting on various drafts of it.

1 This is the reason the verb "focusing" rather than the noun "focus" is used more often in this paper.
2 This does not mean the entities must exist in the "real world." Even so, the statement is not quite correct. In Grosz and Hendrix (1978), we point out that the only kind of object an interpreter can focus on is structures in its memory. The perspective of an outside observer is required to relate these structures to entities in some real or hypothetical world.
3 Although we will concentrate on dialogue, much of what will be said carries to other forms of discourse.
4 For most of these dialogues the expert and apprentice had only limited visual contact.
5 The modifying phrase "in the center" does not distinguish the main wheelpuller screw from the setscrews, but from other screws that are part of the wheelpuller.
6 It is interesting that some people who are not familiar with the compressor or wheelpuller find this sequence confusing: (18) seems to end any concern with screws, and hence (25) is unintelligible. One must know – or infer – that the wheelpuller has a screw for the statement to make sense.
7 The concept of structure used here is similar to that in Levy (1979), but different from that in work on story and text grammars (cf. van Dijk, 1972; Rumelhart, 1975). In particular, we are not interested in such things as generating or recognizing a valid dialogue (the analogy to sentence grammars), but rather in those dynamic aspects of intersentential relationships such as focusing that influence the interpretation and generation of utterances in a dialogue.
8 One of the open problems for incorporating focusing mechanisms in natural language processing systems that bears further investigation is identifying the different kinds of clues to focusing and how they interact. Some aspects of this problem are discussed below in the section on "A focus representation."
9 This segment also illustrates the cooperative nature of task-oriented dialogues: The two participants work together to achieve a shared goal of identifying the object the expert wants the apprentice to locate.
10 Rubin (1978) describes spatial and temporal commonality between speaker and hearer as two dimensions along which language experiences may differ and considers how these dimensions affect the interpretation of deictic expressions.

11 There is a clear indication at the end of the fragment concerning "the conduit," that the expert realizes the importance of shape in the apprentice's orientation: He says he didn't know how to describe the part, apparently meaning that he didn't have a description of its shape (he did describe it functionally, and that description seems to have worked very well).

12 Olson (1970) has shown that the description of an object changes, depending on the surrounding objects from which it must be distinguished. For example, the same flat, round, white object was described as "the round one" when a flat, square object of similar size and material was present, but as "the white one" when a similarly shaped but black object was present. The importance of contrast for distinguishing objects is well established in vision research (e.g., Gregory, 1966). Comparison of differences has also played a crucial role in computer programs that reason analogically (Evans, 1963; similar strategies are used in Winston, 1970).

13 Olson (1970, p. 266) comments on this phenomenon and on the need for further investigation of it.

14 Grosz and Hendrix (1978) examine the question of matching in a more coherent framework. In particular, the notions of processor-dependent interpretation and processor state are used to explain how an expression can refer (in the standard sense) to different entities for speaker and hearer.

15 "A definite description can be used attributively even when the speaker believes that some particular person fits the description, and it can be used referentially in the absence of this belief" (p. 111).

16 There is, of course, the possibility that the speaker meant to say 1977, in which case s/he is referring (wrongly) to an existing entity, but then we are back with the referential case.

17 We have ignored a third issue that arises when considering a computer system for natural language processing: The formalism used for encoding knowledge in the system must be adequate for handling attributive descriptions. For a discussion of this issue, see Cohen (1978) and Webber (1978).

18 In addition, during retrieval and deduction operations, this highlighting enables the system to access more important information first. Grosz (1977) describes this aspect of focusing in relation to identifying the referents of definite noun phrases.

19 Robinson (1978) contains a description of the system and a sample of the kind of dialogue it can currently handle.

20 To avoid complicating the figures and the description, I have used a simplified network notation. The actual network representation used for implementing and testing the focus mechanisms described here is presented in Hendrix (1978). Among the things glossed over are the actual representation of individual instances. Also, time information has been left out. A more detailed presentation of the initial use of partitioned networks for encoding focusing can be found in Grosz (1977) and Walker (1978).

21 Additional information includes the effects and preconditions of the operation. The actual representation also accounts for partial ordering in the task steps (see Hendrix, 1975; Sacerdoti, 1977; Robinson, 1978).

22 This is part of the partitioning that Hendrix (1978) uses for quantification.

23 It is important to note that shifting and focusing are not separable tasks. Focusing is an ongoing process that both influences and is influenced by the interpretation of an utterance. This dynamic aspect of focusing is clear in the interpretation of the phrase "one screw" in utterance (5) of the initial dialogue fragment. The focusing established by the expert in utterance (3) highlights a set of screws from which the one screw can be chosen. The reference to one screw shifts focus to the particular subtask of loosening those screws.

24 The structure need not be that of a task. For example, in describing a house, focus can move from the total house to one of the rooms of the house.

25 Consequently, the reference resolution mechanisms did not use this feature.

REFERENCES

Chafe, W. L. 1979. "The Flow of Thought and the Flow of Language." In T. Givon, ed. *Syntax and Semantics*, Vol. 12. New York: Academic Press.

Cohen, P. R. 1978. "On Knowing What to Say: Planning Speech Acts." Ph.D. thesis, University of Toronto.

Deutsch (Grosz), B. G. 1974. "Typescripts of Task Oriented Dialogs." SUR Note 146, Menlo Park, Calif.: Artificial Intelligence Center, Stanford Research Institute. August 20.

Donnellan, K. 1966. "Reference and Definite Description." *The Philosophical Review*, Vol. 75. Reprinted, 1971. In D. P. Steinberg and L. A. Jakobovits, eds. *Semantics*. Cambridge: Cambridge University Press, pp. 100–14.

Downing, P. A. 1977. "On 'Basic Levels' and the Categorization of Objects in English Discourse." *Proceedings of the Third Annual Meeting of the Berkeley Linguistics Society*, Berkeley, Calif. February.

Evans, T. G. 1963. "A Heuristic Program to Solve Geometric-Analogy Problems." Ph.D. thesis, Massachusetts Institute of Technology, Department of Mathematics.

Fillmore, C. J. 1978. "The Case for Case Reopened." In P. Cole and J. M. Sadock, eds. *Syntax and Semantics*, Vol. 8. New York: Academic Press.

Freedle, R. O. 1972. "Language Users as Fallible Information-Processors: Implications for Measuring and Modeling Comprehension." In J. B. Carroll and R. O. Freedle, eds. *Language Comprehension and the Acquisition of Knowledge*. Washington, D.C.: Winston, pp. 169–209.

Gregory, R. L. 1966. *Eye and Brain: The Psychology of Seeing*. New York: McGraw-Hill.

Grice, J. 1975. "Logic and Conversation." In P. Cole and J. Morgan, eds. *Syntax and Semantics*, Vol. 3. New York: Academic Press, pp. 41–58.

Grimes, J. E. 1975. *The Thread of Discourse*. The Hague: Mouton.

Grosz, B. J. 1977. "The Representation and Use of Focus in Dialogue Understanding." Ph.D. thesis, University of California, Berkeley. Also, Technical Note No. 151, Menlo Park, Calif.: Artificial Intelligence Center, SRI International.

Grosz, B. J., and Hendrix, G. G. 1978. "A Computational Perspective on Indefinite Reference." Presented at Sloan Workshop on Indefinite Reference, University of Massachusetts, Amherst, Mass. December. Also, (in preparation) Technical Note No. 181. Menlo Park, Calif.: Artificial Intelligence Center, SRI International.

Halliday, M. A. 1967. "Notes on Transitivity and Theme in English, Part 2." *Journal of Linguistics* 31:177–274.

Halliday, M. A. Forthcoming. "Language as Code and Language as Behaviour: A Systemic-functional Interpretation of the Nature and Ontogenesis of dialogue." In M. A. K. Halliday, S. M. Lamb and A. Makkai, eds. *Semiotics of Culture and Language.* New York: The Press at Twin Willows.

Halliday, M. A., and Hasan, R. 1976. *Cohesion in English.* London: Longman.

Hendrix, G. G. 1975. "Partitioned Networks for the Mathematical Modeling of Natural Language Semantics." Technical Report NL-28, University of Texas, Austin, Department of Computer Sciences.

Hendrix, G. G. 1978. "The Representation of Semantic Knowledge." In D. E. Walker, ed. *Understanding Spoken Language.* New York: Elsevier North-Holland.

Hobbs, J. R. 1976. "A Computational Approach to Discourse Analysis." Research Report 76-2, City College, CUNY, Department of Computer Sciences. December.

Levy, D. M. 1979. "Communicative Goals and Strategies: Between Discourse and Syntax." In T. Givon, ed. *Syntax and Semantics,* Vol. 12. New York: Academic Press.

Moore, R. C. 1979. "Reasoning About Action and Knowledge." Ph.D. thesis, Massachusetts Institute of Technology.

Olson, D. R. 1970. "Language and Thought: Aspects of a Cognitive Theory of Semantics." *Psychological Review* 77:257–73.

Robinson, A. E. 1978. "Investigating the Process of Natural-Language Communication." Technical Note 165, Menlo Park, Calif.: Artificial Intelligence Center, SRI International. July.

Rubin, A. D. 1978. "A Theoretical Taxonomy of the Differences Between Oral and Written Language." In R. Spiro, B. Bruce, and W. Brewer, eds. *Theoretical Issues in Reading Comprehension.* Hillsdale, N.J.: Erlbaum.

Rumelhart, D. E. 1975. "Notes on a Schema for Stories." In D. R. Bobrow and A. Collins, eds. *Representation and Understanding: Studies in Cognitive Science.* New York: Academic Press.

Sacerdoti, E. D. 1977. *A Structure for Plans and Behavior.* New York: Elsevier North-Holland, Inc.

Sidner, C. L. 1979. "A Computational Model of Co-reference Comprehension in English." Ph.D. thesis, Massachusetts Institute of Technology.

van Dijk, T. A. 1972. *Some Aspects of Text Grammars: A Study in Theoretical Linguistics and Poetics.* The Hague: Mouton.

Walker, D. E. 1978. *Understanding Spoken Language.* New York: Elsevier North-Holland.

Webber, B. L. 1978. "A Formal Approach to Discourse Anaphora." BBN Report No. 3761, Cambridge, Mass.: Bolt, Beranek and Newman Inc. May.

Winston, P. H. 1970. "Learning Structural Descriptions From Examples." MAC TR-76, Cambridge, Mass.: MIT Artificial Intelligence Laboratory.

4

Mental models of meaning

P. N. JOHNSON-LAIRD

Psycholinguists generally assume that in order to understand a sentence a listener has to establish its underlying grammatical structure (see, e.g., Fodor et al., 1974). This "deep structure" specifies the grammatical relations between the constituents of the sentence. Once these relations have been established, they can be used as instructions for combining the meaning of words in order to obtain the meaning of the sentence. In fact, however, there is no unequivocal evidence that deep structure, or any other such syntactic *representation*, plays any role in either comprehension or speaking. Ideally, syntactic processing might better be thought of as yielding meaning without building up explicit syntactic structure except perhaps in the case of elliptical sentences (Johnson-Laird, 1977a, b). But, what is meaning?

There are three main sorts of semantic theory within psychology. First, some psychologists argue that words are represented in a mental dictionary that *decomposes* their meanings into semantic features (see, e.g., Smith et al., 1974). Second, other theorists propose that the mental lexicon takes the form of a *network* that links words according to the semantic relations between them (see, e.g., Collins and Quillian, 1972). Third, an analogous theory has been couched in terms of *meaning postulates*, that is, rules that specify the semantic relations between words (see, e.g., Kintsch, 1974). There is controversy about the extent to which these three sorts of theory differ in substance. They have at least one element in common: None of them is rich enough to provide a psychologically plausible representation of meaning. The aim of this chapter is to explain why. It also offers some tentative arguments in favor of a different conception of meaning.

Decompositional theories of meaning

The central assumption of the decompositional theories of meaning is that the semantic interpretation of a sentence is obtained by replacing

106

its words with their dictionary definitions, and combining them according to the syntactic relations of the sentence. A dictionary definition is made up of a structured set of semantic elements, which decompose the meaning of the word into its semantic constituents. Because a word may have more than one distinct sense, the process of combining meanings is also sensitive to the constraints, the so-called selectional restrictions, that one word may place upon the meanings of the words with which it can be combined (i.e., these words must have a specified meaning). For example, one sense of *handsome* is restricted to human beings and artifacts, and another sense is restricted to conduct: Neither *a handsome prince* nor *a handsome act* is ambiguous because each noun meets the selectional restrictions on only a single sense of *handsome*. Figure 1 presents a simplified example of decompositional analyses of words and the semantic representation of a sentence.

An influential linguistic theory of decomposition was proposed by Katz and Fodor (1963); it was immediately appealing because it appeared to be a natural development of transformational grammar. The theory was taken over by psychologists and inspired a number of experiments, but its psychological implementations have run into a number of criticisms, most of which might equally well be applied to Schank's (1975) decompositional theory developed within the framework of Artificial Intelligence. Let us briefly examine the five major points of the critique.

First, Kintsch (1974) argues that "if one starts to decompose, it is hard to see where to stop." The point seems no more cogent here than it would be in opposing the atomic theory of matter.

Second, according to Fodor, Fodor, and Garrett (1975) (henceforth referred to as FFG), the rapidity with which comprehension occurs is not readily explicable if it consists in replacing words with their decompositional dictionary entries, combining them, and so on. This argument carries little weight; many complicated mental processes can occur with great rapidity.

Third, FFG claim that the decompositional theory makes erroneous predictions about the comprehension of sentences. It predicts, for example, that the sentence *John is a bachelor* should be harder to understand (and occupy more space in memory) than *John is unmarried* because the definition of bachelor should include the meaning of *unmarried* as a proper part. There seems intuitively to be no such difference. Moreover, Kintsch (1974) was unable to find any effects of semantic complexity in a number of tasks (e.g., it had no effect on the time taken to begin to speak a sentence containing a given word). FFG have likewise investigated the times taken to evaluate deductive ar-

Words in the lexicon

man : (noun) HUMAN, ADULT, MALE
      count
child : (noun) HUMAN, NOT(ADULT)
      count
   lift : (verb) CAUSE(ACTIVITY X, UPWARD(MOVE)Y)
      tr
      where X is the underlying subject, Y is the underlying object, and their
      selectional restrictions are as follows: X : $\langle$(HUMAN) OR (ANIMAL)
      OR (MACHINE)$\rangle$, and Y : $\langle$(PHYSICAL OBJECT)$\rangle$.

The representation of a sentence: "A man lifts a child."

CAUSE(ACTIVITY(HUMAN, ADULT, MALE), UPWARD(MOVE)
(HUMAN, NOT(ADULT)).

Figure 1. An example of the representation of meaning in terms of a decompositional theory of semantics.

guments of differing semantic complexity. Some of the deductions hinged on an explicit negation such as:

If practically all of the men in the room are not married, then few of the men in the room have wives.

Other inferences involved lexical items such as *bachelor* with a putative semantic representation containing a negation. The results indicated that such lexical items made an inference reliably easier to evaluate than one containing an explicit negation. This facilitation was significantly greater than that created by a so-called morphological negative such as *unmarried*. FFG conclude that a word such as *bachelor*, unlike *unmarried*, does not seem to contain a negative in its semantic representation though it ought to according to the decompositional theory.

Although such negative findings may be suggestive, they are hardly decisive. Katz (1977) is inclined to dismiss all psychological evidence as irrelevant to linguistic theories. However, it is highly pertinent to the evaluation of related psychological theories. Yet, both Kintsch's and FFG's results are equivocal. There is no reason to suppose that the latency to make up a sentence should be affected by the semantic complexity of words; the latency of speaking does not correlate with the difficulty of defining a word, whether measured in terms of accuracy or subjective difficulty (Johnson-Laird and Quinn, 1976). Kintsch's other experimental tasks probably do not require a subject to decompose the meanings of lexical items in order to perform satisfactorily. This failing applies, for example, to the study in which the recall of a sentence (such as *John was accused of stealing*) was cued by a word denoting a relevant semantic component (such as *guilty*). Such a cue was no better than a close associate of a word in the original sentence (such as *blame*). But when subjects know that their verbatim memory is to be tested, they tend to hold on to a representation of the original words rather than a deeper semantic interpretation (see Johnson-Laird and Stevenson, 1970; Green, 1975). Likewise, FFG's conclusion that the representation of *bachelor* does not include a negative cannot be justified by a mere difference in latency of response; a negation in a dictionary entry may simply be responded to faster than a morphological or explicit negation.

Fourth, FFG argue that decompositional dictionary entries are unable to capture certain inferences that depend on the meanings of words. Even if, for example, *kill* is replaced by "cause to die," then some other machinery is required to mediate the inference from "*x* cause *y* to die" to "*y* die." As a matter of fact, this particular inference does follow from a decomposition of "cause" (see Miller and Johnson-Laird, 1976, p. 506). A related argument, which FFG evidently find most persuasive because it also occurs in J. A. Fodor (1976) and J. D. Fodor (1977), is that there can be no satisfactory dictionary definition of *red*. "Presumably," FFG write, "*x is red* entails *x is colored*. But, surely, there is no property *F* which is logically independent of the property of being colored and such that *x is F and x is colored* entails *x is red*." The fallacy here rests on the assumption that mental dictionaries contain only analyses that are conjunctive in form. It is entirely feasible that *colored* is defined disjunctively as RED or ORANGE or YELLOW or GREEN, and so forth (see Miller and Johnson-Laird, 1976, Section 5.1), in which case *x is red* would entail *x is colored* without the need to postulate some hypothetical property *F*.

Fifth, Kintsch (1974) claims that it is difficult to see why complex words would have evolved if comprehension invariably required their meanings to be decomposed. This is a sensible point, yet there may be economies to be obtained by processing one semantically complex word rather than a synonymous string of simple words.

The case against the dictionary theory is hardly overwhelming. Indeed, FFG themselves claim only that it is sufficiently persuasive to make it worth considering an alternative theory of semantics. In fact, this alternative has a number of antecedents, including the semantic network theories.

Semantic network theories

A variety of semantic theories have been couched in the network format (see, e.g., Quillian, 1968; Collins and Quillian, 1972; Rumelhart et al., 1972; Simmons and Slocum, 1972). Their central

Words in the lexicon

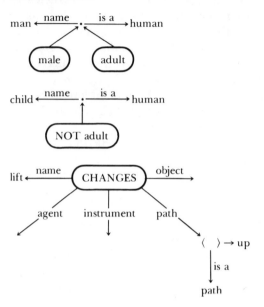

The initial representation of a sentence: "A man lifts a child."

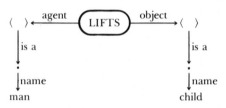

Figure 2. An example of the representation of meaning in terms of a semantic network. *Note:* Nodes represented by black dots correspond to generic nodes; nodes represented by ovals correspond to propositions that apply to other nodes; nodes represented by angle brackets represent specific instances of generic concepts. The different arguments of a verb are here, as in many network theories, assigned labels from Case Grammar (Fillmore, 1968); for some arguments against this practice, see Johnson-Laird (1977a).

assumption is that the lexicon should be treated as a network that interrelates representations of lexical items by a variety of inferential links. "Man," for example, is related by an "is a" link to "human." The initial interpretation of a sentence consists in setting up a similar sort of network with pointers into the appropriate nodes of semantic memory. A simplified version of such a representation is illustrated in Figure 2. The entailments of a sentence can be captured by pursuing the links in semantic memory that emanate from the nodes initially activated.

There is a controversy in the psychological literature over whether semantic network theories are substantially different from decompositional theories. Hollan (1975) takes the view that they are merely notational variants of each other. However, semantic networks are not without their critics, and Woods (1975) has identified a number of profound problems for them, including the need to adopt a consistent notation and to ensure that the links between nodes are not treated in an entirely ad hoc manner.

Woods also draws attention to the lack of any machinery in semantic networks to distinguish between the meaning (or intension) and the reference (or extension) of expressions. Perhaps the point can be most directly made by considering a gerundive construction. An assertion such as:

Ogden's playing of the sonata wrecked the piano

contains a gerundive that refers to an event, Ogden's actual playing. But the assertion:

That Ogden played the sonata is true

contains a complement that refers, not to an event, but to a proposition; its extension is an intension (see Vendler, 1968; Miller and Johnson-Laird, 1976, Section 7.3.1). It is not obvious how the distinction between the intension and the extension of an expression should be captured within a semantic network. In model-theoretic semantics, as developed by logicians and philosophers, an intension of an expression is often treated as a function from possible worlds (and possible times and contexts) to an extension. Given a possible world, the function yields a truth value for a sentence, and a referent for a referring phrase if it has one in that particular possible world. Unfortunately, despite the able championing of Partee (1977), it seems unlikely that the apparatus of a "possible worlds" semantics can be directly adopted for a plausible psychological theory of meaning. Human beings are poor at evaluating the complete set of alternatives to a given situation, and of course the number of such alternatives is usually vast. It is for this reason, and others, that I have proposed a "constructive" account of possibility (see Johnson-Laird, 1978).

The representation of sentences containing quantifiers such as:

Some books have been read by all philosophers

requires special care within semantic networks. Woods points out that quantifiers have often been treated as though they were adjectives that

modify a noun phrase, a failing that is by no means unique to proponents of semantic networks. It is important to be able to capture the
relative scopes of quantifiers in order to be able to distinguish, for
example, the salient interpretation of the sentence above from that of
the following sentence:

> All philosophers have read some books.

Quantifiers present very special problems for psychologists because
although their semantics can be explicitly formulated in model-
theoretic terms, it is not obvious how best to do justice to their everyday interpretations. I shall return to this problem later.

The meaning postulate theory of semantics

The late Yehoshua Bar-Hillel (1967) argued that the decomposition
theory advocated by Katz and Fodor could not account for the
synonymy of such sentences as *John sells books to Peter* and *Peter buys
books from John.* He proposed instead that this relation should be captured by a *meaning postulate,* a device introduced by Carnap (1956) in
order to accommodate analytical truths based on the meanings of
words within a model-theoretic semantics of a formal language. Thus,
the following meaning postulate establishes the appropriate relations
between *buy* and *sell:*

> for all x, y, and z, x sells y to $z \equiv z$ buys y from x.

Although the decompositional theory was reformulated in order to
meet these criticisms, Bar-Hillel's stratagem of replacing dictionary
entries by meaning postulates is the core of a new psychologically
oriented theory of meaning that was first proposed by Kintsch (1974).
He argued that corresponding to each word there is a word concept.
Hence, for the word *red* there is a concept that Kintsch denotes in
capital letters: RED. The logical entailments of a concept are captured, not by dictionary entries that decompose its meaning into
semantic primitives, but by meaning postulates that relate it to other
concepts. This closed conception of the lexicon is broken by allowing
that lexical descriptions may also include sensory information or
motor programs, but not conceptual programs – presumably because
they would amount to a reintroduction of dictionary entries.

A similar theory was proposed by Fodor et al. (1975). They make
three main assumptions:

1. Each morpheme in the surface vocabulary of a natural language is
   represented by a corresponding primitive (i.e., unanalyzed) item
   in the vocabulary of the language of mental representations

Words in the lexicon

man : MAN
child : CHILD
 lift : LIFT

Meaning postulates

FOR ANY X, IF X IS A MAN THEN X IS HUMAN AND X IS ADULT AND X IS MALE.

FOR ANY X, IF X IS A CHILD THEN X IS HUMAN AND NOT (X IS AN ADULT).

FOR ANY X AND Y, IF X LIFTS Y THEN X CAUSES Y TO MOVE UPWARD.

The initial representation of a sentence: "A man lifts a child."

$((A\ MAN)_{NP}\ (LIFTS(A\ CHILD)_{NP})_{VP})_S$

where NP = noun phrase, VP = verb phrase, S = sentence.

Figure 3. An example of the representation of meaning in terms of meaning postulates.

   (henceforth, this language will be called "mentalese"). Thus, the
   formatives of natural language correspond to formatives in mentalese.
2. The process of comprehension consists in translating a sentence into
   its corresponding representation in mentalese – a representation
   that closely resembles the surface form of the sentence and is
   composed of the primitive formatives of mentalese.[1]
3. Those entailments of a sentence that depend on its lexical content are
   established, not in the process of comprehension by the use of
   eliminative dictionary entries, but subsequently in an inferential
   process based on meaning postulates.

It follows that in understanding a sentence such as *A man lifts a child* a
listener translates it morpheme by morpheme into a virtually isomor-
phic mentalese representation. In determining that the sentence entails that a human lifts a child, the listener utilizes a meaning postulate.
Both the initial translation and the meaning postulate are presented
in Figure 3.

To what extent does a meaning postulate theory really differ from a
decompositional theory? Katz and Nagel (1974) argue that a dictionary entry is equivalent to a set of meaning postulates. They also
advance cogent arguments for the meaning postulate theory to be
supplemented by a system of selectional restrictions and by some principles for combining the meanings of words in syntactically complicated sentences. With the addition of this and other related machinery, Katz and Nagel claim that the theory becomes a notational

variant of the decompositional theory. This view is challenged, however, by FFG. They point out at least three crucial theoretical distinctions. First, the theories diverge on the primitive vocabulary of the language of semantic representations. Their theory is committed to a mental language that stands in a one-to-one relation to the vocabulary of natural language; decompositional theories are committed to a language of semantic primitives that need have no such correspondence to natural language. Second, the theories diverge on the question of the abstractness of the semantic level. Their theory postulates less abstract semantic interpretations than those of decompositional theories. This point is amplified by Fodor (1977), who writes that the meaning postulate theory does not propose that sentences are translated into ultimate irreducible components of meaning: "language-specific words can still be represented by language-neutral universal semantic symbols, but the translation would not be any more DETAILED or explicit than the expression it translates. The most abstract level of representation provided by the grammar would be thus less abstract than is implied by decompositional theories" (p. 154). Third, the theories differ on the relation between comprehension and inference. In the meaning postulate theory, initial comprehension is extremely superficial with the entailments of a sentence determined at some later time, whereas decompositional theories make no distinction between understanding a sentence and grasping its semantic entailments: They are one and the same process.

The case against decompositional, network, and meaning postulate theories

There is one major point of agreement between proponents of all three sorts of theory and the present author. We agree about the importance of psychological phenomena for semantic theory. Indeed, I am inclined to accept Fillmore's (1974) dictum that *issues in semantics that have no conceivable application to the process of comprehension cannot be very important for semantic theory.* It is from this standpoint that I propose to criticize the three sorts of theory. The basis of my criticism is that they all are based on the "autonomy" of semantics, that is, they assume that the meaning of any sentence can be established entirely independently from what it may refer to. This assumption of autonomy is self-evident because none of the theories has anything of substance to say about referential matters. Indeed, it is natural to assume that grasping the intension of an expression is a precursor to determining its extension because the intension is so often treated as a function that delivers the extension. Would that it were always so, and that natural language invariably worked in this orderly fashion.

The interaction between meaning and reference is evident in the machinery of selectional restrictions. What has to be constrained is not the meaning of expressions, but their referents (Woods, 1975). An assertion such as *it is pregnant* plainly constrains the referent of *it*, not its meaning; it must either refer to an idea or to a female animal. Moreover, the orthodox specification of selectional restrictions is too rigid to be workable. The constraints are ones that should be taken to hold by default, that is, unless the utterance or its circumstances explicitly override them. A still more critical weakness of the original theory is that it turns out to be impossible to state determinate selectional restrictions for many verbs. Consider, again, the verb *lift*, which was earlier assigned the following constraint on its subject: ⟨(HUMAN) or (ANIMAL) or (MACHINE)⟩. Plainly, this specification is a first approximation. It fails to allow the following acceptable sentences:

> The wind lifted the leaves over the fence
> The magnet lifted the pins
> The sea lifted the flotsam over the jetty
> The rope lifted the weight
> Her little finger lifted the thimble
> Hot air lifted the balloon
> The root lifted the earth

Wind, sea and magnets might be subsumed by FORCE, a finger might be subsumed by BODY PART, but how are hot air, ropes, and roots to be accommodated? As the list grows, it takes on an increasingly ad hoc character, which suggests that some underlying general principle has been overlooked. It might be argued that there are no constraints on the subject of *lift* other than that the noun phrase should not be an abstract one such as *sincerity*. The trouble with this hypothesis, however, is that it fails to establish the oddity of such sentences as "The apple lifted the tree."

The principle underlying the interpretation of sentences is that a listener often has recourse, not to selectional restrictions, but to inferences based on factual knowledge about referents. It is necessary to know that hot air rises, that ropes can support weights, that roots grow, in order to infer that they can lift things; and this knowledge is hardly lexical, but directly concerns matters of fact. The commonplace interpretation of the following sentence:

> He found it difficult to grasp

depends on the referent of *it;* one sense of *grasp* is selected if *it* refers to a mathematical theorem, whereas quite another sense is selected if *it* refers, say, to a boa constrictor. A psychologically plausible theory of meaning must accordingly allow for the *reference* of some expressions to play a role in determining the *meanings* of other expressions.

Reference also plays a critical role in certain logical implications that hold between expressions. The problem arises most immediately in the case of spatial prepositions. It is simple enough to assume that a relation such as *in* is transitive because the conclusion of the following inference is valid:

> Fred is in his office
> Fred's office is in the University
> ∴ Fred is in the University.

Transitivity can be readily captured in a meaning postulate:

> If x is in y and y is in z, then x is in z.

The property of transitivity might, indeed, be stated once and for all in Universal Semantics, as Bar-Hillel (1967) suggested, and *in* specified as being a transitive relation in the semantics of English. Presumably, its transitivity can also be specified in a decompositional dictionary entry, or a semantic network. But, how is a relation such as *on the right of* to be treated? Consider the following inference:

> Matthew is on the right of Mark
> Mark is on the right of Luke
> ∴ Matthew is on the right of Luke

Granted the truth of the premises, the truth of the conclusion depends on how the relevant individuals are spatially arranged. If they are seated along one side of a rectangular table, the conclusion is true, and *on the right of* is transitive. If they are equally spaced around a circular table, the conclusion is false, and *on the right of* is not transitive. It might be suggested that the expression has accordingly two senses, one transitive and the other intransitive, but this maneuver is useless because the problem merely arises again in the selection of the appropriate sense. Moreover, if there were six individuals equally spaced around a circular table, then the above conclusion would be true, but the one below would be false:

> Matthew is on the right of Mark
> Mark is on the right of Luke
> Luke is on the right of John
> ∴ Matthew is on the right of John

Hence, *on the right of* would have a limited transitivity here. In fact, the extent of its transitivity varies as a function of the seating arrangements up to any arbitrary magnitude, and it would accordingly require an infinite number of different meanings in order to cope with each possible extent from zero to infinity. The attempt to treat the problem as a question of ambiguity is plainly unworkable.

Theorists as varied as Montague, Chomsky, Lakoff, Katz, Partee, and the Fodors have argued that the semantic representation of a sentence captures its logical form. But, the entailments of sentences containing such relations as *on the right of, in front of, at, near,* evidently depend on properties of the reference situation. In short, such expressions have a deictic (or indexical) component, a feature of ordinary language that led Bar-Hillel (1963) to argue that logical relations hold between specific statements, questions, and so on, and only derivatively between the sentence-types used to make them.

How are inferences based on *on the right of* to be handled by decompositional dictionary entries, semantic networks, or meaning postulates? The answer is that they cannot be. Such inferences destroy any theory based on the assumption that meaning is autonomous and independent of the reference of expressions. The one remaining option for proponents of the three theories is to argue that such phenomena are not part of semantics proper and should accordingly be disposed of into pragmatics. Unfortunately, this tactic still leaves the contents of the wastepaper basket to be explained. I shall offer such an explanation in the next section, and by all means let the theory be treated as a branch of pragmatics. The fact remains that it works only by allowing meaning to interact with reference in a way that cannot occur within the three theories.

Procedural semantics and mental models

The psychological theory of meaning that I wish to advance assumes that the mental representation of a sentence can take the form of an internal model of the state of affairs characterized by the sentence. Theories of mental models have, of course, been advanced before; one of the earliest and most prescient was proposed by Kenneth Craik (1943) several years before the advent of digital computers. Indeed, the notion has become commonplace with the reemergence of imagery as a respectable topic for scientific investigation. Critics of the concept of imagery, however, have pointed out the problems inherent in the notion that an image is " a picture in the head" (see, e.g., Pylyshyn, 1973). Likewise, sceptics have argued that it is in principle impossible to determine the nature of an internal representation. One cannot investigate mental representations in isolation from the processes that manipulate them; given a theory of process and representation, it is always possible to construct an alternative theory in which differences in the nature of representations are balanced by compensating differences in processes (Anderson, 1976, p. 10). Both of these points are well taken, but neither counts decisively against the existence of mental models.

Utterances provide clues for building mental models. What is important about these models is not their phenomenal or subjective content, but their structure and the fact that we possess procedures for constructing, manipulating and interrogating them. Many of the procedures can take for granted a common background of knowledge including facts about the world, about the language, and about the conventions governing conversation. Obviously, the extent to which a listener actively constructs a mental model is to a considerable extent under voluntary control; he may merely allow a speaker's words to register in a passive way, or he may follow them intently, drawing as many implications for their representation as he can.

It is plausible to suppose that a sentence that describes a spatial relation such as:

> The window is on the right of the door.

can be used to construct a mental model with a corresponding structure. This sort of semantic representation is likely to be necessary in order to make inferences based on spatial relations:

> The window is on the right of the door.
> The drainpipe is between them.

In a simple illustrative computer program that I have written in POP-11 (a high-level list-processing language), simple spatial assertions are interpreted in just such a way. The program builds up a spatial model of the relations between entities, combining the information in separate assertions in order to produce a composite representation. Most of the program consists of general procedures that set up an internal representation of two-dimensional space, add items to it, test for specified relations between them, and so on. There is, for instance, a general procedure for verifying whether a specified relation holds between two items: It looks along a line whose origin is the second of the two items in order to determine whether the first of them is somewhere on that line. The direction of this search is controlled by two variables, which are the values by which the X and Y

coordinates are incremented to successively spell out the locations to be scanned. The actual values of X and Y are determined by the spatial relation expressed in the assertion to be verified.

In fact, the dictionary entries for the spatial relations are extremely simple and in marked contrast to their representation in the three orthodox theories. Instead of a specification of logical properties, the entry for *behind*, for example, simply consists of the following instruction:

FUNCTION (% 1, 0 %);

What this instruction does is to take one of the general procedures for manipulating the array, assign it to the variable FUNCTION, and then "freeze in" values for two of its parameters (as signified by the decorated parentheses). Thus, if the general procedure is the one for verifying the relation between items, a new more specific function is created: Parameters +1 and 0 specify the direction in which to look from one item in order to verify whether another item is *behind* it (i.e., increment the X coordinate and hold the Y coordinate constant). The viewer is accordingly taken to be examining the array as though it were a graph laid out in front of him on a table.

These details are worth dwelling on because they establish that it is feasible to have a semantic system in which the meanings of words in the object language (in this case a very restricted subset of English) are represented in an internal meta language that has no simple, let alone one-to-one, relation to the object language. Such processes as "freezing in" the values of variables cannot be described in the subset of English that the program comprehends – they are difficult enough to express with the full resources of English at one's disposal. The program also establishes that it is possible to represent the meanings of relational terms without having to specify which inference schemata they permit. It is not necessary to specify, for example, that the relation *on the right of* is asymmetric, irreflexive, and transitive to varying degrees. The expression is simply assigned a semantics that makes it possible to build up mental representations from which these logical characteristics emerge (Johnson-Laird, 1975a). A more complex procedure is, of course, required in real life: It is necessary to allow that the locus of points scanned need not be a straight line; the actual shapes and sizes of objects will affect it. It seems that the only way such factors could be taken into account would be by constructing an internal model of the sort described here.

By reflecting on the properties of relations represented in mental models, an individual may come to acquire a higher-order knowledge of them. He may come to realize that many relations such as *taller than* are truly transitive, though this fact need not be a part of his initial procedural representation of the expression. There are certain terms, however, for which such reflective knowledge does not develop, and this phenomenon provides decisive evidence for the psychological reality of mental models. The terms I have in mind are the quantifiers: *all, some, none,* and their cognates.

Martin (1978) has argued against the existence of semantic representations because quantified assertions are represented in the predicate calculus by formulae that fail to mirror their psychological complexity. He accordingly proposes to handle their semantics by way of meaning postulates. But, although he presents a cogent case against an underlying *logical* notation, his arguments for meaning postulates are unconvincing because he omits providing the requisite set. In fact, the semantics of quantifiers cannot be captured in meaning postulates without doing violence to psychological reality. The fundamental point is that systematic errors are often made in reasoning with quantifiers, but if their representation ordinarily took the form of a higher-order reflective knowledge, then such errors should be no more likely to occur than they do with *taller than*. The higher-order knowledge does exist, of course, but only in the minds of logicians. Indeed, logic would not exist as an intellectual discipline if such knowledge were commonplace.

As I have argued elsewhere (Johnson-Laird, 1975a), a psychologically plausible account of interpreting a quantified sentence consists of a process that builds up a semantic representation that directly models the logical structure of the sentence (in much the same way that the representation of spatial sentences mirrors their structure). Thus, a statement such as *All the artists are beekeepers* is represented by imagining an arbitrary number of artists who are taken to represent the relevant class and then mentally tagged in some way to indicate that each of them is a beekeeper. Because there may be beekeepers who are not in the class of artists, it is necessary to add some arbitrary number of such beekeepers to the representation, tagging them in some way as optional. The elements in the representation may be vivid images or abstract items; what is important is not their phenomenal content but their structural relations:

$$
\begin{array}{cc}
a & a \\
\downarrow & \downarrow \\
b & b \quad (b)
\end{array}
$$

where the *a*'s stand for representations of artists, the *b*'s stand for representations of beekeepers, the arrows stand for representations of the relation of identity, and the possibility of beekeepers who are not artists is represented by the parenthesized *b*. These sorts of representation for quantified assertions obviate Martin's criticisms of logical notation because they do not differ markedly in their complexity. The system can be extended in an entirely natural way to cope with such quantifiers as *many, most,* and *few,* and to accommodate multiply quantified assertions (see Johnson-Laird, 1975a).

Inferences can be made from such mental models by combining them according to a simple heuristic: Roughly, try to form connections between as many items as possible. Some such heuristic is required because logical principles do not specify which of a vast set of valid conclusions should be drawn from a given set of premises. Putative conclusions are submitted to a logical test that consists in attempting to destroy the composite model without doing violence to the representations of the individual premises. The theory has been implemented in the form of a computer program, and it is entirely compatible with the sorts of deductions people actually make from quantified assertions. It predicts correctly the systematic errors that are made, and the relative simplicity of those problems for which the heuristic yields a conclusion that remains unmodified by the test procedure. The heuristic also accounts for a pronounced bias in favor of some sorts of conclusions at the expense of other equally valid ones (see Johnson-Laird and Steedman, 1978, for details of the experiments and the computer program). The procedural theory postulates many internal processes that cannot be couched in meaning postulates containing only mentalese tokens corresponding to the lexical items that occur in the object language. It represents the meanings of quantifiers without having to specify which inference schemata they permit, and builds up internal representations in which these logical characteristics are merely immanent.

How to stop decomposing

What psychological processes are involved in the construction of mental models? The programs described in the previous section rely upon dictionary entries that represent the meanings of words in terms of more primitive notions. There are, however, many occasions when it would be unnecessarily wasteful to decompose the meaning of a lexical item. If someone asks you what your name is, for example, you are hardly likely to have to take to pieces the full meaning of the word *name* in order to reply; a fact such as your name is likely to be directly represented in memory. On the other hand, if someone asks you what is meant by the word *name,* then a process of decomposition is necessary in order to answer. The problem accordingly arises as to what information is in general retrieved from the dictionary entry for a word in order to understand a sentence in which it occurs. One conjecture that has some superficial appeal is that:

a listener retrieves no direct information from the lexical entry but merely accesses it and checks that it contains some semantic information. A subsequent retrieval of this information may take place in, say, trying to verify the sentence, but mere access is sufficient for comprehension, provided that there is at least some semantic information stored in the lexical entry. (Johnson-Laird, 1975b)

This sort of access-and-check may occasionally occur; and it would certainly account for the phenomenon of what I call "depth charge" sentences – you lob them into discourse and only later do they go off with a bang. A simple example of one makes the point:

This book fills a much needed gap.

Many people take this sentence to be laudatory. It is only later that they realize that it is the gap, not the book, that is needed. The meanings of the words here seem to be treated initially as prefabricated parts; they are used as cues to build a familiar mental model without an adequate check on how well their meanings fit with what is required.

The information retrieved about a given word probably depends on its context, the illocutionary force of the utterance, and the circumstances in which it occurs. Different components of the meaning of a word become salient as its context is varied:

He peeled a lemon (lemons have skins)
The lemon rolled across the floor (lemons are round)
The lemon ripened (lemons are fruit).

The extent to which the meaning of a word is decomposed also depends on the listener's task. In general, for example, an efficient strategy for answering a question from memory is to search initially for information in a fairly "high-level" form – one checks indeed for one's *name* – without analyzing the meaning of the word. If this search fails, then the meaning of the sentence can be broken down into more primitive constituents, and an attempt can be made to find the requisite component facts. The high-level programming language PLANNER allows a data base to be interrogated in such a way: If a search for a specific assertion fails, an attempt is made to infer it (see Hewitt, 1971). Such degrees of freedom accommodate Kintsch's point about the evolution of semantically complex words: If decomposition is not inevitable, much is to be gained by packing as much meaning as one wants into a word. It need only be unpacked on some occasions; hence, the proliferation of jargon, and the efficacy of euphemisms.

Some psychological conclusions

The case against the three "autonomous" theories of meaning and in favor of a theory of mental models is supported by a variety of experimental findings. Bransford and his colleagues have shown many times that subjects in memory experiments often go beyond what is linguistically given (see, e.g., Bransford and McCarrell, 1975). For example, if subjects are presented with the sentence:

Three turtles rested on a floating log and a fish swam beneath them

they readily assume that the sentence asserted that the fish swam beneath the log. Bransford and McCarrell account for these results on the grounds that "the semantic descriptions created by subjects may often include more information than was expressed in a sentence." Analogous findings have been reported by R. C. Anderson and his colleagues (Anderson et al., 1976). They presented their subjects with such sentences as:

The fish attacked the swimmer

and later tested their memory by presenting them with a recall cue. It turned out that a more specific term such as *shark* was a better cue than *fish,* the general term actually used in the original sentence. Anderson accounts for these results in terms of an "instantiation" hypothesis: A word does not have a small number of determinate meanings, but a whole family of potential meanings. A subject uses the context in which the word occurs, and general knowledge, to infer a more specific meaning; a sense is *instantiated* from among the indefinitely many meanings that the term can have. Anderson and his colleagues clearly and correctly see their findings as creating difficulties for the orthodox theories of meaning that make use of semantic features or networks. However, a more plausible explanation for their results is that subjects construct a mental model of the referents and relations described in the sentence. Suppose, for example, that the original sentence were:

It attacked the swimmer

then doubtless *shark* would be a better retrieval cue than *it.* However, it would be an obvious error to argue that *it* has indefinitely many meanings including *shark*. *It* has a single meaning, but indefinitely many entities that it can refer to including sharks. The instantiation hypothesis confounds meaning and reference. If they are kept separate, its proponents can be seen to have provided some striking experimental results in support of the theory of mental models. This interpretation of the phenomena of instantiation has also been advocated by Garnham (1979), who has obtained similar effects by manipulating verbs.

My case against autonomy and in favor of an interactive theory of sense and reference is now complete. It can be recapitulated in four simple points:

1. Selectional restrictions can constrain the reference of expressions; conversely, the reference of an expression can select the appropriate sense of an ambiguous term. Many selectional restrictions are, in fact, inferences based on factual knowledge about referents.

2. Logical relations often hold directly between specific assertions, requests, or questions, and only derivatively between the sentence-types used in making them. The logical properties of certain terms can be established only by taking into account aspects of the reference situation.

3. The inferential use of quantifiers requires the construction and manipulation of mental models. Their logical properties are known to few ordinary individuals.

4. There is considerable experimental evidence that subjects interpret sentences by constructing mental models in which the relevant events and entities are represented.

NOTES

I am very grateful to Anne Cutler, Alan Garnham, Gerald Gazdar, Stephen Isard, Stanley Peters, Stuart Sutherland, and Arnold Zwicky for their incisive criticisms of earlier versions of this paper. My ideas on meaning were decisively shaped by George Miller, to whom I owe a very considerable intellectual debt. I should also like to thank Jerry Katz, Janet and Jerry Fodor, and Merrill Garrett, who have taken time to argue with me over the years. My research is supported by a grant for scientific assistance from the Social Science Research Council (GB).

1 FFG write (p. 256): ". . . it seems clear that, barring decisive evidence to the contrary, we should assume that the semantic representation of a sentence is as much like the surface form of the sentence as we can." The present author and others (see Forster, 1979) had taken this claim to imply that the semantic representation of a sentence consisted in a mentalese expression similar to the surface structure of the sentence, and that meaning postulates would accordingly be defined over surface structures. However, Jerry Fodor (personal communication) has recently indicated that internal representations are not surface-linear, and that meaning postulates are probably defined over deep structure trees.

REFERENCES

Anderson, J. R. 1976. *Language, Memory and Thought.* Hillsdale, N.J.: Erlbaum.
Anderson, R. C., Pichert, J. W., Goetz, E. T., Schallert, D. L., Stevens, K. V., and Trollip, S. R. 1976. "Instantiation of General Terms." *Journal of Verbal Learning and Verbal Behavior* 15:667–79.
Bar-Hillel, Y. 1963. "Can Indexical Sentences Stand in Logical Relations?" *Philosophical Studies* 14:87–90.
Bar-Hillel, Y. 1967. "Dictionaries and Meaning Rules." *Foundations of Language* 3:409–14.
Bransford, J. D., and McCarrell, N. S. 1975. "A Sketch of a Cognitive Approach to Comprehension: Some Thoughts about Understanding What It Means to Comprehend." In W. B. Weimar and D. S. Palermo, eds. *Cognition and the Symbolic Processes.* Hillsdale, N.J.: Erlbaum.
Carnap, R. 1956. *Meaning and Necessity: A Study in Semantics and Modal Logic.* Chicago: University of Chicago Press.
Collins, A. M., and Quillian, M. R. 1972. "How to Make a Language User." In E. Tulving and W. Donaldson, eds. *Organization and Memory.* New York: Academic Press.
Craik, K. 1943. *The Nature of Explanation.* Cambridge: Cambridge University Press.
Fillmore, C. J. 1968. "The Case for Case." In E. Bach and R. T. Harms, eds. *Universals in Linguistic Theory.* New York: Holt, Rinehart & Winston.
Fillmore, C. J. 1974. "The Future of Semantics." In C. J. Fillmore, G. Lakoff, and R. Lakoff, eds. *Berkeley Studies in Syntax and Semantics,* Vol. I, IV:1–38.
Fodor, J. A. 1976. *The Language of Thought.* Hassocks, Sussex: Harvester Press.
Fodor, J. A., Bever, T. G., and Garrett, M. F. 1974. *The Psychology of Language.* New York: McGraw-Hill.
Fodor, J. D. 1977. *Semantics: Theories of Meaning in Generative Grammar.* Hassocks, Sussex: Harvester Press.
Fodor, J. D., Fodor, J. A., and Garrett, M. F. 1975. "The Psychological Unreality of Semantic Representations." *Linguistic Inquiry* 4:515–31.
Forster, K. I. 1979. "Levels of Processing and the Structure of the Language Processor." In W. E. Cooper and E. Walker, eds. *Sentence Processing: Psycholinguistic Studies Presented to Merrill Garrett.* Hillsdale, N.J.: Erlbaum.
Garnham, A. 1979. "Instantiation of Verbs." *Quarterly Journal of Experimental Psychology* 31:207–14.
Green, D. W. 1975. "The Effects of Task on the Representation of Sentences." *Journal of Verbal Learning and Verbal Behavior* 14:275–83.
Hewitt, C. 1971. "Description and Theoretical Analysis (Using Schemas) of PLANNER: A Language for Proving Theorems and Manipulating Models in a Robot." Ph.D. dissertation, Massachusetts Institute of Technology.
Hollan, J. D. 1975. "Features and Semantic Memory: Set-Theoretic or Network Model?" *Psychological Review* 82:154–5.
Johnson-Laird, P. N. 1975a. "Models of Deduction." In R. J. Falmagne, ed. *Reasoning: Representation and Process.* Hillsdale, N.J.: Erlbaum.
Johnson-Laird, P. N. 1975b. "Meaning and the Mental Lexicon." In A. Kennedy and A. Wilkes, eds. *Studies in Long Term Memory.* London: Wiley.
Johnson-Laird, P. N. 1977a. "Psycholinguistics without Linguistics." In N. S. Sutherland, ed. *Tutorial Essays in Psychology,* Vol. I. Hillsdale, N.J.: Erlbaum.

Johnson-Laird, P. N. 1977b. "Procedural Semantics." *Cognition* 5:189–214.
Johnson-Laird, P. N. 1978. "The Meaning of Modality." *Cognitive Science* 2:17–26.
Johnson-Laird, P. N., and Quinn, J. G. 1976. "To Define True Meaning." *Nature* 264:635–6.
Johnson-Laird, P. N., and Steedman, M. J. 1978. "The Psychology of Syllogisms." *Cognitive Psychology* 10:64–99.
Johnson-Laird, P. N., and Stevenson, R. 1970. "Memory for Syntax." *Nature* 227:412–13.
Katz, J. J. 1977. "The Real Status of Semantic Representations." *Linguistic Inquiry* 8:559–84.
Katz, J. J., and Fodor, J. A. 1963. "The Structure of a Semantic Theory." *Language* 39:170–210.
Katz, J. J., and Nagel, R. 1974. "Meaning Postulates and Semantic Theory." *Foundations of Language* 11:311–40.
Kintsch, W. 1974. *The Representation of Meaning in Memory.* Hillsdale, N.J.: Erlbaum.
Martin, E., Jr. 1978. "The Psychology Unreality of Quantificational Semantics." In W. Savage, ed. *Perception and Cognition: Minnesota Studies in Philosophy of Science,* Vol. 9. Minneapolis, Minn.: University of Minnesota Press.
Miller, G. A., and Johnson-Laird, P. N. 1976. *Language and Perception.* Cambridge, Mass.: Harvard University Press.
Partee, B. H. 1977. "Montague Grammar and Issues of Psychological Reality." Paper prepared for the conference on Language and Psychotherapy of the Institute for Philosophy of Science, Psychotherapy, and Ethics. April. New York.
Pylyshyn, Z. 1973. "What the Mind's Eye Tells the Mind's Brain: A Critique of Mental Imagery." *Psychological Bulletin* 80:1–24.
Quillian, M. R. 1968. "Semantic Memory." In M. Minsky, ed. *Semantic Information Processing.* Cambridge, Mass.: The M.I.T. Press.
Rumelhart, D. E., Lindsay, P. H., and Norman, D. A. 1972. "A Process Model for Long-Term Memory." In E. Tulving and W. Donaldson, eds. *Organization and Memory.* New York: Academic Press.
Schank, R. C. 1975. *Conceptual Information Processing.* Amsterdam: North Holland.
Simmons, R., and Slocum, J. 1972. "Generating English Discourse from Semantic Networks." *Communications of the Association for Computing Machinery* 15:891–905.
Smith, E. E., Shoben, E. J., and Rips, L. J. 1974. Comparison Processes in Semantic Memory. *Psychological Review* 81:214–41.
Vendler, Z. 1968. *Adjectives and Nominalizations.* The Hague: Mouton.
Woods, W. A. 1975. "Syntax, Semantics, and Speech." In D. Raj Reddy, ed. *Speech Recognition: Invited Papers presented at the 1974 IEEE Symposium.* New York: Academic Press.

5

Appropriate responses to inappropriate questions

S. JERROLD KAPLAN

Casual users of Natural Language (NL) computer systems are typically inexpert not only with regard to the technical details of the underlying programs, but often with regard to the structure and/or content of the domain of discourse. Consequently, NL systems must be designed to respond appropriately when they can detect a misconception on the part of the user. Several conventions exist in cooperative conversation that allow speakers to indirectly encode their intentions and beliefs about the domain into their utterances ("loading" the utterances), and allow (in fact, often require) cooperative respondents to address those intentions and beliefs beyond a literal, direct response. To be effective, NL computer systems must do the same. The problem, then, is to provide practical computational tools that will determine both when an indirect response is required, and what that response should be, without requiring that additional domain-specific knowledge be encoded in the system.

This chapter will take the position that distinguishing *language-driven inference* from *domain-driven inference* provides a framework for a solution to this problem in the Data Base (DB) query domain. An implemented query system (CO-OP) is described that uses this distinction to provide cooperative responses to DB queries, using only a standard (CODASYL) DB and a lexicon as sources of world knowledge.

What is a loaded question

A loaded question is one that indicates that the questioner presumes something to be true about the domain of discourse that is actually false. Question (1A) presumes (1B). A cooperative speaker must find (1B) *assumable* (i.e., not believe it to be false) in order to appropriately utter (1A) in a cooperative conversation, intend it literally, and expect a correct, direct response.

127

(1A) What day does John go to his weekly piano lesson?
(1B) John takes weekly piano lessons.
(1C) Tuesday.

Similarly, (2A) presumes (2B).

(2A) How many Bloody Marys did Bill down at the banquet?
(2B) Hard liquor was available at the banquet.
(2C) Zero.

If the questioner believed (2B) to be false, there would be no point in asking 2A – s/he would already know that the correct answer had to be "Zero" (2C).

Both examples (1) and (2) can be explained by a convention of conversational cooperation: that *a questioner should leave the respondent a choice of direct answers*. That is, from the questioner's viewpoint upon asking a question, more than one direct answer must be possible.

It follows, then, that if a question presupposes something about the domain of discourse, as (1A) does, a questioner cannot felicitously utter the question and believe the presupposition to be false. This is a result of the fact that each direct answer to a question entails the question's presuppositions. (More formally, if question Q presupposes proposition P, then each question–direct answer pair $(Q, A\text{i})$ entails P.[1]) Therefore, if a questioner believes a presupposition to be false, s/he leaves no options for a correct, direct response – violating the convention. Conversely, a respondent can infer in a cooperative conversation from the fact that a question has been asked, that the questioner finds its presuppositions assumable. (In the terms of Keenan, 1971, the logical presupposition is pragmatically presupposed.)

Surprisingly, a more general semantic relationship exists that still allows a respondent to infer a questioner's beliefs. Consider the situation where a proposition is entailed by all but one of a question's direct answers. (Such a proposition will be called a *presumption* of the question.) By a similar argument, it follows that if a questioner believes that proposition to be false, s/he can infer the direct, correct answer to the question – it is the answer that does not entail the proposition. Once again, to ask such a question leaves the respondent no choice of (potentially) correct answers, violating the conversational convention. More important, upon being asked such a question, the respondent can infer what the questioner *presumes* about the context.

Question (2A) above presumes (2B), but does not presuppose it: (2B) is not entailed by the direct answer (2C). Nonetheless, a questioner must find (2B) assumable to felicitously ask (2A) in a cooperative conversation – to do otherwise would violate the cooperative convention. Similarly, (3B) below is a presumption but not a presupposition of (3A) (it is not entailed by 3C).

(3A) Did Sandy pass the prelims?
(3B) Sandy took the prelims.
(3C) No.

If a questioner believes in the falsehood of a presupposition of a question, the question is inappropriate because s/he must believe that no direct answer can be correct; similarly, if a questioner believes in the falsehood of a presumption, the question is inappropriate because the questioner must know the answer to the question – it is the direct answer that does not entail the presumption. *In short, the failure of a presupposition renders a question infelicitous because it leaves no options for a direct response, whereas the failure of a presumption renders a question infelicitous because it leaves at most one option for a direct response.* (Note that the definition of presumption subsumes the definition of presupposition in this context. See Joshi et al., 1977.)

Corrective indirect responses

In a cooperative conversation, if a respondent detects that a questioner incorrectly presumes something about the domain of discourse, s/he is required to correct that misimpression. A failure to do so will implicitly confirm the questioner's presumption. Consequently, it is not always the case that a correct, direct answer is the most cooperative response. When an incorrect presumption is detected, it is more cooperative to correct the presumption than to give a direct response. Such a response can be called a *corrective indirect response*.

For example, imagine question (4A) uttered in a cooperative conversation when the respondent knows that no departments sell knives.

(4A) Which departments that sell knives also sell blade sharpeners?
(4B) None.
(4C) No departments sell knives.

Although (4B) is a direct, correct response in this context, it is less cooperative than (4C). This effect is explained by the fact that (4A) presumes that some departments sell knives.

To be cooperative, the respondent should correct the questioner's misimpression with an indirect response, informing the questioner that no departments sell knives (4C). (The direct, correct response 4B will reinforce the questioner's mistaken presumption in a cooperative conversation through its failure to state otherwise.) A failure to produce corrective indirect responses is inappropriate in a cooperative conversation, and leads to "stonewalling" – the giving of very limited and precise responses that fail to address the larger goals and beliefs of the questioner.

Relevance to DB queries

Some NL query systems stonewall, primarily because they are capable only of direct answers to questions. [Perhaps this results from a view of NL questions as high level DB queries (Kaplan, 1978).] Unfortunately, the domain of most realistic DBs is sufficiently complex that the user of a NL query facility (most likely a naive user) may make incorrect presumptions in his or her queries. *A NL system that is only capable of a direct response will necessarily produce meaningless responses to failed presuppositions and stonewall on failed presumptions.* Consider the following hypothetical exchange with a NL query system:

Q: Which students got a grade of F in CIS500 in Spring, '77?
R: Nil. [the empty set]
Q: Did anyone fail CIS500 in Spring, '77?
R: No.
Q: How many people passed CIS500 in Spring, '77?
R: Zero.
Q: Was CIS500 given in Spring '77?
R: No.

A cooperative NL query system should be able to detect that the initial query in the dialogue incorrectly presumed that CIS500 was offered in Spring, '77, and respond appropriately. This ability is essential to a NL system that will function in a practical environment because the fact that NL is used in the interaction will imply to the users that the normal cooperative conventions followed in a human dialogue will be observed by the machine. (The CO-OP query system, described in a later section of this chapter, obeys a number of cooperative conventions.)

Although the definition of presumption given above may be of interest from a linguistic standpoint, it leaves much to be desired as a computational theory. It provides a descriptive model of certain aspects of conversational behavior, but it does not provide an adequate basis for computing the presumptions of a given question in a reasonable way. By limiting the domain of application to the area of data retrieval, it is possible to show that the linguistic structure of questions encodes considerable information about the presumptions that the questioner has made. This structure can be exploited to compute a significant class of presumptions and provide appropriate corrective indirect responses.

Language-driven versus domain-driven inference

A long-standing observation in Artificial Intelligence research is that knowledge about the world – both procedural and declarative – is required in order to understand NL.[2] Consequently, a great deal of study has gone into determining just what type of knowledge is required, and how that knowledge is to be organized, accessed, and utilized. One practical difficulty with systems that attempt to explore these issues is that they may require the encoding of large amounts of domain-specific knowledge (knowledge about the particular domain of the system) to be tested, or even to function at all. It is not easy to determine if a particular failure of a system is due to an inadequacy in the formalism or simply an insufficient base of knowledge. In addition, the collection and encoding of the appropriate knowledge can be a painstaking and time-consuming task.

Most NL systems that follow this paradigm (such as Lehnert, 1977) share a common approach: They decompose the input into a suitable "meaning" representation, and rely on various deduction and/or reasoning mechanisms to provide the "intelligence" required to draw the necessary inferences. Inferences made in this way can be called *domain-driven inferences*[3] because they are motivated by the domain itself.[4]

Although domain-driven inferences are surely essential to an understanding of NL (and will be a required part of any comprehensive cognitive model of human intelligence), they alone are not sufficient to produce a reasonable understanding of NL. Consider the following story:

> John is pretty crazy, and sometimes does strange things. Yesterday he went to Sardi's for dinner. He sat down, examined the menu, ordered a steak, and got up and left.

For an NL system to infer that something unusual has happened in the story, it must distinguish the *story* from the *events the story describes*. A question-answering system that would respond to "What did John eat?" with "A steak." cannot be said to understand the story. As a sequence of events, the passage contains nothing unusual – it simply omits details that can be filled in on the basis of common knowledge about restaurants. As a story, however, it raises expectations that the events do not. Drawing the inference "John didn't eat the steak he ordered." requires knowledge about the use of language in addition to knowledge about the domain. Inferences that require language-related knowledge can be called *language-driven inferences*.

Language-driven inferences can be characterized as follows: They are based on the fact that a story, dialogue, utterance, and so on, is a description, and that *the description itself may exhibit useful properties not associated with the thing being described.*[5] These additional properties are used by speakers to encode essential information – a knowledge of language-related conventions is required to understand NL.

Language-driven inferences have several useful properties in a computational framework. First, being based on general knowledge about the language, they may not require an infusion of knowledge to operate in differing domains. As a result, they tend to be transportable to new domains (new DBs, in the case of NL DB query systems). Second, they do not appear to be as subject to runaway inferencing; that is, the inferencing is driven (and hence controlled) by the phrasing of the input. Third, they can often achieve results approximating that of domain-driven inference techniques with substantially less computational machinery and execution time.

As a simple example, consider the case of factive verbs. The sentence "John doesn't know that the Beatles broke up." carries the inference that the Beatles broke up. Treated as a domain-driven inference, this result might typically be achieved as follows. The sentence could be parsed into a representation indicating John's lack of knowledge of the Beatles' breakup. Either immediately or at some suitable later time, a procedure might be invoked that encodes the knowledge "For someone to not know something, that something has to be the case." The inferential procedures can then update the knowledge base accordingly. As a language-driven inference, this inference can be regarded as a lexical property, that is, that factive verbs presuppose their complements, and the complement immediately asserted, namely, that the Beatles broke up. (Note that this process cannot be reasonably said to "understand" the utterance, but achieves the same results.) Effectively, certain inference rules have been encoded directly into the lexical and syntactic structure of the language – facilitating the drawing of the inference without resorting to general reasoning processes.

Another type of language-driven inferences is those that relate specifically to the structure of the discourse, and not to its meaning. Consider the interpretation of anaphoric references such as "former," "latter," "vice versa," "respectively," and so forth. These words exploit the linear nature of language to convey their meaning. To infer the appropriate referents, an NL system must retain a sufficient amount of the structure of the text to determine the relative positions of potential referents. If the system "digests" a text into a nonlinear representation (a common procedure), it is likely to lose the information required for understanding.

The CO-OP system, described in the following section, demonstrates that a language-driven inference approach to computational systems can to a considerable extent produce appropriate NL behavior in practical domains without the overhead of a detailed and comprehensive world model. By limiting the domain of discourse to DB queries, the lexical and syntactic structure of the questions encodes sufficient information about the user's beliefs that *a significant class of presumptions can be computed on a purely language-driven basis.*

CO-OP: a cooperative query system

The design and implementation of an NL query system (CO-OP) that provides cooperative responses to simple NL questions requesting data retrieval and operates with a typical (CODASYL) DB system has been completed. In addition to producing direct answers, CO-OP is capable of producing a variety of indirect responses, including corrective indirect responses. The design of the system is based on two hypotheses:

1. To a large extent, language-driven inferences are sufficient to drive procedures that detect the need for an indirect response and select an appropriate one.
2. The domain-specific knowledge required to process a significant class of NL DB queries is already present in standard ways in DB systems, if it is augmented by a suitably encoded lexicon.

Consequently, the inferencing mechanisms required to produce the cooperative responses are *domain-transparent* in the sense that they will produce appropriate behavior without modification from any suitable DB system. These mechanisms can therefore be transported to new DBs unchanged. (Transporting CO-OP to a new DB mainly requires the recoding of the lexicon.) To illustrate this claim, a high-level description of the method by which corrective indirect responses are produced follows.

The Meta Query Language

Most DB queries can be viewed as requesting the selection of a subset (the response set) from a presented set of entities (this analysis follows

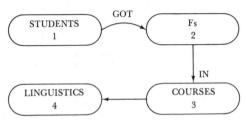

Figure 1. Meta Query Language representation of "Which students got Fs in linguistics courses?"

Belnap and Steel, 1976). Normally, the presented set is put through a series of restrictions, each of which produces a subset, until the response set is found. This view is formalized in CO-OP in the procedures that manipulate an intermediate representation of the query, called the *Meta Query Language* (MQL).

The MQL is a graph structure, where the nodes represent *sets* (in the mathematical, not the DB sense) "presented" by the user, and the edges represent *binary relations* defined on those sets, derived from the lexical and syntactic structure of the input query. Conceptually, the direct response to a query is an N-place relation realized by obtaining the referent of the sets in the DB, and composing them according to the binary relations. Each composition will have the effect of selecting a subset of the current sets. The subsets will contain the elements that survive (participate) in the relation. (Actually, the responses are realized in a much more efficient fashion – this is simply a convenient view.)

As an example, consider the query "Which students got Fs in Linguistics courses?" as diagrammed in Figure 1. This query would be parsed as presenting four sets: "students," "Fs," "Linguistics," and "courses." (The sets "Linguistics" and "Fs" may appear counterintuitive, but should be viewed as singleton entities assumed by the user to exist somewhere in the DB.) The direct answer to the query would be a four-place relation consisting of a column of students, grades (all Fs), departments (all Linguistics), and courses. For convenience, the columns containing singleton sets (grades and departments) would be removed, and the remaining list of students and associated courses presented to the user.

Executing the query consists of passing the MQL representation of the query to an interpretive component that produces a query suitable for execution on a CODASYL DB using information associated for this purpose with the lexical items in the MQL. (The specific knowledge required to perform this translation is encoded purely at the lexical level; the only additional domain-dependent knowledge required is access to the DB schema.)

The MQL, by encoding some of the syntactic relationships present in the NL query, can hardly be said to capture the meaning of the question: It is merely a convenient representation formalizing certain linguistic characteristics of the query. The procedures that manipulate this representation to generate inferences are based on observations of a general nature regarding these syntactic relationships. Consequently, these inferences are language-driven inferences.

Although the MQL, as implemented in CO-OP, has its advantages and disadvantages, it has several characteristics that ought to be present in any representation used for similar purposes:

First, it reflects closely the surface structure of the input (indeed, it is little more than a modified parse tree), and so facilitates the capturing of surface syntactic features. For example, the representation of corresponding passives and actives is not the same. This has an important bearing on the organization of the responses.

Second, it provides a level of description useful for providing explanations that a user is certain to understand. This occurs mainly because each part of an MQL expression is labeled with a lexical item or phrase that the user just used (with minor exceptions). Failures at lower levels of the system can always be localized to the processing of some subset of the MQL, and the offending subset can be explained to the user in his or her own terms.

Third, the MQL representation of a query is invariant under differing organizations of the underlying DB. Many of the organizational options available to a DB designer have no bearing on either the range of questions that can be appropriately posed to the DB or on the content of the responses – they affect only the efficiency of retrieval. Consequently, the options chosen by the DB designer ought to be transparent to the user. In CO-OP, the organization of the response is a function solely of the MQL, and so is not affected by variations in the organization of the DB.

MQL incorporates limited mechanisms for handling negation, quantification, and disjunction, though these details are not included here. (A more complete description can be found in Kaplan, 1979.)

Computing corrective indirect responses

The crucial observation required to produce a reasonable set of corrective indirect responses is that the *MQL query presumes the nonemp-*

tiness of its connected subgraphs. Each connected subgraph corresponds to a presumption the user has made about the domain of discourse. Consequently, should the initial query return a null response, the control structure can check the user's presumptions by passing each connected subgraph to the interpretive component to check its nonemptiness (notice that each subgraph itself constitutes a well-formed query). Should a presumption prove false, an appropriate indirect response can be generated, rather than a meaningless or misleading direct response of "None."

For example, in the query of Figure 1, the subgraphs and their corresponding corrective indirect responses are (the numbers represent the sets the subgraphs consist of):

(1)   "I don't know of any students."
(2)   "I don't know of any Fs."
(3)   "I don't know of any courses."
(4)   "I don't know of any Linguistics."
(1,2)   "I don't know of any students that got Fs."
(2,3)   "I don't know of any Fs in courses."
(3,4)   "I don't know of any Linguistics courses."
(1,2,3) "I don't know of any students that got Fs in courses."
(2,3,4) "I don't know of any Fs in Linguistics courses."

Suppose that there are no linguistics courses in the DB. Rather than presenting the direct, correct answer of "None." the control structure will pass each connected subgraph in turn to be executed against the DB. It will discover that no linguistics courses exist in the DB, and so will respond with "I don't know of any linguistics courses." This corrective indirect response (and all responses generated through this method) will entail the direct answer because they will entail the emptiness of the direct response set.

Several aspects of this procedure are worthy of note. First, although the selection of the response is dependent on knowledge of the domain (as encoded in a very general sense in the DB system – not as separate theorems, structures, or programs), *the computation of the presumptions is totally independent of domain-specific knowledge.* Because these inferences are driven solely by the parser output (MQL representation), the procedures that determine the presumptions (by computing subgraphs) require no knowledge of the DB. Consequently, producing corrective indirect responses from another DB, or even another DB system, requires no changes to the inferencing procedures. Second, the mechanism for selecting the indirect response is identical to the procedure for executing a query. *No additional computational machinery need be invoked to select the appropriate indirect response.* Third, the computational overhead involved in checking and correcting the user's presumptions is not incurred unless it has been determined that an indirect response may be required. Should the query succeed initially, *no penalty in execution time will be paid for the ability to produce the indirect responses.* In addition, the only increase in space overhead is a small control program to produce the appropriate subgraphs (the linguistic generation of the indirect response is essentially free – it is a trivial addition to the paraphrase component already used in the parsing phase).

The MQL also provides a means of selecting the most appropriate set of corrective responses when more than one is applicable. The presumptions of a question can be partially ordered according to an entailment relationship: The failure of some presumptions entails the failure of others. For example, if there are no courses, then there are no Fs in courses, which in turn entails that there are no Fs in Linguistics courses, and so on. It is often the case that several presumptions of a question fail simultaneously, in part because of this partial ordering. In such cases, the most appropriate response is to correct the *least-failing set* of presumptions in this ordering.[6] In the MQL, this ordering manifests itself as a subgraph relation among the subgraphs of the MQL: Some subgraphs are subgraphs of others. By checking the nonemptiness of the subgraphs in a suitable order, the most appropriate response can be formulated. Thus, in the example, it is possible for the system to produce a response such as "I don't know of any Fs, and I don't know of any Linguistics courses." without producing the additional irrelevant facts that there are no Fs in courses, no students got Fs, and so forth.

Corrective indirect responses, produced in this fashion, are language-driven inferences because they are derived directly from the structure of the query as represented by the MQL. If the query were phrased differently, a different set of presumptions would be computed. (This is not a drawback, as it might seem at first; it ensures that the response will be in terms that the user understands.) For these reasons, corrective indirect responses, made possible by a careful choice of representations and associated algorithms, are produced in a domain-transparent fashion with minimal system overhead using knowledge already available in the DB.

Examples

This section contains a few examples drawn from the current implementation of the CO-OP query system. CO-OP was implemented on a DEC KL-10 under TOPS-10 at the Wharton Computational Facility in RUTGERS-UCI-LISP and FORTRAN. It operates with the SEED CODASYL DB system (Gerritsen, 1978). The domain for these examples is a real DB from the National Center for Atmospheric Research (NCAR) in Boulder, Colorado. One of the functions of NCAR is to provide computational resources to researchers across the country working on government grants, mainly in meteorology. The DB tracks the utilization of these resources. It contains information on users, programmers (users that work for the computing facility), divisions (which are organized further into superdivisions), accounts, projects, sponsors, and project advisors, to name a few. To understand the responses, it is important to note that users can be in many divisions, and work on many projects, but the projects are not considered to be in particular divisions. The projects, however, are organized into areas of interest, according to a set of area codes. Figure 2 is a diagram and description of the NCAR DB.

An annotated sample of questions and responses illustrating the salient features of the current implementation follows. Names have been altered in the interest of privacy. "Q" (below) stands for question, "P" for paraphrase, and "R" for response. (The paraphrases are presented to the user for approval prior to execution of the query.) Commentary is in square brackets ([ ]). (Some irrelevant paraphrases and responses are deleted in the interest of brevity.)

Q: Who advises projects in area 36?
P: Assuming that there are projects that are in area 36, who advises those projects?
[The system incorporates a powerful paraphraser,[7] which performs two types of disambiguation: lexical – it will explain its chosen interpretation for vague or ambiguous terms, and syntactic – it explains the clausal dependencies determined by the parser. It is also used for indirect responses, as illustrated below. This component has access solely to the MQL (parser output), and so requires no modification on new domains.]
R: I don't know of any area 36.
[This is an example of a corrective indirect response. Rather than giving a misleading direct answer of "No one." the system produces the appropriate indirect response, using the techniques described above. Note that the system carefully hedges its response with respect to its state of knowledge, rather than assuming either a closed or open world DB (Reiter, 1978).[8]]
Q: Which programmers from the ASD group are in superdivision 5000?
[The programmers are organized into groups, identified by group IDs.]

139

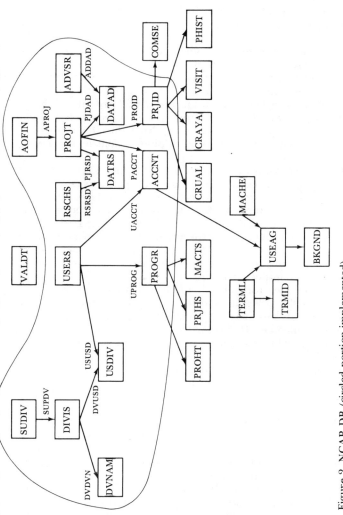

Figure 2. NCAR DB (circled portion implemented).

P: (I am assuming that "ASD" is a GROUP ID.) Which programmers are in superdivision 5000? Look for programmers that are from ASD group.
[This paraphrase illustrates both types of disambiguation, although the lexical disambiguation is probably unnecessary in this example.]

R: I don't know of any ASD group. I don't know of any programmers that are in superdivision 5000.
[This corrective indirect response has two components. Rather than simply correcting all subgraphs of the MQL that denote empty referents in the DB, the system explains only the appropriate ones. For example, because there is no ASD group, it is obvious that there are no programmers in the ASD group. This parsimony is achieved by using the partial ordering technique described above. CO-OP computes and corrects only the least-failing subgraphs in this ordering. Note that this technique is entirely domain-transparent; no additional domain-driven inference is required.]

Q: Which programmers are in division 4111 and 4361?
[The scoping of conjunction is a subtle problem that must be handled in any serious NL query system. Here the parser is faced with essentially three syntactically valid scopes: conjoining the numbers, the divisions (division 4111 and division 4361), or conjoining the programmers (programmers in division 4111 and programmers in division 4361). The system chooses the narrowest scoping that could result in a nonempty response set based on an inspection of the DB schema. The basic structure of the CODASYL formalism is the functional relationship (in-or-above in the DB schema diagram), in this case revealing that divisions can have only one number. On this basis, the narrowest scope is ruled out. However, the schema does admit the possibility of programmers being in two divisions (a many-to-many relationship), and so this interpretation is chosen. The paraphrase makes this choice clear to the user.]

P: Which programmers are in division 4361 and division 4111?
R: . . .

Q: Who sponsors projects not in oceanography?
R: FAILURE. Sorry, but I didn't understand you fully – I have a very limited knowledge of English. My best guess as to what you meant is: Who sponsors projects? Could you please rephrase your question and try again . . .
[This is an example of failure in the system. In principle, the only kind of failure is parse failure – the interpretive components can process any legal output of the parser. (In addition, the parser will reach an interpretation of any syntactically valid input, regardless of its semantic well-formedness.) Consequently, the only type of failure diagnostics that are required are in the parse. During the parse, a current hypothesis regarding the input is maintained at all times. In the event of a parse failure, the best

guess (largest hypothesis) encountered is displayed for the user, in the hope that this will aid the user in localizing the nature of the problem. This approach, to try to explain what went right with the parse rather than what went wrong, is motivated by the fact that the point at which the error actually occurred is often considerably before the point at which the error is detected – English is more than locally ambiguous. Any attempt to diagnose the error at the point of failure is more likely to mystify the user than to help him or her rephrase the question. In this case, the system is unable to process a negation preceding a prepositional phrase.]

Q: Who doesn't sponsor projects in the oceanography area? [Here the user has rephrased the question.]

P: (I am assuming that "oceanography" is an AREA OF INTEREST.) Assuming that there are projects that are in the oceanography area, who doesn't sponsor those projects?

R: (SPONSOR NAME)
CTR NATL DE LA RECHERCHE SCIEN
ERDA/WASHINGTON
NASA/MARSHALL SPACE FLT. CNTR
OFFICE OF NAVAL RESEARCH/ARL.
U.S. NUCLEAR REGULATORY COM.
[This example illustrates two points. First, that the system can process certain types of negation. This is handled by the quantification routines, essentially by counting the number of projects in oceanography sponsored by each sponsor and selecting those that sponsor exactly zero. This is a special case of quantification. Second, the system must decide in such cases just what the set "Who" should appropriately refer to. If it took the set of all people in the DB (i.e., users, advisors, programmers, sponsors, etc.), the response would include a great deal of extraneous information. CO-OP selects as the referent those individuals that could reasonably participate in the unnegated relationship.]

Q: Which users work on projects in area 3 that are in division 200?

P: Assuming that there are projects that are in area 3, which users work on those projects? Look for users that are in division 200. [Relative clause and prepositional phrase attachment is another difficult problem that involves the use of semantic tests in the parsing process. Fortunately, the DB schema provides sufficient information for disambiguation. Syntactically, it is unclear whether the relative clause "that are in division 200" modifies users or projects. The system decides that users is the most likely referent, by scoring the potential referents on three dimensions. The first is the semantic relatedness of the subject and object of the resulting MQL relation, in this case (users, divisions) and (projects, divisions). The semantic relatedness is measured by the distance through the schema between the records denoting those items. In the schema, DIST(USER,DIVIS) = 2, whereas DIST(PROJT,DIVIS) = 4 (recall that projects are not organized into divisions). Second, the distance back in the question from the clause to the potential referent is measured, on the assumption that the modifier is most likely to be near its referent. Third, a prediction is made on the basis of the information content of the lexical items designating the relation (in this case, the word "in" contains little predictive value, and does not affect the decision). This is done by associating with each preposition and verb in the lexicon a (possibly empty) list of probable subjects and objects. For example, a verb like "sponsor" in this domain predicts a sponsor as a subject and a project as an object.]

Conclusion

The problem of producing apparently intelligent behavior from an NL system has often been viewed in Artificial Intelligence as a problem of modeling human cognitive processes, or modeling knowledge about the real world. It has been demonstrated here that such approaches must include a pragmatic theory of the conventions and properties of the use of language to function effectively. Domain-driven inferences must be complemented by language-driven inferences to appropriately process NL. Further, it has been argued that language-driven inference mechanisms help to control the inference process, and can provide a more general and computationally attractive solution to many problems previously thought to require domain-driven inference.

A descriptive theory of one type of cooperative indirect response to inappropriate questions has been presented, and extended to a prescriptive (computational) theory by restricting the domain of application to DB query systems. This theory has been implemented using language-driven mechanisms in the design of CO-OP, a cooperative query system. The result is the generation of appropriate corrective indirect responses in a computationally efficient and domain-transparent fashion.

NOTES

This work was partially supported by NSF grant MCS 76-19466 and ARPA contract MDA 903-77-C-0322. An earlier version of this paper appeared in the proceedings of the Second Workshop on Theoretical Issues in Natural Language Processing, Champaign-Urbana, Illinois, July 1978.

1 This entailment condition is a necessary but not sufficient condition for presupposition. The concept of presupposition normally includes a condition that the negation of a proposition (in this case, the negation of the proposition expressed by a question–direct answer pair) should also entail its presuppositions. Consequently, the truth of a presupposition of a ques-

tion is normally considered a prerequisite for an answer to be either true or false (for a more detailed discussion see Keenan, 1973). These subtleties of the concept of presupposition are irrelevant to this discussion, because false responses to questions are considered a priori to be uncooperative.

2 For example, to understand the statement "I bought a briefcase yesterday, and today the handle broke off." it is necessary to know that briefcases *typically* have handles.

3 "Domain" here is meant to include general world knowledge, knowledge about the specific context, and inferential rules of a general and/or specific nature about that knowledge.

4 Of course, these inferences are actually made on the basis of *descriptions* of the domain (the internal meaning representation) and not the domain itself. What is to be evaluated in such systems is the *sufficiency* of that description in representing the domain.

5 In the story example, assumptions about the connectedness of the story and the uniformity of the level of description give rise to the inference that John didn't eat what he ordered. These assumptions are conventions in the language, and not properties of the situation being described.

6 This is more an empirical observation than a provable fact. This set of failed presumptions provides the most perspicuous way of communicating the nature of the problem to the questioner, following the maxims of Grice (1975).

7 Designed and implemented mainly by Kathy McKeown (McKeown, 1979).

8 A *closed world DB* is one in which the absence of a fact implies the truth of its negation. For example, if a DB does not contain information that John Smith is a manager, then it can be assumed that John Smith is not a manager, under the closed world assumption. In an *open world DB,* this assumption does not hold – if John Smith is not listed in the phone book, it cannot be inferred that he doesn't have a phone number.

REFERENCES

Belnap, N. D., and Steel, T. B. 1976. *The Logic of Questions and Answers.* New Haven: Yale University Press.

Gerritsen, R. 1978. *SEED Reference Manual,* Version C00 – B04 draft. Philadelphia: International Data Base Systems.

Grice, H. P. 1975. "Logic and Conversation." In P. Cole and J. L. Morgan, eds. *Syntax and Semantics,* Vol. 3, *Speech Acts.* New York: Academic Press.

Joshi, A. K., Kaplan, S. J., and Lee, R. M. 1977. "Approximate Responses from a Data Base Query System: An Application of Inferencing in Natural Language." In *Proceedings of the 5th IJCAI.* Cambridge, Mass., pp. 211–12.

Kaplan, S. 1978. "On the Difference Between Natural Language and High Level Query Languages." *Proceedings of the ACM 78.* Washington, D.C. December.

Kaplan, S. 1979. "Cooperative Responses from a Portable Natural Language Data Base Query System." Ph.D. dissertation, University of Pennsylvania, Department of Computer and Information Science, Moore School, Philadelphia.

Keenan, E. L. 1971. "Two Kinds of Presupposition in Natural Language." In C. J. Fillmore and D. T. Langendoen, eds. *Studies in Linguistic Semantics.* New York: Holt, Rinehart, and Winston.

Keenan, E. L., and Hull, R. D. 1973. "The Logical Presuppositions of Questions and Answers." In J. Petofi and D. Frank, eds. *Prasuppositionen in Philosophie und Linguistik.* Frankfurt: Athenäum Verlag.

Lehnert, W. 1977. "Human and Computational Question Answering." *Cognitive Science* 1:1.

McKeown, K. R. 1979. "Paraphrasing Using Given and New Information in a Question–Answer System." In *Proceedings of the 17th Annual Meeting of the Association for Computational Linguistics.* La Jolla, Calif.

Reiter, R. 1978. "On Closed World Data Bases." In H. Gallaire and J. Minker, eds. *Logic and Data Bases.* New York: Plenum Press.

6

A computational theory of human question answering

WENDY G. LEHNERT

Problems in question answering assume a new perspective when question answering is viewed as a problem in natural language processing. A theory of question answering has been proposed from this viewpoint that relies on ideas in conceptual information processing and theories of human memory organization. This theory has been implemented in a computer program, QUALM, which is currently used by two story-understanding systems (SAM and PAM) to complete a natural language processing system that reads stories and answers questions about what was read.

The processes of QUALM are divided into four phases: (1) Conceptual Categorization, (2) Inferential Analysis, (3) Content Specification, and (4) Retrieval Heuristics. Conceptual Categorization guides subsequent processing by dictating which specific inference mechanisms and memory retrieval strategies should be invoked in the course of answering a question. Inferential Analysis is responsible for understanding what the questioner really meant when a question is not intended to be taken literally. Content Specification determines how much of an answer should be returned in terms of detail and elaboration. Retrieval Heuristics do the actual digging in order to extract an answer from memory. All of the inference processes within these four phases are independent of language, operating within conceptual representations.

The theory of question answering represented by QUALM is motivated by theories of natural language processing. Within the context of story understanding, QUALM has provided a concrete criterion for judging the strengths and weaknesses of story representations generated by SAM and PAM. If a system understands a story, it should be able to answer questions about that story in the same way that people do. Although the computer implementation of QUALM is currently limited to answering questions about stories, the theoretical model goes beyond this particular context. As a theoretical model QUALM is intended to describe question answering in its most general form, viewed as a verbal communication device between people.

Conceptual information processing

The theory described here rests on a foundation of theories in natural language processing that range from the conceptual representation of single sentences (see Schank, 1975) to the representation of entire stories (see Schank and Abelson, 1977). Over the last five years various programs have been implemented to test this theoretical background, of which a few major components will be outlined here. It is hoped that the following brief descriptions will motivate the uninitiated reader to seek out these earlier works, which are better suited to providing an initial introduction. In any event, I wish to emphasize that the research orientation behind these theories has always been dedicated to producing cognitive models of human information processing phenomena.

Representing meaning with Conceptual Dependency

Conceptual Dependency is a representational system that encodes the meaning of sentences through decomposition into a small set of primitive actions. When two sentences are identical in meaning, the Conceptual Dependency representations for those sentences are identical. For example, "John kicked the ball" and "John hit the ball with his foot" will have identical Conceptual Dependency representations.

Cognitive memory processes operate on the meaning of sentences, not on the lexical expression of that meaning. It follows that simulations of human cognition must rely on conceptual representations. For example, if memory contains an encoding for "John bought a book from Mary," then the processes that access memory should be able to answer "Did Mary sell John a book?" on the basis of that encoding. This sort of recognition is trivial when "John bought a book from Mary" and "Mary sold John a book" have similar conceptual representations.

All sentences are translated into Conceptual Dependency by means of a conceptual parser ELI (see Riesbeck, 1975). The same parser that produces conceptual representations for declarative sentences is also used to produce conceptual parses of questions. The process that maps conceptualizations into English is called generation. The program used to generate English is modeled after BABEL (see Goldman, 1975). Because the parser and generator are separate processes, it is possible to independently interchange parsers and generators for different languages. If a sentence in English is parsed by an English parser and its resulting conceptualization is fed into an English generator, we have a system that paraphrases English sentences. If the English generator is then replaced by a Russian generator, we have a system that translates English sentences into Russian.

Because Conceptual Dependency is a language-free representation, no changes must be made in the representational system to accommodate parsers and generators for different languages. Our current systems have English, Dutch, Russian, Chinese, and Spanish generators available for the final expression of natural language output. This modularity in the paraphrase (or translation) task also extends to question-answering tasks. Because processes specific to question answering are confined to manipulations of information in Conceptual Dependency representations, an appropriate parser can be used to understand questions in any language, and different generators can be used to produce answers in different languages without making any alterations to the question-answering module.

Story understanding and inference generation

A system that claims to understand a story must do more than merely produce Conceptual Dependency representations for each sentence read. Inferences must be generated to fill in implicit information, and causal connections to tie together individual conceptualizations must be made. If we hear "Mary went to the hospital after John hit her," we infer that Mary was hurt as a result of John's hitting her, and that she went to the hospital to preserve her health. One of the most difficult and most interesting problems in natural language processing concerns the generation of inferences. Where do inferences come from? When are they made? Exactly which inferences are made in any given context?

In attempting to answer these questions, we become involved in problems of human memory organization. Inferences are obviously made on the basis of knowledge about the world. The problem is, how can this knowledge be represented and organized so that appropriate inference mechanisms can access relevant information as needed? A theory that accounts for problems in inference generation must therefore be tied to a theory of general knowledge structures. Some knowledge structures encode mundane information about stereotypic situations, others organize information about human motivations and goals, whereas still others are designed to provide understanding about physical causation and the relationships of physical objects.

Scripts

A script is a theoretical knowledge structure that has been proposed as a model of human memory organization. A vast amount of information appears to be encoded in people in the form of scripts (Schank and Abelson, 1977), and these same constructs are being exploited as a means of organizing world knowledge in a computer.

Scripts are memory units that contain information about situations or activities frequently encountered. They describe the expectations involved in extremely mundane situations such as going to a restaurant, shopping in a grocery store, or stopping at a gas station. People acquire most scripts through experience and use them both operationally (as in actually going to a restaurant) and cognitively (as in understanding stories about restaurants). When you go to a restaurant, you have certain expectations about finding a table, ordering, being served, eating, getting a check, paying the check, and so on. These are so ingrained that you probably don't have to spend much conscious processing time on them. Most likely you only think about them when they fail or deviate from your expectations. If you hear that John went to a restaurant and ordered a hamburger, you will infer that he ate a hamburger unless you hear something to the contrary. You aren't told that he ate a hamburger; you use your scriptal knowledge of restaurants to make the inference. Whereas scriptal knowledge must vary from person to person according to variations of experience, there are quite a few standard scripts that will be held in common as a cultural norm (e.g., most people have the same restaurant script because restaurants are highly standardized).

The scripts that are important for natural language processing are those that a large population hold in common. Whenever a script is shared by people, it can be referenced very efficiently. "I went to a restaurant last night" conveys performance of the entire restaurant script to anyone who has that script.

Scripts are used in story understanding to generate a complete causal chain of events, filling in those events that were not explicitly mentioned but would be inferred by any knowledgeable reader. This story representation is generated at the time the story is read. Subsequent processes like question answering, paraphrase, or summarization can then access this story representation to complete their desired task.

Scripts are only one particular type of knowledge structure. In a comprehensive understanding system, many different knowledge structures may be needed to process a story successfully. The general theory of question answering described here is not restricted to stories understood on the basis of scripts alone. In addition to answering questions about stories understood by SAM (Script Applier Mechanism), QUALM has also been used to answer questions understood by PAM (Plan Applier Mechanism), an understanding system that understands stories requiring knowledge about plans (Schank and Abelson, 1977). As more systems are developed that implement theories of other knowledge structures, we expect to extend the techniques in QUALM as needed without altering the foundational theory.

QUALM

If a computer is going to answer questions in a manner that is natural for human interaction, the computer must have knowledge of how people ask questions and what kinds of answers are expected in return. A competent question-answering system must be based on a theory of human question answering that describes:

1. What it means to understand a question
2. How context affects understanding
3. What kind of responses are appropriate
4. How to extract answers from memory

A theory of conceptual question answering has been developed that addresses these four problems (Lehnert, 1977,1978a,b), and it has been implemented in a computer program (QUALM) that runs in conjunction with the systems SAM (Cullingford, 1978) and PAM (Wilensky, 1976), enabling these systems to answer questions about the stories they read.

The theory behind QUALM extends theories of memory processing that originated with the study of parsing and generation (Riesbeck, 1975; Goldman, 1975). These parsing and generation strategies based on Conceptual Dependency were naturally adopted for question answering without significant alterations. This approach to question answering, which utilizes existing theories of natural language processing, constitutes a major departure from the information-retrieval viewpoint where natural language is considered to be merely a "front end" for a question-answering system.

In order to understand questions, QUALM must interface with a conceptual analysis program that parses an English question into its

Conceptual Dependency representation (Schank, 1975). In SAM and PAM, QUALM interfaces with a parser designed by Christopher Riesbeck (Riesbeck and Schank, 1976). In order to produce answers in English, QUALM also needs a generator that can translate Conceptual Dependency representations into English. The generator used by SAM and PAM is based on a generator designed by Neil Goldman (Goldman, 1975). All of the processing specific to answering questions occurs on a conceptual level that is language-independent. If QUALM interfaced with a Russian parser and a Chinese generator, it would be able to understand questions stated in Russian and produce answers to these questions in Chinese. No changes in QUALM are required to accommodate different languages because the question-answering processes are independent of language.

Conceptual question categories

When QUALM initially receives a question from the parser, the question is represented as a Conceptual Dependency conceptualization. This conceptualization must then be categorized into one of thirteen possible Conceptual Categories. The Conceptual Categories for questions are:

1. Causal Antecedent
2. Goal Orientation
3. Enablement
4. Causal Consequent
5. Verification
6. Disjunctive
7. Instrumental/Procedural

8. Concept Completion
9. Expectational
10. Judgmental
11. Quantification
12. Feature Specification
13. Request

The conceptual parse of a question represents a very literal or naive understanding of the question. Conceptual Categorization constitutes a higher level of interpretation designed to determine exactly what the questioner really means. For example, if a stranger walks up to John on the street and asks:

> Q1: Do you have a light?

John will parse this question into a conceptualization equivalent to asking:

> Q2: Do you have in your immediate possession an object capable of producing a flame?

If John does not interpret the question any further, he could answer:

> A1: Yes, I just got a new lighter yesterday.

and then walk away. This sort of response indicates that John did not have a complete understanding of the question. He understood it on a preliminary level, but he did not understand it in terms of what the questioner had intended. His misinterpretation can be explained as faulty Conceptual Categorization. What John understood to be an inquiry deserving a yes or no answer, should have been understood as a request deserving a performative action. The person asking Q1 didn't just want to know if John had a light; he wanted John to offer him a light (flame). In terms of Conceptual Categories, we would say that the question should have been interpreted as a Functional Request rather than a Verification Inquiry.

If a question is not categorized correctly, it will be impossible to produce an appropriate response.

> *Right*
> Q3: How could John take the exam?
> (an Enablement question)
> A3a: He crammed the night before.
> (an Enablement answer)
> *Wrong*
> Q3: How could John take the exam?
> (an Enablement question)
> A3b: He took it with a pen.
> (an Instrumental/Procedural answer)

Q3 is asking about the enabling conditions for taking an exam. In order to take an exam, one has to be prepared for it, presumably be a student, and so forth. Q3 suggests that the questioner does not believe John satisfied the necessary enabling condition. An appropriate answer to Q3 will address this questioned enablement. (He crammed the night before, or he bribed an administrator.) A3b does not address the Enablement conditions at all. A3b answers the question on a much lower level of instrumentality, indicating that the question was understood to be an Instrumental/Procedural question instead of an Enablement question.

> *Right*
> Q4: How did John die?
> (a Causal Antecedent question)
> A4: He caught the swine flu.
> (a Causal Antecedent answer)
> *Wrong*
> Q4: How did John die?
> (a Causal Antecedent question)
> A4b: Well, first he was alive.
> (an Enablement answer)

This time A4b indicates that Q4 was understood to be an Enablement question. A necessary enablement for dying is being alive. But Q4 should not have been interpreted to be asking about enabling conditions for dying. Q4 is more reasonably understood to be asking about the cause of John's death: Was it an accident? Was he ill? Did he kill himself?

> *Right*
> Q5: How did John get to Spain?
>   (an Instrumental/Procedural question)
> A5a: He went by plane.
>   (an Instrumental/Procedural answer)
> *Wrong*
> Q5: How did John get to Spain?
>   (an Instrumental/Procedural question)
> A5b: He wanted to see Madrid.
>   (a Causal Antecedent Answer)

An appropriate answer to Q5 would specify the transportational means that was instrumental to John's getting to Spain (he took a cruise, he flew, etc.). But A5b tells us what caused John to go to Spain. A5B answers a Causal Antecedent question instead of an Instrumental/Procedural question.

When Q3–5 are represented in Conceptual Dependency, it is easy to see which Conceptual Category should be assigned to these questions. In QUALM, parsed conceptualizations are run through a discrimination net that assigns a Conceptual Category to each question. But Conceptual Categorization does not constitute complete understanding of a question. Each conceptual question is subject to further interpretive processing before a memory search for an answer can begin.

Inferential analysis

Complete understanding of a question often involves inferences in addition to Conceptual Categorization. When interpretation of a question does not include analysis of inference, answers may be produced that are technically correct but completely useless. Suppose John is mixing cake batter, and he asks his wife:

> Q6: Now what haven't I added?
> A6: A pound of dog hair and an air filter.

She's probably right; he probably didn't add a pound of dog hair and an air filter. But her answer is inappropriate because John was "obviously" asking for a list of ingredients that he hadn't but should have added. The intent of this question is obvious only when an interpretive inference mechanism can be invoked to supply an implicit constraint. There is an entire class of questions that require the same type of inferential analysis:

> Q7: Who isn't here?
> (Who isn't here who should be here?)
> Q8: What did I forget to buy?
> (What didn't I buy that I should have?)

In each of these questions, an inference must be made that specifies appropriate constraints for potential answers. When Q7 is asked by a professor upon entering his or her class, appropriate answers refer to members of the class. When Q8 is asked in the context of shopping for a dinner party, appropriate answers refer to those things that are needed for dinner.

The Universal Set Inference, a general inference mechanism, is needed for questions of this class. This mechanism examines the context of a question and determines appropriate constraining factors (see Lehnert, 1978a). But before this mechanism can be invoked, some process must be responsible for recognizing which questions require this particular inference mechanism. The Universal Set Inference should not be summoned for questions like:

> Q9: Who is coming to your party?
> Q10: Isn't this the book you wanted?

The successful application of an interpretive inference mechanism relies on the ability to know when that mechanism is needed. This is one way Conceptual Categorization is exploited. One of the thirteen Conceptual Categories is the class of Concept Completion questions, which correspond roughly to fill-in-the-blank questions. During the interpretation of a question, the Universal Set Inference is applied if and only if:

(1) the question is categorized as a Concept Completion question, and
(2) the conceptual question has MODE = NEG

Q6–8 each satisfy these requirements. Whereas the lexical statement of Q8 does not appear to be negated, the conceptual representation for Q8 is equivalent to asking "What didn't I remember to buy?" which is encoded as an MTRANS with negative MODE. Q9 is a Concept Completion question, but it fails to meet the criteria because it has a nonnegative MODE. Q10 fails because it is a Verification question instead of a Concept Completion question.

A useful system of categorization will provide simple test criteria for inference mechanisms of the sort just described. Different questions require different processing, and a strong categorization system can recognize which processes are required for a given question and dictate subsequent processing accordingly.

Content specification

Once a question has been sufficiently understood, retrieval processes can begin to look for an answer. The first part of the retrieval process decides how much of an answer is needed. Consider the following story:

> John went to a restaurant and the hostess gave him a menu. When he ordered a hot dog, the waitress said they didn't have any. So John ordered a hamburger instead. But when the hamburger came, it was so burnt that John left.

If asked:

> Q11: Did John eat a hot dog?

There are many possible answers. When SAM reads this story, SAM can answer Q11 three different ways:

> A11a: No.
> A11b: No, the waitress told John they didn't have any hot dogs.
> A11c: No, the waitress told John they didn't have any hot dogs and so John ordered a hamburger.

These answers are all different in terms of the amount of information they convey. In fact, answers can vary not only in terms of their relative content, but in terms of the kind of content they communicate. For example, if Q11 had been answered "Yes" in the context of our story where John didn't eat a hot dog, then the content of this answer would be described as wrong.

The decision-making processes that determine what kind of an answer should be returned are part of Content Specification. Content Specification takes into acccount the Conceptual Category of each question and intentionality factors that describe the "attitudinal" mode of the system in order to determine how a question should be answered. A system of descriptive instructions is produced by Content Specification to instruct and guide memory retrieval processes as they look for an answer.

The primary challenge involved in Content Specification is precisely how these instructions to memory retrieval are formalized. It is not enough to say "give a minimally correct answer," or "bring in every-thing you can find that's relevant." The instructions generated by Content Specification must tell the retrieval heuristics exactly how to produce a minimally correct answer and exactly what has to be done to come up with everything that's relevant.

One type of Content Specification mechanism that guides retrieval heuristics is Elaboration Options. Each Elaboration Option has four parts: an Intentionality Threshold, a Question Criterion, an Initial Answer Criterion, and Elaboration Instructions. Intentionality refers to variables within the system that are set with suggestively named values like "talkative," "cooperative," "minimally responsive," and so on. The Intentionality Threshold specifies what sort of Intentionality must be assigned to the system in order for an Elaboration Option to be attached to the question. The Question Criterion describes what Conceptual Category must be assigned to the question in order for it to receive the Elaboration Option. If either the Intentionality of the system or the Conceptual Category of the question fails to meet the specifications of the Intentionality Threshold or Question Criterion, then the Elaboration Option is not used. The Answer Criterion specifies the type of conceptual answer that the memory search must initially return in order for the Elaboration Option to be executed. And the Elaboration Instructions specify exactly how an elaboration is to be extracted from memory and integrated into the conceptual answer.

To see exactly how an Elaboration Option works, we will discuss one of the simpler Elaboration Options that has been implemented in QUALM. Consider the following story:

> John went to New York by bus. On the bus he talked to an old lady. When he left the bus, he thanked the driver. He took the subway to Leone's. On the subway his pocket was picked. He got off the train and entered Leone's. He had some lasagna. When the check came, he discovered he couldn't pay. The management told him he would have to wash dishes. When he left, he caught the bus to New Haven.

After reading this story SAM answers:

> Q12: Did John do to New York?
> A12: Yes, John went to New York by bus.
> Q13: Did John eat?
> A13: Yes, John ate lasagna.
> Q14: Did someone pick John's pocket?
> A14: Yes, a thief picked John's pocket.

These are answers SAM gives when it has a talkative Intentionality. If SAM were running with a less than talkative Intentionality, each of these questions would have been answered with a simple "Yes." The longer answers (A12–14) are the result of the Verification Option. This is a very simple Elaboration Option, which is defined as follows:

The Verification Option. Intentionality Threshold: talkative; Question Category: verification; Answer Criterion: initial answer is "Yes"; Elaboration Instructions: final conceptual answer is "Yes, *X*" where *X* is the conceptualization found in the story representation that matches the question concept.

The retrieval heuristics for a Verification question search the story representation for a conceptualization matching the conceptual question. If it finds a match, the initial answer is "Yes." A conceptualization from the story representation doesn't have to correspond to the question concept exactly in order to match it; it may contain more information than the question concept. This is why A12–14 appear to volunteer information. A12 tells how John went to New York, A13 tells what John ate, and A14 asserts who stole John's wallet.

Retrieval heuristics

Once we know how to search memory for an answer, somebody has to do the actual digging. This is the job of the Memory Search. The Memory Search is defined by a set of default retrieval heuristics. These default heuristics are generally augmented by specific instructions from Content Specification. But if no special guidance is provided by Content Specification, the Memory Search will resort to its standard default processes to produce an answer.

Memory Searches are organized according to three levels of description within a story representation: Script Structures, Planning Structures, and Causal Chain Representations. When a question asks about static properties or features of things, the Memory Search resorts to checking information stored in memory tokens. The heuristics devised are designed to take advantage of a story representation as much as possible. As such they are intimately connected to the specific features and properties of script and plan-generated memory representations. In fact, the design of these story representations has been altered and extended to accommodate retrieval heuristics at the same time that the retrieval heuristics have been designed to fit the story representations.

For the most part, the information needed to produce answers to questions about stories exists within the story representation that was generated at the time of understanding. But there are questions that can only be answered by activating predictive memory processes in conjunction with the story representation. For example, suppose we ask "Why didn't John order a hamburger?" in the context of a story where John orders a hot dog. In order to answer this question we must activate processes that can provide information about why John did what he did instead of something else. This information cannot be found in the story representation alone. Special processes are activated during the memory search when the story representation is not enough. A brief overview of this retrieval technique will be outlined in the following section. But, these situations should be thought of as exceptions to the rule; most questions about a story can be answered on the basis of inferences made at the time of understanding and stored in the story representation.

More problems

Although QUALM provides a framework for a working question-answering module, there are many question-answering phenomena awaiting further study and investigation. Indeed, computer programs based on theories of cognitive processing are especially valuable for the ways in which they fail. After QUALM was implemented, it was much easier to see where the theory behind QUALM was weak or inadequate as a comprehensive theory of human question answering. In the following sections we will discuss a few of these problem areas that require further exploration.

Integrative memory processing

Retrieval heuristics cannot always expect to find the precise information needed to answer a question as a conveniently structured piece of data. Sometimes it is necessary to combine bits of information from different places in memory in order to arrive at the desired answer. As question-answering systems become increasingly sophisticated, we can expect to find more and more retrieval heuristics based on abilities to find and combine information from various places in memory. One such retrieval heuristic was implemented for SAM. We will describe this heuristic as an example of a dynamic memory retrieval technique.

Expectational questions are interesting because they cannot be answered on the basis of a story representation alone. Expectational questions correspond roughly to why-not questions. These questions require "integrative" memory processing. The term integration is very often used in the context of adding new information to memory. A single unit of information is "integrated" into a larger memory structure. But in the context of retrieving information from memory, an integrative process is one that combines information from different sources to produce new information.

After reading the burnt-hamburger story, SAM answers:

Q1: Why didn't John eat a hot dog?
A1: Because the waitress told John they didn't have any hot dogs.
Q2: Why didn't John eat the hamburger?
A2: Because the hamburger was burnt.

These questions are answered by an integrative process that combines the story representation with predictive mechanisms in order to reconstruct expectations that were alive at some time during the understanding process. When John orders a hamburger, we have an expectation that he will eat the hamburger until we hear that the hamburger was burnt and John just left. Expectational questions ask about expectations that were aroused at some point during the understanding process and then subsequently violated by an unexpected turn of events. Had we asked "Why didn't John swim across the lake?" the question would seem unreasonable because we never had any expectations about John going swimming or crossing a lake.

The theories of memory representation implemented in SAM and PAM adhere to the premise that a story representation should encode information about things that happened in the story. This includes inferences about things that probably occurred (but weren't explicitly mentioned) as well as conceptualizations for events that were explicitly described in the input story. But Expectational questions ask about things that didn't happen. To answer an Expectational question, we must use the same predictive processes used during story understanding to reconstruct failed expectations which were alive at some time during understanding. This reconstruction is achieved by an integrative memory process called ghost path generation.

The generation of ghost paths cannot be fully understood without a fundamental understanding of script application (Cullingford, 1977). But some sense of what goes on should be apparent from Figure 1. In this diagram, the chain of events in the center corresponds very roughly to information in the story representation that SAM generated at the time it read the burnt-hamburger story. The two chains on either side correspond to the two ghost paths needed to answer Q1 and Q2.

Ghost path generation effectively reconstructs expectations that were aroused at some time during the understanding process, and

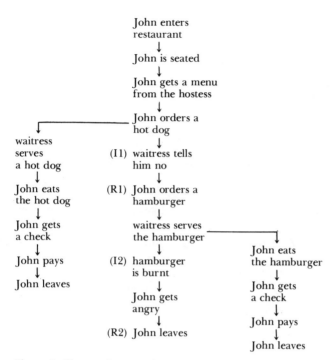

Figure 1. Ghost path generation.

were subsequently violated by later information. This reconstruction is made on the basis of two general kinds of information: (1) the specific story representation at hand, and (2) a general script in permanent memory that was used to understand the story. Only when these two pieces of information are combined by the processes of script application can the answer to an Expectational question be found. In the future we can expect to see more such retrieval heuristics which can combine data to arrive at information that is greater than the sum of its parts.

Knowledge state assessment

In an actual question-answering dialogue, people keep track of the information communicated. No human will be content to loop indefinitely:

Q: Who hit Mary?
A: John.

Q: Who hit Mary?
A: I just told you, John.

The impatience people experience when they are asked the same question twice is a by-product of processes that build and check models of other people's knowledge states.

In coherent question-answering dialogues, questions are not answered in isolation of each other. Answers to questions are produced in accordance with what has and hasn't been said before. In the question-answering dialogues that occur in courtrooms between a lawyer and a witness, the continuity of the questions asked and answers given is so tight that it is possible to see where the examination is heading; after a certain point we can predict what will be asked next (at least in dramatized courtroom dialogues). In the context of answering questions about stories, the continuity of a question-answering dialogue is not so important. Questions about stories are asked only for the purpose of demonstrating comprehension; so the communication is somewhat artificial (because the questioner knows the answers). But even in this situation we can feel disturbed by a lack of continuity:

John took a bus to New York. Then he took the subway to Leone's. He had lasagna. He took the bus back to New Haven.

Q1: How did John go to New Haven?
A1: By bus.
Q2: What did he eat?
A2: He ate lasagna.
Q3: Did John eat?
A3: Yes.
Q4: How did John go to New York?
A4: John went to New York by bus.
Q5: Did John go back to New Haven?
A5: Yes.
Q6: Where did John go?
A6: New York.

This dialogue seems to be lacking direction. The questioner appears to be totally ignorant of the answers given. People would not normally ask a question like "Did John eat?" immediately after hearing "John ate lasagna." The same questions could have been asked in a much more reasonably organized dialogue:

Q6: Where did John go?
A6: New York.
Q4: How did John go to New York?
A4: John went to New York by bus.
Q3: Did John eat?
A3: Yes.

Q2: What did he eat?
A2: John ate lasagna.
Q5: Did John go back to New Haven?
A5: Yes.
Q1: How did John go to New Haven?
A1: By bus.

The lack of continuity in the first dialogue and the apparent continuity of the second dialogue are due to a process of knowledge state assessment. Whenever people answer questions, they try to keep track of what the questioner knows. That is, the answerer maintains a model of the questioner's knowledge state. Whenever a question is answered, the information communicated in that answer is incorporated in this model. If the questioner asks a question that violates our assessment of his knowledge state, we get impatient and wonder what's wrong.

Knowledge state assessment makes the difference between a system that mindlessly answers any question it hears and one that has some sense of when a question is or isn't reasonable. Underlying all Q/A dialogues is an implicit principle: Questions are asked to draw attention to gaps in the questioner's knowledge state; questions are answered to fill those gaps. This principle applies to all Q/A dialogues, even the more artificial ones where people answer questions in order to display their comprehension for the purposes of an evaluation (i.e., testing situations).

Some task domains that involve question-answering capabilities rely on a very sophisticated capacity for knowledge state assessment. For example, a system that answers (or asks) questions in a teaching situation must have a very accurate sense of what the student does and doesn't know in order to be effective (Collins, 1976). A system that answers questions in the context of technical information retrieval will be more effective if it knows how sophisticated the questioner's knowledge state is. When a question is answered on a level that is either too far above or below the questioner's level of competence, the answer will fail to communicate information.

Knowledge state assessment is closely related to theories of conversation, overall memory organization, and issues of short-term versus long-term memory. Even very simple-minded notions of knowledge state models run into severe difficulties in terms of representation and overwriting. For example, suppose we want to create a short-term knowledge state model for a given conversation. We won't even worry about integrating the information in this short-term memory structure into a more permanent memory structure. The simplest structure we can propose is a list of concepts. Suppose that every time a concept is communicated to Mary by John, John adds that concept to his knowledge state list-model for Mary. Even in this short-term memory model, we run into problems of updating. Consider the following dialogue:

> Mary: Does Susan live in New York?
> John: No.
> Mary: Where does she live?
> John: She lives in Washington.

The following entries must be made in John's knowledge state model for Mary:

(1) Susan does not live in New York.
(2) Susan lives in Washington.

We have a duplication of information here. If Mary knows that Susan lives in Washington, it is useless to retain a conceptualization that encodes the fact that Mary knows Susan does not live in New York. But this reduction is only possible if a memory process can determine that living in New York and living in Washington are mutually exclusive possibilities.

Suppose we could update the list-model to eliminate redundancies. Then we would have a knowledge state model that encodes the knowledge Mary acquired in the course of the conversation, but this model would have no trace of Mary's previous knowledge states. After this dialogue, John should be able to conclude that Mary did not know where Susan lived before he told her (unless he has some reason to believe she has been devious with him). Her first question indicated that Mary had some reason to believe Susan might live in New York. If this is important to John or if it is surprising to him for some reason, he is likely to remember that Mary thought Susan lived in New York. A knowledge state model that only records those concepts communicated by the person maintaining the model, and which eliminates redundant communications, will not be adequate for representing previous knowledge states that can be inferred from a question. This raises another issue.

Should a complete running history of Mary's knowledge states be maintained? If not, how much information about previous knowledge states should be kept? Which information? What is really going on here is much more complicated than keeping lists. John is likely to remember that Mary thought Susan lived in New York only if this fact is significant or unexpected for some reason. To determine whether or not a given piece of information is significant or unexpected, a lot of memory interaction must be taking place with John's long-term memory in order to pick out inconsistencies and surprises. Much more has

to be known about overall memory structures and integrative processes before problems of this magnitude can be tackled in a serious
manner.

Answer selection

Whereas Expectational questions are interesting because they cannot
be answered on the basis of a story representation alone, there are
many other types of questions that do not need information outside of
the story representation that are still difficult to answer. Causal Antecedent questions are complicated in this respect. A Causal Antecedent question asks for the reason behind an event. After reading the
Leone's story, consider the following answers:

> Q7: Why did John wash dishes?
> A7a: Because he couldn't pay the check.
> A7b: Because he had no money.
> A7c: Because he had been pickpocketed on the subway.

SAM answers Q7 "Because he had no money." But is this the best
answer of the three? What factors determine the superiority of one
answer over another?

Effective answer selection entails making assumptions about what
the questioner knows. Anyone who asks Q7 can be assumed to know
that John washed dishes. If we go on to assume that the questioner
knows two more things: (1) John washed dishes in a restaurant, and
(2) washing dishes in a restaurant is classically what happens when
someone eats and then can't pay – then the questioner can infer: (3)
John couldn't pay the check. If the questioner can figure out that John
couldn't pay the check, then A7a does not tell the questioner anything
s/he doesn't know to begin with. A good answer must take into account what the questioner does and doesn't know, and address the
questioner's knowledge state by telling him or her something new.

A7b is a weak answer for the same reasons that A7a is weak. If
someone knows that John couldn't pay a check, that individual can
reasonably infer that John didn't have (enough) money. Both inferences:

> (1) John couldn't pay the check.
> (2) John didn't have any money.

can be made by the questioner on the basis of general world knowledge and the fact that John washed dishes in a restaurant. But there is
no way the questioner can infer that John was pickpocketed on the
subway without additional knowledge of the story. Therefore A7c is

the best answer to Q7 as long as we assume the questioner has knowledge about the world and can make inferences on the basis of that knowledge.

If we assumed that the questioner knew nothing about restaurants, A7a would be the best answer. If we assumed that the questioner knew about restaurants but didn't understand about paying for things, A7b would be the best answer. It is impossible to judge various answers to a question without knowing (or assuming) something about the person asking the question.

Rules of conversation

Question-answering dialogues are a form of conversation. There are rules of conversational structure that are used to arrive at correct interpretations and appropriate responses. To get some idea of just how complicated a conversational structure can be, let's look at an example of a nested question-answering dialogue.

> Mary: Do you know anyone who can referee some papers before August?
> John: Is Bill Sand going to be around this summer?
> Mary: Who?
> John: Don't you know the members of the editorial board?
> Mary: Yes, but that name isn't familiar.
> John: I think he just joined. He's a new member.
> Mary: No, I don't think he is.
> John: Then we can't ask him.

In this conversation Mary disagrees with John about somebody named Bill Sand being a member of the editorial board. John seems to give in to her opinion about the matter, and says something that indicates that they shouldn't ask anyone outside of the editorial board to referee papers. The critical juncture in this conversation occurs when John says "I think he just joined. He's a new member," at which point Mary says "No, I don't think he is." Conversational continuity forces us to interpret Mary's statement as a reply to John. Mary seems to be saying that she doesn't think there is a new member of the editorial board named Bill Sand. John's final reply, "Then we can't ask him," is also interpreted in terms of the reply preceding it. John seems to be saying that if the person he is thinking of is not a member of the editorial board, then they can't ask him to referee papers. The conversation makes sense as it stands, and there does not seem to be any confusion about what is being said. But now look what happens when one small alteration is made:

> Mary: Do you know anyone who can referee some papers before August?
> John: Is Bill Sand going to be around this summer?
> Mary: Who?
> John: Don't you know the members of the editorial board?
> Mary: Yes, but that name isn't familiar.
> John: I think he just joined. He's a new member.
> Mary: Oh yes, now I know who you mean. No, I don't think he is.
> John: Then we can't ask him.

The only change is an addition to Mary's last statement, "Oh yes, now I know who you mean." This declaration acts as a signal to tell John that she is resuming a suspended exchange. Without this signal her next statement, "No, I don't think he is," is interpreted as a response to John's "I think he just joined. He's a new member." But with the added signal, "Oh yes, now I know who you mean," we must interpret "No, I don't think he is" as a reply to the earlier suspended question "Is Bill Sand going to be around this summer?" The signal is critical here because the nesting of processes is three deep. People can recover from one level without signals to establish a return to the next level, but when more than one level has to be recovered, clues must be supplied to help the transitions. In Figure 2 we see the same two dialogues with their nested conversational levels.

Without a theory of conversational structures, it is not possible to recognize when a question-answering exchange is being dropped, suspended, or resumed. Questions and answers are merely units of communication within larger conversational exchanges. These exchanges are themselves subject to structural laws of combination that include nesting phenomena. Complete conceptual processing for question-answering dialogues must be sensitive to these larger units of conversational structure.

Memory representation

When people answer questions, their answers sometimes tell us something about the form and organization of conceptual information in human memory. For example, consider the following story:

> John was sitting in a dining car. When the train jerked, the soup spilled.

Suppose we ask:

> Q8: Where was the soup?

Dialogue without level recovery signal

Mary: Do you know anyone who can referee some papers before ——— 0
       August?
       (level 0 question)
John: Is Bill Sand going to be around this summer? ——————— 1
       (level 1 question)
Mary: Who? ——————————————————————————————— 2
       (level 2 question)
John: Don't you know the members of the editorial ——— 3
       board?
       (level 3 question)
Mary: Yes, but that name isn't familiar. ———————
       (level 3 answer)
John: I think he just joined. He's a new member. ———————
       (level 2 answer)
Mary: No, I don't think he is. ————————————————
       (level 2 continuation)
John: Then we can't ask him. —————————————————————
       (level 0 answer)

Dialogue with level recovery signal

Mary: Do you know anyone who can referee some papers before ——— 0
       August?
       (level 0 question)
John: Is Bill Sand going to be around this summer? ——————— 1
       (level 1 question)
Mary: Who? ——————————————————————————————— 2
       (level 2 question)
John: Don't you know the members of the editorial ——— 3
       board?
       (level 3 question)
Mary: Yes, but that name isn't familiar. ———————
       (level 3 answer)
John: I think he just joined. He's a new member. ———————
       (level 2 answer)
Mary: Oh yes, now I know who you mean. ———————
       (signals ends of level 2 exchange)
       (No, I don't think he is. ————————————————
       (level 1 answer)
John: Then we can't ask him. —————————————————————
       (level 0 answer)

Figure 2. Dialogues with nested conversational levels.

This is a specification question that can be answered a number of ways. Two common answers are:

A8a: In a bowl.
A8b: On the table.

A much less natural answer would be:

A8c: On a plate.

A8c is a very odd answer which conjures up an image of a soup puddle on a plate. This is not the scene most people envision when hearing the story. Most people imagine the soup in a bowl on a plate on a table.

The acceptable and unacceptable answers to Q8 tell us something about human memory organization. It never occurs to people to answer "On a plate." Furthermore, when this answer is given, it provokes a wrong image of soup resting directly on a plate. But "On the table" is a natural answer. Why is it that "On a plate" is a bad answer but "On the table" is perfectly reasonable? The soup does not rest directly on the table any more than it rests directly on a plate. Why is the answer acceptable in one case but not the other? This phenomenon must be accounted for in terms of memory organization.

When people hear this story they assume a causality between the train jerking and the soup spilling. (If asked "Why did the soup spill?" people will answer "Because the train moved.") This causality relies on the fact that the soup is physically connected to the train in some way. This physical connection can only be recognized by constructing a path of physical objects between the soup and the train. This path of connections must be accessed in order to answer Q8. If a path is constructed by a computational system in the same way that people build one, it will be easy to retrieve answers to Q8 that seem natural. If the path is built differently, we may end up with an answer like A8c. Suppose we construct a path like the following:

> *A bad path:*
> soup (inside-of)
> bowl (on-top-of)
> plate (on-top-of)
> tablecloth (on-top-of)
> table (on-top-of)
> floor (on-top-of)
> dining car (part-of)
> train

With this memory representation it is not clear how we can extract the answers A8a and A8b without also getting answers like "On a plate" or "On a tablecloth." There is nothing in this memory representation that tells us where the good answers are. What we need is a memory representation that makes it easy to find a bowl and a table but hard to retrieve a plate.

> *A better path:*
> soup (inside-of)
> bowl (part-of)
> placesetting (part-of)
> tablesetting (on-top-of)

table (part-of)
dining area (part-of)
dining car (part-of)
train

This path suggests a very simple retrieval heuristic for producing the answers A8a and A8b; trace the path looking for objects that are connected by either "inside-of" or "on-top-of" links.

The closer a memory representation is to human memory organization, the easier it will be to produce answers that make sense to people. A system of memory representation for physical objects has been proposed (Lehnert, 1978b) that is designed to facilitate inference and retrieval problems of the sort just described. Conceptual descriptions of objects in this system are based on decompositions into a set of object primitives in much the same way that Conceptual Dependency (Schank, 1975) describes actions by decomposing them into a set of primitive acts.

Flexible memory retrieval

This last problem concerns a phenomenon in human memory retrieval that we might expect to be the most difficult one to model in a computer program. When people answer questions, they not only utilize efficient and effective retrieval techniques, but they appear to have a facility for optimizing retrieval tasks as well. This can best be illustrated with a simple example.

If I were giving a talk to a room full of people and I asked them "How many days are in July?" it is quite likely that many of those people would find the answer to that question by means of a little rhyme that most of us learned as children: "Thirty days hath September, April, . . . etc." By internally running through the rhyme until the necessary information is found, the question can be answered. Yet under different circumstances, the same people who would normally use that rhyme, may be able to answer the question with a different retrieval technique. Suppose that it happens to be July 31 and the same question is asked. If one is aware of the date, it will be easier to answer the question with the following reasoning: Today is July 31 so there are at least 31 days in July; but 31 is the maximum number of days a month can have; therefore July must have 31 days. Being aware of the date might very well cause one to adopt a retrieval strategy based on simple deduction rather than the rote memorization of a rhyme. Presumably this deduction is easier and quicker than remembering the verse.

This suggests that the retrieval heuristics people use are not fixed and permanent, but are instead flexible and subject to adjustment for optimal memory manipulations. Because it will be quite some time before a computer can reliably simulate the memory retrieval capabilities of a human under any circumstances, this observation is being made more in tribute to human memory capabilities than as a serious research concern for current retrieval systems.

Conclusions

The overall question-answering process can be intuitively approached in two stages: understanding the question (interpretation) and finding an answer (memory retrieval). Each of these stages is likewise divided into two parts:

> Interpretation
> (1) Conceptual Categorization
> (2) Inferential Analysis
>
> Memory retrieval
> (3) Content Specification
> (4) Searching Heuristics

1. Conceptual Categorization guides the subsequent processing by dictating which specific inference mechanisms, elaboration options, and retrieval heuristics should be invoked in the course of answering a question.
2. Inferential Analysis is responsible for understanding what the questioner really meant when a question should not be taken literally.
3. Content Specification determines how much of an answer should be returned in terms of detail and elaborations.
4. Searching Heuristics do the actual digging in order to extract an answer from memory.

All of the processes within these four phases are specific to question answering per se and are language-independent, operating within a conceptual representation system.

Although many of QUALM's question techniques are designed for answering questions about stories, QUALM is not limited to stories about a specific content domain. QUALM is applicable to any story that can be understood in terms of scripts and plans (Schank and Abelson, 1977). This limitation is not content-specific; it is dependent on the general knowledge structures that are used in text understanding. When new scripts and plans are added to the knowledge base for SAM and PAM, questions can be answered about stories using this new knowledge without any additional alterations of QUALM.

Question-answering phenomena are of special interest to researchers of cognitive processes. By studying the ways in which people answer questions, we can learn about processes in natural language comprehension, the generation of short-term memory structures, and the organization of conceptual information in long-term memory. The task of question answering is inexorably bound to a broad spectrum of cognitive tasks, ranging from the more visible phenomena of conversational structure down to the elusive mechanisms of memory retrieval. It presents psychologists and computer scientists with a rare opportunity to coordinate their research efforts. The pursuit of a comprehensive theory of question answering would be greatly enhanced by the utilization of both experimental data and computational models to substantiate and test proposed theories of underlying thought processes. The value of such an interdisciplinary research effort extends in three directions. (1) Such a theory would enable natural language communication with computer systems that process text. If a computer system were processing tremendous amounts of text, its ability to answer questions about what it read could be used to combat the knowledge explosion in professional fields. (2) Alternatively, a theory of human question answering could profoundly alter our educational methods. Because question answering of one form or another is our primary method for evaluating students, greater sensitivity to the cognitive mechanisms underlying the question-answering process might shed light on specific learning disabilities or problematic social interactions. (3) Finally, the pure scientist who wishes to study human cognition in general would greatly benefit from studying question answering. Question answering touches on many aspects of human cognition, and if studied carefully, it can provide us with a relatively clear window to the workings of the mind. Data can be collected, and computational models can be implemented. Eventually, when general theories of human cognition are proposed, we can expect a theory of question answering to be a major component of such efforts.

Appendix: Output from four computer programs

SAM

John went to New York by bus. On the bus he talked to an old lady. When he left the bus, he thanked the driver. He took the subway to Leone's. On the subway his pocket was picked. He got off the train and entered Leone's. He had some lasagna. When the check came, he discovered he couldn't pay. The management told him he would have to wash dishes. When he left, he caught a bus to New Haven.

Who went to New York?
JOHN WENT TO NEW YORK.

Why did John go to New York?
BECAUSE JOHN WANTED TO GO TO LEONE'S.

Why did John go to Leone's?
BECAUSE JOHN WANTED TO HAVE SOME LASAGNA.

How did John get to New York?
JOHN TOOK A BUS TO NEW YORK.

Did a thief pick John's pocket?
A THIEF PICKED JOHN'S POCKET.

Did John order lasagna?
JOHN ORDERED LASAGNA.

Did John eat a steak?
NO, JOHN ATE LASAGNA.

What did John eat?
JOHN ATE LASAGNA.

Did John order lobster?
NO, JOHN ORDERED LASAGNA.

Did John eat lasagna?
JOHN ATE LASAGNA.

Did John pay the check?
NO, JOHN DIDN'T HAVE ANY MONEY.

Did John leave the waitress a tip?
NO, JOHN DIDN'T HAVE ANY MONEY.

Did John leave Leone's?
JOHN LEFT LEONE'S.

Why did John take the subway from Leone's?
SO JOHN COULD TAKE A BUS TO NEW HAVEN.

How could John take the subway from Leone's?
PROBABLY JOHN HAD A TOKEN.

How did John get to Leone's?
JOHN TOOK A BUS TO NEW YORK AND THEN HE TOOK THE SUBWAY TO LEONE'S.

Did anything unusual happen on the bus?
I DON'T REMEMBER ANYTHING.

Did anything unusual happen on the subway?
A THIEF PICKED JOHN'S POCKET.

What did John order?
JOHN ORDERED LASAGNA.

Who gave John a menu?
THE WAITRESS GAVE JOHN A MENU.

Did anything unusual happen at the restaurant?
JOHN DISCOVERED THAT HE COULDN'T PAY THE CHECK AND SO HE HAD
TO WASH DISHES.

Why couldn't John pay the check?
BECAUSE JOHN DID NOT HAVE ANY MONEY.

Why didn't John have any money?
BECAUSE A THIEF PICKED JOHN'S POCKET.

How did John get back to New Haven?
JOHN WENT FROM LEONE'S BY SUBWAY AND THEN HE WENT TO NEW
HAVEN BY BUS.

How was John able to take the bus to New Haven?
PROBABLY JOHN HAD A TICKET.

John went to a restaurant and the hostess gave him a menu. When he ordered
a hot dog, the waitress said that they didn't have any. So John ordered a
hamburger instead. But when the hamburger came, it was so burnt that John
left.

Did the waitress give John a menu?
NO, THE HOSTESS GAVE JOHN A MENU.

Did John order a hot dog?
YES.

Did John eat a hot dog?
NO, THE WAITRESS TOLD JOHN THEY DIDN'T HAVE ANY HOT DOGS.

What did the waitress serve John?
THE WAITRESS SERVED JOHN A HAMBURGER.

Why didn't John eat the hamburger?
BECAUSE THE HAMBURGER WAS BURNT.

Was John angry?
PROBABLY.

Why didn't John pay the check?
JOHN WAS ANGRY BECAUSE THE HAMBURGER WAS BURNT AND SO HE
LEFT.

Why didn't John eat the hot dog?
BECAUSE THE WAITRESS TOLD JOHN THEY DID NOT HAVE ANY HOT
DOGS.

What happened when John ordered the hamburger?
THE WAITRESS GAVE THE ORDER TO THE COOK, THE COOK PREPARED THE
HAMBURGER. THE COOK GAVE THE HAMBURGER TO THE WAITRESS, THE
WAITRESS SERVED JOHN THE HAMBURGER.

What happened when John ordered the hot dog?
THE WAITRESS TOLD JOHN THEY DIDN'T HAVE ANY HOT DOGS.

Friday evening a car swerved off Route 69. The vehicle struck a tree. The
passenger, a New Jersey man, was killed. David Hall, 27, was pronounced
dead at the scene by Dr. Dana Blauchard, medical examiner. Frank Miller, 32,
of 593 Foxon Rd., the driver, was taken to Milford Hospital by Flanagan

Ambulance. He was treated and released. The passenger was extricated from the vehicle by the Branford Fire Department. No charges were made. Patrolman Robert Onofrio investigated the accident.

Was anyone killed?
YES, DAVID HALL DIED.

Was anyone hurt?
YES, FRANK MILLER WAS SLIGHTLY INJURED.

Why was Frank Miller hurt?
BECAUSE THE AUTOMOBILE HIT THE TREE.

Did Miller go the hospital?
YES, HE WAS IN THE MILFORD HOSPITAL.

How did Miller get to the hospital?
THE FLANAGAN AMBULANCE COMPANY TOOK HIM TO THE MILFORD HOSPITAL.

PAM

John loved Mary but she didn't want to marry him. One day, a dragon stole Mary from the castle. John got on top of his horse and killed the dragon. Mary agreed to marry him. They lived happily ever after.

Why did John get on his horse?
BECAUSE HE WANTED TO BE NEAR MARY.

Why did Mary agree to marry John?
BECAUSE SHE WAS INDEBTED TO HIM.

Why did John kill the dragon?
BECAUSE HE WANTED MARY NOT TO DIE.

John disliked his job as the bank janitor. One day, a thief tried to rob the bank. John jumped on the thief and knocked him out. The bank president made John the bank guard. John enjoyed his new job.

Why did John knock the thief out?
BECAUSE HE WANTED THE THIEF NOT TO HAVE THE BANK'S MONEY.

Why did the bank president make John the bank guard?
BECAUSE THE BANK WAS INDEBTED TO JOHN.

ASP

ASP is a small program that was designed in 1975 to investigate theories concerned with finding the best answer to a question. Its implementation required no efforts outside of my own. ASP is given a set of answers to a question about a story and tries to select the best answer. ASP makes its decision by asking the user to respond yes or no to a sequence of questions about the answers provided. ASP has no memory representation for the story and no understanding of the question or answers given. It chooses an answer on the basis of selection rules that respond to the yes or no answers of the user.

The following dialogue represents an interactive session with ASP. ASP has the answers it was given stored in memory as lists so it can ask questions about pairs of answers by combining those answers with fixed connectives.

Story context:

One morning John noticed his dog was having trouble walking. That afternoon he took it to the vet.

    Q: Why did John take his dog to the vet?
    A1: It was sick or injured.
    A2: It was having trouble walking.
    A3: He wanted to make it well.

The following dialogue represents an interactive session with ASP. For this execution ASP has been given the lexical answers A1, A2, and A3, as initial input to the program.

**** Interactive Session Begins ****

ASP: GIVEN THE CONTEXT OF THE STORY, CAN EITHER
      He wanted to make it well
      OR
      It was sick or injured
      BE INFERRED FROM ONE ANOTHER?
USER: YES
  ASP: DOES IT MAKE SENSE TO SAY
      He wanted to make it well
      BECAUSE
      It was having trouble walking?
USER: YES
  ASP: DOES IT MAKE SENSE TO SAY
      He wanted to make it well
      AND HE KNEW THAT
      It was having trouble walking?
USER: YES
  ASP: THE BEST ANSWER IS BECAUSE
      It was having trouble walking

COIL

COIL was developed at the Xerox Palo Alto Research Center during the summer of 1976. It was written in an experimental implementation of KRL (Knowledge Representation Language) which was developed by Daniel Bobrow and Terry Winograd (Bobrow and Winograd, 1977).

    Unlike SAM and PAM, which answered all of their questions after reading an entire story, COIL interrupts the input story to answer questions.

John picked up a newspaper. He went from the hall into the kitchen and got some milk.

    Where did John come from?
    THE HALL.
    Where did the milk come from?
    THE REFRIGERATOR.

But the milkcarton was empty so he threw it out.

Where did the milkcarton go to?
THE GARBAGE BAG.
Why did John throw the milkcarton into the garbage bag?
BECAUSE THE MILKCARTON WAS EMPTY.

He turned on the light and radio. Then he listened to music and read.

Where did the music come from?
THE RADIO.
What did John read?
THE NEWSPAPER.
Why did John turn on the light?
SO HE COULD READ THE NEWSPAPER.
Why did John turn on the radio?
SO HE COULD HEAR THE MUSIC.

NOTES

The research described here was done at the Yale Artificial Intelligence Project and is funded in part by the Advanced Research Projects Agency of the Department of Defense and monitored under the Office of Naval Research under contract N0014-75-C-1111.

REFERENCES

Bobrow, D. G., and Winograd, T. 1977. "An Overview of KRL, a Knowledge Representation Language." *Cognitive Science* 1, no. 1:3–46.
Collins, A. 1976. "Processes in Acquiring Knowledge." In R. Anderson, R. Spiro, and W. Montague, eds. *Schooling and the Acquisition of Knowledge.* Hillsdale, N.J.: Erlbaum.
Cullingford, R. E. 1978. "Script Application: Computer Understanding of Newspaper Stories." Research Report 116, Yale University, Department of Computer Science.
Goldman, N. M. 1975. "Conceptual Generation." In R. Schank, ed. *Conceptual Information Processing.* Amsterdam: North-Holland.
Lehnert, W. G. 1977. "A Conceptual Theory of Question Answering." In *Proceedings of the Fifth International Joint Conference on Artificial Intelligence.* Cambridge, Mass.
Lehnert, W. G. 1978a. *The Process of Question Answering.* Hillsdale, N.J.: Erlbaum.
Lehnert, W. G. 1978b. "Representing Physical Objects in Memory." Research Report 131, Yale University, Department of Computer Science.
Riesbeck, C. K. 1975. "Conceptual Analysis." In R. Schank, ed. *Conceptual Information Processing.* Amsterdam: North-Holland.
Riesbeck, C. K., and Schank, R. C. 1976. "Comprehension by Computer: Expectation-based Analysis of Sentences in Context." Research Report 78, Yale University, Department of Computer Science.

Schank, R. C. 1975. *Conceptual Information Processing*. Amsterdam: North-Holland.

Schank, R. C., and Abelson, R. P. 1977. *Scripts, Plans, Goals and Understanding: An Inquiry Into Human Knowledge Structures*. Hillsdale, N.J.: Erlbaum.

Wilensky, R. 1976. "Using Plans to Understand Natural Language." *Proceedings of the Annual Conference on the ACM*. Houston, Texas.

7

A computational account of
some constraints on language

MITCHELL MARCUS

In a series of papers over the last several years, Noam Chomsky has argued for several specific properties of language that he claims are universal to all human languages (Chomsky, 1973, 1975, 1976). These properties, which form one of the cornerstones of his current linguistic theory, are embodied in a set of constraints on language, a set of restrictions on the operation of rules of grammar.

This chapter will outline two arguments presented at length in Marcus (1977) demonstrating that important subcases of two of these constraints, the Subjacency Principle and the Specified Subject Constraint, fall out naturally from the structure of a grammar interpreter called PARSIFAL, whose structure is in turn based upon the hypothesis that a natural language parser needn't simulate a nondeterministic machine. This "Determinism Hypothesis" claims that natural language can be parsed by a computationally simple mechanism that uses neither backtracking nor pseudo-parallelism (cf. Woods, 1970) and in which all grammatical structure created by the parser is "indelible" in that it must all be output as part of the structural analysis of the parser's input. Once built, no grammatical structure can be discarded or altered in the course of the parsing process.

In particular, this chapter will show that the structure of the grammar interpreter constrains its operation in such a way that, by and large, grammar rules cannot parse sentences that violate either the Specified Subject Constraint or the Subjacency Principle. The component of the grammar interpreter upon which this result principally depends is motivated by the Determinism Hypothesis; this result thus provides indirect evidence for the hypothesis. This result also depends upon the use within a computational framework of the closely related notions of annotated surface structure and trace theory, which also derive from Chomsky's recent work.

(It should be noted that these constraints are far from universally accepted. They are currently the source of much controversy; for

177

various critiques of Chomsky's position see Postal, 1974 and Bresnan, 1976. However, what is presented here does not argue for these constraints, per se, but rather provides a different sort of explanation, based on a processing model, of why the sorts of sentences that these constraints forbid are bad. Although the exact formulation of these constraints is controversial, the fact that some set of constraints is needed to account for this range of data is generally agreed upon by most generative grammarians. The account that I will present is crucially linked to Chomsky's, however, in that trace theory is at the heart of this account.)

Because of space limitations, this chapter deals only with those grammatical processes characterized by the competence rule "MOVE NP"; the constraints imposed by the grammar interpreter upon those processes characterized by the rule "MOVE WH-phrase" are discussed at length in Marcus (1977), where I show that the behavior characterized by Ross's Complex NP Constraint (Ross, 1967) itself follows directly from the structure of the grammar interpreter for reasons rather different from the behavior considered in this section. Also because of space limitations, I will not attempt to show that the two constraints I will deal with here *necessarily* follow from the grammar interpreter, but instead only that they *naturally* follow from the interpreter, in particular from a simple, natural formulation of a rule for passivization that itself depends heavily upon the structure of the interpreter. Again, necessity is argued for in detail in Marcus (1977).

This chapter will first outline the structure of the grammar interpreter, then present the PASSIVE rule, and then finally show how Chomsky's constraints "fall out" of the formulation of PASSIVE.

Before proceeding with the body of this chapter, two other important properties of the parser should be mentioned which will not be discussed here. Both are discussed at length in Marcus (1977); the first is sketched as well in Marcus (1978).

1. Simple rules of grammar can be written for this interpreter that elegantly capture the significant generalizations behind not only passivization, but also such constructions as *yes/no* questions, imperatives, and sentences with existential *there*. These rules are reminiscent of the sorts of rules proposed within the framework of the theory of generative grammar, despite the fact that the rules presented here must recover underlying structure given only the terminal string of the surface form of the sentence.

2. The grammar interpreter provides a simple explanation for the difficulty caused by "garden path" sentences, such as "The cotton clothing is made of grows in Mississippi." Rules can be written for this interpreter to resolve local structural ambiguities that might

seem to require nondeterministic parsing; the power of such rules, however, depends upon a parameter of the mechanism. Most structural ambiguities can be resolved, given an appropriate setting of this parameter, but those that typically cause garden paths cannot.

The structure of PARSIFAL

PARSIFAL maintains two major data structures: a pushdown stack of incomplete constituents called the *active node stack,* and a small three-place *constituent buffer* which contains constituents that are complete, but whose higher-level grammatical function is as yet uncertain.

Figure 1 shows a snapshot of the parser's data structures taken while parsing the sentence "John should have scheduled the meeting." Note that the active node stack is shown growing *downward,* so that the structure of the stack reflects the structure of the emerging parse tree. At the bottom of the stack is an auxiliary node labeled with the features *modal, past,* and so on, which has as a daughter the modal "should." Above the bottom of the stack is an S node with an NP as a daughter, dominating the word "John." There are two words in the buffer, the verb "have" in the first buffer cell and the word "scheduled" in the second. The two words "the meeting" have not yet come to the attention of the parser. [The structures of form "(PARSE-AUX CPOOL)" and the like will be explained later in this section.]

The constituent buffer is the heart of the grammar interpreter; it is the central feature that distinguishes this parser from all others. The words that make up the parser's input first come to its attention when they appear at the end of this buffer after morphological analysis. Triggered by the words at the beginning of the buffer, the parser may decide to create a new grammatical constituent, create a new node at the bottom of the active node stack, and then begin to attach the constituents in the buffer to it. After this new constituent is completed, the parser will then pop the new constituent from the active node stack; if the grammatical role of this larger structure is as yet undetermined, the parser will insert it into the first cell of the buffer. The parser is free to examine the constituents in the buffer, to act upon them, and to otherwise use the buffer as a workspace.

Although the buffer allows the parser to examine some of the context surrounding a given constituent, it does not allow arbitrary look-ahead. The length of the buffer is strictly limited; in the version of the parser presented here, the buffer has only three cells. The buffer must be extended to five cells to allow the parser to build NPs in a

The active node stack

S1 (S DECL MAJOR S) / (PARSE-AUXCPOOL)
    NP : (John)
    AUX1 (MODAL PAST VSPL AUX) / (BUILD-AUX)
        MODAL : (should)

The buffer

1: WORD3 (*HAVE VERB TNSLESS AUXVERB PRES V-3S) : (have)
2: WORD4 (*SCHEDULE COMP-OBJ VERB INF-OBJ
            V-3S ED=EN EN PART PAST ED) : (scheduled)
    Yet unseen words: the meeting.

Figure 1. PARSIFAL's two major data structures

manner that is transparent to the "clause level" grammar rules, which will be presented in this chapter. This extended parser still has a window of only three cells, but the effective start of the buffer can be changed through an "attention shifting mechanism" whenever the parser is building an NP. In effect, this extended parser has two "logical" buffers of length three, one for NPs and another for clauses, with these two buffers implemented by allowing an overlap in one larger buffer. (For details, see Marcus, 1977.)

Note that each of the three cells in the buffer can hold a *grammatical constituent* of any type, where a constituent is any tree that the parser has constructed under a single root node. The size of the structure underneath the node is immaterial; both "that" and "that the big green cookie monster's toe got stubbed" are perfectly good constituents once the parser has constructed a subordinate clause from the latter phrase.

The constituent buffer and the active node stack are acted upon by a grammar made up of pattern/action rules; this grammar can be viewed as an augmented form of Newell and Simon's production systems (Newell and Simon, 1972). Each rule is made up of a pattern, which is matched against some subset of the constituents of the buffer and the accessible nodes in the active node stack (about which more will be said later in this section), and an action, a sequence of operations that acts on these constituents. Each rule is assigned a numerical *priority*, which the grammar interpreter uses to arbitrate simultaneous matches.

The grammar as a whole is structured into *rule packets,* clumps of grammar rules that can be activated and deactivated as a group; the grammar interpreter only attempts to match rules in packets that have been activated by the grammar. Any grammar rule can activate a packet by associating that packet with the constituent at the bottom of the active node stack. As long as that node is at the bottom of the stack, the packets associated with it are active; when that node is pushed into the stack, the packets remain associated with it, but become active again only when that node reaches the bottom of the stack. For example, in Figure 1 above, the packet BUILD-AUX is associated with the bottom of the stack, and is thus active, whereas the packet PARSE-AUX is associated with the S node above the auxiliary.

The grammar rules themselves are written in a language called PIDGIN, an English-like formal language that is translated into LISP by a simple grammar translator based on the notion of top-down operator precedence (Pratt, 1973). This use of pseudo-English is similar to the use of pseudo-English in the grammar for Sager's STRING parser (Sager, 1973). Figure 2 gives a schematic overview of the organization of the grammar, and exhibits some of the rules that make up the packet PARSE-AUX.

A few comments on the grammar notation itself are in order. The general form of each grammar rule is:

{Rule ⟨name⟩ priority: ⟨priority⟩ in ⟨packet⟩ ⟨pattern⟩ → ⟨action⟩}

Each pattern is of the form:

[⟨description of 1st buffer constituent⟩] [⟨2nd⟩] [⟨3rd⟩]

The symbol "=", used only in pattern descriptions, is to be read as "has the feature(s)." Features of the form "*⟨word⟩" mean "has the root ⟨word⟩," e.g., "*have" means "has the root 'have.' " The tokens "1st," "2nd," "3rd," and "C" (or "c") refer to the constituents in the 1st, 2nd, and 3rd buffer positions and the current active node (i.e., the bottom of the stack), respectively. The PIDGIN code of the rule patterns should otherwise be fairly self-explanatory.

The parser (i.e., the grammar interpreter interpreting some grammar) operates by attaching constituents that are in the buffer to the constituent at the bottom of thé stack; functionally, a constituent is in the stack when the parser is attempting to find its daughters, and in the buffer when the parser is attempting to find its mother. Once a constituent in the buffer has been attached, the grammar interpreter will automatically remove it from the buffer, filling in the gap by shifting to the left the constituents formerly to its right. When the parser has completed the constituent at the bottom of the stack, it pops that constituent from the active node stack; the constituent either remains attached to its parent, if it was attached to some larger constituent when it was created, or else it falls into the first cell of the

(a) The structure of the grammar

Priority	Pattern				Action
		Description of:			
	1st	2nd	3rd	The Stack	
			PACKET1		
5:	[ ]	[ ]	[ ]		→ ACTION1
10:	[ ]			[ ]	→ ACTION2
10:	[ ]	[ ]	[ ]	[ ]	→ ACTION3
			PACKET2		
10:	[ ]	[ ]			→ ACTION4
15:	[ ]			[ ]	→ ACTION5

(b) Some grammar rules that initiate auxiliaries

{RULE START-AUX PRIORITY: 10. IN PARSE-AUX
[=verb] →
Create a new aux node.
Label C with the meet of the features of 1st and pres, past, future, tnsless.
Activate build-aux.}

{RULE TO-INFINITIVE PRIORITY: 10. IN PARSE-AUX
[=*to, auxverb] [=tnsless] →
Label a new aux node inf.
Attach 1st to C as to.
Activate build-aux.}

Figure 2. Rule packets and some sample rules

constituent buffer, shifting the buffer to the right to create a gap (and causing an error if the buffer was already full). If the constituents in the buffer provide sufficient evidence that a constituent of a given type should be initiated, a new node of that type can be created and pushed onto the stack; this new node can also be attached to the node at the bottom of the stack before the stack is pushed, if the grammatical function of the new constituent is clear when it is created.

This structure is motivated by several properties that, as is argued in Marcus (1977), any "non-nondeterministic" grammar interpreter must embody. These principles, and their embodiment in PARSIFAL, are as follows:

1. A deterministic parser must be at least partially data-driven. A grammar for PARSIFAL is made up of pattern/action rules that are triggered when constituents that fulfill specific descriptions appear in the buffer.
2. A deterministic parser must be able to reflect expectations that follow from the partial structures built up during the parsing process. Packets of rules can be activated and deactivated by grammar rules to reflect the properties of the constituents in the active node stack.

3. A deterministic parser must have some sort of constrained look-ahead facility. PARSIFAL's buffer provides this constrained look-ahead. Because the buffer can hold several constituents, a grammar rule can examine the context that follows the first constituent in the buffer before deciding what grammatical role it fills in a higher-level structure. The key idea is that the size of the buffer can be sharply constrained if each location in the buffer can hold a single complete constituent, regardless of that constituent's size. It must be stressed that this look-ahead ability must be constrained in some manner, as it is here by limiting the length of the buffer; otherwise the "determinism" claim is vacuous.

The general grammatical framework: traces

The form of the structures that the current grammar builds is based on the notion of *Annotated Surface Structure*. This term has been used in two different senses by Winograd (1971) and Chomsky (1973); and the usage of the term here can be thought of as a synthesis of the two concepts. Following Winograd, this term will be used to refer to a notion of surface structure annotated by the addition of a *set of features* to each node in a parse tree. Following Chomsky, the term will be used to refer to a notion of surface structure annotated by the addition of an element called *trace* to indicate the "underlying position" of "shifted" NPs.

In current linguistic theory, a trace is essentially a "phonologically null" NP in the surface structure representation of a sentence that has no daughters but is "bound" to the NP that filled that position at some level of underlying structure. In a sense, a trace can be viewed as a "dummy" NP that serves as a placeholder for the NP that earlier filled that position; in the same sense, the trace's binding can be viewed as simply a pointer to that NP. It should be stressed at the outset, however, that a trace is indistinguishable from a normal NP in terms of normal grammatical processes; a trace *is* an NP, even though it is an NP that dominates no lexical material.

There are several reasons for choosing a properly annotated surface structure as a primary output representation for syntactic analysis. Although a deeper analysis is needed to recover the predicate/ argument structure of a sentence [in terms of either Fillmore case relations (Fillmore, 1968) or Gruber/Jackendoff "thematic relations" (Gruber, 1965; Jackendoff, 1972)], phenomena such as focus, theme, pronominal reference, scope of quantification, and the like can be recovered only from the surface structure of a sentence. By means of proper annotation, it is possible to encode in the surface structure the "deep" syntactic information necessary to recover underlying predicate/argument relations, and thus to encode in the same formalism both deep syntactic relations and the surface order needed for pronominal reference and the other phenomena listed above.

Some examples of the use of trace are as follows:

(1a)   What did John give to Sue?
(1b)   What did John give t to Sue?

(1c)   John gave *what* to Sue?
(2a)   The meeting was scheduled for Wednesday.
(2b)   The meeting was scheduled t for Wednesday.

(2c)   ∇ scheduled a *meeting* for Wednesday.
(3a)   John was believed to be happy.
(3b)   John was believed [$_S$ t to be happy].

One use of trace is to indicate the underlying position of the wh-head of a question or relative clause. Thus, the structure built by the parser for (1a) would include the trace shown in (1b), with the trace's binding shown by the line under the sentence. The position of the trace indicates that (1a) has an underlying structure analogous to the overt surface structure of (1c).

Another use of trace is to indicate the underlying position of the surface subject of a passivized clause. For example, (2a) will be parsed into a structure that includes a trace as shown as (2b); this trace indicates that the subject of the passive has the underlying position shown in (2c). The symbol "∇" signifies the fact that the subject position of (2c) is filled by an NP that dominates no lexical structure. (Following Chomsky, I assume that a passive sentence in fact has *no underlying subject,* that an agentive "by NP" prepositional phrase originates as such in underlying structure.) The trace in (3b) indicates that the phrase "to be happy," which the brackets show is really an embedded clause, has an underlying subject that is identical with the surface subject of the matrix S, the clause that dominates the embedded complement. Note that what is conceptually the underlying subject of the embedded clause has been passivized into subject position of the matrix S, a phenomenon commonly called "raising." The analysis of this phenomenon assumed here derives from Chomsky (1973); it is an alternative to the classic analysis which involves "raising" the subject of the embedded clause into object position of the matrix S before passivization (for details of this later analysis see Postal, 1974).

The active node stack (1. deep)

S21 (S DECL MAJOR) / (SS-FINAL)
    NP : (The meeting)
    AUX : (was)
    VP : ↓
C: VP17 (VP) / (SUBJ-VERB)
    VERB : (scheduled)

The buffer

1 : PP14 (PP) : (for Wednesday)
2 : WORD 162 (*. FINALPUNC PUNC) : (.)

Figure 3. Partial analysis of a passive sentence: after the verb has been attached

The passive rule

In this section and the next, I will briefly sketch a solution to the phenomena of passivization and "raising" in the context of a grammar for PARSIFAL. This section will present the Passive rule; the next section will show how this rule, without alteration, handles the "raising" cases.

Let us begin with the parser in the state shown in Figure 3, in the midst of parsing (2a) above. The analysis process for the sentence prior to this point is essentially parallel to the analysis of any simple declarative with one exception: The rule PASSIVE-AUX in packet BUILD-AUX has decoded the passive morphology in the auxiliary and given the auxiliary the feature *passive* (although this feature is not visible in Figure 3). At the point we begin our example, the packet SUBJ-VERB is active.

The packet SUBJ-VERB contains, among other rules, the rule PASSIVE, shown in Figure 4. The pattern of this rule is fulfilled if the auxiliary of the S node dominating the current active node (which will always be a VP node if packet SUBJ-VERB is active) has the feature *passive*, and the S node has not yet been labeled *np-preposed*. (The notation "** C" indicates that this rule matches against the two accessible nodes in the stack, not against the contents of the buffer.) The action of the rule PASSIVE simply creates a trace, sets the binding of the trace to the subject of the dominating S node, and then drops the new trace into the buffer.

The state of the parser after this rule has been executed, with the parser previously in the state in Figure 3, is shown in Figure 5. S21 is now labeled with the feature *np-preposed*, and there is a trace, NP53, in the first buffer position. NP53, as a trace, has no daughters, but is bound to the subject of S21.

{RULE PASSIVE IN SUBJ-VERB
[**c; the aux of the s above c is passive; the s above c is not np-preposed] →
Label the s above c np-preposed.
Create a new np node labeled trace.
Set the binding of c to the np of the s above c.
Drop c.}

Figure 4. Six lines of code captures np-preposing

The active node stack (1. deep)

S21 (NP-PREPOSED S DECL MAJOR) / (SS-FINAL)
    NP : (The meeting)
    AUX : (was)
    VP : ↓
C :   VP17 (VP) / (SUBJ-VERB)
    VERB : (scheduled)

The buffer

1 : NP53 (NP TRACE) : bound to: (The meeting)
2 : PP14 (PP) : (for Wednesday)
3 : WORD 162 (*. FINALPUNC PUNC) : (.)

Figure 5. After PASSIVE has been executed

Now rules will run that will activate the two packets SS-VP and INF-COMP, given that the verb of VP17 is "schedule." These two packets contain rules for parsing simple objects of nonembedded Ss, and infinitive complements, respectively. Two such rules, each of which utilizes an NP immediately following a verb, are given in Figure 6. The rule OBJECTS, in packet SS-VP, picks up an NP after the verb and attaches it to the VP node as a simple object. The rule INF-S-START1, in packet INF-COMP, triggers when an NP is followed by "to" and a tenseless verb; it initiates an infinitive complement and attaches the NP as its subject. (An example of such a sentence is "We wanted John to give a seminar next week.") The rule INF-S-START1 must have a higher priority than OBJECTS because the pattern of OBJECTS is fulfilled by any situation that fulfills the pattern of INF-S-START1; if both rules are in active packets and match, the higher priority of INF-S-START1 will cause it to be run instead of OBJECTS.

Although there is not space to continue the example here in detail, note that the rule OBJECTS will trigger with the parser in the state shown in Figure 5 above, and will attach NP53 as the object of the verb "schedule." OBJECTS is thus totally indifferent both to the fact that NP53 was not a regular NP, but rather a trace, and the fact that NP53

{RULE OBJECTS PRIORITY: 10 IN SS-VP
[=np] →
Attach 1st to c as np.}
{RULE INF-S-START1 PRIORITY: 5 IN INF-COMP
[=np] [=*to,auxverb] [=tnsless] →
Label a new s node sec, inf-s.
Attach 1st to c as np.
Activate parse-aux.}

Figure 6. Two rules that utilize an NP following a verb

did not originate in the input string, but was placed into the buffer by grammatical processes. Whether or not this rule is executed is absolutely unaffected by differences between an active sentence and its passive form; the analysis process for either is identical as of this point in the parsing process. Thus, the analysis process will be exactly parallel in both cases after the PASSIVE rule has been executed. (I remind the reader that the analysis of passive assumed above, following Chomsky, does *not* assume a process of "agent deletion," "subject postposing," or the like.)

Passives in embedded complements: "raising"

The reader may have wondered why PASSIVE drops the trace it creates into the buffer rather than immediately attaching the new trace to the VP node. As we will see below, such a formulation of PASSIVE also correctly analyzes passives like (3a) in the examples above, which involve "raising," but with no additional complexity added to the grammar, correctly capturing an important generalization about English. To show the range of the generalization, the example that we will investigate in this section, sentence (1) below, is yet a level more complex than example (3a) above; its analysis is shown schematically in (2). In this example, which shows simple passive and raising, there are two traces; the first, the subject of the embedded clause, is bound to the subject of the major clause, whereas the second, the object of the embedded S, is bound to the first trace, and is thus ultimately bound to the subject of the higher S as well. Thus the underlying position of the NP "the meeting" can be viewed as being the object position of the embedded S, as shown in (3):

(1) The meeting was believed to have been scheduled for Wednesday.
(2) The meeting was believed [s *t* to have been scheduled *t* for Wednesday]
(3) ∇ believed [s ∇ to have scheduled *the meeting* for Wednesday]

The active node stack (1. deep)

S22 (S DECL MAJOR) / (SS-FINAL)
    NP : (The meeting)
    AUX : (was)
    VP : ↓
C : VP20 (VP) / (SUBJ-VERB)
    VERB : (believed)

The buffer

1 : WORD166 (*TO PREP AUXVERB) : (to)
2 : WORD167 (*HAVE VERB TNSLESS AUXVERB PRES. . .) : (have)

Figure 7. After the verb has been attached

The active node stack (1. deep)

S22 (NP-PREPOSED S DECL MAJOR) / (SS-FINAL)
    NP : (The meeting)
    AUX : (was)
    VP : ↓
C : VP20 (VP) / (SUBJ-VERB)
    VERB : (believed)

The buffer

1 : NP55 (NP TRACE) : bound to: (The meeting)
2 :· WORD 166 (*TO PREP AUXVERB) : (to)
3 : WORD167 (*HAVE VERB TNSLESS AUXVERB PRES . . .) : (have)

Yet unseen words: been scheduled for Wednesday.

Figure 8. After PASSIVE has been executed

We begin our example, once again, right after "believed" has been attached to VP20, the current active node, as shown in Figure 7. Note that the AUX node has been labeled *passive,* although this feature is not shown here.

The packet SUBJ-VERB is now active; the PASSIVE rule contained in this packet now matches and is executed. This rule, as stated above, creates a trace, binds it to the subject of the current clause, and drops the trace into the first cell in the buffer. The resulting state is shown in Figure 8.

Again, rules will now be executed that will activate the packet SS-VP (which contains the rule OBJECTS) and, because "believe" takes infinitive complements, the packet INF-COMP (which contains INF-S-START1), among others. (These rules will also deactivate the packet SUBJ-VERB.) Now the patterns of OBJECTS and INF-S-START1 will both match, and INF-S-START1, shown above in Figure 6, will be

The active node stack (2. deep)

S22 (NP-PREPOSED S DECL MAJOR) / (SS-FINAL)
    NP : (The meeting)
    AUX : (was)
    VP : ↓
VP20 (VP) / (SS-VP THAT-COMP INF-COMP)
    VERB : (believed)
C : S23 (SEC INF-S S) / (PARSE-AUX)
    NP : bound to: (The meeting)

The Buffer

1 : WORD166 (*TO PREP AUXVERB) : (to)
2 : WORD167 (*HAVE VERB TNSLESS AUXVERB PRES . . .) : (have)

Yet unseen words: been scheduled for Wednesday.

Figure 9. After INF-S-START1 has been executed

executed by the interpreter because it has the higher priority. (Note once again that a trace is a perfectly normal NP from the point of view of the pattern-matching process.) This rule now creates a new S node labeled infinitive and attaches the trace NP55 to the new infinitive as its subject. The resulting state is shown in Figure 9.

We are now well on our way to the desired analysis. An embedded infinitive has been initiated, and a trace bound to the subject of the dominating S has been attached as its subject, although no rule has explicitly "lowered" the trace from one clause into the other.

The parser will now proceed exactly as in the previous example. It will build the auxiliary, attach it, and attach the verb "scheduled" to a new VP node. Once again PASSIVE will match and be executed, creating a trace, binding it to the subject of the clause (in this case itself a trace), and dropping the new trace into the buffer. Again the rule OBJECTS will attach the trace NP57 as the object of VP21, and the parse will then be completed by grammatical processes that will not be discussed here. An edited form of the resulting tree structure is shown in Figure 10. A trace is indicated in this tree by giving the terminal string of its ultimate binding in parentheses.

This example demonstrates that the simple formulation of the PASSIVE rule presented above, interacting with other simply formulated grammatical rules for parsing objects and initiating embedded infinitives, allows a trace to be attached either as the object of a verb or as the subject of an embedded infinitive, whichever is the appropriate analysis for a given grammatical situation. Because the PASSIVE rule is formulated in such a way that it drops the trace it

```
(NP-PREPOSED S DECL MAJOR)
NP : (MODIBLE NP DEF DET NP)
     The meeting
AUX : (PASSIVE PAST V13S AUX)
      was
VP : (VP)
     VERB : believed
     NP : (NP COMP)
          S : (NP-PREPOSED SEC INF-S S)
          NP : (NP TRACE) (bound* to: The meeting)
          AUX : (PASSIVE PERF INF AUX)
                to have been
          VP : (VP)
               VERB : scheduled
               NP : (NP TRACE) (bound* to : The meeting)
               PP : (PP)
                    PREP : for
                    NP : (NP TIME DOW)
                         Wednesday
```

Figure 10. The final tree structure

creates into the buffer, later rules, already formulated to trigger on an NP in the buffer, will analyze sentences with NP-preposing exactly the same as those without a preposed subject. Thus, we see that the availability of the buffer mechanism is crucial to capturing this generalization; such a generalization can only be stated by a parser with a mechanism much like the buffer used here.

The grammar interpreter and Chomsky's constraints

Before we turn to a sketch of a computational account of Chomsky's constraints, several important limitations of this work must be enumerated.

First of all, although two of Chomsky's constraints seem to fall out of the grammar interpreter, there seems to be no apparent account of a third, the Propositional Island Constraint, in terms of this mechanism.

Second, Chomsky's formulation of these constraints is intended to apply to all rules of grammar, both syntactic rules (i.e., transformations) and those rules of semantic interpretation that Chomsky calls "rules of construal," a set of shallow semantic rules that govern anaphoric processes (Chomsky, 1977). The discussion here will only touch on purely syntactic phenomena; the question of how rules of semantic interpretation can be meshed with the framework presented in this document has yet to be investigated.

Third, the arguments presented below deal only with English, and in fact depend strongly upon several facts about English syntax, most crucially upon the fact that English is subject-initial. Whether these arguments can be successfully extended to other language types is an open question, and to this extent this work must be considered exploratory.

And finally, I will not show that these constraints must be true *without exception;* as we will see, there are various situations in which the constraints imposed by the grammar interpreter can be circumvented. Most of these situations, though, will be shown to demand much more complex grammar formulations than those typically needed in the grammar so far constructed. This is quite in keeping with the suggestion made by Chomsky (1977) that the constraints are not necessarily without exception, but rather that exceptions will be "highly marked" and therefore will count heavily against any grammar that includes them.

The Specified Subject Constraint

The Specified Subject Constraint (SSC), stated informally, says that no rule may involve two constituents that are Dominated by different cyclic nodes unless the lower of the two is the subject of an S or NP. Thus, no rule may involve constituents X and Y in the following structure if α and β are cyclic nodes and Z is the subject of α, Z distinct from X.

$$[_\beta \ldots Y \ldots [_\alpha Z \ldots X \ldots] \ldots Y \ldots]$$

The SSC explains why the surface subject position of verbs like "seems" and "is certain" which have no underlying subject can be filled only by the subject and not the object of the embedded S: The rule "MOVE NP" is free to shift any NP into the empty subject position, but is constrained by the SSC so that the object of the embedded S cannot be moved out of that clause. This explains why (a) in the following examples, but not (b), can be derived from (c); the derivation of (b) from (c) would violate the SSC.

(a) John seems to like Mary.
(b) Mary seems John to like.
(c) ∇ seems [_s John to like Mary]

In essence, then, the Specified Subject Constraint constrains the rule "MOVE NP" in such a way that only the subject of a clause can be moved out of that clause into a position in a higher S. Thus, if a trace

The active node stack

```
         . . . . .
    S2 . . . / . . .
         . . .
         NP2
         . . .
C :  S1 . . ./. . .
         NP : NP1 (NP TRACE) : bound to NP2
```

Figure 11. NP1 must be attached as the subject of S1 because it is bound to an NP Dominated by a higher S

in an annotated surface structure is bound to an NP Dominated by a higher S, that trace must fill the subject position of the lower clause.

In the remainder of this section I will show that the grammar interpreter constrains grammatical processes in such a way that annotated surface structures constructed by the grammar interpreter will have this same property, given the formulation of the PASSIVE rule that has been presented. In terms of the parsing process, this means that if a trace is "lowered" from one clause to another as a result of a "MOVE NP"-type operation during the parsing process, then it will be attached as the subject of the second clause. To be more precise, if a trace is attached so that it is Dominated by some S node S1, and the trace is bound to an NP Dominated by some other S node S2, then that trace will necessarily be attached so that it fills the subject position of S1. This is depicted in Figure 11.

Looking back at the complex passive example involving "raising" presented in the section on "Raising," we see that the parsing process results in a structure exactly like that shown above. The original point of the example, of course, was that the rather simple PASSIVE rule handles this case without the need for some mechanism to explicitly lower the NP. The PASSIVE rule captures this generalization by dropping the trace it creates into the buffer (after appropriately binding the trace), thus allowing other rules written to handle normal NPs (e.g., OBJECTS and INF-S-START1) to correctly place the trace.

This statement of PASSIVE does more, however, than simply capture a generalization about a specific construction. As I will now argue in detail, the behavior specified by both the Specified Subject Constraint and Subjacency follows almost immediately from this formulation. In Marcus (1977) I argue that this formulation of PASSIVE is the only simple, non–ad hoc, formulation of this rule possible, and that all other rules characterized by the competence rule "MOVE NP" must operate similarly; here, however, I will only show that these constraints follow naturally from this formulation of PASSIVE, leaving

The active node stack

. . . .
C : S123 (S SEC . . .) / . . .

The buffer

. . .
NP 123 (NP TRACE) : bound to NP in S above S123
. . .

Figure 12. Parser state after embedded S created

the question of necessity aside. I will also assume one additional constraint, the *Left-to-Right Constraint,* which will be briefly motivated in the following section as a natural condition on the formulation of a grammar for this mechanism.

> *The Left-to-Right Constraint:* The constituents in the buffer are (almost always) attached to higher level constituents in left-to-right order; i.e., the first constituent in the buffer is (almost always) attached before the second constituent.

I will now show that a trace created by PASSIVE that is bound to an NP in one clause can only serve as the subject of a clause dominated by that first clause.

Given the formulation of PASSIVE, a trace can be "lowered" into one clause from another only by the indirect route of dropping it into the buffer before the subordinate clause node is created, which is exactly how the PASSIVE rule operates. This means that the ordering of the operations is crucially: (1) create a trace and drop it into the buffer; (2) create a subordinate S node; (3) attach the trace to the newly created S node. The key point is that at the time that the subordinate clause node is created and becomes the current active node, the trace must be sitting in the buffer, filling one of the three buffer positions. Thus, the parser will be in the state shown in Figure 12, with the trace, in fact, most likely in the first buffer position.

Now, given the L-to-R Constraint, a trace that is in the buffer at the time that an embedded S node is first created must be one of the first several constituents attached to the S node or its daughter nodes. From the structure of English, we know that the leftmost three constituents of an embedded S node, ignoring topicalized constituents, must be either:

COMP NP AUX

or:

NP AUX [vp VERB . . .]

(The COMP node will dominate flags like "that" or "for" that mark the beginning of a complement clause.) But then, if a trace, itself an NP, is one of the first several constituents attached to an embedded clause, the only position it can fill will be the subject of the clause, exactly the empirical consequence of Chomsky's Specified Subject Constraint in such cases as explained above.

The L-to-R Constraint

Let us now return to the motivation for the L-to-R Constraint. Again, I will not attempt to prove that this constraint must be true, but merely to show why it is plausible.

Empirically, the Left-to-Right Constraint seems to hold for the most part; for the grammar of English discussed in this chapter, and, it would seem, for any grammar of English that attempts to capture the same range of generalizations as this grammar, the constituents in the buffer are utilized in left-to-right order, with a small range of exceptions. This usage is clearly not enforced by the grammar interpreter as presently implemented; it is quite possible to write a set of grammar rules that specifically ignores a constituent in the buffer until some arbitrary point in the clause, though such a set of rules would be highly ad hoc. However, there rarely seems to be a need to remove a constituent other than the first constituent in the buffer.

The one exception to the L-to-R Constraint seems to be that a constituent C_i may be attached before the constituent to its left, C_{i-1}, if C_i does not appear in surface structure in its underlying position (or, if one prefers, in its unmarked position), and if its removal from the buffer reestablishes the unmarked order of the remaining constituents, as in the case of auxilliary inversion. To capture this notion, the L-to-R Constraint can be restated as follows: All constituents must be attached to higher-level constituents according to the left-to-right order of constituents in the unmarked case of that constituent's structure.

This reformulation is interesting in that it would be a natural consequence of the operation of the grammar interpreter if packets were associated with the phrase structure rules of an explicit "base component," and these rules were used as templates to build up the structure assigned by the grammar interpreter. A packet of grammar rules would then be explicitly associated with each symbol on the right-hand side of each phrase structure rule. A constituent of a given type would then be constructed by activating the packets associated with each node type of the appropriate phrase structure rule in left-to-right order. Because these base rules would reflect the unmarked l-to-r order of constituents, the constraint suggested here would then simply fall out of the interpreter mechanism.

Subjacency

Before turning to the Subjacency Principle, a few auxiliary technical terms need to be defined: If we can trace a path up the tree from a given node X to a given node Y, then we say *X is dominated by Y,* or equivalently, *Y dominates X.* If Y dominates X, and no other nodes intervene (i.e., X is a daughter of Y), then *Y immediately (or directly)* dominates X (Akmajian and Heny, 1975). One nonstandard definition will prove useful: I will say that if Y dominates X, and Y is a cyclic node (i.e., an S or NP node), and there is no other cyclic node Z such that Y dominates Z and Z dominates X (i.e., there is no intervening cyclic node Z between Y and X), then *Y Dominates X.*

The principle of Subjacency, informally stated, says that no rule can involve constituents that are separated by more than one cyclic node. Let us say that a node X *is subjacent to* a node Y if there is at most one cyclic node (i.e., at most one NP or S node) between the cyclic node that Dominates Y and the node X. Given this definition, the Subjacency principle says that no rule can involve constituents that are not subjacent.

The Subjacency principle implies that movement rules are constrained so that they can move a constituent only into positions that the constituent was subjacent to, that is, only within the clause (or NP) in which it originates, or into the clause (or NP) that Dominates that clause (. . .). This means that if α, β, and ϵ in the following display are cyclic nodes, no rule can move a constituent from position X to either of the positions Y, where $[_\alpha . . . X . . .]$ is distinct from $[_\alpha X]$.

$$[_\epsilon . . . Y . . . [_\beta . . . [_\alpha . . . X . . .] . . .] . . . Y . . .]$$

Subjacency implies that if a constituent is to be "lifted" up more than one level in constituent structure, this operation must be done by repeated operations. Thus, to use one of Chomsky's examples, the sentence given in (a) below, with a deep structure analogous to (b), must be derived as follows (assuming that "is certain," like "seems," has no subject in underlying structure): The deep structure must first undergo a movement operation that results in a structure analogous to (c), and then another movement operation that results in (d), each of these movements leaving a trace as shown. That (c) is in fact an intermediate structure is supported by the existence of sentences such as (e), which purportedly result when the ∇ in the matrix S is replaced by the lexical item "it," and the embedded S is tensed rather than infinitival. The structure given in (f) is ruled out as a possible annotated surface structure because the single trace could only be left if the NP "John" were moved in one fell swoop from its underlying position to its position in surface structure, which would violate Subjacency.

(a)   John seems to be certain to win.
(b)   ∇ seems [$_s$ ∇ to be certain [$_s$ John to win]]
(c)   John seems [$_s$ John to be certain [$_s$ t to win]]
(d)   John seems [$_s$ t to be certain [$_s$ t to win]]
(e)   It seems that John is certain to win.
(f)   John seems [$_s$ ∇ to be certain [$_s$ t to win]]

Having stated Subjacency in terms of the abstract competence theory of generative grammar, I now will show that a parsing correlate of Subjacency follows from the structure of the grammar interpreter. Specifically, I will show that there are only limited cases in which a trace generated by a "MOVE-NP" process can be "lowered" more than one clause; that is, that a trace created and bound while any given S is current must almost always be attached either to that S or to an S that is Dominated by that S.

Let us begin by examining what it would mean to lower a trace more than one clause. Given that a trace can only be "lowered" by dropping it into the buffer and then creating a subordinate S node, as discussed in the "SSC" section, lowering a trace more than one clause necessarily implies the following sequence of events, depicted in Figure 13: First, a trace NP1 must (a) be created with some S node, S1, as the current S, (b) be bound to some NP Dominated by that S, and then (c) be dropped into the buffer. By definition, it will be inserted into the first cell in the buffer. (This is shown in Figure 13a.) Then a second S, S2, must be created, supplanting S1 as the current S, and then yet a third S, S3, must be created, becoming the current S. During all these steps, the trace NP1 remains sitting in the buffer. Finally, NP1 is attached under S3 (Figure 13b). By the Specified Subject Constraint, NP1 must then attach to S3 as its subject.

But this sequence of events is highly unlikely. The essence of the argument is this:

Nothing in the buffer can change between the time that S2 is created and S3 is created if NP1 remains in the buffer. NP1, like any other node that is dropped from the active node stack into the buffer, is inserted into the first buffer position. But then, by the L-to-R Constraint, nothing to the right of NP1 can be attached to a higher-level constituent until NP1 is attached. (One can show that it is most un-

(a) NP1 is dropped into the buffer while S1 is the current S.

The Active Node Stack

. . . . .
S1 . . . / . . .

The Buffer

1st: NP1 (NP TRACE) : bound to NP Dominated by S1
. . .

(b) After S2 and S3 are created, NP1 is attached to S3 as its subject (by the SSC).

The Active Node Stack

. . . . .
S1 . . . / . . .
S2 . . . / . . .
C: S3 . . . / . . .
NP1 (NP TRACE) : bound to NP Dominated by S1

Figure 13. Lowering a trace more than one clause

likely that any constituents will enter to the left of NP1 after it is dropped into the buffer, but I will suppress this detail here; the full argument is included in Marcus, 1977.)

But if the contents of the buffer do not change between the creation of S2 and S3, then what can possibly motivate the creation of both S2 and S3? The contents of the buffer must necessarily provide clear evidence that both of these clauses are present because, by the Determinism Hypothesis, the parser must be correct if it initiates a constituent. Thus, the same three constituents in the buffer must provide convincing evidence not only for the creation of S2 but also for S3. Furthermore, if NP1 is to become the subject of S3, and if S2 Dominates S3, then it would seem that the constituents that follow NP1 in the buffer must also be constituents of S3 because S3 must be completed before it is dropped from the active node stack and constituents can then be attached to S2. But then S2 must be created *entirely* on the basis of evidence provided by the constituents of another clause (unless S3 has fewer than three constituents). Thus, it would seem that the contents of the buffer cannot provide evidence for the presence of both clauses unless the presence of S3, by itself, is enough to provide confirming evidence for the presence of S2. This would be the case only if there were, say, a clausal construction that could only appear (perhaps in a particular environment) as the initial constituent of a higher clause. In this case, if there are such constructions, a violation of Subjacency should be possible.

   With the one exception just mentioned, there is no motivation for creating two clauses in such a situation, and thus the initiation of only one such clause can be motivated. But if only one clause is initiated before NP1 is attached, then NP1 must be attached to this clause, and this clause is necessarily subjacent to the clause that Dominates the NP to which it is bound. Thus, the grammar interpreter will behave as if it enforces the Subjacency Constraint.

   As a concluding point, it is worthy of note that although the grammar interpreter appears to behave exactly as if it were constrained by the Subjacency principle, it is in fact constrained by a version of the Clausemate Constraint! [The Clausemate Constraint, long tacitly assumed by linguists but first explicitly stated, I believe, by Postal (1964), states that a transformation can only involve constituents that are Dominated by the same cyclic node. This constraint is at the heart of Postal's attack on the constraints that are discussed above and his argument for a "raising" analysis.] The grammar interpreter prevents grammar rules from examining any node in the active node stack higher than the current cyclic node, which is to say that it can only examine clausemates. The trick is that a trace is created and bound while it is a "clausemate" of the NP to which it is bound, in that the current cyclic node at that time is the node to which that NP is attached. The trace is then dropped into the buffer and another S node is created, thereby destroying the clausemate relationship. The trace is then attached to this new S node. Thus, in a sense, the trace *is* lowered from one clause to another. The crucial point is that although this lowering goes on as a result of the operation of the grammar interpreter, it is only implicitly lowered, in that (1) the trace was never *attached* to the higher S and (2) it is *not* dropped into the buffer because of any realization that it must be "lowered"; in fact, it may end up attached as a clausemate of the NP to which it is bound – as the passive examples we examined make clear. The trace is simply dropped into the buffer because its grammatical function is not clear, and the creation of the second S follows from other independently motivated grammatical processes. From the point of view of this processing theory, we can have our cake and eat it too; to the extent that it makes sense to map results from the realm of processing into the realm of competence, in a sense *both* the clausemate/"raising" and the Subjacency positions are correct.

Evidence for the Determinism Hypothesis

   In closing, I would like to show that the properties of the grammar interpreter crucial to capturing the behavior of Chomsky's constraints were originally motivated by the Determinism Hypothesis, and thus, to some extent, the Determinism Hypothesis explains Chomsky's constraints.

The strongest form of such an argument, of course, would be to show that: (a) either (i) the grammar interpreter accounts for *all* of Chomsky's constraints in a manner that is conclusively universal, or (ii) the constraints that it will not account for are wrong; and (b) the properties of the grammar interpreter that were crucial for this proof were *forced* by the Determinism Hypothesis. If such an argument could be made, it would show that the Determinism Hypothesis provides a natural processing account of the linguistic data characterized by Chomsky's constraints, giving strong confirmation to the Determinism Hypothesis.

I have shown none of the above, and thus my claims must be proportionately more modest. I have argued only that important subcases of Chomsky's constraints follow from the grammar interpreter, and although I can show that the Determinism Hypothesis strongly *motivates* the mechanisms from which these arguments follow, I cannot show necessity. The extent to which this argument provides evidence for the Determinism Hypothesis must thus be left to the reader; no objective measure exists for such matters.

The ability to drop a trace into the buffer is at the heart of the arguments presented here for Subjacency and the SSC as consequences of the functioning of the grammar interpreter; this is the central operation upon which the above arguments are based. But the buffer itself, and the fact that a constituent can be dropped into the buffer if its grammatical function is uncertain, are directly motivated by the Determinism Hypothesis. Given this, it is fair to claim that if Chomsky's constraints follow from the operation of the grammar interpreter, then they are strongly linked to the Determinism Hypothesis. If Chomsky's constraints are in fact true, then the arguments presented in this paper provide solid evidence in support of the Determinism Hypothesis.

NOTES

This paper summarizes one result presented in my Ph.D. thesis; I would like to express my gratitude to the many people who contributed to the technical content of that work: Jon Allen, my thesis advisor, to whom I owe a special debt of thanks, Ira Goldstein, Seymour Papert, Bill Martin, Bob Moore, Chuck Rieger, Mike Genesereth, Gerry Sussman, Mike Brady, Craig Thiersch, Beth Levin, Candy Bullwinkle, Kurt VanLehn, Dave McDonald, and Chuck Rich.

This paper describes research done at the Artificial Intelligence Laboratory of the Massachusetts Institute of Technology. Support for the work reported here was provided through a grant by the Defence Advanced Research Projects Agency to the Artificial Intelligence Laboratory.

REFERENCES

Akmajian, A., and Heny, F. 1975. *An Introduction to the Principles of Transformational Syntax*. Cambridge, Mass.: The M.I.T. Press.
Bresnan, J. W. 1976. "Evidence for a Theory of Unbounded Transformations." *Linguistic Analysis* 2:353.
Chomsky, N. 1973. "Conditions on Transformations." In S. Anderson and P. Kiparsky, eds. *A Festschrift for Morris Halle*. New York: Holt, Rinehart and Winston.
Chomsky, N. 1975. *Reflections on Language*. New York: Pantheon.
Chomsky, N. 1976. "Conditions on Rules of Grammar." *Linguistic Analysis* 2:303.
Chomsky, N. 1977. "On Wh-Movement." In A. Akmajian, P. Culicover, and T. Wasow, eds. *Formal Syntax*. New York: Academic Press.
Fillmore, C. J. 1968. "The Case for Case." In E. Bach and R. T. Harms, eds. *Universals in Linguistic Theory*. New York: Holt, Rinehart and Winston.
Gruber, J. S. 1965. "Studies in Lexical Relations." Unpublished Ph.D. thesis, Massachusetts Institute of Technology.
Jackendoff, R. S. 1972. *Semantic Interpretation in Generative Grammar*. Cambridge, Mass.: The M.I.T. Press.
Marcus, M. P. 1977. "A Theory of Syntactic Recognition for Natural Language." Unpublished Ph.D. thesis. Massachusetts Institute of Technology.
Marcus, M. P. 1978. "Capturing Linguistic Generalizations in a Parser for English." In the *Proceedings of the 2nd National Conference of the Canadian Society for Computational Studies of Intelligence*. Toronto.
Newell, A., and Simon, H. A. 1972. *Human Problem Solving*. Englewood Cliffs, N.J.: Prentice-Hall.
Postal, P. M. 1964. "Constituent Structure." Special supplement to *International Journal of American Linguistics*.
Postal, P. M. 1974. *On Raising*. Cambridge, Mass.: The M.I.T. Press.
Pratt, V. R. 1973. "Top-Down Operator Precedence." In the *Proceedings of the SIGACT/SIGPLAN Symposium on Principles of Programming Languages*. Boston.
Ross, J. 1967. "Constraints on Variables in Syntax." Ph.D. thesis, Massachusetts Institute of Technology, Department of Linguistics.
Sager, N. 1973. "The String Parser for Scientific Literature." In R. Rustin, ed. *Natural Language Processing*. New York: Algorithmic Press.
Winograd, T. 1971. "Procedures as a Representation for Data in a Computer Program for Understanding Natural Language." Project MAC-TR 84, Massachusetts Institute of Technology.
Woods, W. A. 1970. "Transition Network Grammars for Natural Language Analysis." *Communications of the ACM* 13:591.

8

Interactions of modality and negation in English

GEORGE A. MILLER and DONNA M. KWILOSZ

In all standard systems of modal logic, the necessity operator L and the possibility operator M are interdefinable. That is, if L is taken as primitive, Mp can be defined as $-L-p$, or if M is taken as primitive, Lp can be defined as $-M-p$. For intuitive support, students are often introduced to this idea with examples phrased in natural language. Take p to be the proposition expressed by the declarative sentence *The sky is blue*. Then these equivalences can be read as follows: *It's possible for the sky to be blue* is equivalent to *It isn't necessary for the sky not to be blue*, and *It's necessary for the sky to be blue* is equivalent to *It isn't possible for the sky not to be blue*. This is not the only way to render these logical forms as English sentences, but it reflects the logician's explicit division of modal propositions into two parts: a modality operator and a propositional operand.

When modal propositions are negated, the scope of the negation can be either broad or narrow. Negation *de dicto* ($-Lp$ or $-Mp$) is the contradictory of the affirmative, whereas negation *de re* ($L-p$ or $M-p$) is the contrary of the affirmative. This difference is also assumed to be reflected in the English sentences: In *It isn't necessary for the sky to be blue*, for example, the scope of *not* is said to be the entire sentence, whereas in *It's necessary for the sky not to be blue* the scope of *not* is said to be limited to the propositional component. From the axiom of interdefinability, of course, it follows that $L-p$ is equivalent to $-Mp$, and $-Lp$ is equivalent to $M-p$. These equivalences are also generally considered to be reflected in the corresponding English sentences: *It's necessary for the sky not to be blue*, for example, would be taken as equivalent in meaning to *It isn't possible for the sky to be blue*.

The logical equivalences are, of course, true by definition. The corresponding equivalences between English sentences, if true, represent empirical facts about English. The first experiment to be described is an attempt to determine whether native speakers of English, in ignorance of the logical formalisms, do judge sentences with *necessary* and *possible* to be equivalent according to the pattern that follows from the assumption of interdefinability.

Experiment 1: Interdefinability

The method of triads (Romney and D'Andrade, 1964) was used to determine the judged similarity of meaning among sentences containing *not necessary, necessary not, not possible,* and *possible not.* With this method, the expressions to be compared are presented to judges three at a time. If there are N expressions, there will be $N!/3!\ (N-3)!$ possible triads; this function grows rapidly as N increases, and therefore the method is convenient only when small numbers of expressions are to be compared. With four sentences, however, there are only four triads to be presented.

Twenty adult, monolingual speakers of English were asked to read each triad carefully and then to mark the sentence that was most different in meaning from the other two (an instruction that is sometimes called "odd man out"). The logical forms, the corresponding sentences, and the number of judges marking each sentence as different from the other two are as follows, for all four triads:

$-Lp$:	It isn't necessary for him to attend the meeting.	14
$L-p$:	It's necessary for him not to attend the meeting.	5
$-Mp$:	It isn't possible for him to attend the meeting.	1
$-Lp$:	It isn't necessary for him to attend the meeting.	0
$L-p$:	It's necessary for him not to attend the meeting.	20
$M-p$:	It's possible for him not to attend the meeting.	0
$-Lp$:	It isn't necessary for him to attend the meeting.	1
$-Mp$:	It isn't possible for him to attend the meeting.	19
$M-p$:	It's possible for him not to attend the meeting.	0
$L-p$:	It's necessary for him not to attend the meeting.	4
$-Mp$:	It isn't possible for him to attend the meeting.	0
$M-p$:	It's possible for him not to attend the meeting.	16

From the middle two triads we see that 39 out of a possible 40 judgments were that the (theoretically interdefinable) pair corresponding to $-Lp$ and $M-p$ are more similar in meaning to each other than either is to the other sentences. From the first and last triads we see that 30 out of a possible 40 judgments were that the other pair, corresponding to $L-p$ and $-Mp$, are more similar in meaning to each other than either is to the other two sentences. Only 11 out of the total of 80 judgments violated the assumption of interdefinability; 9 of these violations consisted of taking $L-p$ to be the semantically odd member of a triad.

Majority vote favored the hypothesis of interdefinability as expressed by these English sentences. A minority, however, did not consider *necessary not* to be equivalent to *not possible.*

Modal verbs of English

By syntactic criteria, there are nine modal verbs in English: *can, could, may, might, must, shall, should, will,* and *would.* Two others, *need* and *dare,* appear as modals in negative and interrogative contexts. Other verbs are commonly used to express intuitively similar meanings, and because the present concern is with semantics rather than syntax, six of these were also included in the study: *has to, has got to, had better, ought to, is to,* and *is going to.*

Discussions of the meanings of these verbs generally divide them into three groups, expressing possibility, necessity, and prediction. It is also generally assumed that each of these three groups can be used in two senses, which are sometimes called the root sense and the epistemic sense. For example, *can* expresses either permissibility (root sense) or possibility (epistemic sense). Thus, the three groups can be labeled: possible/permissible, necessary/obligatory, and predictive/volitional (see, e.g., Leech, 1971). Whenever modals are combined with other auxiliary verbs (*have, be*), the epistemic interpretation is salient.

Disagreement has been expressed as to whether root and epistemic interpretations reflect different senses of each modal verb, or whether the difference arises from different contexts of use. No attempt was made to resolve this dispute in the present experiments. The sentence *He attends the meeting* was taken as the propositional component precisely because its modal forms are ambiguous between these two interpretations. That is, it was assumed that, whichever interpretation a judge adopted, the interaction of the modal verb and negation would be the same. This assumption proved incorrect in one case (*may*), which will be discussed below.

Before considering the interaction of these verbs with negation, however, the assumption that they fall naturally into three broad semantic groups was tested.

Experiment 2: Sorting isolated modals

The method of sorting (Miller, 1969) was used to explore the judged similarity of meanings for modal and related verbs in isolation (not in sentential contexts). The words *can, could, had better, has to, is, is going to, is to, may, might, must, ought to, shall, should, will,* and *would* were typed

Table 1. *Number of judges (out of 20) who judged each pair of expressions similar enough in meaning to be put in the same pile*

	OUGHT TO	SHOULD	HAD BETTER	MUST	HAS TO	IS TO	SHALL	IS GOING TO	WILL	IS	WOULD	MIGHT	MAY	COULD	CAN
OUGHT TO	(2)														
SHOULD	17														
HAD BETTER	10	9	(1)												
MUST	5	4	13												
HAS TO	5	4	14	19											
IS TO	3	3	4	5	5	(7)									
SHALL	1	2	1	4	4	6	(1)								
IS GOING TO	1		1	2	2	5	13	(1)							
WILL				2	1	4	13	16	(1)						
IS				1	1	4	1	2	1	(15)					
WOULD	2						1	1	1	1	(10)				
MIGHT	1										5	(1)			
MAY	1										6	15			
COULD	2					1					5	8	4	(2)	
CAN	1								1	1	2	2	5	11	(4)

on cards, one per card, and 20 monolingual English-speaking judges were asked to sort the 15 cards into piles on the basis of similarity of meaning. No limit on the number of piles or the number of words per pile was imposed.

The pooled results for all judges are shown in Table 1, where the entries in each cell give the number of judges who put the word in that row together in the same pile with the word in that column. It is assumed that these numbers can be taken as indicating the subjective proximities of the meanings of all the possible pairs of expressions. For example, 19 of the 20 judges put *must* and *has to* in the same pile, which can be taken as evidence that these verbs are very similar in meaning, whereas nobody put *must* and *can* in the same pile, which can be taken as evidence that they are different in meaning. The matrix is symmetrical (you cannot put word A in the same pile with word B without also putting B in the same pile with A), and therefore only half of the total matrix is presented in Table 1. The parenthetical entries on the main diagonal show the numbers of judges who put each word in a pile by itself.

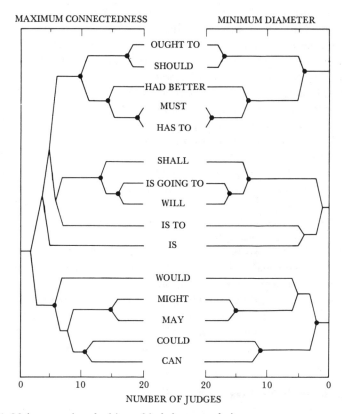

MAXIMUM CONNECTEDNESS   MINIMUM DIAMETER

NUMBER OF JUDGES

Figure 1. Major groupings by hierarchical cluster analysis

Although major groupings can be discovered from inspection of Table 1, a variety of multidimensional scaling techniques are available to make the underlying structure more apparent. The technique used to produce the graphical representation in Figure 1 was Johnson's (1967) hierarchical clustering analysis. This analysis solves the clustering problem twice: One solution maximizes the estimated connectedness between words; the other solution minimizes it. If the data represent a true hierarchy, the two solutions are identical; the extent to which they differ can be taken as a crude indicator of the extent to which the data must be forced into hierarchical form. In Figure 1, those clusters obtained by both solutions are indicated by filled circles at the corresponding nodes of the hierarchy.

The discrepancies between the two solutions can be traced to *is*, which is not a modal verb and which 15 judges put in a separate pile by itself, and to *would*, which also seemed to pose a problem because 10 judges put it in a separate pile.

If we take the minimum diameter analysis (right half of Figure 1) as the more conservative indicator of clustering, there appear to be three major clusters. *Ought to, should, had better, must,* and *has to* are the necessary/obligatory group; *shall, is going to, will,* and *is to* are the predictive/volitional group (*is* was put with *is to* by only four judges); *might, may, can,* and *could* are the possible/permissible group (*would* should be in the predictive/volitional group, according to most linguistic analyses).

It is gratifying that so crude a method yields results corresponding to any serious classification. To the extent that these results confirm the usual semantic analysis of these words, they also confirm that subjective judgments of linguistically untrained people can be used to explore such semantic questions.

Although the results show that people do not spontaneously put predictive/volitional words together with either the necessary/ obligatory or the possible/permissible groups, it is not difficult to devise a two-choice situation in which they are forced to assign them to one group or the other. The advantage of doing so would be that the three semantic groups could be reduced to two, and we might hope to find that all of the modals, like *L* and *M*, are interdefinable.

Experiment 3: Necessary or possible?

Triads were presented to 30 monolingual English-speaking judges. Each triad consisted of one sentence with a verb expressing a modal concept, one sentence with *necessary*, and one sentence with *possible*. For example, they were given the triad:

> He shall attend the meeting.
> It's necessary for him to attend the meeting.
> It's possible for him to attend the meeting.

As before, judges marked the sentence they thought was most different in meaning from the other two.

The verbs that were used in the first sentence were *dare, had better, has got to, has to, is going to, is to, need, ought to,* and *shall*. The second and third sentences were the same in every triad. The only exceptions were *dare* and *need*, which were presented in the interrogative form; for example:

> Dare he attend the meeting?
> Is it necessary for him to attend the meeting?
> Is it possible for him to attend the meeting?

Table 2. *Member of triad marked most different in meaning* ($N = 30$)

	Verb	Necessary	Possible
dare	5	21	4
had better	0	2	28
has got to	0	0	30
has to	0	0	30
is going to	3	10	17
is to	0	2	28
need	0	0	30
ought to	1	4	25
shall	2	7	21

The results are summarized in Table 2, where the number of judges marking each member of each triad is given. They were unanimous in judging *has got to, has to,* and *need* as verbs of necessity; *had better* and *ought to* can also be included in this group. The three that are members of the predictive/volitional group in Figure 1 – *is going to, is to,* and *shall* – are also verbs of necessity by the majority vote, although *is going to* might better be classed as ambiguous. In general, however, when forced to choose, most people assimilate the predictive/volitional group into the necessary/obligatory group. *Dare* is the only modal tested that could be called a verb of possibility; the judges were far from unanimous, but the scatter (five judges voting that *Dare he attend the meeting?* is most different in meaning) suggests that some of the judges may have been unfamiliar with the use of *dare* as a modal auxiliary.

On the basis of these results (and other data not reported here), we propose the following classification of verbs expressing modal concepts:

> Necessity: *had better, has got to, has to, (is going to), (is to), must, need, ought to, (shall), (should), (will), (would)*
> Possibility: *can, could, dare, may, might*

where those in parentheses would usually be classified as a separate predictive/volitional group.

Negation

Although the scope of negation is relatively clear in modal sentences with *necessary* or *possible*, it is not immediately obvious in sentences with modal verbs. The problem can be illustrated with *can't* and *mustn't*.

We have two forms of negation of modal propositions, *de dicto* and *de re*, but only one natural way to introduce negation in a sentence with a modal verb. By artifice, however, we can contrive ways to indicate the scope of negation in sentences with modal verbs. For example, let the nonmodal version *p* be *He leaves,* and take its negation *−p* to be *He stays* (rather than *He doesn't leave*). Then we can take *He can stay* as negation *de re,* or *can −p.* In order to form negation *de dicto,* we can use a clumsy phrase from logic texts: *It is not the case that he can leave* or *−can p.* Now consider the triad:

> *can't p:* He can't leave.
> *−can p:* It's not the case that he can leave.
> *can −p:* He can stay.

Most people agree that *can't p* is more similar to *−can p; can't* is a case of negation *de dicto.* If we construct the same triad for *mustn't:*

> *mustn't p:* He mustn't leave.
> *−must p:* It's not the case that he must leave.
> *must −p:* He must stay.

we obtain the opposite result. *Mustn't p* is more similar to *must −p,* which is negation *de re.*

The same contrast can be shown with triads based on *possible* and *necessary.* Because *can* is a verb of possibility, the appropriate triad for it would be:

> *can't p:* He can't attend the meeting.
> *−Mp:* It isn't possible for him to attend the meeting.
> *M−p:* It's possible for him not to attend the meeting.

where again *can't p* is most similar to *−Mp* (negation *de dicto*). And, because *must* is a verb of necessity, the appropriate triad for it would be:

> *mustn't p:* He mustn't attend the meeting.
> *−Lp:* It isn't necessary for him to attend the meeting.
> *L−p:* It's necessary for him not to attend the meeting.

where again *mustn't p* is most similar to *L−p* (negation *de re*).

The difference in the scope of negation for *can't* and *mustn't* has frequently been noted. From the assumption of the interdefinability of *L* and *M,* it follows that *L−p* is equivalent to *−Mp,* and thus, if the English paraphrases conform to the same logic, that *He can't attend the meeting* means the same as *He mustn't attend the meeting.* As long as we think of these sentences as being used to express a prohibition (root sense), their equivalence is intuitively acceptable. If *can't* is interpreted epistemically, however, the equivalence is less compelling: *He can't* *have attended the meeting* seems stronger than *He mustn't have attended the meeting.* Or, again, *You can't satisfy her insatiable lust* has an interpretation that *You mustn't satisfy her insatiable lust* lacks (Wertheimer, 1972).

The subtleties of these words should not be overlooked, but the present concern is to characterize them broadly by judgments, not of synonymy, but of similarity. We will accept the difference in scope, therefore, without subscribing to the much stronger claim that all the meanings of modal verbs are captured adequately by the axioms of modal logic.

Experiment 4: *De dicto or de re?*

The scope of negation was tested for all the modal verbs and for six verbs expressing related modal ideas by asking 30 monolingual English-speaking judges to compare the negated verbs in triads formed with negated sentences containing *possible* or *necessary*. Those verbs judged in Experiment 3 to be verbs of necessity were tested in triads with *not necessary* and *necessary not;* those that were judged to be verbs of possibility were tested in triads with *not possible* and *possible not.* For example, *ought to* was taken to be a verb of necessity, so *oughtn't to* was tested in the triad:

> He oughtn't to attend the meeting.
> It isn't necessary for him to attend the meeting.
> It's necessary for him not to attend the meeting.

The results are summarized separately in Table 3 for the verbs of necessity and for the verbs of possibility. Those judged as negation *de dicto* are *don't have to, haven't got to,* and *needn't* of the verbs of necessity, and *cannot, can't, couldn't,* and *dare not* of the verbs of possibility. Those judged as negation *de re* are *had better not, is not to, must not, mustn't, oughtn't to, shall not,* and *shouldn't* of the verbs of necessity, and *might not* of the verbs of possibility. There is apparently a tendency for verbs of necessity to take *de re* negation, and for verbs of possibility to take *de dicto* negation, but there are exceptions in both cases.

The interesting cases are those for which judges did not agree as to the scope of negation. Their disagreements over *isn't going to, won't,* and *wouldn't* are not surprising because they are verbs of prediction/ volition that were forced into the necessary/obligatory group. Consider the following triad:

> *won't p:* He won't go.
> *−will p:* It's not the case that he will go.
> *will −p:* He will stay.

Table 3. *Member of triad marked most different in meaning* $(N = 30)$

Verbs	Verb + neg	Not necessary	Necessary not
Of necessity			
don't have to	0	0	30
had better not	2	27	1
haven't got to	0	1	29
is not to	1	28	1
isn't going to	4	14	12
must not	0	30	0
mustn't	1	29	0
needn't	0	1	29
oughtn't to	0	25	5
shall not	1	25	4
shouldn't	0	28	2
won't	3	17	10
wouldn't	7	14	9
Of possibility			
cannot	0	0	30
can't	0	0	30
couldn't	0	0	30
dare not	5	3	22
may not	1	19	10
might not	0	25	5

If *won't* is interpreted in its predictive sense, all three sentences seem to express the same idea; the same can be said about *isn't going to* and *wouldn't*. In this sense, therefore, there is no interaction between the verb and the location of the negative. Compare this situation with *isn't*:

> *isn't p:* He isn't going.
> *—is p:* It's not the case that he's going.
> *is —p:* He's staying.

Here, too, there is no interaction; all three sentences express the same idea. Unlike the verbs of necessity and possibility, the placement of the negative relative to *will* or *be* does not have differential semantic effects.

When *won't* is used to describe intentions (root sense), however, many people feel a difference in meaning between *He won't go* (he refuses to go) and both *It's not the case that he will go* and *He will stay* (he intends to stay). Note, however, that on this volitional interpretation *won't* is neither negation *de dicto* nor *de re*, but seems to have a unique sense of its own. On either the predictive or the volitional interpretation, therefore, *will* behaves more like the nonmodal copula *be* than like the modals *can* or *must*. Semantically, *will* seems to be simply the predictive form of the copula (but see Binnick, 1971).

These observations account for the judgments of *won't, isn't going to,* and *wouldn't* in Table 3, but they raise a new question about *shall not* and *shouldn't*. *Shall* and *should* are also members of the predictive/volitional group, yet the judges were in substantial agreement that they express negation *de re*. Why do *shall* and *should* not behave like *will* and *would*? *Shouldn't*, like *won't*, seems to have picked up a unique meaning of its own, very similar to *oughtn't*, which is one of the necessary/obligatory group. But what about *shall*? Compare:

> *shall not p:* He shall not go.
> *−shall p:* It's not the case that he shall go.
> *shall −p:* He shall stay.

where there is relatively little to choose between the three sentences, with the type of triad that was used in the experiment:

> *shall not p:* He shall not go.
> *−Lp:* It isn't necessary for him to go.
> *L−p:* It's necessary for him not to go.

where most judges agreed that *−Lp* is different in meaning from the other two sentences. In the first triad, the sentences are most easily compared if *shall* is given the predictive sense of *will;* in the second triad, in order to compare *shall* with *necessary* it is easiest to give *shall* an obligatory interpretation: *I'll not allow him to go.*

It seems, therefore, that *shall* and *should* both have more than one sense: One sense would classify them in the predictive/volitional group, and another would classify them in the necessary/obligatory group. When the predictive/volitional sense is salient, there is no semantic effect of the placement of the negative, but when the necessary/obligatory sense is salient, they take negation *de re*.

The judges also failed to agree on the scope of negation for *may not*. Because *may* is a member of the possible/permissible group, this ambiguity cannot be explained in the same way as the ambiguity of *will*. Consider the triad used in the experiment:

> *may not p:* He may not attend the meeting.
> *−Mp:* It isn't possible for him to attend the meeting.
> *M−p:* It's possible for him not to attend the meeting.

The choice will be for negation *de dicto* if *may* is taken in its root sense (*not permissible*), but for negation *de re* if *may* is taken in its epistemic sense (*possible not*). *May* clearly violates the assumption that the scope of negation is independent of the sense assigned to it.

Some of the ambiguity attending *may* probably arises from the fact that its epistemic sense is usually better paraphrased by *possible that* than by *possible for–to*. The epistemic sense of *A student may own a car*, for example, is *It's possible that a student owns a car;* the root sense is closer to *It's permissible for a student to own a car*. If the following triad had been tested:

> *may not p:* The pilot may not own a plane.
> *–Mp:* It isn't possible that the pilot owns a plane.
> *M–p:* It's possible that the pilot doesn't own a plane.

it is likely that the judges would have voted unanimously for negation *de re*. But if the following triad had been tested:

> *may not p:* The pilot may not own a plane.
> *–Mp:* It isn't permissible for the pilot to own a plane.
> *M–p:* It's permissible for the pilot not to own a plane.

it is likely that the judges would have voted unanimously for negation *de dicto*. Judgments of similarity are sensitive to context. Using *possible that* in the experimental triad favors the epistemic interpretation and negation *de re;* using *permissible for–to* favors the root sense and negation *de dicto*.

If this account is correct for *may not*, why is it not needed also for *might not*? When presented with the triad:

> *might not p:* He might not attend the meeting.
> *–Mp:* It isn't possible for him to attend the meeting.
> *M–p:* It's possible for him not to attend the meeting.

only 5 of 30 judges voted for negation *de dicto* (marked *M–p* as the "odd man out"). Apparently the epistemic sense is more salient for *might not* than for *may not*. The root sense can be made salient, however, in such contexts as *From that time on it was agreed that, without the consent of parliament, the king might not levy any taxes*. In principle, therefore, *might not* also has a *not permissible* sense. In use, however, this sense seldom occurs.

From these data it is clear that English modals interact with negation in complex ways that simply have to be learned by speakers of the language – a fact that causes much trouble for people learning English as a second language, and complicates the work of anyone trying to program a computer to answer questions phrased in English.

Table 4. *Tentative classification of English modals*

	Modality	
Scope of negation	Possible/ permissible	Necessary/ obligatory
Broad (*de dicto*)	*can* *could* *dare* *may$_{root}$*	*need* (*has to*) (*has got to*)
Narrow (*de re*)	*may$_e$* *might*	*must* *shall$_{root}$* *should$_{root}$* (*is to*) (*ought to*) (*had better*)

A tentative classification

Judges classified English verbs, first on the basis of modality (possible or necessary) and again on the basis of the scope of negation (*de dicto* or *de re*). In both cases, a group of predictive/volitional verbs – *will, would, be going to, shall$_e$*, and *should$_e$* (where the subscript *e* indicates the epistemic sense) – resisted classification. Although *will, would, shall$_e$*, and *should$_e$* are classified as modal auxiliary verbs on syntactic grounds, they do not qualify as modal operators on semantic grounds.

The rest of the verbs studied are semantic modals. The experimental results suggest the classification by modality and scope of negation shown in Table 4. The root senses of *shall* and *should* appear with obligatory modality and negation *de re*. The epistemic (possible) sense of *may* appears with negation *de re*, whereas the root (permissible) sense of *may* appears with negation *de dicto*. (Verbs that do not satisfy syntactic criteria for modal auxiliaries appear in parentheses.)

Discussion

The modal verbs of English do not lend themselves well to interpretation as logical operators applied to propositional operands because they interact differentially with elements of the operand. At the very least, four operators would be required: one necessity operator with broad and another with narrow scope; one possibility operator with broad and another with narrow scope. The wisdom of following this line appears questionable, however, when it is recognized that the meanings of modal verbs also interact with other propositional elements, for example, with the occurrence of *have* as an auxiliary verb, which makes epistemic interpretations more salient. The interpretation of English modal verbs is, in short, highly dependent on context – unlike logical operators that have fixed semantic effects wherever they can be applied.

It is also apparent that the modal verbs of English did not evolve on a logical pattern of interdefinability. It might be possible to impose such a pattern on *can* and *has to*, where, if *can* is taken to be primitive, *has to* could be defined in terms of it, and vice versa:

$$Lp \equiv -M-p: \text{ He has to leave } \equiv \text{He can't stay}$$
$$Mp \equiv -L-p: \text{ He can leave } \equiv \text{He doesn't have to stay}$$

But even here it is necessary to represent the negation of *leave* as *stay*, rather than as *not leave*, a stratagem that is available only for pairs of antonymous verbs. Most people find *He can't not leave* at least awkward. The awkwardness is exaggerated in such constructions as *He can't speak no French*, where *He has to speak French* is not the salient interpretation.

Modal logic, of course, was never intended as a theory of the English modal verbs. The perils of translating logical formulas into English sentences are well known, even for the logic of propositions. The mismatch between modal logic and modal verbs is so great, however, that psychologists are almost forced to abandon formal logic in favor of a more cognitive account of modal thinking. Following a line taken by some philosophers (e.g., Goodman, 1955; Toulmin, 1958; Wertheimer, 1972), modal verbs might be characterized as marking sentences that are grounded on inference, not on direct knowledge.

Toulmin considers *good* to be a parallel case. The grounds for calling something *good* vary widely depending on the particular nominal expression it qualifies; all that remains constant from one use to the next is a favorable evaluation. In order to understand what is good about a *good red* or a *good view* or a *good knife*, it is necessary to draw on general knowledge of what reds, views, and knives are normally expected to do or be. Similarly, the grounds for calling something *possible* or *necessary* (or even predictable) vary widely from one situation to the next, and in order to understand what is meant it is necessary to draw on general knowledge of the appropriate situation – which goes well beyond any logical or lexical information about the formal interdefinability of these words. All that remains constant from one use to the next is that the speaker has made a particular kind of inference: On the basis of some body of general knowledge, the speaker says that, given the prevailing situation, the proposition that he expresses follows inferentially. As Goodman argues, what is required is a theory of inductive inference, not a theory of possible worlds. And, as Wertheimer points out, the modal verbs are not really ambiguous; they merely seem ambiguous because the grounds for making such inferences vary so widely from one occasion to the next.

The claim that modal verbs are syncategorematic does not, in itself, preclude the possibility of using them in conformity with the axioms of some formal modal logic. The point, however, is that when we discover that modal logic does not provide an adequate account of what people mean when they use these words, we are not left in a theoretical vacuum. Rather, the definition of the theoretical problem is changed from one stated in terms of form to one stated in terms of content. What is needed is a theory of how these words are understood differently in different contexts – a pragmatic, rather than a (narrowly) semantic theory.

If these arguments are correct, how should we think of the entries for these words in the mental lexicon? Not, apparently in terms of meaning postulates that interdefine them. One approach (Miller, 1978) is to formulate their definitions with variables ranging over different bodies of knowledge and different contexts of use. The development of such definitions, however, would take us beyond anything that the experimental data reported here would warrant.

The present data point to an apparently fortuitous variability in the scope of negation for different modal verbs. In the absence of any explicit theory of the meanings of the affirmative forms, it is impossible to say whether any coherent account could be given for this variability. At present, because there is no single general rule for determining the meaning of a negative form from the meaning of its affirmative, we suggest that there are separate entries in lexical memory for affirmative and negative modal verbs. This solution (which may be unique to English) receives some support from the lexicalization of *cannot* and from the existence of contracted forms: *can't, couldn't, mustn't, shan't, won't, wouldn't.* The assumption of separate lexical entries is theoretically untidy, inasmuch as it increases the number of lexical entries a person has to learn, and fails to capture obvious semantic relations between affirmative and negative forms, but it seems to provide the best match to the untidiness of the empirical data.

NOTES

This research was supported in part by grant number BNS77-16612 from the National Science Foundation to The Rockefeller University.

REFERENCES

Binnick, R. I. 1971. *"Will* and *be going to."* In *Seventh Regional Meeting, Chicago Linguistic Society.* Chicago: Chicago Linguistic Society.
Goodman, N. 1955. *Fact, Fiction, and Forecast.* Cambridge, Mass.: Harvard University Press.
Johnson, S. C. 1967. "Hierarchical Clustering Schemes." *Psychometrika* 32:241–54.
Leech, G. M. 1971. *Meaning and the English Verb.* London: Longman.
Miller, G. A. 1969. "A Psychological Method to Investigate Verbal Concepts." *Journal of Mathematical Psychology* 6:169–91.
Miller, G. A. 1978. "Practical and Lexical Knowledge." In E. Rosch and B. B. Lloyd, eds. *Cognition and Categorization.* Hillsdale, N.J.: Erlbaum.
Romney, A. K., and D'Andrade, R. G. 1964. "Cognitive Aspects of English Kin Terms." *American Anthropologist* (special issue) 66:146–70.
Toulmin, S. E. 1958. *The Uses of Argument.* Cambridge: Cambridge University Press.
Wertheimer, R. 1972. *The Significance of Sense: Meaning, Modality, and Morality.* Ithaca, N.Y.: Cornell University Press.

9

It's for your own good: a note on inaccurate reference

C. RAYMOND PERRAULT and PHILIP R. COHEN

Austin (1962) was one of the first to emphasize the distinction between the truth value of a proposition and the use of that proposition within an utterance that is the result of a (speech) *act* performed by some speaker for some hearer(s). Propositions can be true or false; the study of their relation to the world is the domain of classical semantics. Acts can succeed or fail; their success may depend on certain circumstances obtaining, in particular on the speaker holding certain beliefs and having certain intentions. Grice (1957) gives an account of what a *speaker* means when performing an act of communication in terms of the speaker's intention that the hearer should recognize certain intentions of the speaker. Strawson (1964) and Searle (1969) propose slightly different ways of applying Grice's theory to define the illocutionary acts first discussed by Austin.

Following his account of illocutionary acts, Searle also suggests that the sentence-meaning/speaker-meaning distinction can be extended to reference; that is, that there is a difference between what a definite description, say, refers to, and what a speaker intends to refer to by using that description. He then proposes conditions defining the felicitous performance of the reference act.

Cohen and Perrault (1979) and Perrault and Allen (1980) show how certain difficulties with Searle's definitions of the illocutionary acts REQUEST and INFORM can be. overcome by redefining them as operators in a problem-solving system (e.g., see Fikes and Nilsson, 1971). Cohen's OSCAR program (Cohen, 1978) can construct sequences of actions by which one agent can achieve certain goals, and these sequences can involve the performance of REQUESTs and INFORMs. Although OSCAR constructs the propositional content of its illocutionary acts (i.e., what act is being requested, or of what proposition the hearer is to be informed), it does not construct noun phrases by which the speaker can refer to entities as part of performing the referring act.

217

This leads us to seek necessary and sufficient conditions defining when a speaker S can be said to have referred to an entity x in uttering a referring expression E. Much of the difficulty stems from the fact that although the classic examples of referring expressions are proper names and definite descriptions, not all utterances of expressions of these grammatical types are normally said to refer. Well-known examples to the contrary are "Cerebus" and "the Golden Mountain," which presumably never referred, and "the largest prime number," which could not. Some definite descriptions such as "the Prime Minister" can be used to refer to an individual, as in "I met the Prime Minister yesterday," but can also be used intensionally, as in "The Prime Minister is the head of the executive." In the latter use, the truth conditions of the sentence are independent of what individual the definite description identifies, or even of whether there is such an individual.

Searle's analysis, like that of Russell (1905) and of Strawson (1964) before him, is limited to singular definite reference whereby the speaker is assumed to be trying to identify some existing entity for the hearer. We adopt here a similarly restricted view.

It is convenient to accept Searle's distinction between "fully consummated reference," one in which the identification of an object is communicated successfully to the hearer, and "successful reference," where the speaker had all the right intentions and conformed to all the right conventions, although, to use Austin's term, uptake may not have been secured. Restricting himself to the latter, Searle states his "principle of identification" (PI):

(PI.1) A necessary condition for the successful performance of a definite reference in the utterance of an expression is that either the expression must be an identifying description or the speaker must be able to produce an identifying description on demand. (Searle, 1969, p. 88)

In this paper we claim that Searle's PI fails to take into account the fact that *what* the description can be used to identify depends on the beliefs of the speaker and hearer, including the speaker's beliefs about the hearer, and so on. In particular, it does not account for cases where the description used in a successful reference may not only not be satisfied by its intended referent but may be believed by the speaker not to be satisfied.

In the rest of this introductory section we consider a few preliminary objections to PI.1. The second section contains a brief description of the properties of the propositional attitude "belief" on which the rest of the analysis relies. The section "The need for mutual belief" reviews some arguments of Clark and Marshall (Chapter 1 of this volume), who claim that an *infinite* set of beliefs about the entity's satisfying the identifying description is necessary. In the "Overriding mutual belief" section we argue that Clark and Marshall's claim is too strong by giving a series of counterexamples. The section concludes with a refined version of the PI. "A reconsideration" suggests that *how* the description identifies the intended referent must also be considered. The section on "The attributive case" argues that the version of the PI given in the preceding section does not apply to the so-called attributive uses of descriptions, and a final section offers some concluding remarks.

Preliminary objections

Returning to PI.1, Searle's analysis of what counts as an "identifying" description is rather vague. He claims that for a speaker to have identified an object by means of a description means that "there should be no longer any doubt or ambiguity about what exactly is being talked about . . . questions like 'who?', 'what?' and 'which one?' are answered." These answers can be provided in two ways: by demonstrative presentation and by "descriptions in purely general terms which are true of the object uniquely." Descriptions may also rely on a mixture of demonstrative devices and descriptive predicates. "So identification rests squarely on the speaker's ability to supply an expression of one of these kinds, which is satisfied uniquely by the object to which he intends to refer. I shall hereafter call any such description an *identifying description*" (emphasis in the original; Searle, 1969, p. 86).

Nowhere does Searle discuss what he means by a description being "satisfied uniquely" by an object. One objective of this paper is to explore this question.

First, it is clear that "satisfying uniquely" must be considered with respect to some "context" or "focus" (as, e.g., described by Grosz, 1977), created by the conversational process, the physical setting, and probably cultural conventions. The referent of "the man" in "John met a man in the street. He gave *the man* a dime." is the man whom John met and who was mentioned in the previous sentence (Webber, 1978). Searle's claim in his principle of identification that the speaker should provide an identifying description or "be able to produce one on demand" is meant to capture the fact that the speaker should be able to expand the description by explicitly including as much of the context as necessary to identify the object.[1]

Second, it is also clear that the use of a referring expression by a speaker has little or nothing to do with whether it is true that the object he intends to refer to actually satisfies the description and does so uniquely. We can all refer to Roger Bannister as "the first man to run a mile in less than four minutes" even if there may have been a Bantu tribesman who had a long way to go to the nearest tree in escaping one of the neighborhood beasts.

With these refinements in mind, we can now reformulate the principle of identification as follows:

(PI.2) A necessary condition for the successful performance of a definite reference by a speaker S using a description D in a context C is that S believes that D is fulfilled in C.

The introduction of the context C is intended here to account for Searle's "or must be able to produce an identifying description on demand." What context is remains a problem; we will take it to be a set of entities "known" to speaker and hearer. By "D is fulfilled in C" we mean that exactly one entity in C satisfies D; that is, $(Ex) (Ay:C) D(y) \Rightarrow x = y$.

In the rest of this chapter we want to show that this version of the principle of identification is neither sufficient nor necessary. It is not sufficient because it says nothing about the knowledge that H must *share* with S about D. This point is discussed by Clark and Marshall (Chapter 1 of this volume), and their evidence will be reviewed in the section "The need for mutual belief." It is not necessary because in some sense, to be made precise in the section "Overriding mutual belief," it is possible for the speaker to believe (and for the speaker to believe the hearer believes . . .) that D is *not* fulfilled in C, or that it is fulfilled by the "wrong" entity, and yet still use the description in an essential way.

Belief

It will be convenient to formulate the Principle of Identification in terms of statements in a logic of belief. Following Hintikka (1969) we interpret belief as a modal operator B(a,P), where a is the believing agent and P the believed proposition. This is usually written aB(P) or aBP and satisfies the following axiom schemas, where a and P range over agents and propositions, respectively:

B.1   aB(all axioms of the propositional calculus)
B.2 $aB(P) \Rightarrow aB(aB (P))$
B.3 $aB(P) \Rightarrow not\ aB(not\ P)$
B.4 $aB(P \Rightarrow Q) \Rightarrow (aB(P) \Rightarrow aB(Q))$

B.5   E*x* aB(P (*x*)) ⇒ aB(E*x* P(*x*))
B.6   All agents believe that all agents believe B.1 to B.5

It is important to note that the converse of B.5 does not hold.

A sound and complete model for these axioms may be given in terms of possible worlds as suggested by Hintikka (1969).

The need for mutual belief

Clark and Marshall (Chapter 1) give a series of examples[2] that show that for S to refer to H to some entity E using some description D in a context C, it is not sufficient that S believe that D is fulfilled in C, but S must also believe that H believes it is, and that H believes S believes it is, and so on. For S to ask H "How did you like *the movie?*" it is not sufficient for S to believe that H went to exactly one movie; S must also believe that H believes H went to exactly one movie, and so on. If any of these conditions fails *before* the reference act is made, then in order to successfully refer the speaker must be willing to accept that the hearer will attribute all of them to her. Thus no *finite* conjunction of the form

SB(P) & SBHB(P) & . . . & SBHB . . . SB(P)

is sufficient for successful reference, where P is the proposition "E fulfils D in C." We will say that S and H *mutually believe* that P [written MB (S,H,P)], if the *infinite* conjunction

SB(P) & SBHB(P) & SBHBSB(P) & . . .

obtains.[3] We will show in the next section that although an infinite number of conjuncts *are* necessary for successful reference, mutual belief that the description be fulfilled is not. But first, we digress briefly to discuss mutual belief.

Mutual belief is a way of representing facts that humans acquire because they expect other humans' perceptions and deductive processes to be similar to theirs. Lewis (1969) and Schiffer (1972) noted that when two agents S and H together witness some event A (or, to use Clark and Marshall's term, are *copresent* at A), then an unbounded set of propositions seems to be acquired by both. From S's point of view,

S believes that A occurred

and because S saw H witnessing A,

S believes H believes A occurred

and because S saw H see S witnessing A,

> S believes H believes S believes A occurred

and so forth. Assuming rationality on the part of S and H, S must agree to all these propositions (i.e., S and H mutually believe that A occurred).

As a consequence of their copresence and their assumption of mutual rationality, S and H may also be assumed to acquire consistent descriptions of entities involved in some event. For example, if S and H together see a table on which sit a green block G and a red block R, then it is reasonable to conclude

> MB(S,H,R fulfils "the red block on the table")

and

> MB(S,H,G fulfils "the green block on the table")

Overriding mutual belief

Consider now the following example adapted from Donnellan (1966):

> *Example 1:* S and H are at a party. They watch together as water and gin are being poured in two identical glasses and given to women W1 and W2 respectively. Unbeknownst to H, S sees W1 and W2 exchange glasses. Later S tells H: "The woman with the martini is the mayor's daughter."

There is no doubt that in so doing S successfully referred to W2 even though W2 was not drinking a martini, nor did S believe she was, although S believed H believed she was. S could not have been referring to W1 because S does not believe that H could recognize the woman with the martini as referring to W1 because S's knowledge of the exchange is not shared with H. In some sense, S's utterance is misleading because a (perlocutionary) effect of the assertion is that H believes that S believes that W2 is the mayor's daughter. However, neither S's nor H's beliefs about who the woman with the martini is need change as a consequence of S's securing uptake for the referent of "the woman with the martini." S's only fault is in not correcting a previous misunderstanding.

S is thus relying on S and H having shared the drink-pouring experience to construct descriptions of W1 and W2 they could agree to.[4] Immediately following the pouring of the drinks it is true that

> MB(S,H,W1 fulfils "TWWW" & W2 fulfils "TWWM")[5]

Beliefs about objects and their descriptions can also be acquired privately and may override some of the conjuncts of the mutual belief that results from two agents witnessing an event together. In Example 1, S saw W1 and W2 exchange glasses but S does not believe H saw the exchange. Thus the information available to S immediately prior to her assertion can be represented as:

> SB(W1 fulfils "TWWM" & W2 fulfils "TWWW") &
> SB(MB(H,S,W1 fulfils "TWWW" & W2 fulfils "TWWM"))

One might claim that S's reference to W2 was successful because SBHB(W2 fulfils "TWWM") because this follows from SB(MB(W2 fulfils "TWWM")). However, this condition is still too strong. In the rest of this section, we give a series of examples that show that any finite number of conjuncts of the formula

> MB(S,H,W1 fulfils TWWW & W2 fulfils TWWM)

can fail and yet S can still refer to W2 as TWWM.

> *Example 2:* S and H are at a party. They watch together as water and gin are being poured in two identical glasses and given to women W1 and W2 respectively. Later S sees H see the women swap glasses but S believes that H did not see S see H. S then tells H: "TWWM is the mayor's daughter."

We claim that S has successfully referred to W2 and that before she made her assertion it was the case that:

> SB(W1 fulfils "TWWM" & W2 fulfils "TWWW") &
> SBHB(W1 fulfils "TWWM" & W2 fulfils "TWWW") &
> SBHBMB(S,H,W1 fulfils "TWWW" & W2 fulfils "TWWM")

As in Example 1, S could not be referring to W1 because to do so would require S to expect H to understand the reference based on H's private beliefs. But following an argument similar to that given after Example 1, H cannot use private beliefs to understand a reference that S is trying to make. Thus the description may fail in SB and in SBHB. In the next example, it also fails in SBHBSB.

> *Example 3:* S and H are at a party. They watch together as water and gin are being poured in two identical glasses and given to women W1 and W2 respectively. Later S sees H see the women swap glasses, without seeing H see him. S also overhears A telling H that S saw him see the exchange. Later, S tells H: "'TWWM is the mayor's daughter."

Again here S has made a successful reference to W2 and before the assertion it also was the case that:

> SB(W1 fulfils "TWWM" & W2 fulfils "TWWW") &
> SBHB(W1 fulfils "TWWM" & W2 fulfils "TWWW") &
> SBHBSB(W1 fulfils "TWWM" & W2 fulfils "TWWW") &
> SBHBSBMB(H,S,W1 fulfils "TWWW" & W2 fulfils "TWWM")

By now it should be obvious that this game can be played forever. True believers can skip Example 4.

> *Example 4:* S and H are at a party. They watch together as water and gin are being poured in identical glasses and given to W1 and W2 respectively. Later S sees H seeing the women exchange glasses, but S believes H did not see her see the exchange. A, whom S believes to be truthful, tells S that A told H that S saw H see the exchange. S knows that H is listening to their conversation but pretends not to notice. S then tells H: "TWWM is the mayor's daughter."

Here we have:

> SB(W1 fulfils "TWWM" & W2 fulfils "TWWW") &
> SBHB(W1 fulfils "TWWM" & W2 fulfils "TWWW") &
> SBHBSB(W1 fulfils "TWWM" & W2 fulfils "TWWW") &
> SBHBSBHB(W1 fulfils "TWWM" & W2 fulfils "TWWW") &
> SBHBSBHBMB(W1 fulfils "TWWW" & W2 fulfils "TWWM")

In Examples 1–4, reference has been successful, although at some of the "early" levels SB, SBHB, and so on, the desired referent failed to fulfil the description. Beyond this finite set of conjuncts, however, there is mutual belief that the referent *does* fulfil the description. Can a reference act succeed if the description fails at an *unbounded* number of levels? We claim not, although intuitions differ on this point.

> *Example 5:* Two women W1 and W2 are holding martini glasses. S thinks that W1's glass contains water and W2's contains gin, and she has told this to H who has replied that he believes it to be the other way around. Neither is convinced by the other's argument, and neither thinks one would lie to the other. S tells H: "The woman with the martini is the mayor's daughter."

Here we claim that S has failed to refer to *either* W1 or W2, and that S's situation is as follows:

> SB(W1 fulfils "TWWW" & W2 fulfils "TWWM") &
> SBHB(W1 fulfils "TWWM" & W2 fulfils "TWWW") &
> SBHBSB(W1 fulfils "TWWW" & W2 fulfils "TWWM") &
> . . .

Because SB(P) $\Rightarrow$ SB(SB(P)), the infinite conjunction above implies:

> MB(S,H,SB(W1 fulfils "TWWW" & W2 fulfils "TWWM")) &
> MB(S,H,HB(W1 fulfils "TWWM" & W2 fulfils "TWWW")).

Note that S *could* refer to W2 by asserting the following sentence, for then the description is again a mutually believed one:

> "The woman that I believe is holding a martini is the mayor's daughter."

Let us say that S and H *agree* that P (written AGREE(S,H,P)) if

MB(S,H,P) *or* SBMB(H,S,P) *or* SBHBMB(S,H,P) . . .

Notice that AGREE(S,H,P) implies SB(AGREE(H,S,P)).

Examples 1–5 can be accounted for by the following version of the principle of identification:

> (PI.3) A necessary condition for a speaker S to refer for H to some entity E using a description D in a context C is that AGREE(S,H,E fulfils D in C).

Before reexamining the martini examples, note that in them all beliefs are acquired visually. But clearly mutual belief can be acquired verbally as well, and the same "overriding" phenomena can occur. For example, if S tells H "That is the woman with the martini" pointing at E, then if H and S mutually believe S to be sincere and correct, we have MB(H,S,E fulfils TWWM). If H believes S to be sincere but wrong then we have

> HB(E does not fulfil TWWM) &
> HBMB(S,H,E fulfils TWWM)

If H believes S to be lying then

> HB(E does not fulfil TWWM) &
> HBSB(E does not fulfil TWWM) &
> HBSBMB(H,S,E fulfils TWWM)

In any case, E can subsequently be referred to as "the woman with the martini."

A reconsideration

In our interpretation of the martini examples so far we have been assuming that the speaker intends the description "the woman with the martini" to be interpreted with respect to the information S and H share about the event during which the glasses were filled, and with respect to general (shared) information such as "if a person is holding a glass containing a martini at some time t in the past, and if the person continues to hold that glass until the present, and if no change is made to the contents of the glass in the interval, then the person is holding a martini now." Let us call this proposition J the *justification* for the reference.

In the cocktail-party context, S clearly does not intend that the referent of "the woman with the martini" be determined by H's actually *testing* the contents of the glasses. If this were S's intention, then S could not refer to the woman who is actually holding the water as "the woman with the martini." Thus S's ability to use descriptions that are inaccurate but which he knows to be inaccurate depends crucially on *how* the referent is to be determined by H, or of what justification there is for a referent to fulfil a description. This is not captured by the current version of the principle of identification.

How then are we to relate the entity E that S intends to refer to, the description "the *x* such that D(*x*)" uttered by S to H, and the way S intends H to determine the referent? We suggest the following:

> (PI.4) For a speaker S to refer to an entity E by uttering "the *x* such that D(*x*)" to H in a context C, it is necessary that there exist formulas ID(*x*) and J(*x*), called the *initial description* and *justification* formulas respectively such that
> 1. MB(S,H,ID(E)) & (A*x* : C) ID(*x*) $\Rightarrow$ *x* = E)
> 2. MB(S,H,(A*x*) (ID(*x*) & J(*x*) $\Rightarrow$ D(*x*))
> 3. AGREE(S,H,J(E))
> 4. AGREE(S,H, (A*x,y in* C) D(*x*) & D(*y*) $\Rightarrow$ *x* = *y*)
> 5. S intends H to identify E by means of ID and J
> 6. S intends H to recognize S's intention 5

The *initial description* ID is a predicate that S and H mutually believe is fulfilled by E (condition 1). The justification predicate J ensures that if an entity satisfies ID and J, then it also satisfies D, and this fact is mutually believed (condition 2). In the martini examples, we take

> ID(*x*) = woman(*x*) & hold(*x*,G,T) & martini(G,T)
> J(*x*) = (A*t* : [T,NOW]) hold(*x*,G,*t*) & martini(G,*t*)

and

> D(*x*) = (E*g* : glass) & woman(*x*) & hold(*x*,*g*,NOW) & martini(*g*,NOW)

where hold(*x*,*g*,*t*) is true if *x* holds glass *g* at time *t*, and martini(*g*,*t*) if glass *g* contains a martini at time *t*. We take G, T, and NOW to be constants denoting the glass E held, the time at which the martini was poured, and the current time, respectively. [T,NOW] denotes the interval between T and NOW. The truth of condition 2 then follows as a special case of the "frame axiom"

> (A*x*) (A*g*) (A*t*1) (A*t*2) hold(*x*,*g*,*t*1) & martini(*g*,*t*1) &
> (A*t* : [*t*1,*t*2]) hold(*x*,*g*,*t*) & martini(*g*,*t*)
> $\Rightarrow$ hold(*x*,*g*,*t*2) & martini(*g*,*t*2)

which is mutually believed by everyone.

Condition 3 states that S and H AGREE that the justification holds of E; in our case this means AGREEing that E held a martini between the time of pouring and the present. This condition is *not* mutually believed. Condition 4 states that S and H AGREE that at most one entity satisfies the uttered description. This condition does not follow from 1, 2, and 3 because, for example, another woman with a martini might have walked into the room between times T and NOW.

Conditions 5 and 6 are analogous to the Gricean conditions in Searle's definitions of illocutionary acts.[6] It is not sufficient that ID and J should exist: S must also intend that they be used by H. In a Searle-type definition of an illocutionary act, such a condition also includes the qualification that the recognition of intention be done at least in part because of the utterance itself. It is much more difficult to see how the description itself can suggest to the hearer the ID and J that the speaker intends him to use.

The attributive case

In the examples we've examined so far, the speaker and hearer could both identify the entity being referred to, in the sense that both were assumed to have about the referent information that could not be deduced from the description uttered. Their "acquaintance" with the referent gives them descriptions relating appearance, location, time, and so on. Definite descriptions are, however, often used when one or the other party does not have other information to identify the referent (i.e., cannot establish coreference of the definite description uttered with any other one that does not follow from it logically).

For example, a passenger asking an information clerk "What is the departure time of the next train to Montreal?" may not know *anything* about the referent of "the departure time . . ." other than what he has said. He presupposes that a departure time exists, and that it is unique, but the uniqueness here is a consequence of the meaning of "departure time." In no way could he identify the referent; in fact, the more he could, the less likely he would be to ask the question. In this case there seems no way that the speaker could inaccurately refer to "the departure time . . ." as was the case in the martini examples.

Unfortunately, PI.4 is too strong to accommodate this use of the definite description, and we see no way of weakening it while still accounting for the martini examples. Even if ID is taken to be D (and J to be trivially true), condition 1 of PI.4 fails in general because no copresence situation can be assumed to have asserted it previously. At best, $MB(S,H,(Ex)\ (Ay:C)\ D(y) \Rightarrow x = y)$ is necessary. The condition $AGREE(S,H,(Ex)\ (Ay:C)\ D(y) \Rightarrow x = y)$ seems too weak because $SB((Ex)\ (Ay:C)\ D(y) \Rightarrow x = y)$ must be true, and we can find no case where a formula of the form SBHBSB . . . SB((Ex) (Ay : C) D(y) $\Rightarrow x = y$) fails.

Thus there are two quite different uses of definite descriptions, as defined by the knowledge conditions necessary to their utterance, and they appear to correspond to Donnellan's "referential" and "attributive" uses. Only if a description is used referentially can the speaker *not* believe that it is true of the entity he wishes to refer to. (Ironical utterances, as usual, must be treated specially.)

The satisfaction of the conditions for referential use do not imply satisfaction of those for attributive use, unless condition 1 happens to be mutually believed, as well as agreed. This would justify defining two different reference acts.

Ortony and Anderson (1977) make the very suggestive claim that proper names and definite descriptions each have a different *primary* role with respect to reference: Uses of proper names are primarily referential, and uses of definite descriptions are primarily attributive. However, each can *indirectly* play the role of the other.

This proposal is particularly appealing because it is very close in spirit to several proposals (Searle, 1975; Morgan, 1978; Perrault and Allen, 1980) for explaining the relation between the literal, or direct, interpretation of utterances such as "Can you reach the salt?" (as a yes/no question) and their indirect interpretations (e.g., as a request to pass the salt). Unfortunately the steps by which the illocutionary forms can be related (see Perrault and Allen, 1980) do not seem to be the same as those required in the case of reference. However, the prospect of such an explanation is highly enticing.

Defining the reference acts requires specifying the effects of these acts, which traditionally has meant specifying the weakest formula that becomes true when the act is successfully executed. This requires investigating the relation between the reference acts and the illocutionary acts, and remains to be done.

Concluding remarks

It is beyond the scope of this chapter to discuss the logical, psychological, or computational aspects of mutual belief. The difficulties in giving adequate semantics for *belief* are well known. We simply want to point out that the countable number of conjuncts in the definition of mutual belief need not make things worse.

If one considers the change in the state of some agent witnessing some event in the presence of another agent, it is reasonable to assume that the mutual belief will be acquired as a "unit" rather than one conjunct at a time, and that certain deductions can also be made, on the basis of mutually believed information, that result in new mutually believed propositions. This can be represented informally as

$$MB(S,H,P) \ \& \ MB(S,H,P \Rightarrow Q) \Rightarrow MB(S,H,Q)$$

Clark and Marshall (Chapter 1) discuss the acquisition of mutual belief, and Cohen (1978) examines some related computational questions such as data structures that allow finite representations of belief and mutual belief in a program that generates speech acts.

NOTES

This research was supported in part by the National Research Council of Canada under Operating Grant A9285, and by the Advanced Research Project Agency of the Department of Defense and was monitored by the Office of Naval Research under Contract N00014-77-C-0378. Many thanks to Alex Borgida, David Israel, Corot Reason, Candy Sidner, and Bonnie Webber for their comments.

1 One of Searle's objectives is to show that the principle of identification is a special case of his earlier "principle of expressibility," which stated roughly is "What can be meant can be said."
2 A similar argument is made by Schiffer (1972) to show the lack of sufficiency of Strawson's (1964) refinement of Grice's (1957) analysis of speaker meaning.
3 Notice that MB(H,S,P) interchanges H and S in (4) and thus MB(S,H,P) and MB(H,S,P) are not equivalent. However MB(S,H,P) is equivalent to

$$SB(P) \ \& \ SB(MB(H,S,P))$$

4 Searle recognizes that a reference may be successful without the description being true of the object referred to and quotes an example of Whitehead (1920):

> S: That criminal is your friend"
> H: "He is my friend and you are insulting"

He dismisses it because "the word 'that' in 'that criminal' indicates the object either is present or has already been referred to by some other referring expression and that the present reference is parasitic on the earlier. The descriptor 'criminal' is not essential to the identification . . . which is achieved by other means" (Searle, 1969, p. 90).
　In example 1 however, "the woman with the martini" is not parasitic, for although S, H, and W are copresent, no use is made, nor need be made, of deictic expressions for successful reference. The example would work equally well if S and H were each watching the group including W from separate rooms on TV monitors and communicating by telephone.
5 For the rest of the paper "TWWM" will be used as an abbreviation for "the woman with the martini," and "TWWW" will be used as an abbreviation for "the woman with the water."
6 Condition 6 is probably not strong enough to avoid analogues to Schiffer's counterexamples.

REFERENCES

Austin, J. L. 1962. *How To Do Things With Words.* New York: Oxford University Press.

Cohen, P. R. 1978. "On Knowing What to Say: Planning Speech Acts." Technical Report 118, University of Toronto, Department of Computer Science.

Cohen, P. R., and Perrault, C. R. 1979. "Elements of a Plan Based Theory of Speech Acts." *Cognitive Science* 3, 3:177–212.

Donnellan, K. 1966. "Reference and Definite Descriptions." *Philosophical Review* 75:281–304. Reprinted, 1971. In D. Steinberg and L. Jakobovits, eds. *Semantics.* Cambridge: Cambridge University Press.

Fikes, R. E., and Nilsson, N. J. 1971. "STRIPS: A New Approach to the Application of Theorem Proving to Problem Solving." *Artificial Intelligence* 2:189–205.

Grice, H. H. 1957. "Meaning." *Philosophical Review* 66:377–88. Reprinted, 1971. In D. Steinberg and L. Jakobovits, eds. *Semantics.* Cambridge: Cambridge University Press.

Grosz, B. G. 1977. "The Representation and Use of Focus in Dialog Understanding." Ph.D. dissertation, University of California, Berkeley.

Hintikka, J. 1969. "Semantics for Propositional Attitudes." In J. W. Davis et al., eds. *Philosophical Logic.* Dordrecht: Reidel. Reprinted, 1969. In L. Linsky, ed. *Reference and Modality.* New York: Oxford University Press.

Lewis, D. K. 1969. *Convention: A Philosophical Study.* Cambridge, Mass.: Harvard University Press.

Morgan, J. L. 1978. "Toward a Rational Model of Discourse Comprehension." In D. Waltz, ed. *Proceedings of Theoretical Issues in Natural Language Processing.* Urbana: University of Illinois.

Ortony, A., and Anderson, J. 1977. "Definite Descriptions and Semantic Memory." *Cognitive Science* 1, 1:74–83.

Perrault, C. R., and Allen, J. F. 1980. "A Plan-Based Analysis of Indirect Speech Acts." Technical Report, University of Toronto, Department of Computer Science.

Russell, B. 1905. "On Denoting." *Mind.* Reprinted, 1949. In H. Feigl and W. Sellars, eds. *Readings in Philosophical Analysis.* New York: Appleton-Century-Crofts.

Schiffer, S. R. 1972. *Meaning.* London: Oxford University Press.

Searle, J. R. 1969. *Speech Acts.* New York: Cambridge University Press.

Searle, J. R. 1975. "Indirect Speech Acts." In P. Cole and J. L. Morgan, eds. *Syntax and Semantics,* Vol. 3, *Speech Acts.* New York: Academic Press.

Strawson, P. F. 1964. "Intention and Convention in Speech Acts." *Philosophical Review* 73, 4:439–60. Reprinted, 1971. In J. R. Searle, ed. *The Philosophy of Language.* London: Oxford University Press.

Webber, B. L. 1978. "A Formal Approach to Discourse Anaphora." Technical Report 3761, Cambridge, Mass.: Bolt, Beranek and Newman.

Whitehead, A. N. 1920. *The Concept of Nature.* Cambridge.

10

On the inferencing of indefinite-*this* NPs

ELLEN F. PRINCE

On the ignoring of indefinites

Although in the past two decades much has been written within the field of linguistics on the presuppositional behavior of definite noun phrases, far less attention has been paid to the presuppositional behavior of indefinites. One possible reason might be thought to be the fact that indefinites exhibit a wide variety of "ways of referring," in some of which they do not actually refer at all. Consider, for example:

(1)a. *A body* was found in the river yesterday.
   b. *A tiger* has stripes.
   c. John is *a plumber*.
   d. I never saw *a two-headed man*.
   e. He won't say *a word*.

In their most usual readings, only the italicized NP in (1a) can actually be said to be *specific*. The italicized NPs in (1b–e) are all *nonspecific*, though of different types (generic, predicative, attributive, and negative polarity idiom-piece, respectively). However, definite NPs exhibit a similar range of understandings:

(2)a. *The body* was found in the river. (specific)
   b. *The tiger* has stripes. (generic)
   c. Ronald is *the president*. (predicative)
   d. They'll never find *the man that will please them*. (attributive)
   e. He doesn't mean *the slightest thing* to me. (negative polarity idiom-piece)

Those linguists working on the presuppositional behavior of definite NPs (e.g., Karttunen, 1974 and elsewhere; Kempson, 1975; Gazdar, 1976 and elsewhere; Prince, 1978; Clark and Marshall, this volume) have simply assumed that specific definites like the italicized item in (2a) could somehow be formally distinguished from all other types of definite NPs. Thus the mere fact of the existence of a wide range of understandings of indefinite NPs does not explain their having been so largely ignored in the literature.

231

Another, more likely, reason is a general (apparent) pattern of be-havior of indefinites under negation: specific indefinite NPs in object position seem to "lose" their specificity when the sentence in which they occur is negated, in situations where a corresponding definite NP would retain its specificity:

(3)a. John bought *the car*.
   b. John didn't buy *the car*.
(4)a. John bought *a car*.
   b. John didn't buy *a car*.

In (3b), we see that the italicized definite NP remains specific, whereas, in (4b), the italicized indefinite NP seems to lose its specificity. Actually, however, (4b) is *ambiguous* between a specific and a nonspecific reading, the latter being strongly preferred. The nonspecific reading is so strongly preferred, however, that one can be misled into ignoring the existence of the specific reading and assume that the specificity of indefinites is too tenuous to be of any interest (e.g., Kempson, 1975; Gazdar, 1976). Consider, however, the follow-ing:

(5)a. John bought *a particular car*.
   b. John didn't buy *a particular car*.

The italicized NPs in (5) are indefinite and unambiguously specific, and they show that the ambiguity of (4b) is not a necessary feature of negative sentences containing indefinite NP objects.

A class of unambiguously specific indefinite NPs

In this chapter, I shall consider the presuppositional behavior of a class of specific indefinite NPs. Put differently, I shall examine the inferences that a hearer makes upon hearing a certain type of specific indefinite. As I am not concerned here with the problem of how the hearer knows to choose the specific reading in cases of ambiguity, I have chosen not to base the analysis on indefinite NPs like those in (4). Likewise, I have chosen not to consider indefinite NPs like those in (5) because one might argue that NPs containing adjectives are inherently different. Instead, I shall confine the discussion – or at least the claims – to another type of NP, virtually ignored in the literature but very common in speech, though stigmatized as being nonstandard – the indefinite-*this* NP:

(6) "One day last year on a cold, clear, crisp afternoon, I saw *this huge sheet of ice* in the street . . ." (Hockey player; Terkel, 1974, p. 505)

I shall first give evidence for considering such NPs to be in fact a subclass of indefinite NPs, but one that is unambiguously specific. Then I shall show that they are presuppositional, and I shall try to demonstrate that a study of the use of such NPs in discourse and of the inferences that they trigger sheds light on the definite/indefinite and specific/nonspecific distinctions and on the relations between these distinctions. Furthermore, I shall try to show that such constructions have important theoretical implications for any theory that purports to account for natural-language presuppositional phenomena, particularly on the subject of the analysis of presuppositional items in negative and opaque contexts. Finally, it should be noted that whatever a theory of presupposition needs in order to account for indefinite-*this* NPs will be needed anyway in order to account for standard indefinite NPs because (nearly) all sentences containing indefinite-*this* NPs have paraphrases with (some allomorph of) the standard indefinite article.

Indefiniteness of this *this*

(7)a. "It's hard to take pride in a bridge you're never gonna cross, in a door you're never gonna open. You're mass-producing things and you never see the end result of it. [muses] I worked for a trucker one time. And I got *this tiny satisfaction* when I loaded a truck. At least I could see the truck depart loaded." (Steelworker; Terkel, 1974, pp. 1–2)

b. *. . . I got *the tiny satisfaction* . . .

c. . . . I got *a tiny satisfaction* . . .

(8)a. "I work in electronic and auto shows. Companies hire me to stay in their booth and talk about products. I have *this speech* to tell." (Airline stewardess; Terkel, 1974, p. 79)

b. *. . . I have *the speech* to tell.

c. . . . I have *a speech* to tell.

Although demonstrative articles are generally taken to be definite, the occurrences of the demonstrative *this* in (7a) and (8a) are replaceable, not by definite *the*, but by indefinite *a*. The classic test for indefiniteness, occurrence in existential-*there* sentences, shows that this *this* is in fact indefinite:[1]

(9)a. "A long-hair person doesn't bother me, but when you see that radical with the mop and that shanky garbage and you can smell him a block away, that bothers me. A few years ago, *there was this hippie,* long-haired, slovenly. He confronted me . . ." (Policeman; Terkel, 1974, p. 191)

b. "One time I went to the roof of this project and *there's this big black guy about six seven on top of the stairs.* He had his back to me . . ." (Fireman; Terkel, 1974, p. 756)

    c. *"There was this one checker who was absolutely vicious."* (Supermarket box
        boy; Terkel, 1974, p. 373)

Furthermore, as noted in Lakoff (1974), this *this* occurs with
warmth-type NPs, which are only indefinite:

(10)a. He kissed her with this unbelievable passion.
     b. *. . . the unbelievable passion.
     c. . . . an unbelievable passion. [example from Lakoff (1974, p. 347)]

Phonologically, this *this* is, unlike definite *this,* necessarily unstressed,
as pointed out in Perlman (1969).[2] Contra Perlman, however, I claim
that this *this,* an indefinite, is distinct from the unstressed *this*
exemplified in (11a) (Perlman, 1969, p. 80) because the latter can be
replaced by *the* but not by *a* and must, therefore, be considered definite:

(11)a. Who's *this chorus girl* you wanted me to meet?
     b. Who's *the/*a chorus girl* you wanted me to meet?

Lakoff (1974, p. 347) classes both under the rubric "emotional deixis" but considers that the latter type is used to "allude to something,
or someone, already mentioned, but outside the discourse proper,"
whereas the former type "seems to replace indefinites."[3] It should be
noted also that the two types of *this* differ dialectally; the type in (11a),
though perhaps colloquial, lacks the nonstandard flavor of indefinite
this.

    For the remainder of this study, I shall count an occurrence of *this* as
indefinite if and only if it is replaceable by zero when followed by a
number or a plural and by *a/an* in all other environments, preserving
acceptability and truth conditions.

Distribution in discourse

As would be expected of indefinites, indefinite-*this* NPs introduce new
information into a discourse and are, therefore, first-mention.[4] Of the
243 occurrences that I have identified in Terkel (1974), 242 are clearly
first-mention. The one apparent exception is the following:

(12)   "I've been bit once already by a German shepherd. And it was some-
      thing. It was really scary. It was an outside meter the woman had. I
      read the gas meter and was walking back out and heard a yell. I
      turned around and *this German shepherd* was coming at me . . ."
      (Gas meter reader; Terkel, 1974, p. 366)

One could argue, however, that *this German shepherd* in the last sentence is not really anaphoric to *a German shepherd* in the first sentence.

In Donnellan's (1971) terms, the first occurrence is *attributive*, whereas the second occurrence is *referential*. It will be seen below that indefinite-*this* NPs in unmarked contexts are always referential. Note that *this* may be replaced by *a* far more felicitously than by *the* (whence the classification of it here as an indefinite). Furthermore, the first three sentences can be seen as being *about* the story that the speaker is preparing to tell, whereas the actual story does not begin until the fourth sentence. Thus *this German shepherd* is in fact first-mention *within* the story, its very unexpectedness being a crucial narrative feature.

To see what is distinctive about the distribution of indefinite *this* in discourse, however, one must look not at the prior context but at what follows. In 209 out of 243 cases (86%), the referent introduced (evoked) by indefinite *this* is referred to again within a few clauses. In 141 instances (58% of all occurrences), it is referred to explicitly (e.g., 13a), and, in 68 cases (28% of all occurrences), it is referred to implicitly (e.g., 13b):

(13)a. *"This fellow I work with* – I wouldn't call *him* militant, but *he's* perhaps a little more forward than I am – *he* wouldn't respond if you called *him* boy. *He'd* promptly tell 'em. . ." (Washroom attendant; Terkel, 1974, p. 156)

b. "I been on *this one case* now about eight months. The problem [in this case] is bad management, not theft . . ." (Industrial investigator; Terkel, 1974, p. 208)

That is, indefinite *this* often seems to serve to introduce something that is going to be talked about (i.e., a new topic).[5]

There is a very striking parallel between indefinite *this*, obviously related to deictic *this*, and a feature of American Sign Language. In ASL, a signer uses pointing – physical deixis – to "set up" an absent third person on his/her right in order to be able to refer later to that individual. An absent third person that is not intended as a topic for further discussion, but is just mentioned in passing, is not set up in this way.[6]

Specificity of this *this*

For a noun phrase – definite or indefinite – to carry an existential presupposition, it must necessarily be *specific*. Thus the underlined definite NPs in (14), being nonspecific, are nonpresuppositional (in the relevant sense) in their most usual readings (i.e., in those readings shared with 15):

(14)a. *The meek* shall inherit the earth.
b. The job will go to *the man that types 80 words a minute.*

(15)a. *Whichever people, if any, are meek* will inherit the earth.
   b. The job will go to *whichever man can type 80 words a minute, if there is such a person.*[7]

Now compare the following:

(16)a. Mary bought *the pink truck.*
   b. Mary bought *a pink truck.*
(17)a. Mary didn't buy *the pink truck.*
   b. Mary didn't buy *a pink truck.*

The italicized NPs in (16a), (16b), and (17a) are clearly specific – they evoke a particular pink truck that Mary did or didn't buy – whereas the italicized NP in (17b) is at best ambiguous between a specific and a nonspecific reading, the nonspecific reading being preferred. Thus, as has been mentioned, the specificity of indefinite NPs with $a(n)$ seems to vanish or at least blur under negation.

Givón (1978) gives ample cross-linguistic evidence of such blurring and argues that the apparent loss of specific indefinites under negation is a universal phenomenon. It is not clear, however, whether he takes this phenomenon to be semantic or pragmatic. Although he seems to be arguing in terms of truth conditions, he implicates that the phenomenon is in fact a pragmatic one.[8]

This phenomenon of ambiguity between a specific and a nonspecific reading arises also in opaque environments:

(18)a. Mary wants to buy the pink truck.
   b. Mary wants to buy the pink truck but she can't find it. (specific)
   c. *Mary wants to buy the pink truck but she can't find one. (nonspecific)
(19)a. Mary wants to buy a pink truck.
   b. Mary wants to buy a pink truck but she can't find it. (specific)
   c. Mary wants to buy a pink truck but she can't find one. (nonspecific)

Kempson (1975, p. 118), noting such facts, generalizes that this sort of blurring is an inherent feature of indefinite NPs in general. Because specificity is a necessary (though not sufficient) condition for an NP to carry an existential presupposition, she concludes that indefinite NPs are nonpresuppositional and hence do not have to be taken into account in a theory of presupposition, whether semantic or pragmatic. In her particular theory, this means that she can use the syntactic feature [+DEF] to trigger pragmatic presuppositions. The same point of view – that the specificity of indefinite NPs is unstable and that they do not display presuppositional behavior – is present explicitly or implicitly in the bulk of the literature on linguistic presupposition.[9]

However, it turns out that, although this ambiguity/indeterminacy/

blurring may be an inherent feature of indefinite NPs with $a(n)$ (at least so long as they are not modified by adjectives like *particular, certain*) – that is, of *unmarked* indefinites, in Givón's terms – it is not an inherent feature of the class of indefinite NPs as a whole. In particular, indefinite NPs with *this* are unambiguously specific, in negative and opaque environments as well as in affirmative, transparent ones:

(20)a. Mary wants to buy *this pink truck.*[10]
   b. Mary wants to buy *this pink truck* but she can't find it. (specific)
   c. *Mary wants to buy *this pink truck* but she can't find one. (nonspecific)
(21)a. Mary didn't buy *this pink truck.*
   b. Mary didn't buy *this pink truck* because it was too expensive. (specific)
   c. *Mary didn't buy *this pink truck* because she couldn't find one. (nonspecific)

Finally, compare the well-known example in (22) with its analogue in (23):

(22)A: John wants to marry a Norwegian.
   B: Is she tall? (Specific uptake)
   B': Must she be tall? (nonspecific uptake)
(23)A: John wants to marry this Norwegian.
   B: Is she tall? (specific uptake)
   B': *Must she be tall? (nonspecific uptake)

As mentioned above, specificity is a necessary condition for (existential) presuppositionality, but it is not a sufficient one. In particular, an NP can be anaphoric to a nonspecific NP, in which case it is specific but still lacks an existential presupposition in the usual sense. Such is the status of *she* in (22B') above and of *it* in (24a) and *her* in (24b):

(24)a. If Mary finds a pink truck, she'll buy *it,* but I don't think she'll find one.
   b. John wants to marry a Norwegian and take *her* home to mother, but he'll never find one.

Note, however, that these specific nonpresuppositional NPs are second-mention and are, therefore, necessarily definite;[11] indefinite-*this* NPs are first-mention and thus cannot occur anaphorically.

The only other type of specific NP that may be said to lack an existential presupposition is the one that occurs under what Morgan (1969) calls "world-creating predicates," comparable to (at least a subset of) Karttunen's (1973) "plugs":

(25)a. Imagine you're at a party and *the person next to you* passes out.
   b. I dreamt that I was discussing hair transplants with *the King of France.*

However, such definite NPs have been shown to be basically presuppositional but to be in environments in which the presupposition gets "canceled" or "suspended." (See Gazdar, 1976, and elsewhere.) We shall return to them below. At this point, I shall support my claim that indefinite-*this* NPs carry an existential presupposition.

Existence

Let us begin by comparing unmarked indefinite NPs with presuppositional definite NPs (i.e., specific definite NPs that are not anaphoric to nonspecific NPs):

(26)a. John married a Norwegian.
  b. John didn't marry a Norwegian.
(27)a. John married the Norwegian.
  b. John didn't marry the Norwegian.
 (28) There was a Norwegian.

Sentences (26a), (27a), and (27b) clearly entail (28), whereas (26b) does not necessarily. This difference between the entailments of affirmative–negative sentence-pairs with indefinites and those with definites is precisely what has led philosophers and linguists to conclude that certain expressions carry existential presuppositions. Put most neutrally, an affirmative–negative sentence-pair, containing a referring expression (specific NP not anaphoric to a nonspecific NP) is said to *presuppose* the existence of the referent of that NP if each member of the pair entails it. Thus it should follow that, if a sentence entails or presupposes the existence of the referent of some NP and also denies that existence, it should be anomalous. Consider:

(29)a. *John married a Norwegian and there was no Norwegian.
  b. John didn't marry a Norwegian and there was no Norwegian.
(30)a. *John married the Norwegian and there was no Norwegian.
  b. +John didn't marry the Norwegian and there was no Norwegian.

Sentences (29a) and (30a) are thus predictably anomalous and (29b) is predictably acceptable, but (30b) is problematic. Although it does have an anomalous reading in some contexts, for example:

(31)A: Did John marry the Italian?
  B: *Yes, he didn't marry the Norwegian, and there was no Norwegian.

it has, in addition, a less usual but perfectly possible understanding with what has been called *external* or *denial* negation, in which case it is not anomalous, its presupposition being said to have been *canceled,* for example:

(32)A: Did John marry the Norwegian?
  B: No, he didn't marry the Norwegian and there was no Norwegian.

(The symbol ⁺ is used above (30b) to indicate that anomaly arises only if the negation is not understood as being one of denial.)
Now consider:

(33)a. John married this (one) Norwegian.
    b. *John married this (one) Norwegian and there was no Norwegian.
(34)a. John didn't marry this (one) Norwegian.
    b. *John didn't marry this (one) Norwegian and there was no Norwegian.

Note that (34a) entails (28) just as strongly as does (33a), in contrast to the situation obtaining with (26a) and (26b). Thus it seems that indefinite-*this* NPs do in fact carry an existential presupposition. Furthermore, the fact that (34b) is just as unredeemably anomalous as (33b) shows that the existential presupposition it carries cannot be canceled by denial/external negation. Thus it appears that indefinite-*this* NPs are even *more* presuppositional, in a manner of speaking, than are definite NPs, a curious situation. Before presenting the obvious explanation for these facts, however, I shall consider them with respect to a recently proposed theory of presupposition.

Gazdar (1976, 1978, 1979) presents an explicit and ingenious pragmatic theory to account for certain presuppositional phenomena – in particular, for the conditions under which (potential) presuppositions get canceled. Space does not here permit a detailed discussion of this model, but a few points must be mentioned. The model, which operates on sentences (in isolation), processes first all *entailments* by adding them to a *context*, defined as a set of propositions constrained only by consistency; then it processes (i.e., adds to the context) all the (formally specified) *potential implicatures* and, finally, all the (formally specified) *potential presuppositions*. If a sentence contains contradictory entailments (or, presumably, if a sentence contains an entailment that is contradictory with a proposition already in the context), then it will be marked as being anomalous. If, however, a potential implicature or presupposition contradicts something already in the context – which includes all the entailments of the sentence, they having already been added – then that potential implicature or presupposition is automatically canceled. Because implicatures are processed before presuppositions, a potential presupposition that is inconsistent with a surviving implicature is also canceled. Thus, (27a) both entails and first potentially and then actually presupposes (28), whereas (27b) does not entail (28) but does (first potentially and then actually) presuppose it. In contrast, (30a) entails both (28) (first conjunct) and the negation of (28) (second conjunct) and is correctly marked as anomalous, whereas (30b) entails only the negation of (28), which cancels its potential presupposition of (28), and it is marked as well formed.

Now consider the case of indefinite *this*. First, it must be emphasized that Gazdar's model does not deal with indefinite NPs. However, let us assume a model exactly like Gazdar's except that certain indefinite NPs, in particular indefinite-*this* NPs, are marked as carrying potential presuppositions. Such a model would presumably process (33a) and (33b) just as it processes (27a) and (29a), respectively. Likewise, (34a), like (27b), would not entail (28), but it would first potentially and then actually presuppose it. A problem arises, however, in (34b); because all negation is external in such a model, (34b) would be processed just as (30b) is – that is, it would be incorrectly predicted to be well formed.

The problem of course lies in reading the negation as only external or denial. In natural language, denial negation is used to *deny* (i.e., to contradict another's statement), as I have argued elsewhere (Prince, 1978). Thus it follows that what one is denying has already occurred in the discourse. In particular, if one is denying the existence of the referent of a particular NP, then that NP has already been introduced, and if a coreferential NP occurs in the denial, it will necessarily be second-mention. But second-mention (specific) NPs are necessarily definite. In contrast, the relevant NP in (34b) is (specific and) indefinite and necessarily first-mention and, therefore, cannot occur in such a sentence without anomaly arising. That Gazdar's model works as well as it does is contingent upon the fact that it deals with sentences in isolation and that it takes into account only definite NPs, which may always be second-mention. It cannot account for non-second-mention definite NPs (e.g., 31B), and, more strikingly, it cannot be made to account for the presuppositional behavior of specific indefinites without fairly drastic revisions (e.g., permitting an NP to be outside the scope of sentence-negation).

Elsewhere (Prince, 1978), I present an informal outline of a different kind of account of pragmatic presuppositional phenomena, based not on sentences but on discourses. I argue there that potential presuppositions do not get "canceled" in any intuitive sense but get attributed by the hearer as *assumptions*. In the unmarked case, the hearer will attribute them to the speaker, and, if the speaker has a sufficient degree of credibility, the hearer will infer the actual existence of the referent in question. Call this the *Existential Inference*. However, there are also marked cases where they will be attributed not to the speaker but to someone else. Nonanomalous utterances of (29b), for example, will occur only as a direct contradiction of someone else's assumption; that is, when the potential presupposition in question, (28), has already been attributed in the speech-situation to another individual and the utterer of (29b) is using it merely anaphorically in order to deny it. Facts like the anomaly of (34b), where the NP in question cannot be anaphoric, are strong support for such an approach.

Although the existential presupposition of indefinite-*this* NPs does not get canceled under negation, it is not the case that it is absolutely "uncancelable." That is, there are cases in which the speaker will not be attributed with the assumption that the referent in question actually exists. Consider the following:

(35)a. John dreamt that he was in the Eskimo restaurant.
  b. John dreamt that he was in this Eskimo restaurant.
  c. There was an Eskimo restaurant.

Following Gazdar's model, (35a) does not entail (35c) but it does potentially presuppose it, and, because (35c) contradicts nothing in the context, it is added as a presupposition of (35a), all of which is in accord with our intuitions. If indefinite-*this* NPs were added to the list of potential presupposition carriers, however, (35b) would be processed in the same way, which would be incorrect because (35c) is certainly not an assumption that one would want to attribute to the utterer of (35b).

The behavior of the potential presuppositions of indefinites under so-called plugs like *dream* is fairly complex. First, it is apparent that not all plugs work the same way; compare (35b) with (36), in which the potential presupposition, (35c), does seem to "survive," more strongly in (36b) than in (36a):

(36)a. John wanted to eat in this Eskimo restaurant.
  b. John refused to eat in this Eskimo restaurant.

One factor that figures in the difference between (35b) and (36) is the difference between the real world and the world that is created by the plug; dream-worlds are clearly more marked as being different from "real worlds" than are want-worlds. Even within want-worlds, however, the speaker's rating of the credibility of the wanter plays a role; compare the attribution of (35c) in (37a) and (37b):

(37)a. Poor old delusional John wanted to eat in this Eskimo restaurant.
  b. John, who really knows what he's talking about when it comes to eating, wanted to eat in this Eskimo restaurant.

The difference between (36a) and (36b) seems to be one of point of view. In (36a), the speaker may be taking John's point of view, in which case the attribution of (35c) to the speaker correlates with the speaker's judgment of John's credibility, as we have just seen. In (36b), however, the speaker is presenting his/her own point of view, and even a lowering of John's credibility will not prevent the attribution of (35c) to him/her:

(38)a. Poor old delusional John refused to eat in this Eskimo restaurant.
   b. Poor old delusional John didn't want to eat in this Eskimo restaurant.

The fact that (38b) is more like (38a) in terms of attribution ("noncancellation") than it is like (37a) suggests that any attempt to account for the facts of presupposition-survival simply by subdividing the class of so-called plugs will not work, and that notions like credibility and point of view will have to be taken into account.

The difference in potential presupposition survival between (35a) and (35b) has still not been accounted for. Even though dream-worlds are taken to be very different from real worlds, (35c) will be attributed to the utterer of (35a), where it is carried by the definite NP *the Eskimo restaurant*, although it will not be attributed to the utterer of (35b), where it is carried by the indefinite NP *this Eskimo restaurant*. To account for this difference, we shall have to consider the notion of *familiarity*.

Familiarity

We have seen that, in the unmarked case, a hearer, upon hearing an indefinite-*this* NP, makes the inference that the referent of that NP is assumed by the speaker to exist. I have called this the Existential Inference. Existential Inferences are of course made also for specific definite NPs (when not anaphoric to nonspecific NPs) in the unmarked case. The difference between specific definites and indefinite-*this* NPs lies not in the Existential Inferences they trigger but in the fact that specific definite NPs trigger, in addition, certain *Familiarity Inferences,* which indefinite-*this* NPs do not. In Prince (1978), I argued for a rule of Familiarity Inferencing, revised as follows:

   (39) Rule of Familiarity Inferencing:
      A hearer who hears a specific definite NP, which carries an Existential Assumption, infers that the speaker assumes, minimally, that:
      1. the hearer has already in the speech-situation attributed an identical assumption to some individual(s); or
      2. the hearer could have inferred that assumption from other stereotypic and/or particular assumptions in his/her assumption set; or
      3. the hearer already had an identical assumption in his/her assumption-set.

The first part is needed, minimally, in order to account for the inferencing of anaphoric NPs, as in (32B) above and (40a) [akin to Clark and Marshall's (this volume) *linguistic copresence*]. The second part is needed, minimally, in order to account for the inferencing of certain first-mention definite NPs of a relational variety; in (40b) the hearer could have inferred that the speaker assumes that the hearer has a telephone on the basis of a *stereotypic* assumption (*People have telephones*) and a *particular* assumption (*I am a person*). (This is related to Clark and Marshall's *indirect copresence.*) The third part is needed to account for, among other things, the inferencing of (unmodified) proper names, the existence of whose referents is not inferrable from other assumptions; thus the hearer of (40c) is assumed to have already the assumption that Gazdar exists. (This is akin to Clark and Marshall's *cultural copresence.*)

(40)a. I went to see a movie last night. It was terrible.
   b. Excuse me, ma'am, may I use your telephone?
   c. Gazdar really doesn't talk about proper names.

Somewhat surprisingly, the literature on presupposition in natural language, while concentrating its attention on definite NPs and largely ignoring indefinites, has concerned itself almost exclusively with Existential Inferences and has generally neglected that which is peculiar to definite NPs, the Familiarity Inferences. Karttunen (1974) attempts to account for them by positing that the existential propositions carried by the items in question be entailed by the "context." This is too narrow; it would account for felicitous occurrences of sentences like (40c) and, prior discourse being part of the context, (40a), but it would not account in any obvious way for cases like (40b). (These are judged by Karttunen, 1974, to be "leaps and shortcuts," which incorrectly makes them seem less than perfectly felicitous.) Gazdar does not really address the issue; his rule that the existential proposition in question must be consistent with (i.e., must not contradict anything in) the context is really intended for other work and is both too strong – it would mark (32B) as anomalous once (32A) had entered the context[12] – and too weak – it would not mark (40c) as infelicitous where there is no reason to assume that the hearer has ever heard of Gazdar. Karttunen and Peters (1979) stipulate that the proposition in question must be "non-controversial" but do not elaborate on the notion of controversiality.

Let us now reconsider the sentences of (35), which I repeat here for convenience:

(35)a. John dreamt that he was in the Eskimo restaurant.
   b. John dreamt that he was in this Eskimo restaurant.
   c. There was an Eskimo restaurant.

As noted above, the hearer would not attribute the assumption (35c) to the speaker in (35b) but would in (35a). The difference may be explained as follows: In both cases, there is an Existential Inference that the speaker assumes there was an Eskimo restaurant – but only necessarily in the world under discussion: John's dream-world. Because indefinite-*this* NPs trigger only Existential Inferences, this is as far as the hearer of (35b) goes. Definite NPs, on the other hand, trigger also Familiarity Inferences, and the hearer of (35a) must assume that the speaker assumes that at least one part of the Rule of Familiarity Inferencing holds. If we take this sentence in isolation (which is what we have been doing), the most likely way for (39) to hold is if (39.3) holds, that is, if the hearer infers that the speaker assumes that the hearer already *had* (35c) as an assumption. But if the hearer already had (35c) as an assumption, the existence of the Eskimo restaurant cannot be limited to John's dream-world; it must be in some world (assumed to be) shared by the speaker and the hearer (e.g., the "real" world). Thus we see that the apparent survival of the existential presupposition in (35a) is not directly entailed by the Existential Inferencing of specific NPs in general but is a result of the *Familiarity* Inferencing of definite NPs. This is further supported by examples like (41):

(41)   John dreamt that he had gone to a World's Fair where you could get every possible kind of food and that he was in the Eskimo restaurant.

The hearer of (41) would no more infer that the speaker assumed that there was a real-world Eskimo restaurant than would the hearer of (35b). The reason for the difference in the inferencing of the definite NP in (35a) and in (41) is that, assuming a null context, (35a) triggers the third part of the Rule of Familiarity Inferencing, whereas (41) triggers the second part – from the first conjunct, the hearer can have inferred that such a dream-world World's Fair would have an Eskimo restaurant. Thus it is apparent that not even a subcategorization of "plugs" will succeed in predicting the "cancelability" of presuppositions/assumptions, even if the definiteness or indefiniteness of the NP is taken into account.

Uniqueness

As is well known, a presuppositional definite NP often conveys an understanding that there exists just one entity describable by that NP. This uniqueness understanding can be accounted for on the basis of the Familiarity Inferences, without any additional apparatus. (See also Kempson, 1975.) If the first part of the rule is to hold, the hearer must be able to pick out the unique referent of the anaphoric NP in order to determine that the assumption of its existence has already been attributed in the discourse. Thus (42a) and (42b) are, at the very least, extraordinarily uncooperative because the hearer cannot determine the antecedent of the definite NP:

(42)a. There are six boys in my class and the boy is the tallest of them.
   b. You'll find three books on my shelf. Bring me the book.

The question of uniqueness is somewhat different with respect to the third part of the rule, the one required for the inferencing of (among other things) proper names. Assume that A and B each have in their assumption-sets two assumptions:

(43)a. There is a person named Irving Goodman (who lives on Winthrop Street).
   b. There is a person named Irving Goodman (who lives on Lenox Road).

Assume further that A and B each assume the other has these two assumptions. If A then utters (44) to B, all other things being equal, B will be unable to decide which assumption is being evoked:

(44)   I saw Irving Goodman yesterday.

Though not as infelicitous as (42), (44) will call for a repair, that is, for B to ask something like:

(45)   Which one?[13]

However, when the definite NP in question is processed via the second part of the rule – the part needed (minimally) for relational terms – the hearer is in the position not of having to evoke/identify a specific assumption in his/her set but of inferring/building a new assumption on the basis of old ones, and, in such cases, there is no "uniqueness" understanding. That is, the hearer does not infer that the speaker assumes that there is just one entity describably by the italicized NPs in (46):

(46)a. A guy I work with broke *his leg.*
   b. May I use *your bathroom?*
   c. I'm spending the holidays with *my sister.*[14]

This digression into the so-called uniqueness implicatures/ presuppositions of definite NPs has been presented in order to make a prediction about indefinite-*this* NPs: Because they do not trigger

Familiarity Inferences, they will not convey any understanding of uniqueness. The prediction is in fact borne out by the data, where the contrast is striking:

(47)a. *"This fella we had working here,* he tried to hide the fact that he was feminine." (Hair stylist; Terkel, 1974, p. 320)
   b. *The fella we had working here,* he . . .
(48)a. "I got drunk one Friday night and while I was careening around town I ran into *this guy I knew from the past."* (Hockey player; Terkel, 1974, p. 504)
   b. . . . I ran into *the guy I knew from the past.*
(49)a. "I do *this one Jewish party in Skokie."* (Gas meter reader; Terkel, 1974, p. 370)
   b. I do *the one Jewish party in Skokie.*

Note, in addition, that NPs containing *this* (or other demonstratives) used as a true deictic also lack uniqueness understandings:

(50)   I want *this red car,* not that one.

The difference between deictic-*this* NPs and indefinite-*this* NPs is that, upon hearing the former, the hearer can uniquely identify the referent from extralinguistic cues, from the act of pointing, and, upon hearing the latter, the hearer is not expected to identify the referent at all. It is only when the hearer is called upon to uniquely identify a referent solely on the basis of linguistic cues that the uniqueness implicature is present.

So what's this all about?

There are several different directions in which this research can lead. First, it is not at all clear at present what kind of objects "potential presuppositions" are. Obviously, the rules/strategies for attributing them in discourse are pragmatic, but are they? Or are they semantic objects, part of the (truth-conditional) meaning of the sentences in question?[15] Second, what are the implications of the facts of indefinite-*this* NPs for theories that permit only external negation (Kempson, Gazdar), because the assumptions/presuppositions they carry are not cancelable under negation? Third, and in a different vein, if it is true that indefinite-*this* often serves in (nonstandard) colloquial English to introduce a new theme, why is such marking not important in more standard dialects? Or are there other processes that serve a similar function? Fourth, and most basic, what is the relation between the facts of indefinite-*this* NPs and the facts of indefinite NPs in general?

NOTES

This paper was presented at the Sloan Workshop on Indefinite Reference, December 2–3, 1978, University of Massachusetts, Amherst. I wish to thank the following persons for their comments and criticisms: Catherine Ball, Dwight Bolinger, Janet Fodor, Georgia Green, Barbara Grosz, Asa Kasher, William Labov, Jerry Morgan, Keith Stenning, and Bonnie Webber.

1 Though classic, this test is not quite perfect, as pointed out in Bolinger (1977) and Ziv (1978). The NPs in (9), however, are not of the type that is problematic, for example:

   i. There was the usual crowd at the beach last Sunday.

     Note that such definites cannot contain this *this:*

   ii. *There was this usual crowd at the beach last Sunday.

2 I thank William Labov for bringing Perlman (1969) to my attention.

3 Note, however, that, although indefinite *this* may occur instead of *a*, it cannot be said to actually replace *a*, as it very commonly occurs with numbers, with which *a* is in complementary distribution. See, for example, (9c) above and:

   i. "I was with *this one cop,* he wanted to sneak up on cars. . ." (Fireman; Terkel, 1974, p. 751)

   ii. "She used to say she had *these five brothers* . . ." (Hospital aide; Terkel, 1974, p. 621)

4 Somewhat surprisingly, perhaps, an examination of naturally occurring discourse reveals that not all indefinites introduce new information in a discourse. In particular, generic indefinites may represent old information, as in:

   i. "With *stone* we build just about everything. *Stone* is the oldest and best building material that ever was. *Stone* was being used even by the cavemen that put it together with mud. They build out of *stone* before they even used logs. . ." (Stonemason; Terkel, 1974, p. 17)

Specific indefinites, however, cannot represent old information in this way, and I shall argue that indefinite-*this* NPs are necessarily specific.

5 Some occurrences of indefinite *this* may, however, constitute a special subclass. While they introduce new information in the discourse, they also do something else: They are *necessary* for marking the NP as an entity (specific and referential) rather than as part of an attribute (nonspecific and attributive):

   i.A: Why do you like him?
      B: Oh he has *these eyes* . . .
      B': *Oh, he has *eyes.* . .
      (B'': *Oh, he has *the eyes* . . .)
   ii.A: Why did you buy such an expensive car?
      B: Well, you see, it had *these hubcaps* . . .
      B':*Well, you see, it had *hubcaps* . . .
      (B':*Well, you see, it had *the hubcaps* . . .)

My shaky intuition is that such occurrences of *this,* though colloquial, are quite standard, another reason for distinguishing them. I do not, however,

have sufficient naturally occuring data to be anything more than very
tentative about them.

6 I thank Carole N. Frankel and Mark Mandel for confirming these facts
about American Sign Language.

7 However, sentences containing nonspecific superlatives like (i) and (ii) are,
in some practical way, presuppositional, although they are nonreferential;
that is, they lack a paraphrase containing an *if any*–clause:

    i. *The last one in* is a monkey's uncle (*if anyone is the last one in).
    ii. The job will go to *the one that types the fastest* (*if anyone types the fastest).

It is not clear to me, however, what kind of presupposition such NPs carry.

8 In particular, Givón (1978, p. 71) states: "there is nothing LOGICALLY
wrong with [a specific] interpretation of [negative] sentences . . . , but
nevertheless it is not the preferred interpretation."

9 One possible exception is Heringer (1969), where specific indefinites in
opaque contexts are considered. It is argued that, in sentences like (19b),
the subject (*Mary*), though not the speaker, must assume the existence of
the referent of the NP in question (*a pink truck*). However, he ignores the
possibility that specific indefinites may be presuppositional in the way that
specific definites are, from the speaker's point of view.

A second and far more relevant exception is Partee (1972), where it is
stated that referential indefinite NPs carry an existential presupposition
(p. 418) and even that some indefinite NPs (*a certain X*) are always used
referentially. However, Partee's concern is not primarily with a presuppositional account, and negative environments are not considered.

A third exception is Kasher and Gabbay (1976), which has come to my
attention since the original writing of this chapter and with which the
present chapter coincides on a number of points. Immediately relevant is
the authors' claim that "the distinction between specific and non-specific
expressions is, *in every case,* a linguistic distinction which reflects ambiguity
rather than vagueness" (p. 159).

10 I remind the reader to read these examples with *indefinite this* (i.e., with the
this that is more or less paraphrasable by *a*). If this proves difficult, the
reader may replace *this pink truck* in each example with *this one pink truck*.

11 See Partee (1972) and Donnellan (1978) for a discussion of such coreference or *anaphoric chains*.

12 Nothing in Gazdar's model – or in Karttunen's or Karttunen and Peters's –
leads one to infer more than one "context" per speech situation. What
is actually needed, of course, is some notion of individual assumption-
sets.

13 Sentence (44) is less infelicitous than (42a) probably because it is far easier
to think that the utterer of (44) had forgotten about the existence of all but
one of the possible referents than it is to think the same thing about the
utterer of (42a).

14 However, some of the male participants in the Old/New Information
Workshop, July–August 1978, Urbana, claimed that they would in fact
infer uniqueness upon hearing:

    i. My ball itches.

More research is required.

15 Kempson (1975) is clear in claiming that there is no semantic basis for potential presuppositions, Gazdar does not take a stand (although he implicates that they have no semantic import), and Kasher and Gabbay (1976) argue strongly that they are represented in the semantics. It is interesting to note that, of the three, only Kasher and Gabbay consider indefinites, whose "presuppositionality," once recognized, is far more difficult to ignore.

REFERENCES

Bolinger, D. 1977. *Meaning and Form.* London: Longmans.
Clark, H., and Marshall, C. 1978. "Definite Reference and Mutual Knowledge." Presented at the Sloan Workshop on Computational Aspects of Linguistic Structure and Discourse Setting. University of Pennsylvania. May 24–27.
Donnellan, K. 1971. "Reference and Definite Descriptions." In D. Steinberg, and L. Jakobovits, eds. *Semantics.* Cambridge: Cambridge University Press, pp. 100–14.
Donnellan, K. 1978. "Speaker References, Descriptions, and Anaphora." In P. Cole, ed. *Syntax and Semantics,* Vol. 9, *Pragmatics.* New York: Academic Press, pp. 47–68.
Gazdar, G. 1976. "Formal Pragmatics for Natural Language. Implicature, Presupposition, and Logical Form. Ph.D. dissertation, University of Reading.
Gazdar, G. 1978. *Pragmatics.* New York: Academic Press.
Gazdar, G. 1979. "A solution to the projection problem." In C.-K. Oh, and D. Dinneen, eds. *Syntax and Semantics,* Vol. 11, *Presupposition.* New York: Academic Press, pp. 57–90.
Givón, T. 1978. "Negation in Language: Pragmatics, Function, Ontology." In P. Cole, ed. *Syntax and Semantics,* Vol. 9, *Pragmatics.* New York: Academic Press, pp. 69–112.
Heringer, J. 1969. "Indefinite Noun Phrases and Referential Opacity." *Papers from the Fifth Regional Meeting, Chicago Linguistics Society,* pp. 89–97.
Karttunen, L. 1973. "Presuppositions of Compound Sentences." *Linguistic Inquiry* 4:169–93.
Karttunen, L. 1974. "Presupposition and Linguistic Context." *Theoretical Linguistics* 1:182–94.
Karttunen, L., and Peters, S. 1979. "Conventional Implicature." In C.-K. Oh, and D. Dinneen, eds. *Syntax and Semantics,* Vol. 11, *Presupposition.* New York: Academic Press, pp. 1–56.
Kasher, A., and Gabbay, D. 1976. "On the Semantics and Pragmatics of Specific and Non-specific Indefinite Expressions." *Theoretical Linguistics* 1:139–57.
Kempson, R. 1975. *Presupposition and the Delimitation of Semantics.* Cambridge: Cambridge University Press.
Lakoff, R. 1974. "Remarks on *This* and *That.*" *Papers from the Tenth Regional Meeting, Chicago Linguistics Society,* pp. 345–56.
Morgan, J. 1969. "On the Treatment of Presupposition in Transformational Grammar." *Papers from the Fifth Regional Meeting, Chicago Linguistics Society,* pp. 167–77.

Partee, B. 1972. "Opacity, Coreference, and Pronouns." In D. Davidson and G. Harman, eds. *Semantics of Natural Language*. Dordrecht: Reidel, pp. 415–41.

Perlman, A. 1969. " 'This' as a Third Article in American English." *American Speech* 44, 1:76–80.

Prince, E. F. 1978. "On the Function of Existential Presupposition in Discourse." *Papers from the Fourteenth Regional Meeting, Chicago Linguistics Society*, pp. 362–76.

Terkel, S. 1974. *Working*. New York: Avon.

Ziv, Y. 1978. "On Existential *There* in Hebrew and English." Presented to the Pragmatics Workshop. Urbana, Illinois. July.

11

Abstract theories of discourse and the formal specification of programs that converse

STANLEY J. ROSENSCHEIN

In this chapter we develop a small fragment of discourse theory to illustrate how abstract models of mental state can formally link the theory of language to the theory of computation. We view an individual's beliefs as a set of sentences in a formal language that change over time in response to events (including perceived utterances). Then, by a shift of perspective, we show how our theory can be taken as the abstract specification of a computer program that uses language. In principle, such a specification could be used to rigorously demonstrate that a computer implementation is consistent with linguistic or pragmatic facts.

In studying discourse from a computational viewpoint it is natural to concentrate on providing adequate descriptions of mental state. The very basis of discourse is people's ability to partially control one another's mental states using cultural and linguistic conventions – which themselves exist, ultimately, in the minds of individuals. Because computation is conventionally described in terms of state sequences, it is possible to identify "computational state" with "state of mind" and develop a vocabulary that spans both.[1]

The theory of abstract program specification is well suited to bridging the conceptual gap between computational state and mental state. This body of research is aimed at providing convenient tools for defining abstract machines and processes and for producing concrete realizations that provably capture the properties of the abstract machines. This technique has received attention for its usefulness in the generation of reliable software (Dijkstra, 1976). It has much to recommend it as a theoretical framework for cognitive science as well.[2]

Formalizing the description of discourse in terms of mental states can be expected to benefit both the theory of language and applied computational linguistics. Language theory will benefit from a coherent account of pragmatic and semantic phenomena embedded in a more inclusive theory of purposive behavior. Language processing

251

will gain precise methods for describing computer programs as embodying this or that discourse theory, which should make the analysis and synthesis of conversational programs more systematic.

The plan of the chapter is as follows: Section 1 develops a fragment of discourse theory as a set of formal axioms and presents a brief example of their use. Section 2 discusses the interpretation of the formal theory as a partial specification for a computer program, and section 3 contains a small sample program as an illustration of these ideas. Conclusions and areas for future research are given in section 4.

1. Fragment of a formal model of discourse

In this section we attempt to formalize some of the properties a person engaged in discourse might exhibit. Because our purpose is to illustrate an approach rather than to establish an empirically valid theory, we shall present a very simplified, schematic model.

Discourse theory is primarily concerned with how linguistic events are interpreted and initiated for pragmatic effect, and for this reason much of our model concerns general, nonlinguistic aspects of understanding and action. Our primary modeling technique is to describe the relationship maintained over time among the beliefs, goals, and actions of an individual. In brief, we assume these entities to be interrelated in the following way: *At each instant in time a person acts in a way he believes will achieve his goals.* By giving technical meanings to the terms "belief" and "goal" this informal (and rather shallow) assertion about human action can become a surprisingly powerful component of a formal model.

Beliefs are modeled as (potentially infinite) sets of sentences in a formal language. Each set of sentences represents a particular view of the world, especially the evolving mental world of other speakers.[3] To realistically model discourse, the language of beliefs and goals will have to contain recursively nested assertions about beliefs and goals of other individuals. (See, e.g., Cohen, 1978.) An individual's belief set ordinarily varies over time – in fact, from instant to instant. If x believes sentence p at time t, we write $B(x, p, t)$ and define $Bel(x, t) = \{p \mid B(x, p, t)\}$.[4]

Goals are modeled in a way similar to beliefs, that is, as a set of sentences in the same formal language. If x wants p at time t, we write $G(x, p, t)$ and define $Goals(x, t) = \{p \mid G(x, p, t)\}$.

To avoid misunderstanding, let us clarify the intended status of "beliefs" and "goals" in the model. These terms are used to denote theoretical entities and have technical meanings that the names merely suggest. In some cases our use of these terms may deviate from their accepted meanings in ordinary language. Also, no claim is being made for a direct correspondence between these entities and any psychological process. "Having" a set of formal belief sentences, then, is like "having" a generative grammar; both are abstractions that simplify the task of describing what people know.

Informal discussion of the assumptions

Our model consists of a set of assumptions, or axioms, divided into the following general categories: (1) internal constraints on beliefs and goals (CONSISTENCY, CLOSURE, MOTIVATION, and DECISIVENESS); (2) axioms of environmental contact (AWARENESS and CONTROL); and (3) assumptions of a cultural and linguistic nature (READINGS, DECLARATIVES, and COMMON KNOWLEDGE). We shall explain the intent of these axioms before proceeding with the formal presentation.

CONSISTENCY and CLOSURE axioms are required to drive the underlying logical machinery. These axioms should not be interpreted as claims that people are always "consistent" or know the "consequences" of their beliefs in some more general, informal sense.

The DECISIVENESS axiom ensures that actions are always selected, and the MOTIVATION axiom provides a general mechanism for stipulating what *kinds* of actions are taken. By describing a fundamental relationship that must be preserved, this axiom allows a direct assertion about one component of the belief–goal–action triad to serve as an indirect assertion about the other two.

The axioms of environmental contact (AWARENESS and CONTROL) relate mental events to nommental events and provide the machinery for mediating events in several minds. These axioms serve as a formal description of how, for example, deciding to utter a sentence might imply that the sentence is actually uttered, which in turn might imply that the hearer believes it was uttered.

The axiom of READINGS is meant as an entry point into general semantic theory. In this view, discourse theory contains semantics as a proper subtheory. The semantic subtheory defines what counts as a valid reading for a sentence, where "valid reading" is a distinguished relation (between sentences and interpretations) shared by all members of the language community.

The DECLARATIVES axiom provides a way of passing from assertions about the propositional content of a sentence to assertions about people's beliefs. Because it is clearly not the case that people believe exactly what they are told, we have proposed a weaker view of the effect of declarative sentences, namely, that their propositional content enters the hearer's beliefs at the least level of indirection that maintains consistency with his other beliefs. Thus, for example, if someone hears p, knows that p is not the case, but has no reason to believe the speaker doubts p, then he will accept that the speaker believed p. (This axiom is proposed as a plausible hypothesis about discourse rather than as a strong claim.)

The COMMON KNOWLEDGE axiom allows us to use these same axioms in reasoning about beliefs at any level of embedding.

Formalization of the axioms

Before presenting the formal axioms, we shall introduce some notation.

Primitives

$B(x, p, t)$, $Bel(x, t)$, $G(x, p, t)$, $Goals(x, t)$ – as explained above.

$S \vdash p - p$ "follows from" the set of sentences, S.

$A(x,t)$ – a distinguished class of sentences naming actions that an individual x can take at time t.

$DO(x, a, t) - x$ performs, at time t, the action described by sentence a.

$ENGL\text{-}RDG(s, r) - r$ is a valid English reading for sentence s.

int-rdg(x, s, t) – the reading that, at time t, x intended for the hearer to recover upon hearing sentence s.

$UTTER$ $(x, s, y, t_1, t_2) - x$ utters declarative sentence s at time t_1 intending that y hear it at time t_2.

Definitions

$$NEST(n, p, x, y, t_1, t_2) = \begin{cases} P & \text{if } n = 0 \\ B(x, NEST(n - 1, p, y, x, t_2, t_1), t_1) & \text{if } n > 0 \\ \text{undefined} & \text{if } n < 0 \end{cases}$$

We sometimes write $NEST(n, p, v)$ – and later $ENTERS(n, p, v)$ – where it is clear from context that $v = \langle x, y, t_1, t_2 \rangle$.

$ENTERS(n, p, v) \Leftrightarrow [NEST(i, p, v)$ is false for $0 < i < n$ and true for $i = n]$.

$SHARED\text{-}K(p, x, y, t, t') \Leftrightarrow$ for all $n > 0$ $NEST(n, p, x, y, t, t')$.

$COMMON\text{-}K(p) \Leftrightarrow$ for all s, y, t, t' $SHARED\text{-}K(p, x, y, t, t')$.

We now present the axioms themselves together with informal glosses.

Internal constraints on beliefs and goals

(CONSISTENCY) $B(x, p, t) \Rightarrow {}^{\sim}B(x, {}^{\sim}p, t)$

[A person cannot simultaneously believe a sentence and its negation.]

(CLOSURE) $Bel(x, t) \vdash p \Rightarrow B(x, p, t)$

[Logical consequences of beliefs are believed.]

(DECISIVENESS) $| Bel(x, t) \cap A(x, t) | = 1$

[At each instant there is exactly one action a person believes he is taking.]

(MOTIVATION) $DO(x, a, t) \Rightarrow$

    Exists g s.t. $G(x, g, t)$ & $B(x, a \Rightarrow g, t)$

[A person acts in a way he believes achieves a goal.]

Environmental axioms

(AWARENESS SCHEMA) $E(t) \Rightarrow B(x, E(t), t')$,
          where $E(t)$ describes a certain event
          occurring at time t, and $t' > t$.
[A person knows if events of certain types occur.]
(CONTROL) $a \in A(x, t)$ & $B(x, a, t) \Rightarrow DO(x, a, t)$
[For "action" sentences, believing them makes them happen.]

Cultural and linguistic assumptions

(READINGS) $UTTER(x, s, y, t, t') \Rightarrow ENGL\text{-}RDG(s, \text{int-rdg}(x, s, t))$
[Every uttered sentence has an intended reading, which is one of the valid
English readings for that sentence.]
(DECLARATIVES) $UTTER(x, s, y, t_1, t_2) \Rightarrow$ Exists $n > 0$ s.t.
          $ENTERS(n, \text{int-rdg}(x, s, t_1), x, y, t_1, t_2)$
[A person who utters a declarative sentence believes his intended reading
enters his hearer's beliefs (at some level).]
(COMMON KNOWLEDGE)   COMMON-K(p),
          for $p \in \{(\text{CONSISTENCY}), \dots ,$
          $(\text{DECLARATIVES})\}$
[The above axioms are common knowledge.]

Some simple consequences of the axioms

We shall illustrate how the axioms provide a natural way of combining
semantic and pragmatic constraints in a unified framework. Observe
that the DECLARATIVES axiom ensures that an intended reading
enters the hearer's beliefs at some level. This fact, together with the
CONSISTENCY requirement, will serve to enforce semantic constraints on the selection of readings.

For example, assume Al utters to Bill the English sentence $s =$ "Carl
hit the ball," for which there are two English readings:

p_1 = Carl made an appearance at the dance.
p_2 = Carl struck the spheroid.

Assume also that Al and Bill share the belief (are aware they share
the belief . . .) that for someone to make an appearance at the dance
he would have to leave home – and Carl never left home. (Let
p_3 = Carl left home.) We conclude Al meant that Carl struck the
spheroid.

The formal derivation goes as follows. We wish to prove B(Bill,
int-rdg(Al, s, t_1) = p_2, t_2) using the assumptions:

(a1)   SHARED-K($p_1 \rightarrow p_3$, Al, Bill, t, t') for all t, t'
(a2)   SHARED-K($\neg p_3$, Al, Bill, t, t') for all t, t'
(a3)   B(Bill, UTTER(Al, s, Bill, t_1, t_2), t_2)
(a4)   SHARED-K(ENGL-RDG(s, r) $\rightarrow r = p_1/r = p_2$)

Let I = int-rdg(Al, s, t_1). By assumptions (a3), (a4), and CLOSURE,

  (b)   B(Bill, $I = p_1 \bigvee I = p_2$, t_2)

This can also be written:

  (c)   B(Bill, $I \neq p_1 \Rightarrow I = p_2$, t_2)

from which it follows (by CLOSURE) that to prove our theorem it suffices to prove B(Bill, $I \neq p_1$, t_2). We know (from DECLARATIVES and COMMON-KNOWLEDGE) that Bill believes that if p_1 is the intended reading, then it enters at some level, call it k.

  (d)   B(Bill, $I = p_1 \Rightarrow$ ENTERS(k, p_1, Al, Bill, t_1, t_2), t_2)

By the definition of ENTERS,

  (e)   B(Bill, $I = p_1 \Rightarrow$ NEST)k, p_1, A1, Bill, t_1, t_2), t_2)

But by assumptions (a1), (a2), and the definition of SHARED-K,

  (f)   B(Bill, NEST(k, $p_1 \rightarrow p_3$, Al, Bill, t_1, t_2), t_2)
        B(Bill, NEST(k, $\tilde{} p_3$, Al, Bill, t_1, t_2), t_2)

CLOSURE guarantees:

  (g)   B(Bill, NEST(k, $\tilde{} p_1$, Al, Bill, t_1, t_2), t_2)

CONSISTENCY requires B(x, $\tilde{} p$, t) $\Rightarrow$ $\tilde{}$B(x, p, t), which we can apply k times to the definition of NEST to yield:

  (h)   B(Bill, $\tilde{}$NEST(k, p_1, Al, Bill, t_1, t_2), t_2)

This with the contrapositive form of (e) refutes the hypothesis that Bill believes p_1 was intended.

  (i)   B(Bill, $I \neq p_1$, t_2)

He must therefore believe that p_2 was intended, and our theorem is proved: B(Bill, int-rdg(Al, s, t_1) = p_2, t_2). Informally, then, Bill believes Al meant to say that Carl struck the spheroid.

2. From formal models to program specifications

By giving a formal proof we do not mean to imply that a language-understanding program is best organized as a theorem prover. On the contrary, formal deduction is probably not the right implementation mechanism. What, then, is the relationship between our formal apparatus and actual conversational programs? This section addresses that question from the perspective of program correctness theory.

By interpreting the formal discourse model as a program specification, programs can be proved to possess certain discourse properties. The key is to view the axioms as meta-assertions *about* a language-understanding program rather than as formal objects to be manipulated *by* the program. A program could be constructed that probably behaves as the axioms require but does not contain representations of the axioms as data objects.

Program verification theory is the branch of computer science concerned with formally (and, in some cases, automatically) proving that programs conform to their authors' stated intentions. Typically these intentions are expressed as a formal input–output specification, but the theory has been applied to nonterminating programs (like computer operating systems) which do not define simple input–output functions and to concurrent processes (Brinch-Hansen, 1973).

Many verification methods exist (Manna, 1974; Manna and Waldinger, 1977), the best-known being the inductive assertions method (Floyd, 1967). This technique involves reducing the correctness of the program to the truth of a set of verification conditions derived from assertions (called *invariants*) attached to intermediate points in the program. Proving the verification conditions guarantees that whenever control reaches one of these points, the associated invariant will be true. (For programs with loops these proofs often proceed inductively; hence the name "inductive assertion.") The truth of the verification conditions guarantees that the program does indeed compute the specified input–output function for all valid inputs. In practice, the naturalness and tractability of the technique is profoundly influenced by the choice of invariants, so that abstractions that simplify the invariants and the proofs are of considerable utility.

By describing the program's operation as consisting of abstract operations performed on abstract data objects, the input–output specification can be made more manageable. The correctness proof, too, is simpler because it consists of two independent parts: proving that the abstract program correctly transforms the abstract objects, and proving that the concrete program correctly implements the abstract one. There has grown up in the past few years an entire subdiscipline concerned with abstract specifications and their use in proving program correctness, with special attention to abstract data structures (Dijkstra, 1976; Liskov and Zilles, 1975; Guttag, 1977).

To use these techniques in applying our model to language programs, we need to define program counterparts to the primitive notions of the model (e.g., Bel(SYSTEM, t), Goals(SYSTEM, t), UTTER). Let us consider how Bel(SYSTEM, t) might be operationalized. For convenience we shall consider program time to be discrete. Furthermore, because we are concerned with ongoing behavior, let us postulate a point in the program (the *"cycle point"*) to which control will return an infinite number of times, possibly by different paths. Whenever we predicate something of the system at time i, for example B(SYSTEM, p, i), we shall interpret this as an assertion about the state of the system the ith time it reaches the cycle point.

The program would have one or more variables that "contain" the beliefs of the system. For simplicity, let us assume there is a single distinguished variable, BEL, whose value at reaching the cycle point for the ith time is a finite encoding of Bel(SYSTEM, i). This encoding might be as a set of symbolic assertions whose deductive closure equals Bel(SYSTEM, i). Alternatively, some specialized storage structure might be used. We only require the existence of a function b-closure(BEL) that maps the finite object BEL onto the potentially infinite belief set. Note that the closure function need not be implemented; it is simply a way of conceptualizing what the value of the variable BEL stands for. Goals(SYSTEM, i) would be handled in a similar way with GOALS as the system variable and g-closure(GOALS) as the conceptual function.

The action set A(SYSTEM, i) can be translated into a corresponding set of computer actions that can be taken at the cycle point. For instance, A(SYSTEM, i) can include UTTER(SYSTEM, s,i) and LISTEN(SYSTEM, i), the first denoting the production of "s" as system output immediately after the cycle point, and the latter receiving input at that point. By the DECISIVENESS axiom there must be exactly one sentence that is both an action and a system belief at time i. This sentence can be computed by the function act(BEL), with the function PERFORM(act) actually performing the action denoted by the sentence.

The following program structure reflects the ideas described above.

```
begin
  i : = 0;
  BEL : = BEL0;
  GOALS : = GOALS0;
  while (true) do begin
    i : = i + 1;          [i is the time index]
                          [*** this is the cycle point ***]
    PERFORM(act(BEL));
    . . .
    BEL : = . . . ;
    . . .
    GOALS : = . . . ;
    . . .
  end;
end;
```

The cycle point of this program would be right after the increment of the time index. PERFORM would be a procedure with side effects (especially input and output). Updates to BEL and GOALS could be interspersed throughout the program; and although we have portrayed these as assignments, they could be achieved by structure-modifying operations as well.

To prove that a program having this structure actually conforms to our model it is necessary to translate each axiom into an invariant associated with the cycle point. For example, the CONSISTENCY axiom would be translated into

$$p \in \text{b-closure(BEL)} \Rightarrow {}^\sim p \notin \text{b-closure(BEL)}$$

This could be verified inductively, showing that it holds for BEL.0 and is preserved by the updates along each path leading back to the cycle point. Note that probabilistic assignment can occur (to BEL, say) and still satisfy this invariant. This means that uncertainty can be introduced into a system that still provably captures the theory; assignments to BEL might involve a random draw, all outcomes of which satisfy the invariant.

By the DECISIVENESS, CONTROL, and MOTIVATION axioms we know that the following relationship must hold at the cycle point:

Exists $g \in$ g-closure(GOALS) such that
$(\text{act(BEL)} \Rightarrow g) \in$ b-closure(BEL)

Similar invariants would be dictated by the other axioms of the model.

Although from a formal standpoint it is clear what is required, the model in its most general form would be difficult or impossible to implement with full accuracy. The reason for this has to with decidability issues surrounding the CLOSURE axiom. However, by suitably restricting the range of BEL and GOALS, variants of the model could be built and verified. In addition to easing the decidability issues, these variants could exhibit useful special properties.

For instance, we can define a predicate $\text{COOP}(x, y, t)$ that asserts that x is "cooperative" toward y at time t in the sense of adopting as his own goals whatever he perceives y's goals to be. More formally,

$$\text{COOP}(x, y, t) \Leftrightarrow [B(x, G(y, g, t), t) \Rightarrow G(x, g, t)]$$

The assertion that a particular program is always cooperative can now be translated into the following cycle point invariant to be proved:

$$G(y, g, i) \in \text{b-closure(BEL)} \Rightarrow g \in \text{g-closure(GOALS)}$$

Again, operations that change the values of BEL or GOAL during program operation have to be such that this cycle invariant is maintained.

3. Example

In this section we present a short "conversational" program and describe how one would prove that it satisfies the MOTIVATION axiom and the COOPERATIVITY property. The detailed development of a program and of a complete proof lie outside the scope of this chapter. Instead, we show how possession of the properties in question can be reduced to verifying that certain key subfunctions (notably "parse" and "deduce") possess other, simpler properties. To do this, we make use of the abstract auxiliary functions b-closure and g-closure, as described in the previous section. Again, our goal is to focus on the applicability of certain methods rather than the program's behavior per se.

Briefly, the program operates by accepting sentences, parsing them, and updating its beliefs (partitioned into two data structures called PRIVBEL and SHAREDBEL) and its goals. At each cycle, the belief set is guaranteed to contain a formula naming an action the program can perform. The program then performs this action, resulting either in the production of a sentence as output or in the reading of an input sentence for further processing.

In presenting the program, several liberties are taken to simplify the exposition. The representation of time is ignored for the most part, and computer operations are sometimes specified in informal language. Additionally, subfunctions whose definitions could be considered either obvious or tangential to our main purpose are used but not defined. Nonetheless, the form of the arguments would be substantially the same for a more elaborate system.

Before presenting the program text, it is necessary to make a few remarks about the representation of beliefs. Our program maintains its (explicit) beliefs as a set of propositional formulas in a PLANNER-style data base. Some formulas are atomic, whereas others are simple conditional formulas with variables that are assumed to be universally quantified. There is a subfunction called *deduce* (⟨form⟩, ⟨database⟩, ⟨resourcebound⟩). If ⟨form⟩ contains no variables, then *deduce* returns "true" if it can prove ⟨form⟩ from ⟨database⟩ without exceeding ⟨resourcebound⟩ (measured in time or space), "false" if its negation can be proved, and "unknown" if neither can be proved. If ⟨form⟩ contains free variables, *deduce* returns a sequence (possibly null) of bindings for the free variables of ⟨form⟩ that would make ⟨form⟩ provable from ⟨database⟩. The sequence contains those bindings that can be discovered within ⟨resourcebound⟩.

For concreteness, our program's initial set of beliefs assert that the program (denoted by the symbol *I*) is in a restaurant with a friend named John. They have just finished eating and are about to pay the check.

```
begin
    i : = 0;
    PRIVBEL : = ⟨initial nonshared beliefs . . .⟩;
    SHAREDBEL[*I*, JOHN] : =
                        ⟨initial beliefs shared with John . . .⟩;
    GOALS : = {HEAR(*I*)};

while (true) do begin
        i : = i + 1;
        PRIVBEL : = insert(findact(select(i, GOALS,
                            PRIVBEL, SHAREDBEL[*I*, JOHN])),
                        PRIVBEL);
        ALLBEL : = union(PRIVBEL, SHAREDBEL);
        a : = act(ALLBEL)

    { *** this is the cycle point *** }

        PERFORM(a);
        if a = LISTEN(*I*) then begin
        p : = extractlastinput (SHAREDBEL[*I*,JOHN]);
            PRIVBEL : = insert(entry(p,ALLBEL),PRIVBEL);
            GOALS : = updategoals(extractgoals(JOHN,ALLBEL),
                        GOALS, PRIVBEL, SHAREDBEL[*I*, JOHN]);
            end; else
        if a = UTTER(*I*, s)
            then SHAREDBEL[*I*, JOHN] : =
                insert(entry(s, extractbels(JOHN, ALLABEL)),
                    SHAREDBEL[*I*, JOHN]);
    end;
end;

procedure PERFORM(a)
begin
    if a = LISTEN(*I*)
    then SHAREDBEL[*I*, JOHN] : = insert(HEARD
                    (*I*, parse(read())), i), SHAREDBEL[*I*, JOHN])
    else if a = UTTER(*I*,s) then print(generate(s));
    return;
    end;
```

A representative set of initial beliefs might be:

PRIVBEL : =   { ~HAVE-MONEY(*I*),   ~BELIEVE
                (JOHN, ~HAVE-MONEY(*I*)) }

SHAREDBEL[*I*,JOHN]: =

{IN-RESTAURANT(*I*),	~PAY-CHECK(x) ⇒ ~LEAVE(x),
IN-RESTAURANT(JOHN),	~HAVE-MONEY(x) ⇒
	~PAY-CHECK(x),
FINISHED-EATING(*I*),	FRIENDS(x, y) &
	~HAVE-MONEY(x) &
~PAY-CHECK(*I*),	HAVE-MONEY(y) ⇒
	WANT(y,PAY-CHECK(y))
~PAY-CHECK (JOHN),	FINISHED-EATING(s) ⇒
	WANT(x,LEAVE(x))
FRIENDS(*I*, JOHN),	FRIEND(x,y) & LEAVE(x) ⇒
	LEAVE(y)
HAVE-MONEY (JOHN) }	

Consider the following exchange:

> John: I'm finished now.
> System: I don't have any money.

Let us trace through the first cycle of the program's intended operation. If we assume GOALS, PRIVBEL, and SHAREDBEL are initialized as described, we want select(i, GOALS, . . .) to return HEAR(*I*) as the goal being pursued. The function "findact," in turn, should return LISTEN(*I*) as the action intended to achieve this goal. The expression act(ALLBEL) evaluates to this same action, which PERFORM then executes, causing the input "I'm finished now" to be read, parsed, and stored as HEARD(*I*, FINISHED-EATING(JOHN)).

Back in the main program, the formula FINISHED-EATING(JOHN)) is retrieved by extractlastinput and assigned to p. The function "entry" calculates the entry level of p, in this case causing p to enter PRIVBEL as is because p does not contradict any other beliefs. The deductive component is presumed to be invoked by extractgoals, which infers WANT(JOHN, LEAVE(JOHN)). The function updategoals then adds LEAVE(JOHN) to the program's GOALS because we assume cooperativity.

Execution returns to the beginning of the while loop, with select(. . .) choosing LEAVE(JOHN). It is now findact's job to return a form that implies LEAVE(JOHN). In this case it chooses

UTTER(*I*,~HAVE(*I*,MONEY)). The reason for this is as follows: By the initial belief set, for John to leave requires that *I* leave, which in turn requires that *I* pay – or that John pays, which he will do (cooperatively) if he believes that *I* has no money; hence the choice of action. This choice eventually causes PERFORM to call generate, resulting in the sentence "I don't have any money" being printed.

The two invariants we are concerned with have to do with the preservation of the MOTIVATION and COOPERATIVITY properties. In the case of the former, the primary burden of verification rests on findact (presuming that the "act" function is a reliable selector function). What needs to be verified is that (findact(g, b_1, b_2) $\Rightarrow$ g) is in b-closure(b_1, b_2), where b-closure(b_1, b_2) is the deductive closure of the finite set of propositions b_1, with all proper nestings of the formulas in b_2. This is a clear enough requirement, though one that may have to be weakened in practice.

As far as COOPERATIVITY is concerned, the relevant functions are extractgoals and updategoals. Here there are two invariants to be proved: (1) g-closure(extractgoals(JOHN, b) = $\{x \mid$ WANT(JOHN, x) is in b-closure(b)}, and (2) g is contained in updategoals(g, . . .). The latter can be trivially accomplished through the proper definition of updategoals, though the former may be harder to achieve.

4. Conclusion

This chapter has attempted to describe some points of contact between formal discourse theory and the specification of computer programs for understanding language. The relationship is based on interpreting assertions about mental state during discourse as if they were assertions (especially inductive assertions) describing the computational state of a conversational program. This method can be used to formally verify that programs conform to particular linguistic theories or exhibit discourse properties like cooperativity.

Additional research should be directed toward the discovery of classes of discourse models whose special features facilitate their instantiation as computer programs. Some possibilities include restricting the beliefs to be of a certain form (e.g., all beliefs that are not shared knowledge can be nested only to depth k), or considering systems with fixed (or cooperatively adaptive) goal sets. An attempt should be made to incorporate more empirically accurate assertions into the model so that truer characterizations of discourse can replace the rough approximations proposed in DECLARATIVES and READINGS.

In a sense, discourse theory and semantics can be viewed as elaborate subcomponents of a theory like the one we have sketched; although these theories do not often deal explicitly of the speakers' states and behavior over time, these notions are clearly in the background. Making them more explicit may provide the key to translating large amounts of linguistic knowledge into usable program specifications. This possibility presents a variety of methodological and substantive challenges to both linguistic and computational theory.

NOTES

I have profited from many long discussions with Norman Shapiro on the subject of modeling and from the helpful comments of Phil Klahr.

1 This perspective is adopted in much of the research of John McCarthy (McCarthy, 1977; McCarthy and Hayes, 1969), although there has been no attempt to apply it to discourse theory, nor has the connection with recent work in program specification and verification been made explicit.
2 Burstall (Burstall and Goguen, 1977) has used theories to form specifications. His constructs were theories (in the formal sense) but were not motivated by a specific empirical domain such as linguistics or psychology.
3 Although we have not done so, it is clear how one could use a formalization of belief sets to express facts about perception, sudden realization, developmental change, forgetting, and so on.
4 We have intentionally mixed levels of language to avoid technical complications. A more rigorous treatment, however, would require that we distinguish in our notation between expressions in our language and those in the belief of an individual being modeled.

REFERENCES

Brinch-Hansen, P. 1973. *Operating System Principles*. Englewood Cliffs, N.J.: Prentice-Hall.
Burstall, R. M., and Goguen, J. A. 1977. "Putting Theories Together to Make Specifications." *Proceedings of the Fifth International Conference on Artificial Intelligence*. Cambridge, Mass., pp. 1045–58.
Cohen, P. R. 1978. "On Knowing What to Say: Planning Speech Acts." Technical Report No. 118, University of Toronto, Department of Computer Science.
Dijkstra, E. W. 1976. *A Discipline of Programming*. Englewood Cliffs, N.J.: Prentice-Hall.
Floyd, R. W. 1967. "Assigning Meanings to Programs." In J. T. Schwartz, ed. *Mathematical Aspects of Computer Science*. Providence, R.I.: American Mathematical Society, pp. 19–32.

Guttag, J. 1977. "Abstract Data Types and the Development of Data Structures." *Communications of the ACM* 20:396–404.

Liskov, B., and Zilles, S. 1975. "Specification Techniques for Data Abstractions." *Proceedings of International Conference on Reliable Software. SIGPLAN Notices* 10:72–87.

McCarthy, J. 1977. "Epistemological Problems of Artificial Intelligence." *Proceedings of the Fifth International Joint Conference on Artificial Intelligence.* Cambridge, Mass., pp. 1038–44.

McCarthy, J., and Hayes, P. J. 1969. "Some Philosophical Problems from the Standpoint of Artificial Intelligence." *Machine Intelligence* 4:463–502.

Manna, Z. 1974. *Mathematical Theory of Computation.* New York: McGraw-Hill.

Manna, Z., and Waldinger, R. 1977. *Studies in Automatic Programming Logic.* New York: Elsevier North-Holland.

12

Generating and understanding scene descriptions

DAVID L. WALTZ

A semantic theory having no contact with the world, a mere translation of one set of words into another, is a ladder without rungs. (Miller and Johnson-Laird, 1976)

The research reported here is part of a larger project whose goal is to link language and perception, and in this effort to provide a deeper understanding of what it means to *understand*. Computer vision and language researchers have to date had little to say to each other. However, without a connection to the real world via perception, it is difficult to say in what sense a natural language system could be said to understand descriptions of the physical world. If an entity (human or computer) understands scene descriptions, it should be able to make predictions about likely futures; it should be able to judge certain scene descriptions to be implausible; it should be able to point to items in a scene, given a description of the scene; and it should be able to say whether or not a description corresponds to a given scene. This requires that it have a vision system that can generate scene representations that can be compared with scene representations generated from natural language descriptions. This in turn requires that the entity be able to pay attention to what is important in context, be able to note events and cause–effect relationships over time, and in general be able to find patterns in (or impose organization on) visual data.

This chapter explores design issues for a system that has both vision and language, in particular, a system that addresses both the problem of selecting appropriate words and sentences to describe a particular perceptual event, and the related problem of making appropriate inferences about a natural language description of a perceptual event. I first consider the problem of understanding scene descriptions, and concentrate on the problems of judging the plausibility of described scenes and of making inferences about the causes and effects of described events. To account for our ability to handle these problems, I introduce "event simulations," procedures that model events. I then consider scene description generation, providing some connections between processes of perception and processes of description generation. In particular, I argue that perceptual processes also activate event simulations in the perceiver; and that scene descriptions are often stated in terms of the names of event simulations because the event simulations can associate and refer compactly to a number of scene items and relationships, and also because a major goal in scene description is to help a hearer set up event simulations similar to those of the speaker/perceiver. Finally, I give a brief historical perspective on related research, and speculate on how my research might be extended to make possible language/vision systems that could learn from experience.

The domain of interest

Our earliest language is primarily concerned with describing the perceived world. For both infants and adults the outside world is always filtered through and confounded with an internal world of interpretation: The outside world is alternatively interesting, boring, peaceful, threatening, pleasurable, and painful; items in the outside world are in varying degrees similar to other items seen or remembered. Nonetheless, it *seems* to us that we learn early to factor out a neutral outside world from our internal world, so that we can produce descriptions of the outside world that are intelligible to others, and so that we can understand others' descriptions of objects, events, and relationships between them. It is the perception of this "neutral" outside world as expressed in language, and the understanding of language describing this outside world, that are the central concerns of this chapter.[1]

I will explore the following questions:

1. What processes allow me to understand and describe scenes I encounter? How do I decide what to include in a description?
2. If I hear a sentence (e.g., "The car hit the boy.") what inferences can I make about the perceptual world of the speaker?
3. Under what perceptual circumstances is it appropriate to use particular words and sentences; that is, what things could I be looking at to appropriately report a sentence like "The car hit the boy."?
4. What knowledge and procedures would be necessary for a program to produce and understand this sort of language?

In concentrating on perceptual circumstances, I am explicitly deemphasizing important questions about why it would be appropriate to utter a description of the world; for now I would like (as much as possible) to factor out issues of intent in making utterances, and concentrate on the issues involved in "accurate reporting" only. As we will see, it is difficult to separate these issues.

Components

What would a total system be like? I suggest that it would at least have to include components[2] for handling each of the following subproblems:

Syntax and semantics. We need the ability to parse natural language about the physical world, the ability to choose appropriate senses of words (though this may often involve only the process of choosing the "physical interpretation" of a word from the lexicon), and the ability to organize the information into an appropriate "deep structure" (first-order predicate calculus or some other adequate form). I will not say much directly about these components, although some of the issues and examples I discuss have a bearing on the design of these components.

Pragmatics. As mentioned above, I wish as much as possible to factor out consideration of the motives and goals for uttering scene descriptions. However, under the section on "appropriateness" are included various factors and criteria for deciding which words to use in describing a scene, and these items have a distinctly pragmatic flavor.

Vision. I assume the possibility of designing a vision system substantially different from those that have been constructed to date. The chief difference is that the system I want does not perform a total analysis of each static "frame" of a scene, but instead (1) works on a constantly moving scene image, and (2) alternately *attends* to an "item" – some small portion of the overall scene – and *shifts attention* to another item, by moving through some trajectory. The vision system needs criteria for deciding where to look next; such decisions are to be based partially on what is most "interesting" in the periphery of the current visual field, and partially on the current goals, tasks, and hypotheses of the system. We are a rather long way from constructing a vision system of this sort; although I have some ideas on the design of such a system, I will not be concerned here with the details of how it might be done.

World knowledge – epistemology. The major emphasis in this paper is on the representation and use of world knowledge. I am particularly interested in how a scene description is built up and organized, and in how comparable structures could be constructed from language inputs.

Fitting the pieces together

I believe it is important to consider fitting together all the components mentioned in the previous section. First, it will be practically impossible to actually build a system of the sort I am describing unless the design is considered in toto. But more important, the kinds of solutions offered to each of the areas (syntax, semantics, pragmatics, epistemology, vision) may be totally incompatible if each area is only considered independently; in addition there is a danger that important problems may "fall between the cracks" separating the areas, and never be considered at all.

Understanding scene descriptions

In this section I argue that scene descriptions are most naturally treated by representations that are, at least in part, only awkwardly viewed as propositional; such representations include coordinate systems, trajectories, and event-simulating mechanisms.

Compare the following sentences:

(S1) My dog bit the mailman.
(S2) My dog bit the mailman's leg.
(S3) My dachshund bit the mailman's ear.

(S1) and (S2) do not seem to require visualization for understanding (although they may evoke mental images for some people). SCRIPT-like formalisms (Schank and Abelson, 1977) seem at least on the surface to be extendable for expressing such sentences internally, although a BITING script would involve a dog's goals rather than the human goals found in most scripts. However, I believe that many (possibly most) people would note that something is wrong or peculiar about sentence (S3). Even if people did not catch the fact that (S3) is peculiar, once the sentence is pointed out, it does seem to "require an explanation" because it is not possible to figure out with certainty how the dachshund was able to bite the mailman's ear without further information. (Possible explanations: The mailman fell while trying to get away from the dog; the mailman was kneeling or squatting to pick up a dropped item or to pet the dog.) How can we judge that an explanation is needed? What mechanisms could we use to understand an explanation, and what is the relationship between an explanation and the thing explained?

One possible answer to the first question is that we have saved all biting sites ever encountered as possible fillers of a slot in a biting script. When we encounter a bitten ear, we note that it is unusual or never before encountered. This possibility seems to be ruled out, at least as a full explanation, because

(S4) My Doberman bit the mailman's ear.

does not seem peculiar in the sense that (S3) does. It seems that we really make a judgment that a dachshund could not reach a person's ear ordinarily. The possibility that we store ahead of time information of the form (⟨dog type⟩, ⟨part of the body⟩) for each type of dog and reachable part of the body seems to me too remote to consider seriously.

Event simulation

If we don't prestore such lists of possibilities, the only alternative seems to be to compute them when needed via some mechanisms. But if we believe (or can show via psychological testing) that people readily catch physically unlikely sentences like (S3), then it may be that we compute physical plausibility *always* (unconsciously), or that event-simulation mechanisms are invoked by higher-level exception-trapping mechanisms. In any case, it seems to me that event-simulating mechanisms are necessary for full understanding of language about the sensory world.[3] I say this for the following reasons:

1. We are able to make plausibility judgments about descriptions.[4]
2. Something like event simulation seems necessary for the resolution of anaphoric reference. Event simulations could help both in setting up expectations and in attempting to set up plausible "pictures" for the purpose of comparing various pronoun reference candidates.[5]
3. Event simulations may allow us to circumvent short-term-memory limitations. It seems to be possible to remember entire pictures as though they were rather like single chunks. To the extent that items and events can be pictured, it may be possible to enlist perceptual apparatus in reasoning, and thereby achieve greater power and efficiency. Along similar lines, experts in memorization have long used visual imagery to aid retrieval of items (Luria, 1968; Bower, 1970; see also Chafe, 1979).
4. There are also likely to be ties between this work and current research on "mental imagery" (Kosslyn et al., 1979). Although I see no compelling argument that event simulation must give rise to

mental images, the existence of mental imagery seems to me to require the existence of some mechanisms like those of event simulation.

Let us return to the dachshund example, and be more specific about what event simulation would involve in this case. The "event simulation" would: (1) "create" a mailman and dachshund in default positions (both standing) on level ground outdoors with no special props other than the mailman's uniform and mailbag; (2) test to see if the dachshund could reach the mailman's ear with its mouth directly (no); (3) see if the dog could stretch or jump high enough to reach the ear (no); (4) see if the mailman would ordinarily get into positions where the dog could reach the ear (no); (5) judge that the mailman could not be bitten as stated unless default states and movement ranges were relaxed. Because there is no clearly preferred way to relax the defaults, more information should have been included in the description, according to the criteria for scene descriptions listed in the next section. Speakers should realize the need for more information because they should run event simulations on their own output; if for some reason a speaker has not kept track of the picture suggested to the hearer, the speaker should be able to construct the picture rapidly if the hearer hasn't understood the description.

Some other examples of sentences that fail event simulation verification are listed below. Some of these (e.g., S5 and S6) are probably answered via recourse to "world knowledge" rather than actual event simulation.

(S5) I ate 50 eggs for breakfast yesterday.
(S6) My cat killed an elephant.
(S7) I divided the birthday cake 1000 ways.
(S8) The mouse ran across the hood of my car and dented it.
(S9) The rock floated toward the shore.
(S10) A 747 flew so low that it knocked the top of my chimney off.
(S11) The small urn of oil burned for eight days.
(S12) We managed to stuff twenty people in a phone booth.
(S13) The tree grew four feet overnight.
(S14) My car hit the telephone pole at 55 miles per hour, but wasn't damaged.
(S15) Butterflies surrounded us while we skated on the pond.
(S16) I dropped a rock from the window and ran downstairs to catch it.
(S17) The hot water I spilled melted the stove.

Many of these examples are reminiscent of the *Guinness Book of World Records* or of miracles from the Bible. In each case our simulation of the described event is at least difficult to believe, in all cases contrary to ordinary experience.

Proposed mechanisms for event simulation and
scene description generation

I have been working on a sketch of a design for a system to provide event simulations, given sentences as input. The system depends on: (1) a large taxonomy of event types, with structural inheritance links so that events may be treated with a wide range of precision or generality; (2) time-sequencing information for events, so that events may be ultimately broken down (if necessary) into very low-level "primitives" or aggregated into larger event units, and so that a program can predict effects of events and can infer likely causes of events. This taxonomy is built so that it can function as a kind of decision tree for perceptual processes; however, it has words attached to event types in the taxonomy in such a way that it can be used both to simulate events during text understanding, and to generate "appropriate descriptions" and expectations for scenes and events if driven by a perceptual system.

One major piece of a system to run event simulations is Rieger's CSA ("commonsense algorithm") system (Rieger, 1975). CSAs break the world into STATES, STATECHANGES, ACTIONS, TENDENCIES, and GOALS; these can be interconnected with about twenty different causing and enabling relationships (e.g., continuous causation, as pressure causing flow; gated enablement, as in an open valve enabling flow; one-shot causation, as in pushing the flush handle on a toilet; etc.). Although a full discussion is beyond the scope of this chapter, CSAs have been used to model some physical systems (electronic circuits, a toilet, the process of combustion). It will at least be necessary to augment CSAs via: (1) the addition of time and quantities in general –CSAs are now primarily qualitative; (2) the addition of spatial information – coordinate systems, dimensions, and so on.

Deciding what to include in a description

In this section, I want to consider the problem of choosing appropriate words to describe events in a scene, concentrating particularly on verb choice. Much of what I say here may apply as well to the choice of other words and to the form of sentences (e.g., which item is chosen as syntactic subject, which material is put in relative clauses and which in main clauses, etc.). Basically I argue that:

1. Scene descriptions should include items noticed or inferred, and subsequently judged to be important.

2. Scene descriptions should satisfy certain criteria of "appropriateness" which ensure that a hearer will be able to build a plausible, coherent internal representation of the description.
3. Scene descriptions depend on available vocabulary and language production procedures.
4. Scene descriptions always serve some goals of the speaker.

This last point deserves added emphasis. I contend that there is no such thing as a purely objective scene description. What we call "objectivity" can more accurately be described as realizing the goal of reporting on *all* the objects and events in a scene, and at the same time concealing one's opinions and evaluations of the scene. Even for simple scenes it is impossible to cover all the things that could be said about the objects and events in it; n objects in a scene can be grouped in $n!$ ways, and each of the groups may be describable in many ways (e.g., by focusing on different elements in a group), and the groups may be considered in any order, as can choices of focus. Furthermore, the plausible origins of the scene, the expected future of the scene, the reasons why the speaker is generating the description in the first place, and the reasons why the speaker has chosen the particular order of description, all add open-ended possibilities for scene description that cannot be neatly separated from the scene per se.

Attention and salience

Items can be part of a description only if they have been noticed, or if they can be inferred from what has been noticed. What is noticed is in turn a complex function of one's goals and the context of the scene. A number of factors can affect what we attend to, infer, and remember – the "raw material" of descriptions:

External factors. Motion, contrast, size, color, complexity, symmetry, asymmetry, density of interesting features, plus many other scene characteristics can attract attention or camouflage items. We sometimes say of striking items "You can't miss it" (though we often do).

Internal factors. At the same time, goals, desires, habituation, familiarity, novelty, and other internal factors affect attention. (In the words of a proverb: "A thief looks at a saint and sees pockets.") Some items probably seem important to us because they activate mechanisms that have been evolved or conditioned to decide whether a scene contains items that are valuable to us or that threaten us. (As Bill

Woods has put it, we constantly ask the questions: "Can I eat it? Can it eat me?")

However, most internal factors are goal-dependent. For example, consider a particular outdoor scene; we notice very different items and relationships depending on our current goals. If I am looking for a lost wallet, I will attend to places in the scene where I think I have been, objects that might be the wallet, and objects that might obscure the wallet. The processing will be very different, however, if I am looking for a good place to have a picnic, or trying to figure out where I am, or hunting for firewood, or playing hide-and-seek with my children (and then somewhat different depending upon whether I am the hider or the seeker).

Vantage point. One's position with respect to an event affects the relationships one sees between objects in the visual field; the inability to see parts of a scene can lead to hedged descriptions as in "I think that John hit Mary first." However, at least to a degree, we can "see" events independent of viewpoint. For example, we see (and describe) "two cars approaching one another" and not "one car moving left to right and another car moving right to left." We can also include point of view in our descriptions by using orienting phrases whose meaning can be shared (e.g., "toward the north," "away from the house," "on his left," etc.).

Appropriateness

To be "appropriate," descriptions of a scene should meet the following interrelated criteria. [Note: These criteria have close ties with Grice's principles of cooperative conversation (Grice, 1975); however, I arrived at these criteria by looking at a number of examples of descriptions, and generalizing my observations.]

(A)   Descriptions should include all items attended to and subsequently judged to be important.

(B)   Descriptions should be as economical in the use of clauses and words as possible.[6]

(C)   Descriptions should use words and structures whose implications and attached default assumptions are actually true of the scene. If the words one wants to use invite inaccurate inferences, the inaccurate inferences must be explicitly ruled out or modified.

It is on criteria (B) and (C) that I would like to concentrate. By (B), we would prefer description (S18) to description (S19):

(S18)   He knocked the glass onto the floor.
(S19)   He hit the glass and knocked it onto the floor.

because "He hit the glass" can be inferred from (S18). Similarly, criterion (B) favors (S20) over (S21):

(S20) Two cars collided head-on.
(S21) One car was moving on the road and another car was moving on the road in the opposite direction, and the two cars hit each other.

(S20) is preferred because it paraphrases (S21) and uses many fewer words and clauses.

Criterion (C) is more subtle. Suppose that an automobile just grazed a boy or hit just his finger as it went by. Strictly speaking, it would be possible in either case to say:

(S22) The car hit the boy.

However, this description is misleading because the default assumption one would make if (S22) were heard out of context is that a major part of the boy's body was struck (more precisely, that the boy's center of mass was probably situated within the volume defined by projecting the car's frontal cross section forward along the car's trajectory).

Example sentence (S3),

(S3) My dachshund bit the mailman's ear.

is also inappropriate if uttered out of context because in order to understand (S3) one must invoke explanations that violate default assumptions (e.g., that the mailman is standing, the dachshund is of ordinary size and on the ground, etc.). One cannot complete the internal representation of the scene corresponding to (S3) with any confidence that the completion represents the actual situation in the world.

Understatement and overstatement are also violations of criterion (C). The sentence

(S23) My car was damaged in an accident.

would be inappropriate if the car were a total loss because "damaged" entails the possibility of repair, unless specifically excluded as in the phrase "damaged beyond repair."

Expressibility

Items can only appear in the same clause if they all belong to a single perceptual pattern (e.g., event or cause–effect relationship), and if words are available to predicate this patterned relationship between items. Obviously one can simply list all the items present in a scene whether related or not – here the perceptual pattern is simply: "present in the same scene." If the items cannot be seen as part of a single event, however, they have to be described separately, using structures such as: "⟨event-description-1⟩ and meanwhile ⟨event-description-2⟩." Expressibility may seem to be a rather amorphous factor, but I do want to include some indication that our descriptions are constrained by our ability to see the items in a scene as an instance of a pattern, and are also constrained by our vocabulary (lexical and structural) for referring to such patterns.

Speech acts

The scene descriptions we generate may be more or less inappropriate or may be modified because our goals (conscious or unconscious) can affect our choice of items to attend to, and can also change our evaluation of the importance of scene items attended to.

The effects of human values are also evident in both the items attended to and in our judgment of the "appropriateness" of descriptions. For example, in a description of an accident where a car hit a boy, we would expect the consequences to the boy to be described first, even if he were not injured. To describe damage to the *car* first, unless the damage were particularly unusual, would seem at least inappropriate, and possibly perverse. Furthermore, one's description of an accident would almost certainly exaggerate its seriousness if the victim were one's child and the driver a stranger, but minimize its seriousness if the victim were a stranger and the driver a friend. One would look for evidence to support the belief that the stranger in each case was responsible for the accident, and one would probably also attend especially to the consequences of the accident for one's friend or relative.

Sometimes context can make ordinarily inappropriate descriptions appropriate. For example, if one were asked as an accident witness about whether or not a car had contacted the boy, it might be appropriate to say (S22) ("The car hit the boy.") even if the car had only grazed him.

Miscellaneous factors

The choice of specific words and sentences may also be influenced by a large number of other factors, including: rhymes or close associations with words used earlier in a discourse; parallel syntactic structures; consistent use of same voice (i.e., active or passive); "Freudian slips" (i.e., unintended use of inappropriate words that are related to a speaker's suppressed goals); and so on. Although such factors are clearly important for an overall theory of cognition and scene description, I will not treat them further here.

Why are scene descriptions important?

On the surface it may seem that focusing on the domain of physical events is very restricting. After all, most language is not about the physical world per se, but about the "abstract world" of goals, theories, explanations, stories, reports of combined inner and outside world experience, and so on. Nonetheless, I think that the domain of physical events is of central importance, and I will attempt to explain why in this section.

Historical perspective

Most efforts in language processing, in both artificial intelligence (AI) and linguistics, have concentrated on transforming strings of words into trees or other structures of words (sometimes surface words, sometimes "primitive" words) or, conversely, on producing strings of words from these structures. Most language programs "define" nouns as a conjunction of semantic markers (e.g., animate, human, physical object, and so on). At this time in history, AI vision and natural language researchers have little to say to each other; most of the work that treats language and perception[7] together would, I think, be considered to lie in the realms of philosophy or psychology.

Moreover, the areas of language processing that *could* have a bearing on perception have been largely ignored. Very little work has been done on programs to understand language about space, spatial relations, or object descriptions. (But see Boggess, 1978; Waltz and Boggess, 1979; Waltz, 1979.)

By the same token, current computer vision systems are not able to describe what they "see" in natural language; in fact, very few programs can even identify objects within a scene (except for programs that operate in very constrained universes). Furthermore, no vision programs are able to tailor their performance to given questions or tasks (e.g., "Where could a lost object be in the current scene?", "Where am I?", "How can I find a path to take to get to some object in the scene?", etc.). Most vision systems simply produce scene segmentations, labelings, or 3-D interpretations of scene portions. Programs are universally capable of only a single mode of operation; there is no analogue of an attention mechanism or task-dependent performance. Similarly, no programs I know are able to locate or "point to" scene items, given a natural language description of scene items or their whereabouts.

Piaget (1967) has long argued that an understanding of the sensory-motor world is a critically important first step in developing schemas for concepts in abstract worlds. Jackendoff (1976) and Gruber (1965) have suggested in some detail how sensory-motor schemas might be transferred to abstract worlds via the treatment of abstract items as "metaphorical locations." Other researchers have recognized the importance of these problems. Especially noteworthy is the landmark volume *Language and Perception* by Miller and Johnson-Laird (1976). Other work of note in this area includes that of Minsky (1975), Woods (Chapter 14 of this volume), Clark (1973), Bajcsy and Joshi (1978), Soloway (1978), Simmons (1975), Novak (1976), Kuipers (1977), and Johnson-Laird (Chapter 4 of this volume).

Toward programs that learn from experience

The simulation of cognitive processes has been approached in the past by means that are at the extremes of a spectrum. At one end of the spectrum are "adaptive" approaches which assume that systems begin with a blank slate ("tabula rasa"), and that evolutionary, trial-and-error mechanisms will allow the systems to "learn by experience," much as people do (see, e.g., Holland and Reitman, 1977; Minsky and Papert, 1967). At the other end of the spectrum are artificial intelligence approaches, which generally attempt to model the knowledge of an adult directly, and ignore problems of learning. It has been argued that "in order for a program to be capable of learning something it must first be capable of being told it" (McCarthy, 1968), and thus research has concentrated primarily on problems in the representation of knowledge. Learning programs (e.g., Winston, 1970; Sussman, 1973) are extremely narrow in their competence, and depend on having a good teacher – hardly like learning from experience. However, there seems to be little hope that adaptive approaches will be even as successful as AI approaches; the search space of possibilities is so large that unless programs begin with enough structure to exhibit interesting behavior at the outset, it is overwhelmingly unlikely that the programs will ever evolve to the point of exhibiting interesting behavior.

What can be done? I suggest that by examining the problem of designing a system that integrates vision, language, and memory we can begin to work from an approach that is somewhere between the two extremes of AI and adaptive modeling. The basic argument is this: We humans are able to learn only because we begin with a great deal of structure in our perceptual systems (and probably other systems as well). A good starting point for a learning program would be a system that could generate rich procedural descriptions of events in the physical world, and associate language about the physical world with these descriptions. Learning could then be explored in at least two novel ways: (1) The system could add knowledge of specific events to its memory, and attempt to generalize its experience; and (2) we could use it to investigate the use of rich perceptual schemas for interpreting abstract events.

Of course this is only a starting point. In order to be able to eventually learn about abstract worlds as well, a system must be able to bootstrap itself in some way. Jackendoff (1975) and Gruber (1965) have pointed out evidence that linguistic schemas we develop to describe GO, BE, and STAY events in the sensory-motor ("position") world are later transferred via a broad metaphor to describe events in abstract worlds (possession, "identification," and "circumstantial"). Thus we learn to use parallel surface structures for conceptually very different sentences like:

(1a)   The dishes stayed in the sink (position).
(1b)   The business stayed in the family (possession).
(2a)   His puppy went home (position).
(2b)   His face went white (identification).
(3a)   She got into her car and went to work (position).
(3b)   She sat down at her desk and went to work (circumstantial).

Along these same lines, there are striking parallels in the structures of Schank's (1975) conceptual dependency diagrams for PTRANS, ATRANS, and MTRANS. Reddy (1977) has described what he calls the "conduit metaphor" for linguistic communication, in which we typically speak of ideas and information as though they were objects that could be given or shipped to others who need only to look at the "objects" to understand them. Thus we say "You aren't getting your message across," "She gave me some good ideas," "He kept his thoughts to himself," "Let me give you a piece of advice," etc. (Reddy has compiled a very long list of examples.)

These examples suggest many deep and fascinating questions. It seems clear that the same words and similar syntactic structures can be transferred to describe quite different phenomena. What internal structures (if any) are also transferred in such cases? What perceptual criteria are used to classify events to begin with? Ultimately? How does a child transfer observation to imitation? How are memories of specific events generalized to form event types, and how are the representations of event types related to memories of specific events?

There is also a great deal of prima facie evidence of close ties between perception and the language used by adults to describe abstract processes such as thinking, learning, and communicating, and to describe abstract fields like economics, diplomacy, and psychology. Witness the wide use of basically perceptual words like: start, stop, attract, repel, divide, separate, join, connect, shatter, scratch, smash, touch, lean, flow, support, hang, sink, slide, scrape, fall, grow, shrink, waver, shake, spread, congeal, dissolve, precipitate, roll, bend, warp, wear, chip, break, tear, etc., etc. Although we obviously do not always (or even usually) experience perceptual *images* when we use or hear such words, I suggest that much of the machinery used during perception is used during the processing of language about space and is also used during the processing of abstract descriptions. I do not find it plausible that words like these have two or more completely different meanings that simply share the same lexical entry.

Conclusions

I have examined a number of issues in scene description generation and scene description understanding. This work is part of a larger effort to model via computer programs our understanding of the sensory-motor world. I have argued especially for procedural rather than static representations for knowledge, and have attempted to show the intimate connections between discourse about the sensory-motor world, perceptual processes, and "event simulation" mechanisms. I believe that this research can have important consequences in that, compared with the study of isolated components (e.g., vision, syntax, semantics), the design of a complete vision/language system adds many more constraints on the possible for components. I also believe that a thorough understanding of the sensory-motor world is a necessary precursor to a satisfactory handling of abstract worlds, which are understood via metaphorical reference to the sensory-motor world. In turn, solving these problems is essential if we are ever to be able to model "learning from experience" and to understand understanding.

NOTES

This work was supported by the Office of Naval Research under Contract ONR-N0005-C-00612. I would like to thank Bill Woods for providing office space, computer time and moral support, Jeff Gibbons, Brad Goodman, and Candy Sidner for helpful comments on an earlier draft, Bonnie Webber for her patience and confidence in me, and Bonnie Waltz for her loving support.

1 I will argue (in the section "Deciding what to include in a description") that neutrality is impossible because we always act because of goals, and these goals affect every aspect of cognition from attention to interpretation.
2 Alternatively one could argue for a totally integrated system with no distinct component boundaries. Very little of my discussion depends on the assumed decomposability of the problem.
3 I am aware of the dangers in postulating the existence of mechanisms on the basis of our behavior in exceptional cases [e.g., understanding sentences such as (S3)]. It might be possible to get more convincing evidence through psychological testing. If event simulation shares resources with the visual system, then it should be possible to show interference between the understanding of scene description and perceptual tasks.
4 Plausibility judgment may perhaps be usefully viewed as a deeper analogue of grammatical and semantic judgments.
5 I am grateful to Candy Sidner for pointing this out to me.
6 Obviously with children or people who are unlikely to understand certain words (e.g., technical terms), one uses nonoptimum descriptions. I used to tell my children "Our ride will be as long as Captain Kangaroo's show" because they didn't understand directly how long an hour is.
7 Although I intend perception to refer in the human examples to all the senses – vision, hearing, touch, smell, taste, and kinesthetic – in the case of computers, only vision has been explored in more than a cursory manner.

REFERENCES

Bajcsy, R., and Joshi, A. 1978. "The Problem in Naming Shapes: Vision–Language Interface." In D. Waltz, ed. *Theoretical Issues in Natural Language Processing – 2*. New York: Association for Computing Machinery.
Boggess, L. C. 1978. "Computational Interpretation of English Spatial Prepositions." Unpublished Ph.D. dissertation, University of Illinois, Urbana, Computer Science Department.
Bower, G. H. 1970. "Analysis of a Mnemonic Device." *American Scientist* 222, 5:104–12.
Chafe, W. L. 1979. "The Flow of Thought and the Flow of Language." In T. Givon, ed. *Discourse and Syntax*. New York: Academic Press.
Clark, H. H. 1973. "Space, Time, Semantics and the Child." In T. E. Moore, ed. *Cognitive Development and the Acquisition of Language*. New York: Academic Press, pp. 27–63.
Grice, H. P. 1975. "Logic and Conversation." In P. Cole and J. L. Morgan, eds. *Syntax and Semantics*, Vol. 3, *Speech Acts*. New York: Academic Press, pp. 41–58.
Gruber, J. S. 1965. "Studies in Lexical Relations." Unpublished Ph.D. dissertation, Massachusetts Institute of Technology.
Holland, J. H., and Reitman, J. S. 1977. "Cognitive Systems Based on Adaptive Algorithms." Tech. Report No. 201, University of Michigan, Computer and Communication Sciences Department.

Jackendoff, R. 1975. "A System of Semantic Primitives." In R. Schank and B. Nash-Webber, eds. *Theoretical Issues in Natural Language Processing.* Arlington, Va.: Association for Computational Linguistics.

Jackendoff, R. 1976. "Toward an Explanatory Semantic Representation." *Linguistic Inquiry* 7, 1:89–150.

Kosslyn, S. M., Pinker, S., Smith, G. E., and Shwartz, S. P. 1979. "On the Demystification of Mental Imagery." *Behavioral and Brain Sciences* 2:535–81.

Kuipers, B. J. 1977. "Representing Knowledge of Large-Scale Space." Tech. Report AI-TR-418, Cambridge, Mass.: Artificial Intelligence Laboratory, MIT.

Luria, A. R. 1968. *The Mind of a Mnemonist.* New York: Basic Books.

McCarthy, J. 1968. "Programs with Common Sense." In M. Minsky, ed. *Semantic Information Processing.* Cambridge, Mass.: The M.I.T. Press.

Miller, G. A., and Johnson-Laird, P. 1976. *Language and Perception.* Cambridge, Mass.: Harvard University Press.

Minsky, M. L. 1975. "A Framework for Representing Knowledge." In P. Winston, ed. *The Psychology of Computer Vision.* New York: McGraw-Hill.

Minsky, M. L., and Papert, S. 1967. *Perceptrons.* Cambridge, Mass.: The M.I.T. Press.

Novak, G. S. 1976. "Computer Understanding of Physics Problems Stated in Natural Language." Tech. Report NL-30, University of Texas, Austin, Department of Computer Science.

Piaget, J. 1967. *Six Psychological Studies.* New York: Vintage.

Reddy, M. 1979. In A. Ortony, ed. *Metaphor and Thought.* New York: Cambridge University Press.

Rieger, C. 1975. "The Commonsense Algorithm as a Basis for Computer Models of Human Memory, Inference, Belief and Contextual Language Comprehension." In R. Schank and B. Nash-Webber, eds. *Theoretical Issues in Natural Language Processing.* Arlington, Va.: Association for Computational Linguistics, pp. 180–95.

Schank, R. C. 1975. "The Primitive ACTs of Conceptual Dependency." In R. Schank and B. Nash-Webber, eds. *Theoretical Issues in Natural Language Processing.* Arlington, Va.: Association for Computational Linguistics.

Schank, R. C., and Abelson, R. P. 1977. *Scripts, Plans, Goals, and Understanding.* Hillsdale, N.J.: Erlbaum.

Simmons, R. F. 1975. "The Clowns Microworld." In R. Schank and B. Nash-Webber, eds. *Theoretical Issues in Natural Language Processing.* Arlington, Va.: Association for Computational Linguistics.

Soloway, E. 1978. "Learning = Interpretation + Generalization: A Case Study in Knowledge-Directed Learning." COINS Tech. Report 78-13, University of Massachusetts, Amherst.

Sussman, G. J. 1973. "A Computational Model of Skill Acquisition." Tech. Report AI-TR-297, Cambridge, Mass.: MIT AI Lab.

Waltz, D. L. 1979. "Relating Images, Concepts, and Words." *Proc. of the NSF Workshop on the Representation of 3-D Objects.* University of Pennsylvania, Philadelphia.

Waltz, D. L., and Boggess, L. C. 1979. "Visual Analog Representations for Natural Language Understanding." *Proceedings of IJCAI-79.* Tokyo.

Winston, P. H. 1975. "Learning Structural Descriptions from Examples." In P. Winston, ed. *The Psychology of Computer Vision.* New York: McGraw-Hill.

13

Discourse model synthesis: preliminaries to reference

BONNIE LYNN WEBBER

The past few years have seen growing interest in questions of how people manage to understand definite anaphora[1] and of how machines might be made to do the same. Interest in the latter is due in part to the prevalance of anaphora in natural language discourse, including the kinds of dialogues in which we expect to engage information- and support-providing machines.

In this chapter, I will examine one aspect of understanding definite anaphora in light of the following five assumptions[2] about text understanding in general and definite anaphora in particular:

1. One objective of discourse is to enable a speaker to communicate to a listener a model s/he has of some situation. Thus the ensuing discourse is, on one level, an attempt by the speaker to direct the listener in synthesizing a similar model.
2. Such a discourse model can be viewed as a structured collection of entities, organized by the roles they fill with respect to one another, the relations they participate in, and so on.
3. A speaker uses a definite anaphor to refer to an entity already in his or her discourse model (DM_S).[3] In doing so, the speaker assumes (a) that on the basis of the discourse thus far, a similar entity will be in the listener's model (DM_L), and (b) that the listener will be able to access and identify that entity via the given definite anaphor, where different types of anaphor will provide different clues.
4. The referent of a definite anaphor is thus an entity in DM_S, which the speaker presumes to have a counterpart in DM_L. Discourse entities may have the properties of individuals, sets, events, actions, states, facts, beliefs, hypotheses, properties, generic classes, typical set members, stuff, specific quantities of stuff, and so on.
5. In deciding which discourse entity a definite anaphor refers to, a listener's judgments stem in part from how the entities in DM_L are described. (When a discourse entity E is the referent of a definite anaphor A, one might distinguish that description of E conveyed to the listener by the immediately preceding text and consider it A's antecedent.)

283

The point of making these assumptions explicit is to stress that, insofar as reasoning about discourse entities is mediated by their descriptions, the ability to identify and describe discourse entities appropriately is critical to understanding anaphora.

One consequence of these assumptions about definite anaphora is that the listener's job in understanding them can be decomposed into the following complementary tasks:

1. Deciding whether a definite pronoun or definite description is truly anaphoric (i.e., is intended to refer to some entity presumed to be in the listener's discourse model already), or whether it fills some other role in the discourse.
2. Synthesizing a discourse model that is similar to that of the speaker and inhabited by similar discourse entities.
3. Constraining the possible referents of a given anaphoric expression down to one possible choice – the "anaphor resolution" problem.
4. Determining what other functions a definite description is intended to fill besides enabling the listener to construct or get to its referent.

Here I will only be addressing the second task – that of synthesizing an appropriate discourse model and, hence, correctly determining what the speaker assumes to be available for anaphoric reference.

There are two sources of information feeding into the model synthesis process – the text itself and the listener's store of knowledge and beliefs. The latter includes functional knowledge of the world (what roles things play with respect to one another), structural knowledge of the world (part–whole relations, etc.), and intentional knowledge of people (what people do and why they do it). There are many people actively studying how people employ these types of knowledge and beliefs in understanding discourse. [In this volume, see in particular Grosz (task-based knowledge), Perrault and Cohen (plan-based knowledge), Lehnert (script-based knowledge), and Waltz (vision-based knowledge). See also Winograd (1975), Charniak (1975), Schank and Abelson (1977), and Rumelhart and Ortony (1977).]

In this chapter, I am going to concentrate on the text and show how indefinite noun phrases contribute to the model synthesis process.[4] This will involve identifying (1) where a new discourse entity will be evoked, independent of any higher-level expectations, and (2) how that new discourse entity will initially be described. I am going to claim that this initial description (*ID*) is critical to both model synthesis and anaphor resolution because it provides both a handle onto the discourse entity and a basis for determining that entity's role in higher-level expectations. Moreover, if the discourse entity's role assignment turns out at any point to be incorrect, then it is its *ID* that allows the listener to reassign it to another role with respect to his or her revised expectations.

More specifically, in the following section I will consider indefinite noun phrases with respect to the discourse entities they evoke and how those entities are described. I will contrast them briefly with nonanaphoric definite noun phrases vis-à-vis IDs and then raise the question of whether these two ID patterns (that of definites and that of indefinites) are sufficient to characterize the discourse entities evoked by all nonmass noun phrases. In a third section I will show how this approach to definite anaphora in terms of discourse models, discourse entities, and their descriptions can accommodate certain problematic cases that have been discussed in the linguistics and philosophic literatures – the famous "donkey" sentence (see Bartsch, 1976; Edmondson, 1976; Hintikka and Carlson, 1977) and the problem of disjunctive noun phrases and clauses (see Karttunen, 1977).

Indefinite noun phrases and discourse entities

"Naturally evoked" discourse entities

The first point I want to make is that by virtue of its actual wording the text can evoke certain discourse entities "naturally," independent of any expectations. Moreover, every one of these "naturally evoked" entities is accessible to anaphoric reference in the form of a definite pronoun. To see this, consider the sentence

1. Each third-grade girl brought a brick to Wendy's house.

In each continuation given in example 2, the referent of the definite pronoun is one of those entities "naturally evoked" by sentence 1.

2a. *She* certainly was surprised.
      she = Wendy
 b. *They* knew she would be surprised.
      they = the set of third-grade girls
 c. She piled *them* on the front lawn.
      them = the set of bricks, each of which some third-grade girl brought to Wendy's house
 d. She was surprised that they knew where *it* was.
      it = Wendy's house

Notice that texts identical at the conceptual level may not be identical vis-à-vis the discourse entities they evoke, even though their phrasing differs only minimally; compare:

3. John traveled around France twice.
   ?? *They* were both wonderful.
4. John took two trips around France.
   They were both wonderful.

Initial discourse entity descriptions

Except after a copula, any indefinite noun phrase[5] may evoke a new discourse entity into a listener's discourse model.[6] What I want to focus on here is *IDs* for these new entities. Consider the following sentences:

5a. Wendy bought a yellow T-shirt that Bruce had liked.
 b. *It* cost twenty dollars.
6a. Each third-grade girl brought a pelican to Wendy's house.
 b. She is roosting *them* on her front lawn.
7a. If Bruce manages to catch a fish,
 b. he will eat *it* for dinner.
8a. John didn't marry a Swedish princess.
 b. *She* was Norwegian.
9a. Whether Bruce buys a mini-computer or an Advent TV,
 b. he will have to do the repairs on *it* himself.
10. Every man who owns a donkey beats *it*.

I claimed earlier that the *ID* of a newly evoked discourse entity is critical to both model synthesis and anaphor resolution because it mediates all reasoning about that entity until the entity's assignment to some role within the model being synthesized. An entity's *ID* should imply neither more nor less about it than is appropriate. Now consider what an appropriate description would be for the discourse entity that "it" refers to in sentence 5b. It is not "the yellow T-shirt that Bruce had liked" because sentence 5a could be uttered truthfully even if Bruce had liked several yellow T-shirts (and both speaker and listener were aware of that fact). Nor is it "the yellow T-shirt that Bruce had liked and that Wendy bought" because sentence 5a could be truthfully uttered even if Wendy had bought several such T-shirts. What is an appropriate description for the referent of "it" is something like "the yellow T-shirt that Bruce had liked and that Wendy bought and that was mentioned in utterance 5a."

What I am claiming is that in the case of a singular indefinite noun phrase that is not within the scope of either negation, a universal quantifier, a hypothetical (e.g., "if," "suppose"), or one of several other special contexts (see Webber, 1978a), the entity it evokes will be described appropriately via a conjunction of (1) the description inherent in the noun phrase (e.g., "yellow T-shirt that Bruce had admired"); (2) a predicate that embodies the remainder of the sentence (e.g., "which

Wendy bought"); and (3) a predicate that relates that entity to the utterance (sentence token) evoking it (e.g., "which was mentioned in (or evoked by) utterance 10a").[7] This is the description that I am calling the entity's "initial description" or *ID*. What I will now claim is that this *ID* can be simply derived from an appropriately structured logical representation of the sentence. Such a representation is described in detail in Webber (1978a).

Using a somewhat simplified version of that formalism, a simple rule can be stated for forming the *ID* of an existentially evoked discourse entity:

$$[\text{RW-1}] \quad \frac{(\mathrm{E}x : \mathrm{C}) \cdot \mathrm{F}_x \Rightarrow}{\mathrm{S}} \qquad (\mathrm{E}z) \cdot Z = \mathrm{i}x : \mathrm{C}x \ \& \ F_x \ \& \ \text{evoke } \mathrm{S},x$$

Here $(\mathrm{E}x : \mathrm{C})$ is an example of restricted quantification, where C represents an arbitrary predicate that x satisfies. F_x represents an arbitrary open sentence in which x is free; i stands for Russell's definite operator, iota; and S is the label assigned to the utterance whose propositional contents appear on the left-hand side of the arrow. Informally, [RW-1] says that if an utterance S states that there is a member x of class C that makes F_x true, then there exists an individual describable as "the C that F's that was evoked by utterance S." This individual is taken to be the discourse entity evoked by the existential noun phrase. For example, let Y stand for the predicate corresponding to "yellow T-shirt that Bruce had liked."[8] Then utterance 5a can be represented simply as

$$(\mathrm{E}x : Y) \cdot \text{Bought Wendy}, x$$

Because this matches the left-hand side of the above rule, it follows that

$$(\mathrm{E}z) \cdot z = \mathrm{i}x : Y \, x \ \& \ \text{Bought Wendy}, x \ \& \ \text{evoke } \mathrm{S}_{5a}, x$$

That is, there is an individual describable as "the yellow T-shirt that Bruce had liked, that Wendy bought and that was evoked by utterance 5a." The discourse entity so described is the referent of "it" in sentence 5b.

Examples 6–10 illustrate singular indefinite noun phrases in some of the special contexts noted above. Although I will only be discussing examples 9 and 10 in this chapter, notice that in all five cases, the entity evoked by the indefinite noun phrase is appropriately described by taking into account the three factors mentioned above. That is, in example 6 the referent of "them" can be described as "the above-mentioned set of pelicans, each of which some third grade girl brought to Wendy's house."[9] In example 7, the referent of "it" can be described uniquely as "the fish mentioned in utterance 7a that Bruce has managed to catch, if Bruce has managed to catch a fish." In example 8, the negation appears intended to scope only "Swedish." Thus the discourse entity referent of "she" can be described uniquely as "the princess mentioned in utterance 8a that John married." (We later learn in sentence 8b that she is Norwegian rather than Swedish.) *ID*s for the two other existentially evoked discourse entities in examples 9 and 10 will be discussed in the next section.

Notice that a definite noun phrase in the same context as an indefinite noun phrase will also evoke a discourse entity, but one whose *ID* is somewhat different from that in the indefinite case. To see this, consider the following sentences:

11a. Wendy bought the yellow T-shirt that Bruce had liked.
  b. *It* cost twenty dollars.
12a. Each third-grade girl has seen the pelican on Wendy's lawn.
  b. They prefer *it* to the plastic flamingo she had there before.
13a. John didn't marry the Swedish princess.
  b. He threw *her* over for a Welsh ecdysiast.

In each case, an appropriate description for the discourse entity evoked by the singular definite noun phrase is just that singular definite noun phrase itself – "the yellow T-shirt that Bruce had liked," "the pelican on Wendy's lawn," "the Swedish princess." Although it is certainly true that the definiteness of these noun phrases may be contingent on context (i.e., identifiability within the speaker's model of the underlying situation), nevertheless unlike entities evoked by indefinite noun phrases, those evoked by definites do not depend for their *ID*s on the particular sentences the definite noun phrases appeared in.

The same characteristic behavior of definites and indefinites just discussed for singular noun phrases holds for plural noun phrases as well. That is, although both indefinite and definite plural noun phrases evoke discourse entities, the unique initial descriptions that can be assigned to those entities will differ in the two cases. To see this, consider the following examples:

14a. I saw *the* guys from "Earth Wind & Fire" on TV today.
  b. I saw *the three* guys from "Earth Wind & Fire" on TV today.
  c. I saw *all three* guys from "Earth Wind & Fire" on TV today.
  d. I saw *some* guys from "Earth Wind & Fire" on TV today.
  e. I saw *three* guys from "Earth Wind & Fire" on TV today.
15. *They* were being interviewed by Dick Cavett.

Sentences 14a–c contain a definite plural noun phrase. That noun phrase should evoke a discourse entity into the listener's discourse model, one appropriately described as "the (set of) guys from 'Earth

Wind & Fire.' " This can be verified by following either of these sentences by sentence 15 and considering what is the referent of the definite pronoun "they."[10]

Sentences 14d&e, on the other hand, contain an indefinite plural noun phrase. That noun phrase will evoke a discourse entity appropriately described as "the (set of) guys from 'Earth Wind and Fire' that I saw on TV today *and* that was mentioned in sentence 14d(e)." This is so because either utterance is consistent with there being other members of "Earth Wind & Fire" whom I didn't see on TV today, as well as other members whom I did see but whom I don't mean to include in my statement.[11] Notice again that the set size information provided in sentence 14e is not necessary for describing that set uniquely. However, it too may be useful later in resolving definite anaphora.

Here I want to raise an unresolved question: whether these two *ID* patterns (that associated with indefinites and that associated with definites) embrace the *ID*s of all textually evoked, nongeneric, nonmass discourse entities. If they do (and they seem to), the question then is which pattern is appropriate to the entity evoked by any given noun phrase? (In some cases, it seems that the same noun phrase can evoke a discourse entity that is sometimes appropriately described one way, sometimes the other.) Consider the following examples:

16a. Many linguists smoke, although *they* know it causes cancer.
 b. A few linguists smoke, although *they* know it causes cancer.
17a. Few linguists smoke, because *they* know it causes cancer.
 b. Few linguists were at the party, but *they* drank more than the entire Army Corps of Engineers.
18a. Not many linguists smoke, because *they* know it causes cancer.
 b. Not many linguists were at the party, but *they* drank more than the entire Army Corps of Engineers.

In example 16, the noun phrases determined by "many" and "few" seem to pattern after the indefinite plural: The referent of "they" can be appropriately described as "the just-mentioned set of linguists who smoke." (One also learns that this set is larger (or smaller) than the speaker expects or, alternatively, feels the listener might expect.) On the other hand, noun phrases determined by either "few" or "not many" seem capable of following either pattern. In sentences 17a and 18a, the referent of "they" is the discourse entity appropriately described as "(the entire set of) linguists." That is, both "few $\langle x \rangle$s" and "not many $\langle x \rangle$s" behave similarly to the definite noun phrase "the $\langle x \rangle$s." However, as the corresponding "b" sentences show, they can also pattern after the indefinite plural: The referent of "they" is the entity appropriately described as "the just-mentioned set of linguists who were at the party." Of course, for those noun phrases that can pattern either way, the question of what contextual factors determine which pattern is appropriate still needs solving.

Two interesting reference problems

Recall that one purpose of this chapter is to argue for a particular view of the place of the text in explicating definite anaphora. This view takes as given the notion that a listener is using both the discourse and some structured knowledge of the world to synthesize a model of what s/he believes to underlie the discourse. The text indicates where a new discourse entity should be evoked and how that new discourse entity should initially be described. Both of these functions are critical for later anaphor resolution. Definite anaphora are viewed as means by which the speaker refers to entities in DM_S that are presumed to have counterparts in Dm_L. What I want to show in this section is that this approach to definite anaphora can accommodate not only straight forward cases as above, but certain problematic cases as well.

Parameterized individuals

The problem of formally characterizing the referent of "it" in examples like 10 below has often been discussed in the linguistics and philosophy literatures (see Bartsch, 1976; Edmondson, 1976; Hintikka and Carlson, 1977).

    10. Every man who owns a donkey beats *it.*

The problem has been taken to be that although "it" intuitively seems related to the embedded noun phrase "a donkey," there is no way to represent this logically in terms of simple quantifier scoping. What I shall show is that an approach in terms of discourse entities and their *ID*s makes this intuitive relationship simple both to explain and to represent.

First notice that this problem arises independently of how the matrix noun phrase is determined.

    19. A man I know who owns a donkey beats *it.*
    20. The man who owns a donkey beats *it.*
    21. Which man who owns a donkey beats *it?*
    22. No man who owns a donkey beats *it.*

In all these examples, "it" seems intuitively related to "a donkey." Informally, one might describe its referent as "the just-mentioned donkey he owns," where "he" is bound to whatever value that "(each, a, the, which, no) man who owns a donkey" may take. But this is just a discourse entity of a rather special type – one with a parameterized *ID*, rather than a rigid one. I call such entities "parameterized individuals," borrowing the term from Woods and Brachman (1978).[12]

Notice that parameterized individuals behave somewhat differently from other discourse entities. That is, parameterized individuals all have the *same ID*, independent of how the noun phrase containing the relative clause is determined, whereas the other discourse entities evoked by these sentences do not. For example:

23a. Every man who owns a donkey beats it.
   it = the donkey he owns
   b. However, *the donkeys* are planning to get back at *them*.
   the donkeys = the set of donkeys, each of which some man who owns
      a donkey owns
   them = the set of men, each of whom owns a donkey
24a. The man I know who owns a donkey beats it.
   it = the donkey he owns
   b. But *the donkey* is planning to get back at *him*.
   the donkey = the just-mentioned donkey that the man I know
      who owns a donkey owns
   him = the man I know who owns a donkey
25a. Which man who owns a donkey beats it?
   it = the donkey he owns
   – "None"
   b. *Are *the donkeys* planning to get back at (*him, them,* ???)?
   the donkeys = ???
   c. *Is *the donkey* planning to get back at (*him, them,* ???)?
   the donkey = ???

To show that the same approach to definite anaphora in terms of discourse entities and their descriptions can explicate "donkey" sentences as well, I will have to introduce a bit more of the formalism described in Webber (1978a). That bit involves an extension of restricted quantification (cf. [RW-1] above). In restricted quantification, a quantification operator (e.g., $\forall$, E), the variable of quantification, and the class it ranges over (noted implicitly as a predicate) constitute a structural unit of the representation – that is, $(Qx : P)$ where Q is a quantification operator, x the variable of quantification, and P a predicate. For example, "Every boy is happy" can be represented as

$$(\forall x : \text{Boy}) \cdot \text{Happy } x$$

This is truth-functionally equivalent to

$$(\forall x) \cdot \text{Boy } x \Rightarrow \text{Happy } x$$

Similarly "Some boy is happy" can be represented as

(Ex : Boy) · Happy x

which is truth-functionally equivalent to

(Ex) · Boy x & Happy x

My extension to restricted quantification permits the representation of noun phrases with relative clauses as well as that of simple noun phrases. Semantically, a relative clause can be viewed as a predicate, albeit a complex one. One way to provide for arbitrarily complex predicates is through the use of the abstraction operator, represented as "λ" by Hughes and Cresswell (1968), following Church (1941). For example, the noun phrase "a peanut" can be represented as

(Ex : Peanut)

Whereas the noun phrase "a peanut that Wendy gave to a gorilla" can be represented as

(Ex : λ(u : Peanut)[(Ey : Gorilla) · Gave Wendy,u,y]

This follows the same format (Qx : P) as above. In this case

λ(u : Peanut)[(Ey : Gorilla) · Gave Wendy,u,y]

names a unary predicate which is true if its argument is a peanut that Wendy gave to some gorilla.

Using this notation, sentence 10 can be represented as

(∀x : λ(u : Man)[(Ey : Donkey) · Own u, y]) · Beat x, IT

By applying rule [RW-1] to the embedded clause [(Ey : Donkey) · Own u], the entity evoked by the existential would be identified as

iy : Donkey y & Own u, y & evoke S$_{10.1}$,u
"the just-mentioned donkey that u owns"[13]

As I mentioned above, the semantics of restricted quantification is such that the variable of quantification, here x, satisfies the predicate in the restriction. Thus if x satisfies λ(u : Man)[(Ey : Donkey) · Own u, y], it follows that there is an entity identifiable as

iy : Donkey y & Own x, y & evoke S$_{10.1}$, y
"the just-mentioned donkey x owns"

This is a parameterized individual – parameterized by the variable in (∀x : · · ·) – that is a possible referent for "it" in the matrix sentence; that is,

$(\forall x : \lambda(u : \text{Man})[(\text{E}y : \text{Donkey}) \cdot \text{Own } u, y]) \cdot$
$\quad\quad \text{Beat } x, iy : \text{Donkey } y \,\&\, \text{Own } x, y \,\&\, \text{evoke } S_{10.1}, y$
"Every man who owns a donkey beats the just-mentioned donkey he owns"

It has been noted[14] that sentence 10 does not imply one donkey beating per donkey owner; rather, more than one donkey owned implies more than one donkey beaten. Hence the bizarreness of a sentence like

26. Every man who has a daughter will leave her all his vintage port.

I want to explicate this now in terms of the above presentation.

I noted earlier that the "evoke" term in an *ID* is a preliminary attempt to link an entity in the listener's discourse model with its presumed counterpart in the speaker's model. By itself, it does not commit either the speaker or the listener to believing that there is only one such *x* that has the other properties given in its *ID*, or that the entity corresponds to something that exists in the real world. That is, it reflects not what the situation is, but how it is described. For example, if a class is discussed in terms of a stereotypic member, subsequent references to the class can be made via that singular entity. If it is discussed in terms of a set, subsequent references can be made via that nonsingular entity. Compare:

27. The beaver is a dam builder.
    The dams *it* builds rival those of MIT engineers.
28. Beavers are dam builders.
    The dams *they* build rival those of MIT engineers.

However, if one discusses classes in terms of a single instance, this can lead to interpretation problems when what is predicated cannot in fact be true of all instances, as in sentence 26 above. Here, the description computed for the referent of "her" is "the above-mentioned daughter he has," where "he" ranges over men who have a daughter. This is, I claim, correct. However, after resolving it so, world knowledge will remind one that whereas a man who owns a donkey can beat each one of the donkeys he owns, a man who has a daughter cannot leave each one *all* his vintage port.

The final point I want to make about "donkey" sentences and discourse entities concerns anaphora found in subsequent sentences. For example, a sentence like "Every man who owns a donkey beats it" can easily be followed by a sentence like "However, *the donkeys* are planning to get back at them" (see example 23). Given that one can account for the referent of "it" in the first sentence in terms of discourse entities and their formally derivable IDs, can one do the same for the referent of "the donkeys" in the second?[15]

To show that it can, I need to present the rule for dealing with class-dependent definite descriptions that I mentioned in note 9. This rule is motivated by examples such as 29, where the referent of "them" is presumably the discourse entity evoked by the noun phrase "the flower she picked," where "she" stands for the variable bound by "each girl in the class."

29a. Each girl in the class gave Ivan the flower she picked.
  b. He arranged *them* artfully in an empty Glenfiddach bottle.

This is a definite noun phrase, but because of its binding to the distributively quantified noun phrase "each girl," it will evoke a discourse entity with the properties of a set rather than an individual (cf. example 12). In this case, it will be "the set of flowers, each of which was the flower that some girl in the class picked." Simplifying for brevity here, this rule can be written

$$(\forall x : K) \cdot P\ x, iy : c\ x, y \Rightarrow (Ez) \cdot z = \{u \mid (Ex : K) \cdot u = iy : C\ x, y\}$$

where K represents an arbitrary unary predicate that x satisfies and both P and C represent arbitrary binary predicates. The right-hand side of this rule implies that in case the left-hand side matches some sentence, there will be a discourse entity roughly describable as "the set of u's, each of which is the thing that stands in relation C to some member of K."

Notice now that after the "it" is resolved in "Every man who owns a donkey beats it" (see above), the sentence matches the left-hand side of the above rule – that is, "Every man who owns a donkey beats *the just-mentioned donkey he owns.*" Thus it follows that there is a discourse entity describable as "the set of donkeys, each of which is the just-mentioned donkey that some man who owns a donkey owns":

$$\{w \mid (Ex : \lambda(u : \text{Man})[(Ey : \text{Donkey}) \cdot \text{Own}\ u, y])$$
$$w = iz : \text{Donkey}\ z\ \&\ \text{Own}\ x, z\ \&\ \text{evoke}\ S_{17}, z\}$$

This is a possible referent for "the donkeys" in sentence 23b.

Disjunction

The other class of problematic examples that I want to discuss here in terms of discourse entities and their descriptions is one I first encountered in Karttunen (1977). Karttunen presents examples like the following:

30. If Wendy has a car or Bruce has a bike, *it* will be in the garage.
31. Bruce can choose between a bike and a car, but he must keep *it* in the garage.
32. Either Bruce has a new car or he has borrowed his brother's. In any case, *it* is blocking my driveway.
33. Whether Bruce buys a car or his brother buys a bike, he will have to keep *it* in the garage.

The problem is again to determine just what it is that "it" refers to.

I see two ways of approaching this problem in terms of discourse entities and their *ID*s. One way holds that in each sentence, each term of the disjunction evokes a different discourse entity into the listener's model, each with a different *ID:*

(30) "the car that Wendy has (if she has a car)"
      "the bike that Bruce has (if he has a bike)"
(31) "the bike that Bruce will have (if he chooses a bike)"
      "the car that Bruce will have (if he chooses a car)"
(32) "the new car that Bruce has (if Bruce has a new car)"
      "Bruce's brother's car"
(33) "the car Bruce will have bought (if he buys a car)"
      "the bike Bruce's brother will have bought (if Bruce's brother buys a bike)"

The truth of the disjunction (which seems in each case to be interpreted as exclusive "or") then guarantees there being one and only one entity in the model to which "it" refers. Notice that if the terms were conjoined rather than disjoined, the truth of the conjunction would imply the simultaneous existence of two entities within the model. In that case, either the referent of "it" would be ambiguous, or the sentence would just be bizarre.

The other, I think nicer, way of approaching the problem holds that each sentence evokes only a *single* discourse entity, with the indecision (i.e., the disjunction) embodied in its *ID*. That *ID* is of the form "A if P, otherwise B." For example, the entity evoked by sentence 30 would be describable as "the car that Wendy has (if she has a car) or the bike that Bruce has otherwise"; that evoked by sentence 31 would be describable as "the bike that Bruce will have (if he chooses a bike) or the car that Bruce will have otherwise"; that evoked by sentence 32, as "the new car that Bruce has (if he has a new car) or Bruce's brother's car otherwise"; and that evoked by sentence 33, as "the car Bruce will have bought (if he buys a car) or the bike Bruce's brother will have bought otherwise."

One advantage to this approach is that additional properties that truthfully follow from either part of the description can be ascribed to the entity without first having to determine which part is or will be true. The advantage shows up clearly when attempting to resolve later anaphora. For example, in sentence 32, the subject of "block my driveway" is presumably a physical object, preferably large and somewhat mobile. This condition is satisfied by the disjunctively described discourse entity evoked by sentence 32, independent of which disjunct is or will be true.

Although there may be other ways to approach the problem of disjunction, the "donkey" problem, and the whole problem of definite reference in general, what I hope I showed in these two sections is the robustness of an approach based on discourse entities and their formally derivable descriptions.

Conclusion

In this chapter, I have tried to reveal an aspect of understanding definite anaphora that precedes the more frequently discussed problem of "anaphor resolution." This aspect involves accounting for what it is that definite anaphors refer to and how such things become available. My account is based on the notion of discourse models, and I have concentrated on the role of the text in their synthesis. In particular, I have shown how indefinite noun phrases evoke new discourse entities into the listener's discourse model, and, equally important, how appropriate descriptions can be computed from a formal representation of the text. The approach seems capable of dealing with complex cases as well as simple ones. I have not discussed here how the listener's assumed knowledge and beliefs contribute to what becomes referenceable or how other aspects of discourse, like its spatio-temporal context, do the same. I have noted research in these areas, all of which will enhance our ability to improve man/machine discourse and, possibly, to understand our own discourse as well.

NOTES

1 Although I will soon explain what I mean precisely by "definite anaphora," the term basically denotes a function that some types of syntactic expressions can serve. Expressions that can function as definite anaphors include definite pronouns and definite descriptions. Other roles that definite pronouns and descriptions can fill are discussed in Geach (1962), Partee (1972), Norman and Rumelhart (1975), and Webber (1978a).

2 These assumptions are discussed in more detail in Webber (1978a).

3 A similar assumption is made by Karttunen (1976), Levin and Goldman (1978), Lyons (1977), and Stenning (1975).

4 For other work on the role of the text in model synthesis, in particular in the control of the listener's attention or "focusing," see Sidner (1979) and Reichman (1978).

5 I will often refer to these as "existentials" because of their logical interpretation as existential quantifiers.

6 An indefinite noun phrase following a copula functions together with the copula as a predicate; for example:

Beverly is a bargain hunter.
Bruce became a librarian.

As such, it is purely descriptive and does not refer to any particular librarian or bargain hunter (see Kuno, 1970).

7 This last component links the entity not only to the point in the discourse where it was evoked ("You know that shirt I mentioned awhile ago? Well . . .") but also to the person ascribing that description to it. This absolves the listener from a commitment to the truth of the given description. ("It wasn't yellow – it was beige.") See Webber, 1978b.

8 I will soon be more precise about the representation of relative clause containing noun phrases. Here, where the descriptive part of the noun phrase can be treated as an unanalyzed unit, the predicate name Y is an adequate representation.

9 A rule similar to [RW-1] is given in Webber (1978a) for existentials scoped by universals. In all, six such rules are given, covering

1. independent existentials (sg/pl)
"I saw (*a cat, three cats*) on the stoop."
2. definite descriptions (sg/pl)
"I saw *the (cat, cats) which hate(s) Sam.*"
3. distributives
"*Each cat on the stoop* hates Sam."
"*The three cats each* scratched Sam."
4. universally quantified existentials
"Each boy gave each girl (*a peach, three peaches*)."
5. class-dependent definites
"Each boy gave a woman he knew *the (peach, two peaches) she wanted.*"
6. class-dependent distributives
"Each boy I know loves *every woman he meets.*"

10 Although sentences 14b&c provide the additional information that the number of guys in "E.W.F." is three (not actually true), that information is not needed in order to describe the set so as to distinguish it from some other set of guys from "E.W.F." However, it should not be ignored, as it may be needed later in resolving a definite anaphor like "the three guys."

11 This latter point is a subtle one, and usage may vary from person to person. That is, some people intend an indefinite plural noun phrase contained in a sentence S – "Some $\langle x \rangle$s P" – to refer to the maximal set, namely, "the set of $\langle x \rangle$s that P." Other people intend it to refer to some subset of that set – "the set of $\langle x \rangle$s that P that I (the speaker) intended to mention in utterance S." For a system to cope with this variation in usage, it would be better for procedures to derive the latter, nonmaximal set description, which is always appropriate. If a system is sophisticated enough to associate a "belief space" with the speaker (Perrault and Cohen,

this volume, other procedures can later access that belief space (if necessary or desirable) to judge whether the maximal set interpretation might
have been intended.

12 The phrase "parameterized individual" is being used somewhat loosely to
include "parameterized" sets, stuff, and so on. For example,

   (i) No man who owns two donkeys beats them.
       them = the two donkeys he owns

13 In labeling each clause in a complex sentence, I use the following convention: If the matrix clause is labeled S, its leftmost embedded clause will be
labeled S.1, the leftmost embedded clause in S.1 will be labelled S.1.1, and
so forth.

14 Barbara Partee, in her opening remarks to the Sloan Workshop on Indefinite Reference, University of Massachusetts, Amherst MA, 1978.

15 I shall not take the time here to discuss the path from the phrase "every
man who owns a donkey" to the discourse entity informally describable as
"the set of men, each of whom owns a donkey" because it is rather
straightforward (see Webber, 1978a). This entity is a possible referent for
"them" in sentence 23b.

REFERENCES

Bartsch, R. 1976. "Syntax and Semantics of Relative Clauses." In R. Bartsch,
   J. Groenendijk, and M. Stokhof, eds. *Amsterdam Papers on Formal Grammars.* The Netherlands: University of Amsterdam.

Charniak, E. 1975. "Organization and Inference in a Frame-like System of
   Common Knowledge." In B. Nash-Webber and R. Schank, eds. *Theoretical
   Issues in Natural Language Processing.* Cambridge, Mass.: Association for
   Computational Linguistics.

Church, A. 1941. *The Calculi of Lambda Conversion.* Princeton, N.J.: Princeton
   University Press.

Edmondson, J. A. 1976. "Semantics, Games and Anaphoric Chains." In R.
   Bartsch, J. Groenendijk, and M. Stokhof, eds. *Amsterdam Papers on Formal
   Grammars.* The Netherlands: University of Amsterdam.

Geach, P. 1962. *Reference and Generality.* Ithaca, N.Y.: Cornell University Press.

Hintikka, J., and Carlson, L. 1977. "Pronouns of Laziness in Game-
   Theoretical Semantics." *Theoretical Linguistics* 4(1/2):1–30.

Hughes, G., and Cresswell, M. 1968. *An Introduction to Modal Logic.* London:
   Methuen.

Karttunen, L. 1976. "Discourse Referents." In J. McCawley, ed. *Syntax and
   Semantics,* Vol. 7. New York: Academic Press.

Karttunen, L. 1977. "Whichever Antecedent." *The CLS Book of Squibs.*
   Chicago: Chicago Linguistics Society, University of Chicago.

Kuno, S. 1970. "Some Properties of Non-Referential Noun Phrases." In R.
   Jakobson and S. Kawamoto, eds. *Studies in General and Oriental Linguistics.*
   Tokyo: TEC Company Ltd.

Levin, J., and Goldman, N. 1978. "Process Models of Reference." Unpublished ms. Marina del Rey, Calif.: Information Sciences Institute.

Lyons, J. 1977. *Semantics.* Cambridge: Cambridge University Press.

Norman, D., and Rumelhart, D. 1975. *Explorations in Cognition.* San Francisco: Freeman.

Partee, B. H. 1972. "Opacity, Coreference and Pronouns." In G. Harman and D. Davidson, eds. *Semantics of Natural Language.* The Netherlands: Reidel.

Reichman, R. 1978. "Conversational Coherency." (CSR-95) Urbana: Center for the Study of Reading, University of Illinois.

Rumelhart, D., and Ortony, A. 1977. "Representation of Knowledge." In R. Anderson, R. Spiro, and W. Montague, eds. *Schooling and the Acquisition of Knowledge.* Hillsdale, N.J.: Erlbaum.

Schank, R., and Abelson, R. 1977. *Scripts, Plans, Goals and Understanding.* Hillsdale, N.J.: Erlbaum.

Sidner, C. 1979. "A Computational Model of Coreference Comprehension in English." (MIT-AI TR-537) Cambridge, Mass.: Artificial Intelligence Laboratory, MIT.

Stenning, K. 1975. "Understanding English Articles and Quantifiers." Unpublished doctoral dissertation, The Rockefeller University.

Webber, B. L. 1978a. "A Formal Approach to Discourse Anaphora." (Technical Report 3761) Cambridge, Mass.: Bolt Beranek and Newman Inc.

Webber, B. L. 1978b. "Jumping Ahead of the Speaker: On Recognition from Indefinite Descriptions." Presented at the Sloan Workshop on Indefinite Reference. University of Massachusetts, Amherst.

Winograd, T. 1975. "Frame Representations and the Declarative-Procedural Controversy." In D. G. Bobrow and A. M. Collins, eds. *Representation and Understanding: Studies in Cognitive Science.* New York: Academic Press.

Woods, W. A., and Brachman, R. J. 1978. "Research in Natural Language Understanding – Quarterly Technical Progress Report No. 1. (Technical Report 3742) Cambridge, Mass.: Bolt Beranek and Newman Inc.

14

Procedural semantics as a theory of meaning

WILLIAM A. WOODS

For quite a few years researchers have been attempting to construct artificially intelligent machines that understand and use natural language. In their effort, a number of problems that have interested philosophers for centuries have suddenly taken on a new practical importance, among them the problem of meaning. If a machine is to understand questions and commands and take appropriate actions in response to them, then it needs some well-specified criteria to determine what those questions and commands mean.

In searching the philosophical literature for a suitable explication of meaning to use as a foundation for such a system, I acquired many useful insights, but no really adequate notion of what a "meaning" might be or how one might capture it in a computer. The closest notion that I could find was a concept of truth conditions that purported to characterize the circumstances in which a (declarative) sentence would be true and those in which it would be false (Carnap, 1964; Church, 1964).

However, these truth conditions are usually viewed as arbitrary functions from possible worlds or abstract models into truth values, following a tradition begun apparently by Frege (1892) and formalized and codified by Tarski (1944).

The Tarskian model theory provides a formal characterization of the circumstances in which a complex logical statement constructed from Boolean operators ("and," "or," "not") and universal and existential quantification would be true as a function of the truth values of their constituent elementary propositions (i.e., those not composed out of logical operators). The "circumstances" under which such expressions are either true or false are defined by abstract "interpretations" (or "models") consisting of an assignment of a truth value to every possible application of a predicate to every individual in an assumed universe of individuals and predicates. No account is given of how such infinite assignments can be finitely represented or how they could be related to the actual state of the world.

300

In attempting to give a concrete and finitely representable explication to the notion of truth condition, I settled on the notion of a procedure as a familiar example of a finitely specifiable way to characterize an infinite set, and having the advantage of also permitting the definition of truth conditions for elementary propositions in terms of primitive operations of sensory perception. (The "sensory perceptions" of the machines that I first constructed were quite limited, but the theory was chosen with larger goals in mind.) This approach also had the advantage of providing a sensible characterization of the meanings of imperatives and questions as well as simple propositional assertions.

This approach, which I dubbed "procedural semantics," was developed in the context of a hypothetical airline information system (Woods, 1967, 1968) and received its first significant application in the LUNAR system (Woods et al., 1972), a system that answered natural English questions about the chemical analyses of the Apollo moon rocks. In an approximately cotemporal development, Terry Winograd used very similar techniques to build his blocks world system SHRDLU (Winograd, 1972), which simulates a robot moving blocks on a table in response to natural English commands.

Since then, the concept of procedural semantics has generated considerable interest and, I fear, some confusion. In this chapter, I want to discuss some of the things that procedural semantics isn't (at least to the extent that the term refers to an attempt to explicate the notion of "meaning"), to present a number of subtleties that must be dealt with if an adequate theory of meaning is to be obtained, and to outline what I feel are the beginnings of such a theory.

Studies of semantics have traditionally taken one of two forms – either the specification of semantic interpretations of ordinary language in some more or less well-defined notation, or the formal specification of the truth conditions or proof procedures for formal languages. However, the two activities are usually carried on independently almost as if they were unrelated fields of study. When one attempts to design computer systems to understand natural language, one must not only attack both of these problems in a compatible way, but one must also address the basic problem of how the truth conditions of sentences relate to the sense experience of the computer. In addressing this problem, it is difficult not to be interpreted as espousing traditional theories of verificationism and reductionism, but, what I propose is significantly different from those traditions. Although verificationist theories are generally discredited, almost everyone concedes that truth conditions are somehow "related" to perceptions.

However, almost no one seems willing to be specific about what this relationship is. The approach I will present here is the best one I have found to date that attempts to account for this relationship.

In what I am about to say about procedures as devices for specifying the relationship between truth conditions and perception, I am not espousing anything quite like any existing verificationist or reductionist theory. In particular, the abstract procedures that I advocate as devices for linking truth conditions to perceptions are not procedures that people can usually execute to determine the truth of a proposition, and they are certainly not intended to be substitutable for those propositions (so that the behavior of natural language semantics is simply reduced to the rules of computation of machines). Although I will take the computation of machines as a foundation on which to build descriptions of the semantics of natural language, those descriptions in no way follow from the principles of computation, but are rather an independent theory embodied in a computational medium in much the same way that theories of many kinds can be expressed in the predicate calculus.

In general, the procedural semantics approach is a paradigm or a framework for developing and expressing theories of meaning, rather than being a theory of meaning itself. It is possible to formulate obviously false theories of meaning within this framework, as well as (I will argue) correct ones. I will demonstrate that some of the most direct applications of the idea of identifying the meanings of utterances with procedures are not in fact adequate as theories of meaning. In particular, it is not sufficient to identify the meaning of an utterance with whatever procedure a machine happens to execute in response to it, with the procedure used to make incremental changes to a machine's memory store, with the procedures used to carry out a command, or even necessarily with the procedures normally used to decide whether to believe an assertion to be true. All of these procedures are important for a language-understanding system to have and for scientists to explicate, but they do not correspond to the thing to which we seem to refer when we use the ordinary language term "meaning."

In what follows, I shall be discussing problems that I believe hold equally for human beings and machines if they are to adequately use and understand natural language utterances (although I have encountered them in the context of designing artificially intelligent machines). That is, I will be discussing problems that must be faced by any system (human, machine, alien, or whatever) that is to deal with natural language utterances in somewhat the same way that humans currently do, a process we ordinarily refer to as "understanding" and "appropriately using."

Intelligent systems

It is helpful to begin an investigation of the semantics of English with a fairly clear image of the role of language in relation to the overall mental activity of the system that uses it. I will start with a brief outline of a theory of intelligence put forward by Daniel Dennett (1974), which I find highly satisfying and a useful precursor to a theory of the evolution of natural languages. Dennett presents a plausibly mechanistic account for an array of increasing levels of intelligence based on a view of hypothesis formation and testing as a kind of internal natural selection. Moreover, he presents an argument for this as a kind of mental organization that could itself plausibly result from natural selection. Specifically, he points out that for sufficiently low-order organisms, the behavioral characteristics of the organisms in response to stimuli are essentially "wired in" by their genes, and their overall behavioral program is only altered by genetic selection over many generations of individuals. He points out the evolutionary advantages for an organism to have an internal model of the world against which to test hypothesized courses of action prior to carrying them out. Specifically, such an internalized evaluation of hypothetical actions permits one's theories to die instead of oneself. The advantage that such intelligence provides a species is the ability to adapt to a changing environment within the lifetime of a single individual.

An intelligent animal, by this account, would have a behavioral program that was not completely determined by its genes, but which was generated by some internalized behavioral program hypothesizer (or program modification hypothesizer) and evaluated by some internalized behavioral program evaluator. These program hypothesizers and evaluators could either be determined genetically, or could themselves be the result of internalized program hypothesizer hypothesizers, program hypothesizer evaluators, and so on, giving rise to higher and higher levels of intelligence as the number of levels of internalized adaptation increased. This account not only gives a plausible explanation of how complex intelligent behavior could evolve from understood mechanisms, but also nicely predicts such facts as the increasingly long period of maturation of children as a function of the level of intelligence of a species, the development of pathological patterns of behavior as a result of exposure to certain kinds of environments during maturation, and a limitation on the degree of intelligence that can be obtained in this way (i.e., by repeated iterations of selecting the selectors, etc.) by virtue of the limited lifetime of the individual.

Interestingly, Dennett's account also motivates the evolutionary potential for culture and natural language. That is, given this perspective, it is only a short step beyond Dennett's account to see the development of a language for communication as a means for some of this rapidly acquired adaptation to transcend the lifetime of a single individual, thus saving each succeeding generation from having to learn everything from scratch. A culture then becomes a kind of higher-level organism with a collective memory, and can be viewed as a means of escaping the limited lifetime of a single individual.

From this point of view, we see that a particularly useful component of the behavioral program evaluator is a model of the external world that can be used to predict the outcome of actions without actually having to carry them out. We will assume that at least in humans, almost certainly in many monkeys and apes, and probably to a lesser extent in most mammals, there is a genetically determined program either for acquiring such a model or for producing a program to acquire such a model. (The manifestations of this program in our behavior are generally referred to as "curiosity.")

In order to store such a model internally, an intelligent system will need to have some internalized "notation" or "representation" for expressing believed and hypothesized facts about the world. (I hesitate to use the term "language" at this point because of connotations of similarity to a surface language that I deliberately want to avoid. Specifically, I do not want to invite attributions to this internal notation of properties such as temporal word order, structural or semantic ambiguities, situationally dependent meaning, composition out of English words, discrete rather than analogue representation, or anything leading to assumptions of homunculi inside the head that are interpreting the internal notations in ways analogous to the way we understand English. However, subject to these qualifications, I will subsequently refer to this as the "internal language.")

Internal and external language

The thrust of the preceding discussion of intelligence, which may at first seem somewhat of a digression, is to motivate a notion of an internal language that both logically and temporally precedes the development of external language, and in terms of which the meanings of external language expressions are defined. This internal language itself requires a semantics, and I would maintain that without some understanding of its semantics, one cannot have a complete semantic account of an external language. I will argue that this internal language is capable of vastly more discriminative subtlety than one's external language, which has evolved to a suitable compromise between the need for discrimination and the economic costs of inventing and learning a large vocabulary and inventory of syntactic conventions, and of composing, articulating, and understanding long external sentences. As evidence for this, consider the ability of this internal language to store the criteria for discriminating a particular familiar face versus the apparent inability to convey such criteria by means of the external language.

In general, I will argue that human communication relies in a critical way on an ability of the receiver to deduce a much more precise understanding of the intended meaning of an utterance than is conveyed by the words alone and the syntactic structure in which they are incorporated. Moreover, I will argue that this is not just an unfortunate characteristic of natural language, but is in fact an economic solution to the problem of communication in a situation in which it is not economic to develop external terms and conventions for all of the discriminations that one can make internally.

The role of (external) language

If intelligence was evolved by natural selection and Dennett's account is correct, then one should find that the development of the capability for external language evolved in a similar way. Moreover, one should find that the capacity for external language is selected to support the transferral of world models and behavioral strategies from individual to individual, in the way and of the kinds that I have outlined. One might then expect that other "higher level" uses of language, such as poetry, song, and so forth, would derive in some natural way from this basic need (possibly as a result of a higher-level evaluator that values skill in the use of language in general, as an indirect way of achieving the more specific goal of world model transference).

Although there are many different kinds of use of language, I will assume in the rest of this chapter that its uses for factual communication, explanation of principles, and complex instructions for behavior are the primary ones that motivate its evolution. Although I will be concerned specifically with the "literal meanings" of utterances, as opposed to the various things that a speaker might intend to convey by an utterance (threats, irony, etc.), nothing I say will be inconsistent with an account of the pragmatic interpretation of speech acts in contexts other than literal factual communication. I will maintain, in fact, that an understanding of the literal semantics of an utterance is often essential to determining its intended pragmatic meaning. For example, the correct understanding of the statement "It's a lovely day" uttered when it is in fact pouring rain requires the knowledge that the sentence is not literally true.

With these preliminary caveats in hand, let me now devote my attention to the interpretation of literal meanings, and primarily to the interpretation of factual assertions.

Role of sense ambiguity

In my account of the semantics of external language, I will make heavy use of the notion of ambiguity, by which I mean the presence of alternative distinct interpretations in the internal language that the speaker may have intended to convey and among which the hearer must in some sense try to choose the meaning that the speaker intended. I will thus demand of my internal language that it have the capability to represent explicitly and unambiguously any and all of the distinctions that one is capable of making in resolving an ambiguity in a surface utterance as well as being able to represent any of the more abstract (or vague) interpretations that one can make. I will assume that what is understood in response to most (but not necessarily all) utterances is something that is much more precise and less ambiguous than those utterances in isolation would permit. The additional information used to determine this more precise understanding comes from the current values of indexical expressions such as "here," "now," and "current speaker," from knowledge of the world, and from knowledge of various speech act conventions, rules of the language game, emotional state of the speaker, and so on. Whereas the determination of the current interpretation of the speaker's intended meaning will be considered fallible and in some sense "fuzzy," the meaning of each possible sense of the utterance will be assumed to be relatively precise.

I claim that from this point of view most words in English are highly ambiguous, and that the intended sense is selected by context. As an illustration, consider the classical example "bachelor," which by the conventional wisdom has a number of senses, including certain kinds of fur seals and baccalaureate degrees (Katz and Fodor, 1964), but is usually considered to have only one sense – an "unmarried adult male human." However, as Winograd (1976) points out, even this sense has many different subtle shadings, including whether the person referred to "lives the life-style of a bachelor," is eligible for marriage, comes from a culture that permits several wives but has not yet filled his quota, and so forth. Thus, what we take someone to mean by a sentence (in Winograd's example, "Do you know any nice bachelors I could invite [to my party]") is characterized by uncertainty. I will claim that this uncertainty is due to a fundamental parsimony of the external language vis-à-vis the internal language (to be discussed further later in this section) and that each of the distinguishable senses must be explicitly expressible in the internal language. Notice that this account does not necessitate any fundamental assumptions of fuzziness of meaning of the internal language.

By contrast, consider Winograd's account of this example, which rests on the notion of a prototype or "exemplar" of the general concept of bachelor to which various individuals can be matched with varying degrees of closeness of match. By this account, the concept of bachelor itself is a fuzzy concept in the sense of Zadeh (1974), in which different individual instances satisfy different numbers of the features associated with the exemplar. This account does not explain the fact that when a person is asked the above question, something fairly precise is understood without necessarily attempting to match any particular individuals to the concept. Understanding this sentence correctly, it seems to me, requires a particular sense of the word (defined perhaps by a particular allocation of importance to the features from Winograd's list) to be selected as the intended sense. One does not just understand by this sentence some vague notion of an approximate match to the exemplar that is fundamentally the same regardless of context. Rather one must characterize in some way what match criteria must be met, or at least which criteria are more important. Some residual ambiguity may remain as to whether the host(ess) specifically wanted "eligible" males that are likely prospects for marriage, or merely men who are living the life-style of a bachelor, but such ambiguity can be kept distinct from a fuzziness in knowing exactly what the different senses mean.

Acquisition of meanings

Just as what we take someone to mean by a sentence is characterized by uncertainty, so is the process of learning what people mean by a term from the occasions of its use and/or its "definitions" in dictionaries. It may be possible to formulate quite precise and well-defined concepts in the internal language with which to try to model the use of a term as we have been exposed to it; the problem in language acquisition (with respect to the meanings of terms) is to discover which such concept or concepts to take as the meaning(s) of a given term. Once again, our uncertainty in knowing the meaning of a term as other people use it does not necessitate any fundamental fuzziness in the meaning of the concepts of the internal language.

The general state of someone in the process of learning the meaning of an external language term (and I believe this to be the normal state for many if not most of the terms even in the vocabulary of an adult) must consist in holding some hypotheses about the meaning of that term as others use it. Such a hypothesis could be expressed by an explicit set of (fully specified) internal concepts, one or more of which is hypothesized to be what other people mean by the term. Alternatively, one could express such a hypothesis by a collection of ("meta") statements about the hypothesized meaning (i.e., meta-statements in the sense of statements in a meta language about the language in question). Such a characterization would implicitly determine a set of possible internal concepts, but would not require their explicit formulation. In this mode it would be possible to express hypotheses that characterized an infinite class of possible meanings and to express beliefs about the distributions of likelihoods of those hypothesized possible meanings being correct. (It would also be possible to express inconsistent hypotheses that could not be satisfied by any well-defined concept – and it is almost certainly the case that people can do this and do so without realizing it. I think this is especially likely to happen when one coins a term for a concept in scientific theory formation and in philosophy.)

The formulation of meta hypotheses about the meanings of a term also permits the expression of relative likelihoods or likelihood distributions for the different hypotheses, reflecting their degrees of confirmation or disconfirmation. Again, this does not entail any fundamental assumption of fuzziness in the semantics of the internal language expressions, although it does imply a rather complex process for determining the meaning to take for a sentence involving the use of a term for which one only has hypothetical meta-statements to constrain its meaning. In the worst case, one may only be able to deduce hypothetical meta-statements about the meaning of such a sentence.

Parametric ambiguity

If one is to use the notion of ambiguity to account for the uncertainty in the meanings of terms as people use them, then in addition to the usual notion of (discrete) ambiguity, it seems necessary to introduce a notion of ambiguity that is continuously variable over a potentially infinite range of possibilities. This seems necessary, for example, for an account of the ambiguity of various "measure" predicates such as "tall" and "contain" (i.e., predicates that can take qualifiers of amount and admit questions such as "How tall is John?" or "How much does it contain?"). When such terms are used in simple declarative assertions), they seem to assert that the appropriate measure (e.g., height) exceeds some threshold, I will treat such sentences as ambiguous with respect to this threshold, and will refer to such cases as "parametrically ambiguous."

The traditional account of such sentences as "John is tall" is to consider them discretely ambiguous with respect to various classes to which John might belong, taking the necessary threshold from the normative height for each class (e.g., "John is tall for a fifteen-year-old"). However, this account fails to explain a residual ambiguity in what counts as a significant deviation from the norm. That is, whatever threshold one picks for the normative height, there remains some intended scale of what counts as a significant difference that must also be inferred in order to know what the speaker intended to say. One assumes that one millimeter over the normative height would not count as "tall," nor would an additional meter of height be required (for humans, not for buildings). Somewhere in between is a level of discrimination that the speaker was intending his hearer to assume, and we need to infer some value of this parameter in order to fully determine what assertion the speaker was making (e.g., what fact about the world he wanted the hearer to believe).

It is usually not critical in practice to get this value precisely right, but some value needs to be assumed. In many cases, the utterance of such a sentence about a person whose height is known to the hearer is in fact used to "calibrate" the speaker with respect to this ambiguity (i.e., to specify what the speaker considers tall). In other cases, what the hearer presumably encodes in response to such an assertion is a specification of a range of parametric ambiguity which (s)he is unable to resolve, pending some future situation in which it may be further resolved or may make a difference. In general, it seems to be psychologically difficult for a hearer to maintain more than a few discrete ambiguous interpretations of an input utterance, and one can easily imagine how this is a costly operation for a mechanical system. For a parametric ambiguity, however, the encoding of the ambiguity requires only the lack of choice of a value for the parameter or some description of a range of possible values (e.g., the end points of an interval), perhaps accompanied by some description of a likelihood distribution for the possible values. One would therefore not expect the same level of difficulty for holding open this kind of ambiguity.

The economic necessity of ambiguity

When one thinks of it from the perceptual point of view, a linguistic speech act is merely another kind of perceived entity. Moreover, the structural decomposition of a sentence into its individual constituents and their relationships to each other is an intimate part of its perception as a sentence. (Notice that ambiguity enters the picture here as an aspect of perception in exactly the same way that certain diagrams and visual scenes are ambiguous and can be perceived in more than one way.) When viewed in this way, it becomes clear that the perceptual complexity of words and constructions (as spoken waveforms or patterns of ink on paper) is comparable in some sense to the complexity of other perceived entities such as boxes, people, automobiles, and so on.

From the preceding, it follows that characterizing the perceptual conditions for some concept plus also characterizing the perceptual conditions for some word that is uniquely associated with that concept is approximately twice as much effort as representing the perceptual conditions for the concept alone. Specifically, the process of forming a concept by the modification or combination of other concepts is comparable in complexity to the process of forming a lexical concept by the modification of some existing word or the composition of phonetic elements, syllables, or some such constituents. Moreover, the process of forming a named concept requires not only this doubling of complexity in what is stored, but also the effort involved in coining and remembering a suitable external name – a process that involves appropriate problem-solving tasks such as generating candidate names and testing them for memorability, potential misleading associations, previous use for other concepts, and so forth.

Given the situation just presented, it should not be surprising that one in general has many more concepts than one has external names, or that one habitually uses the same external name for many different but related concepts (especially where confusion is not likely to result, but also in places where it is). As an example of the former, consider the concept of the small cylindrical projection on the end of a shoelace that keeps it from unraveling and makes it easier to thread through holes. I expect that you have little difficulty in identifying the concept that I have in mind, although the above description falls far short of completely specifying the concept to someone who has never seen a shoelace. (In a more specific context, such as while displaying a shoelace without one, I would be able to get the point across with as little as "the end is missing," which, given the nature of strings, it would be absurd to take literally.)

The multiple use of the same word for different concepts is so frequently done, and the nuances of meaning shift are sometimes so subtle, that we are largely unaware that it is happening. Only the more glaring examples that are listed in dictionaries as multiple senses seem to make their presence known. However, there are a number of very subtle, systematic uses that are not normally listed as separate word senses in dictionaries. One of these is the use of a word both to refer to an object and to refer to a representation of that object in a picture or diagram (highlighted in such ambiguous phrases as "painting nudes").

This principle of economy also predicts the use of regular system-atic devices for coining names for concepts without having to coin completely new words. Examples are the frequent use of a noun to name an action that is related to it in some way (e.g., "to land a plane," "to dock a ship," "to chair a meeting," etc.) and the highly productive use of so-called noun–noun modifiers to form multiword names for concepts (e.g., "dog house," "pot cover," "ambiguity tester," "idle-speed adjusting screw," "eight-track stereo cartridge tape player," etc.).

In a similar way, the same economy principle motivates the use of devices such as anaphoric reference, ellipsis, and other locutions in-volving a degree of lack of specificity. That is, one must assume that the internal language has little difficulty in making repeated refer-ences to an internal concept by some unique "handle" or pointer, in much the same way as if it had a unique proper name for that concept. The external language, however, has no such simple facility, and uses instead such devices as pronouns and other anaphoric expressions. The uses of deixis, ellipsis, and various other such techniques are all motivated by the differential economics of having something in mind versus expressing it explicitly in the external language.

In summary, unlike Montague (1970, 1973), who claims that one could in principle give an adequate semantic theory of a natural lan-guage directly, as if it were a formal language, I maintain that natural languages have an essential difference from formal languages that necessitates a two-stage account of their semantics. The first stage must cope with the ambiguity inherent in natural languages, whereas the second stage consists of giving a formal semantics for the underlying meaning representation in which the alternative senses of ambiguous sentences are expressed. In fact, even Montague's accounts involve an intermediate entity (an analysis tree) that serves this disambiguation function.

Semantic interpretation

Given the hypothesis of an internal language in which the interpretation of English sentences is expressed, the problem of semantic characterization of English becomes a two-stage process. The first stage consists of assigning to an imput sentence one or more possible interpretations in the internal language, whereas the second consists of characterizing the semantics of the internal language. Historically, the first stage, which we will call semantic interpretation, has been the domain of most concern to the linguistic semanticist, and the second has traditionally been of more concern to the philosopher. I will argue that both rules for assigning interpretations to sentences and the characterization of the meanings of the internal language expressions can be modeled by means of procedures. However, the nature of the two kinds of procedures and the way that they are used are quite different.

Semantic interpretation procedures as defined above are essentially translation procedures that are executed as part of the understanding of a sentence to produce a set of possible interpretations of the sentence. This process can be modeled by a variety of automata such as ATN grammars (Woods, 1970) or systems of rewrite rules as in a Transformational Grammar (Chomsky, 1965). I (Woods, 1978a) have given an exposition of how such translation is accomplished by means of formal semantic interpretation rules in the LUNAR system.

As I have pointed out, the sentences in the external language are in general highly ambiguous, although many different factors can be invoked by the understanding system to attempt to determine which meaning was intended. It seems that at least conceptually, the performance of semantic interpretation involves the use of a fairly regular system of conventionalized literal semantic interpretation rules that determine a range of possible literal meanings, from which a variety of pragmatic considerations determine the intended meaning of the utterance in context. Sometimes this latter is done by simply selecting from among the possible literal meanings, but often it is done by the further application of various more or less conventionalized pragmatic or "speech act" rules.

I say the above organization is the conceptual organization in order to avoid the implication that there is necessarily an actual serial process in which the alternative semantic interpretations are explicitly enumerated before the pragmatic rules operate. In particular, one may want pragmatic rules to operate in the selection of which semantic interpretation rules to apply, or to interact with the semantic interpretation process in some other way. In most cases, however, a literal interpretation (or parts of one) appears to play an important role in the application of speech act rules. For example, in recognizing irony, it is necessary to conclude that the speaker is not intending to express the literal meaning, but rather its opposite.

Although there is a great deal of work required to characterize both the conventionalized semantic rules and the conventionalized pragmatic rules (as well as a range of nonconventionalized problem-solving activities that are often used in determining intended meaning), there is no difficulty in principle in knowing what kinds of things such rules are. That is, they can be characterized as formal translation rules of some sort that can be expressed as computer programs or any of a variety of abstract automata. In particular, they can be embodied in an Augmented Transition Network grammar. When one turns to the semantics of the internal language, however, things are not quite so clear-cut.

Semantics of the internal language

In the remainder of this chapter, I will be concerned with the specification of the semantics of the internal language in terms of which the semantics of external sentences are to be defined. Our previous discussion of intelligence suggests that a principal use of this internal language is to develop a taxonomy of the kinds of objects, events, situations, and so on, that can occur in the external world and to formulate hypotheses about the properties of such entities and the cause-and-effect relationships among them. It is almost certainly necessary that this internal language be extensible in the sense that new concepts can be created out of old ones and then used as components of the specification of still newer concepts. That is, one should not visualize the internal language as having a closed vocabulary.

What must be primitively present in the internal language are some basic concepts and an inventory of fundamental operators that can be used to construct new concepts from old ones. Moreover, principles of economy (and perhaps also logical necessity) dictate that such new concepts must be usable as elements in the internal language in much the same way that the basic concepts are used. They should not be visualized simply as abbreviations for more complex expressions that are to be substituted for them. The utility of creating new concepts in a taxonomy comes from thereafter being able to use a new concept as a single entity rather than copying out its definition on every use. (The distinction I am trying to make here is similar to the way that "closed" subroutines in a computer program may be "used" in several places although only one copy of the subroutine is explicitly stored. "Open" subroutines or "macros" on the other hand are "expanded in place," resulting in a separate copy of the macro definition for each use.)

It is important for the internal language to be able to develop concepts that express very precise and subtle distinctions between classes of objects and situations. A man's life in the jungle (or, for that matter, an ape's) can depend on the ability to distinguish subtle differences between otherwise similar plants and animals, some of which are edible and others toxic or dangerous. Moreover, by the above account, what makes this discrimination ability advantageous to an intelligent animal is the ability to associate cause–effect (or "if–then") predictions with the various concepts in the taxonomy (e.g., "If you eat this, you will get sick," or "If you eat this, it will satisfy your hunger"). The two most important aspects of this internal representational system would thus seem to be its ability to specify precise perceptual conditions for a concept and to characterize the "if–then" associations among such concepts (including concepts of various internal states such as hunger and sickness).

Although in what follows I will be primarily concerned with the semantics of this internal language, rather than its representational conventions and capabilities, the kinds of representations that I will be assuming are somewhat like those of Ron Brachman's "structured inheritance networks" (Brachman, 1978, 1979; Woods and Brachman, 1978), within which is represented what I have been calling a "taxonomic lattice" (Woods, 1978b). This lattice of concepts is used as a "conceptual coat rack" on which to hang various hypotheses and conclusions about different classes of entity.

Brachman's structured inheritance networks are a generalization of Quillian's notions of semantic networks (Quillian, 1966, 1968, 1969; Bell and Quillian, 1971), in which, among other things, generic information about concepts can be stored at its most general level of applicability and "inherited" by more specific concepts below (e.g., information about physical objects can be stored at a very high level, whereas specific information about rocks, animals, birds, etc., can be stored at more specific levels). Economic principles of memory organization suggest some such hierarchical or network organization in which information common to many concepts is shared.

The most salient feature of Brachman's networks is their treatment of inheritance for complex structured entities. These networks explicitly represent not only the subsumption relationship between two concepts, but also the correspondence of parts, attributes, and properties between them. Space does not permit a full exposition of these structures here, but the details of the representations are not critical to anything that follows. The use of such representations, in which given pieces of information are shared or inherited by many different concepts, contributes to the economic efficiency of an intelligent system, and answers a possible objection to my account arising from apparent combinatorial problems in storing the necessary information, but is not essential to a discussion of what the concepts in the internal world model mean.

In the following arguments, I will not present any details of representation suitable for the internal language, but rather will use a mixture of English, traditional predicate calculus notations, and some programming concepts from the language LISP (Berkeley and Bobrow, 1964; Weissman, 1967), which I hope will be clear. The syntax of the LISP language consists of expressions in so-called Cambridge Polish notation, in which a functional operator appears to the left of its operands and the whole is enclosed in parentheses to indicate the grouping of function with arguments [e.g., "(PLUS 2 3)" is the LISP notation equivalent to the "infix" notation 2 + 3, and the conventional notation f(x) would be represented as "(f x)" in LISP].

Motivations for a procedural account of meanings

An interpretation procedure that translates surface sentences into representations in an internal language is clearly procedural, but it is not necessarily "semantic." In order for such a translation process to have anything to do with semantics, the semantics of the resulting representation must be understood. The latter must eventually be specified by something other than just another such translation process. Procedural semantics, at least as I use the term, refers not to the translation process of semantic interpretation, but to the use of procedures to characterize such things as truth conditions (for propositional assertions), conditions of satisfactory response (for imperatives and questions), and conditions of appropriate use (for various social speech acts, etc.).

Although it seems clear that truth conditions for a term can be said to define its semantics, it is not necessary (at least it doesn't seem to be necessary) to interpret them as procedures. However, there are a number of motivations for using procedures as an explication of the notion of truth conditions, some of which were mentioned in the introduction. (They are discussed more fully in Woods, 1967.) Whereas most of the arguments have to do with issues of efficiency or methodological advantages such as concreteness and clarity of understanding, the following argument seems to justify the approach for an account of how people work:

If a person (fully) understands a term characterizing a class of entity and is presented with a clear instance of a member of that class, (s)he can recognize it and say "yes." Likewise (s)he can reject a clear nonmember. If we believe that in doing this, the brain is functioning as some kind of physical/electrical machine, then clearly there is some procedure that is being executed that recognizes members of the class and rejects nonmembers. If we recognize this process not as a physical/electrical one, but rather as the product of some uniquely mental "stuff," we may not necessarily be forced to admit the existence of such a procedure, but neither are we blocked from it. However, to avoid it would seem to require some direct and unexplained form of "knowing" independent of the functioning of the brain, the eyes, the visual cortex, and other sense organs. Although I can't directly rule out such an account, it seems implausible and somewhat sterile as an account of ordinary human behavior. Therefore, a procedural account would appear to have significant face validity.

One of the major methodological advantages of the procedural semantics approach to meaning is that one does not encounter as many dilemmas when confronting things whose meanings do not seem to characterize truth values (things such as commands, promises, measure predicates, etc.). That is, the kinds of things that can be constructed out of the basic procedural elements of a universal machine constitute a richer inventory of conceptual entities than those that can be constructed out of the primitives AND, OR, NOT, and universal and existential quantification (at least without embedding a different conceptual system within a first-order predicate calculus and specifying a set of axioms to characterize that system).

Moreover, the procedural primitives of a higher-level programming language such as LISP provide what seems to be a useful basic set of operations out of which to construct potential "meaning functions" (by which I mean the functions that define the truth conditions of propositions, satisfaction conditions for imperatives, etc.). For example, the procedural paradigm permits one to construct "primitives" for measuring such things as strength of pattern matching, statistical correlations, and weighted sums out of the same basic procedural primitives that one uses to characterize the meanings of the logical terms AND, OR, and EVERY.

Of course, one still has to determine whether a new conceptual operation such as weighted combinations of different measurements is necessary or suitable to account for the meanings of certain terms or expressions, and one still has to characterize which terms and expressions are so interpreted. All that a procedural semantics approach does is to increase the inventory of conceptual apparatus that one can utilize in accounting for meanings without requiring each new such conceptual mechanism to be introduced as a new primitive element or undefined concept.

I view the procedural approach to the problems of semantics not as an alternative to the more traditional Tarskian model-theoretic account, but rather as a means to supplement that account with what in computer terminology would be called an "upward compatible" extension. That is, I view the Tarskian account as a particular special case of a procedural account – one in which the procedures involved are the definitions of the quantifiers and logical connectives as procedures for assigning truth values to complex propositions as a function of the truth values of their constituents. The Tarskian account, however, stops short of attempting to specify the truth conditions of elementary propositions, and falls short of an adequate account of the various "opaque context" operators such as "believe" and "want," whose truth values are determined by something more than just the truth values of their constituents. I believe that by viewing the operations of Tarskian model theory as abstract procedures, and making the extension to permit a more diverse range of procedural primitives from which to construct the meanings of utterances, one can obtain an adequate semantic account, not only of propositional utterances, but also of various other speech acts. Moreover, within the same framework, one can extend the range of semantic explanation beyond an account of truth conditions in terms of abstract models (as in a classical model theory) to include an account of how these models relate to the actual world via sensory perception.

Some inadequate theories of procedural semantics

As I stated earlier, a number of theories could be formulated within the procedural semantics framework that are clearly wrong. At this point, I would like to point out two of them, which I will call the "induced effect" theory and the "criteria for belief theory." The first is a theory that whatever procedure the machine carries out in response to a sentence constitutes its meaning. Among other things, this theory would dictate that if a declarative sentence causes some representation of itself to be stored in memory, and if a question causes some searching and matching procedure to be executed to try to find a matching statement in the memory, then these procedures for storage and searching would be the meanings of the sentences in question.

Now there is no question that the effects of many sentences are to invoke such storage and searching operations. What is in question here is whether those operations can sensibly be taken as an explication of the ordinary use of the word "meaning." The answer is that of course they can't, for one quickly realizes that the meaning of a sentence such as "It is raining" really has something to do with whether it is raining, and not whether a representation equivalent to that sentence is stored in one's head (no matter how strongly it might be believed). Thus, the procedures by which a representation of this sentence is constructed and stored will not serve as an explication of its meaning.

The "criteria for belief" theory takes the meaning of a sentence to be the criteria for deciding whether to believe it. Although this is somewhat closer to the mark, a little reflection will convince one that the situation is quite the other way around. That is, the criteria for belief may include some appeal to the meaning of a sentence, but this is not the only criterion for deciding what to believe. Other criteria include such things as credibility of the source. One should certainly distinguish such criteria for belief from the meaning of the sentence.

Both of the above "theories" attempt to identify the meaning of a sentence with something that is done when the sentence is understood. In fact, unlike the semantic interpretation procedures, the procedures that characterize the meanings of sentences are usually not executed as part of the understanding of a sentence. Rather, their importance lies in being available for execution and/or for simulated execution in hypothetical situations. They serve to define the standard of what a concept refers to, even when input sentences merely make reference to such procedures without requiring their actual execution. For example, many assertions can be viewed as statements of a relationship between two procedures, neither of which is executed as part of the process of understanding, but which are nevertheless critical parts of the meanings. Specifically, "Snow is white" can be interpreted as an assertion of a particular relationship (sometimes referred to as "holding") between the meaning function for "white" and the extension of the meaning function for "snow." To understand the meaning of such sentences, it is not necessary to execute these procedures but only to have them.

In addition to avoiding the above two specifically false interpretations of what a procedural account of meaning might be, there are a number of other, somewhat subtle, interpretations of the notion of procedure that need to be made if one is to give an adequate procedural account of the semantics of English. I will argue that in order to adequately model our pretheoretic notion of meaning, one has to depart in several respects from a "straightforward" interpretation of the meanings of expressions as procedures (i.e., as analogous to a piece of computer program that can be executed in any given situation to determine the truth value or referent of the expression in question). Specific problems have to do with the extent to which the procedures can actually be executed in a given situation, and the notion of what aspects of the specification of a procedure in some representation count as essential parts of the meaning. In the next few sections, I will discuss a number of alterations to the "straightforward" notion of procedural semantics that need to be made in order for such a notion to be an adequate theory of meaning. Many of these issues have been touched upon in a previous paper (Woods, 1973).

Before proceeding further, let us first deal with an often raised question relating to the possibility of achieving the goal.

A fallacious criticism of the procedural approach

A long-standing criticism of any attempt to formally set out the truth conditions for ordinary terms such as "dog," "chair," and "alive" is that although various people have attempted such definitions, no one has succeeded in giving any that are satisfying. I think that the argument I will give shortly for the necessity of partial procedures that do not attempt to account for all of the pathological entities that are "neither fish nor fowl" accounts for a major component of such failures. A second component, I believe, is a rather limited view of the possible devices out of which such a definition could be constructed. In particular, one argument for the impossibility of characterizing the meanings of such terms in terms of more primitive properties goes roughly as follows:

If one attempts to characterize the meanings of ordinary terms such as "dog" as having specific definitions in terms of more primitive properties such as having four legs, hair, certain kinds of teeth, eating meat, and so on, in almost all such cases one can imagine (or actually encounter) entities to which the term should apply that fail to have one or more of these properties. One can imagine dogs with three legs (as a result of either a physical accident or a congenital abnormality), without hair (singed or shaved or somehow bald), with no teeth, and so forth. It seems that none of the supposed defining properties are absolutely necessary. Moreover, if there were some absolutely necessary properties (animate? – no, a dead dog is still a dog), their combination would be extremely unlikely to characterize the desired meaning. That is, even if there were some absolutely necessary conditions for being a dog, their combination would not be sufficient to define what a dog is, but only some much larger class of entities.

The fallacy in the above argument is an implicit assumption that the way that the defining properties are combined to make the definition is by simple conjunction. Such implicit assumptions can easily be (mis?)read into discussion such as the following:

> . . . we can define a class on the basis of some property (or set of properties) which they (sic) have in common. Suppose, for example, we summarize the set of properties assumed to be essential for something to qualify as a dog . . . Then we can say that the class of dogs comprises all those objects in the universe that have this, no doubt very complex . . . set of properties . . . the intension of a term is the set of essential properties that determines the applicability of the term. (Lyons, 1977, p. 158)

However, it is not the case that the only way to define a class of objects in terms of properties is to conjoin them. In particular, a procedural combination of elementary properties could involve conditional checking of some properties dependent on the values of others, as in the following hypothetical example (in a hopefully intuitive procedural language), where A, B, and C are assumed to be tests of elementary properties:

> If A and B, then conclude true;
> else if not A and not B, conclude false;
> else if C, conclude true;
> else conclude false.

In this definition, none of the properties A, B, or C is a necessary property for truth, but they are nevertheless the defining properties.

The above example could of course be represented as a disjunction of conjunctive cases without recourse to a notion of procedures. However, procedures in general permit convenient specification of such operations as testing whether the number of properties from a set of possible ones is greater than some threshold, testing whether the number of confirming properties exceeds the number of disconfirming ones, computing weighted sums of some kind of measures of importance of properties, and applying functions to values of continuous parameters such as height and weight. In such formulations, the connection between some defining property and the ultimate truth value that would be assigned to a proposition could be quite remote and intricate.

Arguing impossibility on the basis of an implicit assumption that limits one's ability to achieve the supposedly impossible goal is a very easy trap to fall into. Even as sophisticated a proceduralist as Winograd appears to be prone to a form of this fallacy (presumably in weak moments). In his account of the previously mentioned "bachelor" example, he says, "In normal use, a word does not convey a clearly definable combination of primitive propositions, but evokes an exemplar . . ." (Winograd, 1976). Here, "clearly definable combination of primitive propositions" is apparently blocked from including such a clearly defined combination as a pattern match with some matching criterion against an exemplar.

One of the advantages of the procedural approach to semantics (as Winograd is taking pains to point out in the above quote) is that procedures do provide for the clear definition of a concept in terms of more basic properties in ways other than simple conjunction, and (in particular) in ways involving such things as testing whether the number of properties an object has in common with some prototype is above some threshold. Moreover, it permits generalizations of such comparisons to comparisons with several alternative prototypes, selectively counting some properties as more criterial than others, and assigning various notions of approximate truth or degrees of satisfaction of a pattern. One of the major advantages of the procedural semantics paradigm, from my point of view, is that it permits such a range of devices with which to attempt to account for the meanings of words and utterances and their use in language.

Partial functions

One of the first adaptations that must be made to the straightforward procedural semantics account is to realize that one must in general permit meanings to be defined by partial functions that in some cases assign neither true nor false. The necessity for such functions is most strongly motivated by predicates such as "Sentence x is false," from which one can construct sentences that cannot be given any consistent truth value. For example, one of Russell's paradoxes (a version of the "Liar's paradox" of Epimenides) consisted of writing on one side of a piece of paper "The sentence on the other side of this paper is true" and writing on the other side "The sentence on the other side of this paper is false." Neither of these sentences can be assigned either of the values true or false without thereby inducing a logical inconsistency, although either sentence by iteslf seems meaningful and can be true or false for other possible values of "the sentence on the other side of this paper."

The problem with this pair of sentences is partly due to the fact that their truths are purportedly mutually defined in terms of each other with no other foundation (i.e., the definition is genuinely circular). Notice that if the pair of sentences both said "The sentence on the other side of this paper is true," either the assignment of both true or both false would be consistent, but there is no principle for choosing one or the other. Worse still, if both sentences were "The sentence on the other side of this paper is false," then the assignment of true to one and false to the other is consistent, although by symmetry one would expect that both sentences should get the same truth value. It seems necessary, therefore, that if we are to give any semantics at all to ordinary English, it must admit the possibility of certain predicates being defined by partial functions that fail to assign truth values at all in some cases (or equivalently have a "third truth value" that is neither true nor false).

The use of partial functions as meaning criteria, once one has been forced to permit it, solves another troublesome problem in the semantics of ordinary terms such as "chair," "dog," and "alive." Unlike formally defined terms such as "bachelor," these ordinary terms do not have a straightforward definition in terms of other words. Instead, they are learned by induction from our experience. As I mentioned, actual attempts to formally characterize the meaning of such terms seem always to fall short of completely delineating the class of objects to which one would want to apply the term. This is claimed as a demonstration of the impossibility of characterizing the meanings of such terms by such means. However, another possible interpretation of the data is that the criterion for the meaning of the term that people have in their heads is in fact partial, although capable of extension to resolve new unanticipated cases. Some psychological experimentation lends credence to this interpretation because it can be demonstrated that people have difficulty deciding whether to assign the term "chair" to various chairlike objects that violate one or more of the ordinary defining characteristics of "chairhood" (e.g., the absence of a back) (Miller and Johnson-Laird, 1976).

A possible account of these psychological results is that the meaning function for "chair" is in fact a partial procedure that assigns truth in some cases and falsity in others, but has simply never been extended to cover all of the possible sensory stimuli that it could be given as arguments. In this view, what goes on when such a novel instance of chair-like object is presented is that a kind of problem-solving activity is invoked to determine whether to extend the meaning of the term to include this new kind of object or not. These problem-solving processes consider such factors as similarity of the candidate object to various prototypes, the severity (on some scale) of the violations of formerly necessary conditions, the risk of overgeneralization, the utility of the resulting extended meaning, consistency with already held beliefs about classes of objects, estimates of how other people would use the term, and so on. In this view, the process of extending the meaning of a term or sharpening its discrimination is a creative act that is voluntarily taken by a person in certain circumstances. Moreover, if we look at the way that people acquire meanings, it seems clear that some such processes are essential. The meanings of most terms are acquired by extensive exposure to examples of their use and a gradual induction of their meaning. Moreover, those few terms that aren't acquired this way are ultimately defined in terms of ones that are.

If the above view is correct, then the notion of partially defined meaning function is not a strange anomaly of certain abstract theoretical concepts, but rather a ubiquitous characteristic of the meaning of words.

Accessibility

Another subtle requirement for an adequate procedural account of meaning has to do with the question of applicability of the procedures in worlds where the system does not have privileged access to all facts in the world, but must deal with the potential difference between what is true in the world and what the system thinks it knows. Current applications of procedural semantics in systems such as the LUNAR system and Winograd's SHRDLU do not face such problems because, by definition, the meanings of their expressions refer to the states of their internal computerized models. These systems thus have privileged access to the true state of their worlds in a way that humans (and mobile robots) do not. In the artificial worlds of these two systems, the primitive "perceptual" routines that measure states of the world not only do not make errors, but also have complete and total access to everything that is true of their world.

There are a number of artifacts of a procedural semantics for such completely accessible worlds that do not extend to the situation that human beings find themselves in in the real world. The most notable of these is the ability actually to execute the procedure that defines the meaning of an expression. In the real world, such procedures frequently are not executable because of lack of access to some of the data on which they operate. For example, even if one has a well-defined procedural specification of the meaning of a color term in terms of the output of a spectral analyzer or the sensors in one's eye, one can fail to be able to execute this procedure in practice because there is no light or the object in question is inside a locked box or is halfway around the world, etc. Moreover, the object may have existed in the past but exists no longer, or it may be a predicted future object, in which case there is no way even in principle (at least within our current technology and beliefs about what is possible) to carry out the procedure.

Nevertheless, even in this most extreme case of inaccessibility of the data on which the procedure would have to be operated, the procedure itself still seems to be a suitable entity to take as the characterization of the meaning of the term. Even in these cases, the representation of the procedure as a structured entity can serve as a source of inferences about what its outcomes would have been in certain circumstances. For example, the truth conditions for (the most common sense of) the word "bachelor" involve quantification over moments in past time to determine that the individual in question has never been the groom in a marriage ceremony. This is a perfectly well-defined procedure in spite of the fact that the relevant perceptions in past time, if they were not made at that time, are not available for retrospective testing in the present. One can, and does, of course look for evidence at a later time of the truth of a given fact at an earlier time, but this is not what characterizes the meaning or truth conditions of assertions about the past (because the failure to find such evidence does not imply the falsity of assertion, and fraudulent evidence could be planted).

Idealized access

It seems, then, that the English language permits us to talk about quantification over moments of past and future time, although our access to these moments in time is severely constrained. Likewise, it permits us to talk about arbitrary points in space, where our access (although less limited than in the case of time) is also constrained. For example, the language permits us to talk about such things as whether certain structures are present inside human cells, even though the actual perception of such cells and their contents requires the technical augmentation of a microscope – a feat not possible prior to the invention of the microscope. Nevertheless, before the invention of the microscope, the theory that the human body is composed of cells could have been described and understood by means of an abstract notion, by focusing one's attention on smaller and smaller scale in this abstract model of space and time, without specific mention of a practical method for actually gaining such access.

In a similar way, our use of words such as "believe" and "want" to apply to other people seems to apply to an idealized world in which we can focus our attention on the beliefs and perception of others, directly perceiving their internal mental events. Again, this is not possible in practice (with present technology), but appears to be what we mean by many English locutions.

As a consequence of these accessibility limitations, it is clear that if procedures are to be taken as explications of meanings, one cannot expect to just blindly execute them. Rather, in some (most??) cases, an intelligent inference component is required in order to deduce useful information from the procedural specification. This in turn dictates that the procedural specifications must be useful for more than just execution as "black box" procedures with input–output conditions. They must have internal structure that is accessible to inferential procedures.

Knowing how versus knowing whether

There is another artifact of the procedural semantics used in LUNAR and SHRDLU that will not extend to the general situation. This is the ability to treat the meanings of commands as procedures for carrying them out and the meanings of nouns as procedures for enumerating the members of the corresponding class. (For example, the meaning of "rock" to LUNAR is a procedure for enumerating all of the lunar samples in its data base, and the meaning of PRINTOUT is a procedure for printing out answers.) Although such procedures are useful when one has them, they are too strong to demand as a criterion for meaning. In the general case, the meaning for a nominal concept must be something weaker, which can tell an instance of the concept when it is presented, but may not be able to find or enumerate all (or even any) instances. (In real life, a person can recognize a rock upon seeing one, but could hardly begin to enumerate all existing ones.) In a similar way, the meaning function for (the propositional content of) an imperative sentence must be something weaker than a procedure for actually carrying it out because one can perfectly well understand the meaning of sentences such as "open the box" even when the box in question has a trick latch and one cannot figure out how to open it. Thus, the meaning function for an imperative seems to be something like a procedure for recognizing its successful completion rather than actually carrying it out.

There is no questioning the utility of having a procedure for a given verb that knows how to carry it out or cause it to be true, or the utility of having a procedure for finding instances of a given noun. These procedures, however, are practical skills, not criteria for the meanings of the terms they are associated with.

Meaning functions versus recognition functions

Although one would at first expect that the procedure defining the meaning of a concept would be the procedure that one would use to recognize instances of that concept, because of economic considerations and logical necessities (such as the previously discussed accessibility limitations) this is not usually the case. That is, the procedure that we normally use for determining whether something we perceive is an instance of a concept involves considerably less than checking out the full procedure that defines the meaning of the concept. It is this fact that permits us to be fooled by objects that are not what they appear to be. For example, the meaning of "telephone" requires more than just the appearance of a telephone because if I examine what appears to be a telephone and discover that it has no mechanism inside it but is instead filled with plaster, I will not consider it to be a telephone. Nevertheless, if I have not so examined it, I will treat it in every respect as a telephone until I discover the inconsistency. (Even knowing the inconsistency, in communication with someone else I may still refer to it as a telephone, but in such a case it will be another sense of the word that I will be using.)

One must assume then that concepts in the system's taxonomy will in general have two associated procedural functions – a meaning function and a recognition function. The meaning function defines the "bottom line" truth conditions for the concept, but in general may be difficult or impossible to execute in practice. The recognition function is the procedure that we ordinarily use to determine or estimate the applicability of a concept in practical situations, although this procedure may be fooled. The meaning function constitutes the criterion with respect to which the recognition function is calibrated for reliability. For example, although the meaning function for vertebrates may involve something like dissection, one ordinarily recognizes an animal as a vertebrate from external visual characteristics (e.g., identification of the animal as a member of a known class). The validation of the use of this recognition function consists of dissection experiments (or something equivalent) that justify the assertion that those recognition characteristics imply the truth of the meaning function (apparently the converse is not required). A methodological test for distinguishing a meaning function from a recognition function is to consider under what circumstances one would admit to having been fooled about whether a concept was satisfied by an entity. In such situations, the recognition function has been satisfied, but the meaning function has not.

Note: I expect that it is psychologically possible for people to use a term for which they have induced a recognition function or part of one, but for which they have no meaning function or only the most nebulous idea of what the meaning function is. (For example, they have only some meta beliefs about the nature of the meaning function.) It would follow from this that it is possible for an entire culture to make use of a term whose meaning function has not been adequately characterized by anyone, and for which there is no criterion for calibration of the recognition function. In particular this could happen when everyone is under the assumption that there is such a meaning function although they don't fully understand it (and even when some people think they do fully understand it). It is probably even possible for this to be done when there is something fundamentally inconsistent in the meta beliefs about the meaning function that people hold.

Abstract procedures

Still another subtlety that intrudes on a straightforward procedural account of meanings in English has to do with the level of detail that we wish to have considered as part of the meaning of a term. If one considers, for example, the term "vertebrate," then the procedure involving its definition would involve something like gaining access to the interior of the animal and seeing whether it has a backbone. However, to the extent that this procedures adequately characterizes the meaning of the term, it should not include details such as how the incision is made, what kind of scalpel is used, or the position or angle of the head in looking into the opening. To serve as an adequate model of meaning, such procedures will have to be expressed as very high-level programs that specify subtasks in general terms without commitment to details. There is an increasing tendency in high-level computer programming languages toward exactly this kind of abstraction so that programmers need specify only the essential characteristics of what is to be done without specifying details that don't make a difference to the outcome.

The kind of abstract procedures required here may be thought of as programs whose subroutines may have alternative procedural realizations with respect to which the calling function "doesn't care" which is used. A particularly simple example of this kind of don't-care condition would be the order in which different clauses of a conjoined condition were tested. Again, the traditional Tarskian account already provides us with a notion of an abstract procedural operation for conjunction in which the order of testing the conjuncts is not considered relevant (although any given axiomatization will essentially specify an order or set of possible orders in which to do things). In exactly the same way, we can think of the statement of an AND operation in a procedural definition not as a single ordered sequence of tests (the way it would be implemented in most programming languages) but rather an abstract specification of a set of alternative possible orders in which those conditions could be tested.

It is a nontrivial undertaking to construct a suitable procedural expression language that clearly indicates what details are important, and what are irrelevant. In fact, this is one of the current research goals of one segment of programming language theorists. However, it is not too difficult to characterize an abstract semantics for such procedures as essentially corresponding to an equivalence class of more detailed procedures, any one of which will serve as a specification of the truth conditions.

Working out the details of what counts as a significant difference between two procedural representations at the level of abstraction that one would like to use for characterizing meaning functions will probably be a difficult task. Moreover, it will involve a heavily empirical component – attempting to characterize and formalize people's pretheoretic intuitions about sameness of meaning. I suspect that the level of abstraction that turns out to be satisfactory will have something to say about the structure of knowledge representation in human memory (and/or vice versa). Future work in knowledge representation structures hopefully will develop some insights into these issues.

Abstract procedures as intensional objects

We have now argued against two extreme interpretations of procedural semantics – a black-box approach in which the internal structure of a meaning function is inaccessible (only the input–output relations are available), and a low-level detail approach in which every detail of the operation of the meaning function procedure is considered a "part of the meaning." The former gives rise to a sense of equivalence between meaning functions that is too weak (in the sense of strong and weak equivalence of formal language theory), in that it counts as equivalent meaning functions whose input–output relations are the same (in all possible situations) regardless of the means by which those extensions are determined. As a simple example of the consequences of this kind of weak equivalence, the propositions "Either the moon is made of green cheese or it isn't" and "Sir Walter Scott is Sir Walter Scott" would mean the same thing because they are both tautologies.

The low-level detail interpretation is at the opposite extreme of this spectrum. Its sense of equivalence is so strong that it counts two meaning functions as different if they differ in any detail of their operation regardless of the extent to which they effectively do the same thing. The notion of abstract procedure that is required for the characterization of meaning functions appears to lie somewhere between these extremes – providing a degree of internal structure that is considered significant, while leaving certain low-level details unspecified (or specified with suitable don't-care conditions).

For reasons similar to the above, Carnap (1964) introduced the notion of the "intension" of a predicate to serve as the thing that characterized the truth conditions of the predicate but also contained some "intensional" structure beyond that possessed by an abstract set of input–output pairs. (He referred to the latter as the "extension" of the predicate.) In these terms, our black-box account can be thought of as a kind of extensional account, whereas our notion of abstract procedure can be taken as an attempt to explicate the notion of intension.

Toward a theory of meaning functions

In light of the previous discussions, one can now begin to outline a theory of meaning within the procedural semantics framework that I believe might be adequate. To begin with, it would assume that the meanings of terms are defined as abstract procedures built upon a basic set of perceptual primitives that are essentially those of our own direct perceptions (including internal perceptions of beliefs, desires, emotional states, etc.) but are treated as if these primitives could be applied in arbitrary contexts of time, space, and perceiver.

On top of these primitives are built more abstract predicates, propositions, and functions by use of the compositional operators of some universal machine (in the Turing machine sense) such as recursive function theory, Post production systems, or a modern high-level programming language such as LISP. Such a foundation will permit one to construct meaning functions that take into account such factors as numbers of features shared with some prototype, differential diagnosis between two similar concepts, probabilistic calculations, thresholding decisions, and so on, as well as the simple combination of truth values by means of logical operations such as AND and OR and universal and existential quantification.

These composite procedures are not simply black boxes (or abstract sets of input–output conditions), but rather have an intensional structure that permits the intelligent system not only to execute them against the external world in particular situations of time and place (with the system itself as perceiver) but also to simulate them in hypothetical situations, including situations involving other perceivers and/or times and places that are not available to direct perception.

These procedures are abstract in the sense that they are expressed at a level of abstraction that "hides" (or declares nonessential) certain low-level details of operation with respect to which two procedures that otherwise compute the same thing are considered the same.

There are associated with a given term two fundamentally different procedures – a meaning function and a recognition function. The recognition function is the function that is normally used to recognize instances to which the term applies, whereas the meaning function is the standard against which the recognition function is measured for reliability and from which (in certain theoretical situations) possible recognition functions can be derived.

Given such a set of notions to work with, it now becomes possible to talk about meanings that are in some sense anchored to actual perceptual operations via an assembly of recursively defined procedural specifications, without the meaning function necessarily being executable in practice in all situations. In particular, if we want to characterize the meaning of some past-tense statement that would otherwise be a directly perceptible fact were it expressed in the present tense, then the assertion has the effect of claiming that if the corresponding procedure had been executed at that time, then its computed value would have been true. This can be expressed abstractly in terms of abstract time and place setting operations followed by an evaluation of the procedure in that abstract setting.

Conclusions

In the previous discussion, I have argued that a notion of procedural semantics can serve as an upward compatible generalization of the Tarskian semantics of truth conditions, and that specifically it provides natural extensions of similar techniques to kinds of meanings that are not directly expressible as having truth conditions. Moreover, it permits the extensions of semantic theories to account for the way in which the truth conditions of elementary "atomic" propositions connect to our perceptual experiences. However, I have raised a number of issues with respect to which the most natural and straightforward notions of procedural semantics are inadequate, and have outlined the direction in which I think an adequate solution lies.

I believe there are good methodological reasons to adopt a procedural semantics approach to the characterization of meaning. Specifically, there now exists a sizable body of intuitive understanding of the nature of procedures, sharpened by the rigors of making a machine actually perform as intended in response to procedural specifications – especially to make a machine perform (albeit in limited ways) in tasks normally thought of as higher-level mental processes (parsing sentences, answering questions, proving theorems, etc.). I believe these intuitions and insights are invaluable in stretching one's view of what kinds of internal mental processes are possible. Moreover, theoretical results in automata theory and computability give a depth of theoretical understanding to some of the issues that arise that is not available for less concrete notions of propositions, predicates, intensions, and so on.

It's not only that the notion of a procedure is admirably well-suited to this kind of analysis. Rather it seems that there is no other mathematical entity as well understood as that of a procedure that one can use to construct a more adequate explanation of the phenomena. Calling such things "propositions" does not help because we have no independent explication of what a proposition is. Calling them functions (in the abstract mathematical sense of sets of ordered pairs) is merely a black-box account that refuses to deal with the contents of the black box (i.e., how the function in fact assigns values to arguments).

However, one should be aware that the notion of procedure, although somewhat more concrete than the abstract notion of proposition, is nevertheless a fairly subtle concept in its own right, and its invocation as a mechanism for modeling semantics is not as straightforward as it might first appear. The final point that I would like to make is that adopting a procedural semantics approach does not automatically provide a solution to all of the classical problems and paradoxes of semantics, saying that the meanings of English expressions are abstract procedures does not eliminate the need for concern over how such procedures are represented, and how expressions of similar meaning share common meaning elements. It merely answers the question of what kinds of things these representations can be interpreted to be and what functions they serve.

Much remains to be done to work out an adequate model of meaning. In a sequel to this chapter (Woods, forthcoming), I discuss a number of difficult problems of semantics from a procedural perspective. Some of these problems (opaque contexts, presuppositions, the uniqueness of identity, theoretical concepts) are traditional problems in the philosophy of language. Some others (abstract procedures, infinite quantification) are problems unique to the procedural approach.

In advancing our understanding of human cognition (just as in Dennett's account of intelligence), there seem to be two important components – hypothesizing models (or aspects of models) and developing criteria by which such models are to be judged. In this chapter, I hope that I have accomplished a little of both.

NOTE

The first draft of this paper was written while I was on sabbatical at the University of Sussex, under the auspices of a Fulbright-Hays Fellowship. Special thanks are due to Christopher Longuet-Higgins and Stuart Sutherland, who provided the environment for this work, to Mary Walton, who heroically (and with exceptional skill) typed the first draft under great pressure, and to many people who read and commented on the draft, including especially Eugene Charniak, Daniel Dennett, Gerald Gazdar, Steven Isard, David Israel, Philip Johnson-Laird, and Aaron Sloman (none of whom can be held responsible, of course, for the opinions expressed herein). Special thanks are also due to John Lyons for valuable discussions.

REFERENCES

Bell, A., and Quillian, M. R. 1971. "Capturing Concepts in a Semantic Net." In E. L. Jacks, ed. *Associative Information Techniques.* New York: American Elsevier.

Berkeley, E. C., and Bobrow, D. G., eds. 1964. *The Programming Language LISP: Its Operation and Applications.* Cambridge, Mass.: The M.I.T. Press.

Brachman, R. J. 1978. "A Structural Paradigm for Representing Knowledge." Ph.D. dissertation, Harvard University, Division of Engineering and Applied Physics. Also, BBN Report No. 3605, Cambridge, Mass.: Bolt Beranek and Newman, Inc. December.

Brachman, R. J. 1979. "On the Epistemological Status of Semantic Networks." In Nicholas V. Findler, ed. *Associative Networks – The Representation and Use of Knowledge in Computers,* New York: Academic Press.

Carnap, R. 1964. *Meaning and Necessity.* Chicago: University of Chicago Press.

Chomsky, N. 1965. *Aspects of the Theory of Syntax.* Cambridge, Mass.: The M.I.T. Press.

Church, A. 1964. "The Need for Abstract Entities in Semantic Analysis." In J. J. Katz and J. A. Fodor, eds. *The Structure of Language: Readings in the Philosophy of Language.* Englewood Cliffs, N.J.: Prentice-Hall.

Dennett, D. C. 1974. "Why the Law of Effect Will Not Go Away." Read to the first meeting of the Society for Philosophy and Psychology, October 26, 1974 at M.I.T. Reprinted, 1978. In *Brainstorms: Philosophical Essays on Mind and Psychology.* Montgomery, Vt.: Bradford Books.

Frege, G. 1892. "Uber Sinn und Bedeutung." *Zeitschr. f. Philosophie und Philosoph. Kritik* 100:25–50. English translation: "On Sense and Reference," in P. Geach and M. Black, eds. *Translations from the Philosophical Writings of Gottlob Frege.* Oxford: Oxford University Press.

Katz, J. J., and Fodor, J. A. 1964. "The Structure of a Semantic Theory." In J. Katz and J. Fodor, eds. *The Structure of Language: Readings in the Philosophy of Language.* Englewood Cliffs, N.J.: Prentice-Hall.

Lyons, J. 1977. *Semantics,* Vol. 1. London: Cambridge University Press.

Miller, G. A., and Johnson-Laird, P. N. 1976. *Perception and Language.* Cambridge, Mass.: Harvard University Press, and London: Cambridge University Press.

Montague, R. 1970. "English as a Formal Language." In B. Visentini et al. (eds.) *Linguaggio nella Società e nella Tecnica* (Proceedings of a symposium, "Language in Society and the Technical World," held in Milan in October 1968). Milan: Edizioni de Comunita, pp. 189–224.

Montague, R. 1973. "The Proper Treatment of Quantification in Ordinary English," in J. Hintikka, J. M. E. Moravcsik, and P. Suppes, eds. *Approaches to Natural Language.* Dordrecht, Holland: Reidel.

Quillian, M. R. 1966. "Semantic Memory." Report No. AFCRL-66-189, Cambridge, Mass.: Bolt Beranek and Newman, Inc. October. (More extensive than the Quillian, 1968 paper by the same name.)

Quillian, M. R. 1968. "Semantic Memory." In M. Minsky, ed. *Semantic Information Processing.* Cambridge, Mass.: The M.I.T. Press.

Quillian, M. R. 1969. "The Teachable Language Comprehender: A Simulation Program and Theory of Language." *Communications of the Association for Computing Machinery* 12:459–76.

Tarski, A. 1944. "The Semantic Conception of Truth and the Foundation of Semantics." *Philosophy and Phenomenological Research* 4:341–76.

Weissman, C. 1967. *LISP 1.5 Primer.* Belmont, Calif.: Dickenson.

Winograd, T. 1972. *Understanding Natural Language.* New York: Academic Press.

Winograd, T. 1976. "Towards a Procedural Understanding of Semantics." Memo AIM-292, Stanford, Calif.: Stanford Artificial Intelligence Laboratory. November.

Woods, W. A. 1967. "Semantics for a Question-Answering System." Ph.D. thesis, Harvard University, Division of Engineering and Applied Physics. Also, Report NSF-19, Harvard Computation Laboratory. September. (Available from NTIS as PB-176-548, and reprinted with a new preface in 1979 by Garland Publishing, New York, as a volume in the series: *Outstanding Dissertations in the Computer Sciences.*)

Woods, W. A. 1968. "Procedural Semantics for a Question–Answering Machine." *Proceedings of the Fall Joint Computer Conference.* Montvale, New Jersey: AFIPS.

Woods, W. A. 1970. "Transition Network Grammars for Natural Language Analysis." *Communications of the Association for Computing Machinery* 13, 10:591–606.

Woods, W. A. 1973. "Meaning and Machines." Published, 1977. In A. Zampolli, ed. *Computational and Mathematical Linguistics.* Proceedings of the International Conference on Computational Linguistics, Pisa, Italy, August 1973. Florence, Italy: Leo S. Olschki.

Woods, W. A. 1978a. "Semantics and Quantification in Natural Language Question–Answering." In *Advances in Computers,* Vol. 17. New York: Academic Press, pp. 2–87. Also, Report No. 3687, Cambridge, Mass.: Bolt Beranek and Newman, Inc.

Woods, W. A. 1978b. "Taxonomic Lattice Structures for Situation Recognition." In *TINLAP-2.* Conference on Theoretical Issues in Natural Language Processing-2, University of Illinois at Urbana-Champaign, July 25–27. (Also in *American Journal of Computational Linguistics,* Microfiche 78, 1978:3.)

Woods, W. A. Forthcoming. *Problems in Procedural Semantics.*

Woods, W. A., and Brachman, R. J. 1978. "Research in Natural Language Understanding – Quarterly Technical Progress Report No. 1, 1 September 1977 to 30 November 1977. Report No. 3742, Cambridge, Mass.: Bolt Beranek and Newman, Inc. January. (Now available from NTIS as AD No. A053958.)

Woods, W. A., Kaplan, R. M., and Nash-Webber, B. L. 1972. "The Lunar Sciences Natural Language Information System: Final Report." Report No. 2378, Cambridge, Mass.: Bolt Beranek and Newman, Inc.

Zadeh, L. A. 1974. "Fuzzy Logic and Approximate Reasoning." Electronics Research Laboratory Memorandum No. ERL-M479, University of California, Berkeley, College of Engineering.

Index

Abelson, R. P., 19, 51, 54, 146, 148, 149, 169, 269, 284
abstract procedures, 301–2, 327–9
access-and-check, 122
acquisition of meaning hypothesis, 308
active node stack, 179–80
affirmative-negative sentence pairs, 238
agent deletion, 187
Akmajian, A., 195
alethic/epistemic propositions, 69
Allen, J. F., 217, 228
Allwood, J., 73
ambiguity, 308–10
American Sign Language, 235
analytical truths, 112
anaphora, 42–5; definite, 4, 283, 284; indefinite this–noun phrases, 234–5; specific/nonspecific noun phrases, 237
anaphoric reference, resolution of, 270
Andersen, E. S., 31
Anderson, J. R., 19, 51, 118, 228
Anderson, R. C., 19, 123
annotated surface structure, 177, 183, 192, 196
anomalous sentences, 238–9
answer, selection, 163–4
associativity, 41
assumption sets, 245
attention assumption, 33
augmented truncation heuristics, 28
Austin, J. L., 65, 217, 218

BABEL, 146
backtracking, parsers, 177
Bajcsy, R., 278
Barenboim, C., 31
Bar-Hillel, Y., 112, 116, 117
Bartsch, R., 285, 290
belief, as a modal operator, 220–1
beliefs, 251–2
Bell, A., 314

Benjamin, R., 75
Berkeley, E. C., 315
Bobrow, D. G., 174, 315
Boer, S. E., 60
Boggess, L. C., 277
Bower, G. H., 270
Brachman, R. J., 291, 314
Bransford, J. D., 123
Bresnan, J. W., 178
Brinch-Hansen, P., 257
broad metaphor, 279
Brown, P., 79n3
Bruce, B., 54
buffer constituents, 194
Bunnick, R. I., 211
Burstall, R. M., 264

Carlson, L., 285, 290
Carnap, R., 112, 300
Carpenter, P. A., 53
Chafe, W. L., 44, 89, 270
Charniak, E., 284
Chomsky, N., 117, 177, 178, 183, 184, 187, 190–1, 194, 195, 198–9, 312
Christopherson, P., 22, 45
Church, A., 292, 300
Clark, E. V., 21, 31, 47, 53
Clark, H. H., 5, 20, 21, 24, 41, 47, 51, 54, 75, 219, 220, 221, 229, 231, 242–3, 278
Clausemate constraint, 198
CLOSURE, 253–4
cognitive models, 146
cognitive processes, 157, 170; simulation of, 278
Cohen, P. R., 5, 7, 17, 21, 101, 103n17, 217, 229, 252, 284
Collins, A. M., 106, 109, 161
commitment-slates, 69
common ground, 20, 69; see also shared knowledge; mutual knowledge
COMMON KNOWLEDGE, 253, 255

335